MYSTERIES
IN THE
PROPHETIC WRITINGS

MYSTERIES
IN THE
PROPHETIC WRITINGS

GOD'S ETERNAL PURPOSE REVEALED

BY

HENRY HON
DOUGLAS KRIEGER

ONE

BODY LIFE

www.onebody.life

Copyright © December 2025 by Henry Hon.

Published in the United States of America.

ISBN- 978-1-954436-11-4

Unless otherwise indicated, Scripture quotations taken from the New King James Version [NKJV]

TABLE OF CONTENTS

Now to Him who is able to establish you according to my gospel and the preaching of Jesus Christ, according to the revelation of the mystery kept secret since the world began but now made manifest, and by the prophetic Scriptures made known to all nations, according to the commandment of the everlasting God, for obedience to the faith— to God, alone wise, [be] glory through Jesus Christ forever. Amen.

— Romans 16:25-27

PREFACE

The Greeks invented democracy (Cir. 600 BC), a government of the people, by the people, and for the people. Their forum for making democratic decisions was the ekklesia. Therefore, ekklesia was a democratic legislative assembly – diverse and participatory. The Lord Jesus appropriated this polity, ekklesia, and said He would build His own Democratic Assembly (Ekklesia) juxtaposed to the governance of the Greeks' democracy.

Jesus said in Matthew 16:18: "I will build my Ekklesia (aka 'church')." Democracy has two main characteristics: diversity (inclusion) and freedom of speech (no one dominating or controlling, as a king or dictator). While secular democracy has often deepened divisions and even fostered hatred among people with differences, the Lord's Ekklesia (Democratic Assembly), as envisioned by Jesus, is designed to exalt love and oneness, where people from the most dramatically diverse backgrounds can unite in harmony. No wonder Scriptures call the Lord's Ekklesia a lampstand shining in this dark and hopeless world (Rev. 1:20).

The value and position of God's Democratic Assembly are elevated to the zenith as a unique counterpart to God. She is destined to be the Bride of Christ, the Body of the God-man who fills all things. She is composed of all God's children with His life, nature, and expression (reflecting the Godhead but not intrinsic within the Godhead). She fulfills God's eternal purpose by manifesting God's manifold wisdom. She is the one commissioned to defeat and crush God's enemy, Satan. She is God's eternal Kingdom – His crown uplifted as a banner before principalities and powers wherein she is embedded as His crown's jewels (Zech. 9:16).

God's Ekklesia is a revealed mystery coming into its fullness through the death and resurrection of Jesus Christ. His Democratic Assembly started *manifesting* herself on the day of Pentecost. She is the goal of all apostolic work. Since God's Ekklesia is His eternal purpose, the Hebrew Scriptures reveal not only the Messiah's sufferings and glories (I Peter 1:10) but are also replete with archetypes and prophecies concerning God's Ekklesia. That is why Paul concluded in Romans 16:26 that the hidden mystery is now disclosed via the prophetic Scriptures. It is also why Peter confirmed that the Spirit of Christ spoke through these same prophets of "this salvation" produced through the "sufferings of the Messiah". He also spoke of "the glories that would follow" (1 Pet. 1:10) and Paul declared "unto Him be glory in the Ekklesia" (Eph. 3:21).

According to both John 5:39 and Luke 24:27, the entire Hebrew Scriptures speak of Jesus Christ. Therefore, Bible teachers have written many books dedicated to unveiling the archetypes and figures revealing Christ in the Tanakh — the Hebrew Scriptures. Therefore, Jesus Christ, as the Lord and Savior, depicted in the Hebrew Scriptures, will not be the exclusive focus of this book. Rather, this text will contribute to expanded enlightenment and fresh understanding concerning God's eternal purpose relating to His diverse people — His called-out ones — being built up as His Democratic Assembly. From the protoevangelium in Genesis 3:15 — where the Seed of the woman is promised to crush the serpent's head — to the fulfillment of that promise in Romans 16:20, where the feet of His Ekklesia crush Satan underfoot, we see the original gospel declared and completed.

This book will focus on the archetypes and prophecies concerning God's Democratic Assembly (Ekklesia), which Jesus was sent to build. The followers of Messiah — the Christ, our Lord and Savior, should earnestly cooperate with the Spirit of God in the building up of God's Kingdom by manifesting His New Covenant with His New Commandment upon the earth.

Although most students of the Bible would only consider the "prophetic writings" to be those of the major and minor prophets in the Old Testament, this text will include the entire Hebrew Scriptures (Old Testament), starting from Genesis, since it is also prophetic. The reason is that Moses was called a prophet (Deut. 34:10) and his writings of the Torah (the first 5 books of the Hebrew Scriptures) are full of prophecies. The first prophecy concerning the coming of Jesus Christ, crushing the serpent, Satan, was Genesis 3:15: *"I will put enmity between you and the woman, and between your offspring and her offspring; he shall bruise your head, and you shall bruise his heel."*

The fulfillment of this prophecy started with Jesus Christ being the offspring of the Virgin Mary. He destroyed Satan on the cross and took away his power of death (Heb. 2:14). In the Lord's resurrection, His believers became part of Him as the corporate "seed of Abraham." His diverse people in unity are the consummate fulfillment of the first prophecy in the Bible. Much has been written and taught concerning Jesus Christ's fulfillment and triumph over Satan. However, the corporate Christ as the ultimate fulfillment of prophetic writings may be quite lacking. We hope to bring to light something new and old in the unveiling of the mysteries hidden in the prophetic writings concerning the corporate Christ.

ACKNOWLEDGEMENT

My family and I arrived in San Francisco from Hong Kong by ship in late November 1962. That very evening, after disembarking, we attended a small Christian conference held in a home. I didn't know what was going on, having just turned nine years old. Only recently, in September 2025, I discovered that Doug Krieger was also present at that same gathering. He was twenty-one at the time. It's astonishing to think that, sixty-three years later, we would co-author a book together.

We reconnected in 2017, when Doug heard my presentation on the Lord's Ekklesia — understood as a democratic assembly — in 1 Corinthians 11, and the significance of "greeting" in Romans 16. The message resonated deeply with him and aligned with his heart for the unity of the Body of Christ. Since then, we've labored together to proclaim the gospel of peace for the building up of the Lord's ekklesia.

Doug brings insight into the Hebrew Scriptures, having written a number of books on them. His understanding of the uniting of Jews and Gentiles as the rebuilding of the Tabernacle of David (Acts 15:16–17) inspired me to explore the Lord's Ekklesia throughout the Hebrew Scriptures. Over the years, we've fellowshipped around fresh unveilings from the Word, and we remain grateful to God for the continual light He shines upon it.

Although I structured and wrote this book around the mysteries revealed by the Apostle Paul, Doug graciously joined as co-author. Through almost three years of research and writing, I've gained new perspectives and a profound understanding — insights I believe are vital for grasping and practicing God's eternal purpose. However, without Doug's initial agreement to partner up, I doubt I would have embarked on this journey. After editing the manuscript, he contributed additional reflections in the footnotes and the Appendix.

Henry Hon

1

THE HIDDEN MYSTERIES OF THE UNIVERSE

Now to him who is able to strengthen you according to my gospel and the preaching of Jesus Christ, according to the revelation of the **mystery** that was kept secret for long ages 26 but has **now been disclosed and through the prophetic writings** has been made known to all nations, according to the command of the eternal God, to bring about the obedience of faith—

– Rom. 16:25-26, ESV

This entire universe, including the Earth, is full of mysteries. As astrophysicists and astronomers scan and explore the universe, it is a mystery as to its origin and size. It is still expanding with an innumerable number of stars. Then, going the opposite way by diving into the subatomic level, scientists are discovering more infinitesimal particles. When the mystery (unexplainable) of how positively charged protons (at the center of an atom, which should explode) are held together, they call it "nuclear glue" or gluons. This "glue" is holding the entire universe together.

If the physical universe is mysterious, how can the things of God not be super mysterious? Therefore, the Scriptures use the word "mystery" in multiple passages, attributing it to God and Christ. The Greek word for mystery is *mystērion*, which means hidden, secret thing, not obvious to understanding (Thayer's). Who or what is God? What are His attributes? Where is He? What are His plans? Even with Christ, what is He doing now, where is He, what are His present characteristics? What is their relationship with mankind? These are mysteries that have been hidden – but are now revealed.

To understand the mysteries of the universe, man (male and female) has blasted off telescopes into space and built particle accelerators to break down sub-atomic structures. Billions of dollars have been spent, together with lifetimes of brilliant minds, on these endeavors. Shouldn't believers who embrace the gospel spend some time reading and understanding the mysteries of God? While the physical mysteries require billions of research dollars and PhD-level scientists to uncover the secrets of the universe, God's mysteries, though far more mysterious and awesome to ponder, can be comprehended. This is possible if believers read Paul's epistles and the rest of the Scriptures with an open heart and seek to be enlightened by the Holy Spirit (Eph. 3:3-4).

The apostle Paul was enamored with the mysteries relating to God. Out of all the epistles (Revelation is not considered to be an epistle[1]), Paul was the only one who used the word *mystery (mystērion)*. Additionally, the word was used in relation to the understanding of the awesomeness of God's heart and eternal purpose, which certainly qualified as the deepest mysteries. Paul was the one who sought to know and was given the revelation to understand these mysteries.

As can be seen in Romans 16:25, Paul used the term "the mystery" as singular; however, in other portions, he used the plural "mysteries." He considered himself in 1 Corinthians 4:1 as a steward of the *mysteries* of God. The mystery is comprised of multiple mysteries. This is like the Trinity, where the one God is distinctly Father, Son, and Holy Spirit. When the various mysteries are designated or disclosed, then the mystery is understood. Paul's entire stewardship revolved around these mysteries as a service to both God and man. If ministers of Christ do not dive into and teach these mysteries, then their services are insufficient. It is due to the lack of teachings and even interest in these mysteries of God that proper apostolic stewardship is deficient among Christians. Therefore, God's eternal purpose is sorely neglected among believers.

According to Romans 16:25-26, the apostles and the prophetic writings have now disclosed the mystery that has been kept in secret for past ages. The apostles received revelation to understand God's eternal purpose and the related mysteries. However, they drew the core of their understanding from the prophetic writings in the Hebrew Scriptures. Thus, the mystery became known through apostolic revelation after the first advent of Christ and their knowledge of the prophetic writings. It can be said that the prophetic writings painted the pictures through archetypes and figures, and "a picture is worth a thousand words." The Holy Spirit led the prophets to ascertain not only those portions relating to the Messiah's coming but the very purpose of His redemptive work and its expansion and continuation on the earth! However, the New Testament apostles supplied the clear utterance to make the mysteries plain and known. This is like watching a silent movie with subtitles. Therefore, both the apostles' epistles and the prophetic writings were necessary for making the mystery known, following the command of the eternal God. Wonderful!

---

1   Although John's Revelation of Jesus Christ was written to the "seven churches in the province of Asia," its composition is by far not in the style of the other apostolic epistles and is more in keeping with a "prophetic vision" of the Son of Man in His immediate and eternal accomplishments.

The Hebrew Scriptures are often misunderstood and have caused conflict and division among Christians. Some would maintain that believers of Jesus should keep the laws of Moses as best as they can. That would be the ten commandments, including the keeping of the Sabbath, the Passover, and the various annual feasts. There is also a growing group of Christians who advocate for "unhitching" completely from the Old Testament. They would say, Christians have nothing to do with the Old Testament Scriptures – today, all we believers need is the New Testament. Salvation comes from Jesus Christ alone, even if one never reads the Old Testament. They may continue: The God of the Old Testament is a different God from the New; the Old is one of judgment and revenge; the New is one of mercy and love. The Old is for Jews only, the New is for Christians!

Salvation is indeed from Jesus Christ alone, even if one never reads the Bible (both old or new). However, God's desire is not just that all men would be saved, but that they would also come to the knowledge of the truth (1 Tim. 2:4). When it is a matter of knowledge, then the Scripture is necessary. At the time of Acts and the New Testament epistles, only what is known today as the Old Testament was Scripture[2]. Without the scriptures, salvation by itself is not complete (2 Tim. 3:16). It is the written law in the Hebrew Scriptures that testify of God's attributes (Exo. 31:18). Therefore, those more noble among believers are those who examined the Scriptures daily concerning Jesus Christ (Acts 17:11). In fact, Peter declared that the Scriptures are more sure or trustworthy than hearing a direct voice from God in the heavens (2 Pet. 1:17-21). The knowledge of God and all the items related to Him are written in the Scriptures of both the Old and New Testaments.

It is illogical for some Christians to say that the Old Testament is not necessary to read. Jesus read and studied the Hebrew Scriptures, knowing Hebrew and Koine Greek of His day (Viz, the Septuagint or Koine Greek version of the OT). Therefore, He Himself quoted from the Hebrew scriptures about 78 times. Shouldn't He be the pattern for all Christians? Every writer of the New Testament quoted from the Hebrew Scriptures. The apostle Paul quoted it about 89 times. The point is that the Hebrew Scriptures provide extensive knowledge of the mystery of God.

However, if the readers do not have their hearts turned to the Lord Jesus, then in the reading of the Hebrew Scriptures, it will be like having a veil over one's face (2 Cor. 3:14-16). This veil becomes a blinder to cover the knowledge of Christ (2 Cor. 4:3-4). Jesus said that all Scriptures testify of Him (John 5:39; Luke 24:27). Therefore, it is critical that believers read all the Scriptures (old and new), and it is essential when

---

2   https://www.blueletterbible.org/study/misc/quotes.cfm - There are over 263 direct quotations of the OT found in the NT; however, there are nearly three times that many "allusions" of the same—therefore, upwards of 1,000 passages found in the NT are taken from the OT.

reading to focus on the Person of Jesus Christ and His work on this earth. Believers are not to just understand what may be apparent in the writings concerning laws, customs, festivals, personalities, and history (with remarkable stories). Yes, those who desire to "search the Scriptures" may find comfort and strength in knowing the God who supernaturally came to save. Nevertheless, the challenge is to go beyond seeking personal blessings and peace of mind and to dive into and consider the mysteries, unveiling the knowledge of God and His eternal purpose. Those are the hidden secrets in the Hebrew Scriptures.

"Mystery" by definition means "a hidden thing." The mysteries of the things of God are hidden within the words of the Hebrew Scriptures. Secrets are not apparent — they are purposefully hidden and must be discovered and understood. Returning to the illustration of a painting, a wall painting of expansive scenery may have many elements: a forest, a lake, animals, a blue sky with the sun shining through one cloud, and finally, a couple of young bike riders having a picnic. Everyone standing up close who focuses on one or a couple of these elements will have a different interpretation of the painting. Not until the entire painting is viewed from a distance can the entire scene be appreciated.

There are many elements in the Old Testament painting: Adam and Eve, the Serpent, two trees, the patriarchs, Noah's ark, Abraham, Isacc, Jacob, 12 Tribes of Israel, Egypt, Passover, Red Sea, Moses, the law of God's covenant, manna, the good land, God's anger, God's forgiveness, an abundance of judgments and destructions, wars, the judges, priests, prophets, David, Solomon, all the kings, the temple, the division of Israel, Assyria, Babylon, the second temple, many prophecies, and much more. This is a huge painting that took about 1500 years to create.

The characters embedded in this painting are merely elements in the hands of the Artist. They have no consciousness of what the finished painting would look like since it took 1500 years for the Painter and Architect to accomplish. Logically, that is why Paul said the mysteries (this painting) were not revealed to anyone until 500 years later (Eph. 3:5, 9; Luke 10:24). Yes, the entire painting was there — but now it had to be revealed, unveiled to all, even to the universe! It is when the apostles, with the light of Christ looking back from afar, could finally see the entire painting. They could not only view the 1500-year-long painting, but the reality of what this painting actually depicts: Christ and His Democratic Assembly (Ekklesia)[3] — His Person and His Work.

---

3   Ekklesia (Greek: ἐκκλησία) is capitalized throughout this work to emphasize its theological significance as the democratic legislative assembly of God's people. The term *Ekklesia* will be used interchangeably with "democratic assembly" throughout this text. Unlike institutional or denominational uses of "church," *Ekklesia* here refers to a participatory, diverse, and inclusive community in which no person or group dominates—a people who embody Christ's life, nature, and purpose.

The entire painting became clear: the mystery hidden in the Hebrew Scriptures is unveiled. It is only due to the coming of Christ with His death, resurrection, ascension, and the outpouring of the Spirit that the story is fulfilled and able to be understood and comprehended. Paul and the other apostles could, during their time, write the captions explaining this vast and intricate picture.

Even today, when most Christians read the Scriptures, they may receive a hodgepodge of assorted topics but not a stereoscopic breadth of vision. These different topics can range from heaven and hell, salvation, holiness, Satan, morality, self-sacrifice, judgments, law, church, righteousness, miracles, demonic possessions, wars, prophecies, love stories, and many how-to items (how to have a good marriage, raise children, overcome addictions, financial gains, etc.). To most, there may not be a cohesive story unfolding the mystery from Genesis to Revelation. However, it is not the understanding of these specific topics, but the comprehension of the entire scope of this mystery of the things of God, which can establish and ground a person in the faith to do the will of God in their lifetime.

Paul was steeped in the study of the Hebrew Scriptures. He was a trained lawyer and a Pharisee, so he had a firm grasp of the prophetic writings. However, before the revelation of Jesus, his knowledge of the law was used to persecute Christians. When the light came and he turned His heart to the Lord Jesus, then his deep knowledge of the Hebrew Scriptures became a source of revelation. The mysteries in the Old Testament became known to him, and he used the Scriptures to unveil them. The light of Jesus Christ made these Hebrew Scriptures new to him. The law that Paul used to persecute Christ became a tutor to bring souls to Christ! (Gal. 3:24).

Romans may be considered as Paul's complete theology. Romans 16:25-26 (reference above) is at the very end of this epistle, and yet every chapter of this epistle cites or refers to the Hebrew Scriptures. It was as if he stitched together quotes and references throughout the Hebrew Scriptures, together with commentaries on how they are related to true faith in Jesus Christ — this became his theology of the New Testament. In other words, Paul's New Testament theology concerning Jesus Christ is completely rooted and grounded in the Hebrew Scriptures. Therefore, his conclusion is logically accurate: the **mystery** kept secret from ages past has **now been disclosed — and through the prophetic writings!**

Paul, in that same verse, says His preaching of Jesus Christ is based on the unveiling of the mystery. Therefore, without seeing and including the mysteries unveiled in the prophetic writings, the preaching of Jesus Christ is woefully inadequate. The entire epistle of Romans was Paul preaching the gospel, and the mysteries are included. Additionally, understanding these mysteries brought about the obedience of faith. Most Christians desire obedience, a sign of maturity and being a disciple. However, without recognizing these mysteries relating to God, believers would not even understand what they are to obey. Therefore, knowing these mysteries leads to obedience and being established in the complete gospel of Jesus Christ.

To be saved by faith is effortless. Salvation is immediate at the moment a person receives faith to accept Jesus Christ as God Who became man, died for the sins of the world, resurrected on the third day, and ascended to be the Lord of all. That is the simplicity of being saved by grace and not by works (Eph. 2:8-9). However, to grow and mature as a believer, there is a pressing need for knowledge of the truth. In 2 Peter 1:5, Peter said that to grow, to have the maturity of "agape" love, all diligence or effort is needed to add to faith, virtue, and knowledge. Faith is a gift from God, but diligence is needed to read and study, to retain knowledge.

It is remarkable that Peter, one of the first recipients of the Spirit on the day of Pentecost and through whom the Spirit performed many signs and wonders, focused his last letter on knowledge. In this short letter of three chapters (2 Peter), he mentions knowledge seven times. The knowledge here is not just general Biblical knowledge, but specifically the knowledge of God and Jesus Christ (2 Pet. 1:2). This knowledge is explicitly derived from the Scriptures (2 Pet. 1:20). The last verse in this epistle is "but grow in the grace and knowledge of our Lord and Savior Jesus Christ." Peter uplifted and directed believers to pursue knowledge through the Scriptures. "Spirit" was only mentioned once, and it concerns the Spirit being the inspiration behind the writing of Scriptures in contrast to the present Spirit. This shows the importance of understanding the mysteries of God and Christ in the Scriptures. The Spirit is certainly needed today for the believers' power and living. Nevertheless, the Spirit of God is in the receiving and understanding of the Lord's words (John 6:63). Believers possess more of the Spirit as they increase in the knowledge of the truth (John 14:17).

The Eight Mysteries

This text is dedicated to unveiling the picture painted for all people to know God's mystery, aka His eternal purpose. However, it will be shown in eight different pictorials, telling various stories to unveil eight different mysteries, whereby, when combined, they will unveil the scope of **the mystery** in the Prophetic writings.

Mystery of God—Christ

> That their hearts may be encouraged, being knit together in love, to reach all the riches of full assurance of understanding and the knowledge of God's mystery, which is Christ,
>
> – Col. 2:2, ESV

God is a mystery. He dwells in unapproachable light (1 Tim. 6:16). No one can approach and see Him. How mysterious! However, Christ came to declare all that God is. He came as the Word of God (John 1:1). As the *logos* (Gk.) of God, Jesus Christ came to explain and make God understandable. No one has seen God; yet Jesus Christ made Him known (John 1:18). Jesus said in John 14:9: If you have seen me, you have seen the Father. Therefore, Paul declared that the mystery of God is Christ.

That is also the experience of every believer. Through Jesus Christ, they know God's love, kindness, mercy, righteousness, wisdom, triumph, and all His attributes. When they believe *into* Jesus, they come into God Himself (John 14:6). God becomes real in Jesus Christ. People who do not know Christ can only grope about for the "unknown god" (Acts 17:23). It is when men (male and female) come to know and enjoy Christ that their fear of God is reversed into love. The Greek word for *religion* (Gk. *thrēskeia*) has a meaning that is based on fear. However, fear is turned to love when Christ is known, because the love of God is in Jesus Christ (Rom. 8:39). Belief in God is no longer a religion, but a loving relationship with a Person. The more Christ is known, God becomes intimately approachable and lovable. This is why the mystery of God is Christ.

"In the past, God spoke to our ancestors through the prophets at many times and in various ways, but in these last days, he has spoken to us by His Son, whom he appointed heir of all things, and through whom also he made the universe. The Son is the radiance of God's glory and the exact representation of his being, sustaining all things by his powerful word" (Heb. 1:1-3a). Yes, it is only through the Son as God's very radiance that God's glory and exact representation are known.

The first writings of the Hebrew Scriptures, the book of Job, started before 1445 BC. Jesus Christ came about 430 years after the last book, Malachi, was written. However, the Hebrew Scriptures are filled with archetypes and figures pointing to and unveiling Jesus Christ. Jesus said that all Scriptures are about Him (John 5:39). Therefore, Paul declared that Adam, the beginning of the creation story, is a type or figure of Jesus Christ (Rom. 5:14). The very last verse of the Hebrew Scriptures (Mal. 4:6) is prophetic concerning the coming of Christ: *"And he will turn the hearts of the fathers to the children, and the hearts of the children to their fathers"* (Luke 1:16-17).

So, from the creation story in Genesis to the last verse in the Hebrew Scriptures, the New Testament writers were enlightened to understand God through Christ in these prophetic writings. Although the focus of this book is not on this first mystery concerning the mystery of God — Christ — since theologians have written many books on this aspect over the last several hundred years. Nevertheless, one chapter will be dedicated to unveiling this mystery throughout the Hebrew Scriptures.

The Great Mystery—Christ and His Democratic Assembly (Ekklesia)

> "Therefore a man shall leave his father and mother and hold fast to his wife, and the two shall become one flesh." 32 This mystery is profound, and I am saying that it refers to Christ and the church [ekklesia-democratic assembly].
>
> – Eph. 5:31-32, ESV

The apostle Paul quoted from Genesis regarding Adam and Eve being joined together in marriage (Gen. 2:24). It was the first joining together between a man and a woman. This portion of Ephesians 5 is common and popular for Christian marriage counseling. It is often used to define the role of a Christian husband to love and for a wife to submit. This view has also sparked conflict in the current age between husbands and wives. Indeed, this portion in Ephesians is about a husband and a wife, but Paul made clear he was not talking specifically about husbands and wives. No, he was revealing the relationship between Christ and His Democratic Assembly by using the example or illustration of a husband and his wife.

For a husband and wife to leave their father and mother to be joined together is not a mystery at all. Thousands upon thousands of couples are married every week on Earth. Whether in the East, the West, Africa, or Latin American countries, men and women have come together for marriage for millennia. However, Paul says that the joining of Christ as the husband with His Democratic Assembly as the wife is a *great mystery*. Not just a mystery, but a **great** one.

According to Paul, the marriage in Genesis was prophetic: unveiling the mystery of the joining into one between Christ and His diverse people. How can Jesus Christ, being the Living God Himself, and man (male and female), being a creature, become joined in marriage? It is understandable that man should serve and worship God, but to be joined in marriage and become one? That is outlandish!

God is divine, supernatural, eternal, and the Creator, while man is a finite, natural, and feeble creature. They do not match — they appear incompatible. They are as far apart as the east is from the west. Even in nature, mating is between those of the same species. It would be ludicrous to imagine a great ape mating with a mouse or a fish. Yet, the Scriptures reveal that God and man are to be joined together in marriage: "the two shall become one." No wonder Paul said this is a "great mystery."

The prophetic writings hid this mystery from Genesis through the major and minor prophets. This marriage is there in plain sight, clearly written; yet, what does this mean, and why is it such a secret? Notwithstanding these quandaries, looking back with the light of Jesus Christ in the New Testament, a wonderful romantic story was woven through the prophetic writings for all to grasp this profound mystery.

The Mystery of Godliness—God Manifested in the Flesh

> If I delay, you may know how one ought to behave in the household of God, which is the church [ekklesia – God's democratic assembly] of the living God, a pillar and buttress of the truth. 16 Great indeed, we confess, is the **mystery of godliness**: He was manifested in the flesh, vindicated by the Spirit, seen by angels, proclaimed among the nations, believed on in the world, taken up in glory.
>
> – 1 Tim. 3:15-16, ESV

> And he put all things under his [Christ] feet and gave him as head over all things to the church [ekklesia – democratic assembly], 23 which is his body, the fullness of him who fills all in all.
>
> – Eph. 1:22-23, ESV

Certainly, believers of Jesus Christ have faith that He is God manifested in the flesh. Jesus is the mystery of God who became flesh to manifest God to man. However, the above verses define godliness not exclusively to the individual God-man Jesus, but to include His Democratic Assembly. Now that is even more mysterious. Christians can readily accept Jesus as the sinless Son of God to be God manifest in the flesh. But to include a divergence of people who are redeemed sinners (now sons and daughters of the Living God) with conflicting perspectives and cultural and societal distinctions to be God manifested in the flesh, now that is truly a mystery!

Notice that in 1 Timothy 3:15, Paul speaks of the Household of God, which is His Democratic Assembly (Ekklesia). Then in verse 16, the sequence of events defining godliness did not stop with Jesus becoming flesh, but it also included the preaching to the nations, His believers in the world, and the rapture of His Household in glory. Additionally, Paul mentioned in Ephesians 1 that He is no longer the individual Jesus, but He has a Body. His Body is His Democratic Assembly, which is the fullness of Him who fills all in all. Who can fill all in all if not God Himself? A mystery transpired with Christ's death, resurrection, and ascension – His followers became His very Family and Body on this earth!

The word "flesh" in the Scriptures (especially in the New Testament) is negative. God created a body for man, but flesh refers to the fallen, sinful man. It is so harmful that Paul said "*nothing good dwells*" in the (my) flesh (Rom. 7:18). He added that the flesh cannot please God (Rom. 8:8). All people on earth are of the flesh; yet God chooses to manifest Himself in the flesh. Amazingly awesome mystery!

Nevertheless, this was also shown in the prophetic writings. God called Abraham to take a journey. This was not just a journey of decades or centuries; the final goal did not end until 1070 years later when Solomon built God's temple. The temple was God's house on earth. His glory came and dwelt among His people. God was homeless from eternity: *Heaven is my throne, and the earth is my footstool; what is my house, the place of my rest* (Isa. 66:1)? Solomon's temple was the most significant archetype of God dwelling in man — God manifested in the flesh.

The temple represented God's people, His family or household. After over 1,100 years of being called from the land of idols, that one man, Abraham, became a collection of men (male and female) with a diverse ancestry, including an assortment of enemies and even those cursed and condemned by God. These impure and disparate [mixed] people became one man under Joshua, and then, under King David, conquered all their enemies. The temple was the testament of their oneness, and God's glory came and filled the house.

That was God's first and final goal in calling forth Abraham: to have a motley people in which He could find His home. From Abraham to Solomon, this narrative is a prophetic story of the mystery of God manifested in the flesh. None of the characters in this nearly 1,100-year journey knew the entire picture that God was painting. They played their part, but now readers of the Hebrew Scriptures (with the help of Paul and others) could appreciate God's mystery hidden therein. In the following chapters, major events and characters will be highlighted in this painting to unveil the mystery of godliness.

The Mystery of His Will Fulfilled by His Economy (Oikonomia)

> Having made known to us the mystery of his will, according to his good pleasure which he hath purposed in himself: 10 That in the **dispensation** [**oikonomia**] of the fullness of times he might collect in one all things in Christ, both which are in heaven, and which are on earth; [even] in him:
>
> – Eph. 1:9-10, WEB

> And to make all men see what is the **dispensation** [oikonomia] of the mystery which for ages hath been hid in God who created all things.
>
> – Eph. 3:9, ASV

Paul says that the mystery hidden has a dispensation or "*oikonomia*." The Greek word *oikonomia*, which is anglicized to "economy," has an essential function in the New Testament. The verses above show that *oikonomia* is how the mystery of God's will is accomplished within an allotted time. In other words, God's *oikonomia* accomplishes God's mysterious will to "sum up" or "collect in one" all things in Christ. Here is another crucial Scripture using this word: "*I became minister, according to the **dispensation** [oikonomia] of God which is given me towards you to complete the word of God, the mystery which [has been] hidden from ages and from generations . . . which is Christ in you the hope of glory*" (Col. 1:25-27).

This word, "*oikonomia*," literally means "management of a household" (Thayer's Greek English Lexicon). This management refers to food distribution to a large household, whereby they will grow and mature as a family unit. Since this word is multifaceted, Bible translators have used various English words to describe oikonomia, such as plan, stewardship, administration, and dispensation. In the New Testament, this word is used prominently with God's eternal purpose since His family needs food and nourishment to grow and mature into His Kingdom. According to Ephesians 3:1 and 8, the "food" that needs to be dispensed to God's children is grace, the unsearchable riches of Christ. This is the regular and required lifelong nourishment to grow and mature as God's family.

This mystery of God's plan to dispense food to His people to fulfill His purpose is unveiled throughout the Hebrew Scriptures. Immediately after creating Adam and Eve, they were placed in a garden where there were every tree that was good for food, and in the center was the tree of life (Gen. 2:9). Then, Joseph was recorded as a prominent steward for dispensing food to the 12 tribes of Israel during a famine. There in Egypt, they grew from 75 people to a huge family of over 2 million when they left Egypt. After that, there was the eating of the Passover lamb, the daily nourishment of manna, and the enjoyment of the rich assortment of food in the promised land. Additionally, as part of God's commandments, the Israelites were to eat some of their offerings to God and feast for seven days three times a year.

It is abundantly clear that God desires that His people be fed, and it is out of this feeding, *oikonomia*, that He gained a grown-up family. When His family in the Hebrew Scriptures matured, He was glorified by the building of Solomon's temple. Since the real food for God's people to grow and mature is Jesus Christ, the assortment of foods for God's people in the Hebrew Scriptures was the archetypes of Christ.

The Hidden Mystery—Christ in You, the Hope of Glory

I now rejoice in my sufferings for you, and fill up in my flesh what is lacking in the afflictions of Christ, for the sake of **His body**, which is the church [**ekklesia** – democratic assembly], 25 of which I became a minister according to the stewardship [oikonomia] from God which was given to me for you, to fulfill the word of God, 26 the **mystery which has been hidden** from ages and from generations, but now has been revealed to His saints. 27 To them God willed to make known what are the riches of the glory of this mystery among the Gentiles: which is **Christ in you**, the hope of glory.

– Col. 1:24-27

The apostle Paul suffered for the sake of the Lord's Body, His Democratic Assembly, and it is for her that he received the stewardship [oikonomia] to fulfill or complete the Word of God. Isn't Jesus' death, resurrection, and becoming Lord of all, the completion of God's purpose? Paul had to fill up or complete the Word of God because the completed word is "*Christ in you*." It is not just Christ who ascended to the heavens on the throne. It is Christ in you ("you all"-plural), in His corporate Body. The *oikonomia* Paul received is to dispense the riches of God's glory, which is Christ in you. The unsearchable riches of Christ in the believers are essential for the maturity of the Lord's democratic assembly, His family.

Christ is God who came in the flesh. He is 100% God and 100% man with both divinity and humanity. What a mystery this Christ, via the Spirit of Christ, is in all His believers. He is not just next to or watching over them, He is literally in them. To many Christians, Christ in them may be figuratively similar to, "I have my boyfriend in my heart," or "Football is dear to my heart." What they mean is that they are always thinking about it and greatly love it, so it is in their heart. Is Christ in His people in that type of way because they are always praying and thinking about Him, or is He actually in them? Jesus Christ is truly and literally in them.

Jesus said: He who eats my flesh and drinks my blood abides in me and I in him (John 6:56). He is in the believers the same way He is in the Father (John 14:20). Then Paul said: Jesus Christ is in all those who are in the faith (2 Cor. 13:5). These are just a sampling of wonderful and powerful verses declaring that Jesus Christ is in His people. That is mysterious! How can that be? Yet, this is true. The simple faith in Jesus Christ brings into the believers His eternal life and divine nature with His attributes and person.

Even though this indwelling did not happen until after the death and resurrection of Christ, this was prophesied in words, archetypes, and figures in the Hebrew Scriptures. It was there in Genesis and the rest of the Torah, in the Psalms, and the prophets. Ingesting food is an example of receiving something from outside a person and assimilating it to become the person's physical body. He is the living food, and when ingested, His Spirit remains alive and living in those who receive Him.

Ezekiel prophesied explicitly that God would give them a new spirit and put His Spirit into His people (Eze. 36:26-27). This is the very nature or inward writing of the law of God placed into His people: This is the New Covenant (Jer. 31:31). Those hearing these prophecies in those days would have no idea what it meant. They knew the exterior God in heaven, Whom they worshiped and to Whom they made offerings. They knew how to fear God and His judgments. However, to have God's Spirit in them — the very nature of God's law integrated into their human spirit, heart, and nature was simply unimaginable — too mysterious.

However, this is the secret needed for all the other mysteries relating to God's Democratic Assembly: The Bride of Christ, godliness — God manifested in the flesh, and "joint heirs, joint body, and joint partakers" (see Eph. 3:3-6 below). Without seeing and understanding this matter of "Christ in you," it is impossible to have a diverse people in oneness expressing God. The life and nature of the Trinity (Christ in you) is the only enabler for people of distinct differences to have the freedom to act individually. Yet, they love one another and are truly one — as the Father and the Son are one.

Brethren, do you see this "hidden mystery" NOW revealed? Yes, there is/was the promise of the New Covenant and that it would be written on our hearts and that He would put His Spirit within us — but how would He do it? Praise God: By the death, resurrection, ascension, and the Spirit of the glorified Christ in His people . . . He found the only way one could live and love was by His New Commandment. He would have to do that in and through them by His Life-giving Spirit . . . THAT'S THE HIDDEN MYSTERY. "Lord, open the inner eyes of our hearts so that we might apprehend this hidden mystery in us!"

The Mystery of Christ—Joint heirs, Joint Body, and Joint partakers

> That by revelation the **mystery** has been made known to me, (according as I have written before briefly, 4 by which, in reading it, ye can understand my intelligence in the **mystery of the Christ**,) 5 which in other generations has not been made known to the sons of men, as it has now been revealed to his

> holy apostles and prophets in spirit, 6 that [they who are of] the nations
> should be joint heirs, and a joint body, and joint partakers of [his] promise
> in Christ Jesus by the glad tidings; . . . 21 to him be glory in the assembly
> [ekklesia — democratic assembly] in Christ Jesus unto all generations of the
> age of ages. Amen).
>
> — Eph. 3:3-6, 21, DBY

When Jesus Christ was alive on the earth, it was easy to know Him . . . at least for those who had the privilege of being close to Him. They knew His kindness, power, love, boldness, honesty, patience, wisdom, selflessness, sinlessness, suffering, and more. They witnessed how He cared for the sick, extended Himself to those rejected, forgave all kinds of sinners, and loved all people. However, even then, there was a mysterious side to Him. His disciples did not understand what He meant when He said He would die and rise on the third day (Luke 18:31-34). Multiple times, Jesus spoke of His death and resurrection. It was a mystery to the disciples. When Peter objected to Jesus speaking of His death out of His concern for Jesus' well-being, Jesus called him *Satan* (Matt. 16:21-23).

The discourse Jesus had with His disciples at the Last Supper, recorded in John chapters 13-17, could only be described as mysterious. They had no idea what Jesus was speaking of: going away and returning (John 16:17-18). Jesus said they would not understand where and why He would be going until after He returned as the Spirit of Truth (John 16:12-13). Therefore, Christ is a mystery, and it was primarily unveiled through Paul.

It took a revelation in spirit or by the Spirit that the mystery was revealed to Paul. This mystery was hidden from all men until the New Testament apostles came on the scene. By reading Paul's writings, believers can truly grasp the mystery as was shown to him. This is a fundamental reason for reading and studying the Scriptures, both the prophetic Scriptures in the Old Testament and those in the New Testament — especially Paul's epistles.

The mystery in this part is focused specifically on the mystery of Christ: that those of the nations (Gentiles) *together* with the Jews become joint heirs, a joint body, and joint partakers. These two people who had been enemies for centuries, full of hatred, envy, and jealousy, would come together as one to inherit all that God is, becoming one Body, united together, and joint partakers of all God's promises in and through Christ.

Here is a brief history leading up to the prophetic writings on this mystery: The building up of David/Solomon's temple was the zenith of Israel, displaying a picture of God manifested in the flesh. However, Solomon fell into God's judgment for worshipping all kinds of idols (1 Kings 11:1-13). God pronounced judgment upon King Solomon's "indiscretions" by tearing apart David's kingdom into two houses. The house of Judah would retain one tribe (Benjamin) because according to the prophecy of Jacob: *"The scepter will not depart from Judah, nor the ruler's staff from between his feet, until he to whom it belongs shall come (lit. "until Shiloh come")"* (Gen. 49:10). Meanwhile, the other 10 tribes would be given to one of Solomon's servants, Jeroboam, of the tribe of Ephraim. This took place when Solomon's son, Rehoboam, refused to lower taxation and end labor exploitation demanded by the ten tribes of the north, henceforth known as Ephraim, Israel, Jezreel, and Samaria. The ten tribes separated from the kingdom of David, while the southern two tribes were called Judah (and those of these two tribes, plus the tribe of Levi, were called "Jews" or *Yehudah*[4]).

These two kingdoms became enemies and never came back together as one kingdom until after Christ's death and resurrection. Due to Jeroboam's insecurity that Israel might return to Judah, he institutionalized a division between the two kingdoms. This was the "sin of Jeroboam" that God remembered because it kept Israel away from worshipping with the other two tribes in Jerusalem and the temple. Without the God-ordained assemblies to feast with all the tribes as one people, Israel lost God's blessing and fell deeper and deeper into idolatry. Indeed, there was not even one good or godly king in all of Israel's 19 recorded kings for about 188 years of its history (931-722 BC). The Assyrian Empire conquered them, and their capital, Samaria, was destroyed over several years — beginning in 727 BC and culminating in 722 BC. The majority of the ten tribes were then exiled from their homeland, dispersed throughout Assyria, while foreign peoples were brought in to repopulate the land of Israel. The ten tribes got swallowed and disappeared in the Assyrian empire (Hos. 8:7-9). The strategy for the Assyrians to maintain control of a conquered land was to swap out and dilute the remaining population. The conquered people would lose their identity. The Samaritans in the New Testament were people who had no relationship with the Jews (John 4:9).

About 115 years later, from 607-586 BC, Judah and Benjamin (the remaining two tribes) were defeated by the Babylonians and were exiled to Babylon with the destruction of the Solomonic Temple in 586 BC. This timeframe was prophesied by Jeremiah in Jeremiah 25 and affirmed by Daniel 9:2. This was the 70 years of Babylonian captivity. In 538-537 BC, about 50,000 from the tribes of Judah, Benjamin, and some Levites returned to Jerusalem to rebuild the temple and the city. About 500 years later, Jesus was born of the descendants of those of Judah who returned.

---

4   It was during the Babylonian Captivity that the term "Jews" designated the two tribes and the tribe of Levi who were taken into Babylonian Captivity from 607-537 BC (70 years). Strictly speaking, the term "Yehudah" (Jew) which means "Praise" or "Thanksgiving" was not in use until this time and thereafter.

To the Jews at the time of Jesus, even though they were descendants of only two tribes (plus Levites), they considered themselves the continuation of all Israel since the other 10 were deported and disappeared. Speaking of "Jewish-Israel" Paul says in Romans 9:4-5 that they are special as God's people (Deut. 7:6), God's son (Hos. 11:1), the keeper of God's glory (1 King 8:11), the covenanted people with God's law (Exo. 34:27; Neh. 9:13), God gave them promises, they are uniquely servants of God (Exo. 12:25), and from whom Christ came. All the other people on earth are considered unclean and overt sinners (Gal. 2:15).

There was a tall and wide wall separating and dividing the Jews and those of the nations (Gentiles). This separation was called the wall of hatred or hostility (Eph. 2:14), built up for over 900 years. The Jews were forbidden by law even to associate with or visit a Gentile's home (Acts 10:28). Again, the Jews' separation from the Gentiles/Nations included the descendants of the ten northern tribes whose genetics had been diluted among the nations for over 700 years of intermarriage.

How astounding and miraculous that these two enemies would become joint heirs, a joint body, and joint partakers. Nevertheless, this is the mystery of Christ, which was prophesied numerous times in the Hebrew Scriptures. Both the major and minor prophets spoke of the ten tribes of Israel (Ephraim) and the two tribes of Judah (the Jews) coming back together again for the rebuilding of David's United Kingdom. When reading these prophecies, a person familiar with Israel's history will say, "No way, this can never be." It is unbelievable that all twelve tribes can somehow come back together according to these prophecies. The northern ten tribes (aka Ten Lost Tribes) are gone, disappeared, so how is it possible for the United Kingdom of David (aka "the Tabernacle of David") to be restored? The prophets are simply wrong.

No wonder Paul said it took a revelation for him to understand this mystery of Christ. He thoroughly understood the prophetic writings concerning this mystery. Thus, he composed his epistles so that believers in the New Testament era might likewise recognize the validity of the prophecies and understand that they were accurately and fully fulfilled. The mystery of Christ is revealed as His Democratic Assembly!

The Mystery of the Gospel and the Mystery of Faith

> And for me, that utterance may be given to me, that I may open my mouth boldly to make known the mystery of the gospel,
>
> – Eph. 6:19-20

> Holding the mystery of the faith with a pure conscience.
>
> – 1 Tim. 3:9

The gospel means good news. Faith is closely related to the gospel. Although the gospel is preached, it only benefits those who have faith. If a person does not believe the good news, then that news does not affect him. Both the gospel and faith of Jesus were hidden in the Hebrew Scriptures but fully proclaimed in plain words in the New Testament. The death and resurrection of Jesus Christ made the gospel and faith fully realized and experiential.

In the Hebrew Scriptures, after man (male and female) succumbed to the Serpent's temptation and partook of the Tree of Knowledge of Good and Evil, God came to proclaim judgment on them. It can be inferred that God's judgment on Satan, the woman, and Adam happened when all three parties were present. Therefore, the condemnation of Satan was the gospel to Adam. God proclaimed to the Serpent, *"And I will put enmity between you and the woman, and between your seed and her Seed; He shall bruise your head, and you shall bruise His heel"* (Gen. 3:15). On one hand, this prophecy was bad news for the Serpent since he would be crushed. On the other hand, for Adam, it was good news since the woman would live and have a seed to deal with Satan. God preached the first gospel (protoevangelium). Adam believed the good news that his wife is going to have a seed and called her "Eve," which means "living" or "life-giving."

Then God preached the gospel to Abraham, telling him that he would have a seed (Gen. 15:5). He believed, and it was counted to him as righteousness (Gen. 15:6). Finally, God told Israel they would have their land and made a covenant with them on Mount Sinai, which was the gospel to all Israel. However, they did not receive this gospel by faith; consequently, they died in the wilderness (Heb. 4:2).

When the gospel of Jesus Christ was finally proclaimed in the New Testament, it was rich and multifaceted. Therefore, it was described as: the gospel of God, the gospel of the grace of God, the gospel of peace, and the gospel of the kingdom. In the chapter entitled "The Mystery of the Gospel," the complete gospel will be explored. The gospel of God can be simple in the form of a seed; however, within it are the unsearchable riches of Christ. This is the knowledge of the truth God desires all men to obtain.

In this text, a chapter will be dedicated to the gospel, and another will be on faith. Faith is joined together with the gospel. It is two sides of the same coin. The gospel or the knowledge of the truth preached is the object for Christians to believe (objective faith). So, how do people receive the ability to believe in the first place (subjective faith)? This subjective faith is a gift from God. This chapter will explore how faith is received, how to grow in faith, the testing of faith, and the work of faith. This is the common faith in which all believers unite as the Lord's one Body.

2

MYSTERY OF GOD – CHRIST

> That their hearts may be encouraged, being knit together in love, to reach all the riches of full assurance of understanding and the knowledge of God's mystery, which is Christ,
>
> – Col 2:2, ESV

The mystery of God is Christ. Christ explains and declares who God is. Without Christ, God would remain a hidden mystery. If people do not know Christ, God would remain a mystery to them. The prophetic writings reveal Christ in types and figures. By understanding these archetypes, one would know who Christ is and His mission. Here are some of the more notable unveilings of Christ in the prophetic writings starting from Genesis.

Adam Is a Type of Christ

> Nevertheless death reigned from Adam to Moses, even over those who had not sinned according to the likeness of the transgression of Adam, who is a type of Him who was to come.
>
> – Rom. 5:14

> And so it is written, "The first man Adam became a living being." The last Adam [became] a life-giving spirit. . . . 47 The first man [was] of the earth, [made] of dust; the second Man [is] the Lord from heaven.
>
> – 1 Cor. 15:45, 47

In Romans 5:14, Paul clearly states that Adam is an archetype of Christ. And the last Adam, Jesus Christ, became a life-giving Spirit through His death and resurrection. The word "type" in Greek means a mark of a stroke or a blow (Thayer's). It is an imprint formed by an impression. This means the archetype, Adam, was not the real figure. He was the imprint of the real figure, Jesus Christ. Adam was created in the image and likeness of God; however, Jesus was the real image of the invisible God (Col. 1:15). When God created Adam, He had in view the coming of Jesus Christ, Who is the reality of God's image.

Adam was to subdue and have dominion over all the earth, but through disobedience, he failed. Instead, He was subdued by God's enemy, Satan. Jesus — God incarnate in the flesh — is the one who defeated Satan as a man and has everything subdued under His feet (Heb. 2:14). Therefore, Hebrews 2:8-9 says, *"You [God] have put all things in subjection under his [man's] feet. For in that He put all in subjection under him, He left nothing [that is] not put under him. But now we do not yet see all things put under him. But we see Jesus, who was made a little lower than the angels, for the suffering of death crowned with glory and honor . . . ."*

Universally, in God's perspective, there are only two men in the cosmos. The first is Adam, who is made of the dust of the earth. The second is not Cain or Abel, but Jesus, the Lord from heaven. However, this second man is also the last Adam. There will not be another man or Adam after Him. So, Paul said:

> Therefore, as through one man's [Adam's] offense judgment came to all men, resulting in condemnation, even so through one Man's [Jesus Christ] righteous act the free gift came to all men, resulting in justification of life.
>
> — Rom 5:18

The first man Adam sinned, resulting in divine condemnation and judgment. Hallelujah, the second Man, Jesus Christ, came and through His righteous act on the cross, He gave the free gift of justification unto eternal life to all who believe in His name. If people stay in their original forefather of the first Adam, they are already condemned, sentenced, and awaiting final judgment. However, through faith in accepting His pardon through Jesus Christ, people are transferred to the second Man who ended the sentence of death upon the Adamic race. In Christ, His followers partake of His eternal divine nature (2 Peter 1:4 NKJV) and are now enjoying eternal life.

Jesus Christ came as a man, died as a man, resurrected, ascended as a man, and is seated as the Lord of lords as a glorified man. He is the Man Whom God desired from eternity. He is the man in God's image and likeness — the One who defeated Satan. Juxtaposed to the first Adam, the last Adam was *". . . obedient unto death, even the death of the cross"* (Phil. 2:8). God has now *". . . highly exalted Him and given Him the name which is above every name, that at the name of Jesus, every knee should bow, of those in heaven, and of those on earth, and of those under the earth, and that every tongue should confess that Jesus Christ is Lord, to the glory of God the Father"* (Phil. 2:9-11 NKJV).

The Tree of Life

> And out of the ground the LORD God made every tree grow that is pleasant to the sight and good for food. The tree of life [was] also in the midst of the garden, and the tree of the knowledge of good and evil.
>
> – Gen. 2:9

> "I am the true vine, and My Father is the vinedresser."
>
> – John 15:1

> Jesus said to her, "I am the resurrection and the life. He who believes in Me, though he may die, he shall live."
>
> – John 11:25

The next significant type of Christ (after Adam) is the Tree of Life. Eating this tree would cause a person to live eternally (Gen. 3:22). Certainly, this is speaking of receiving God's eternal life by ingesting the fruit of this tree. God put this tree squarely amid the garden so that man had many opportunities to partake of God's eternal life. The Tree of Life, as described in Revelation 22:2, is so accessible that it spreads like a vine-tree since it can be on both sides of the river, which spirals down from the throne at the peak to the gates at the bottom. Giving man this divine-eternal life was God's desire from the very beginning when He placed the first Adam in front of the Tree of Life; therefore, His life as typified by the Tree of Life was readily available.

However, when man partook of the Tree of Knowledge of Good and Evil, he ingested sin and death, the nature of Satan. Due to this degradation of man, God could not allow man to simultaneously partake of the Tree of Life and live forever with sin and death in his flesh. Therefore, God guarded the way to the Tree of Life and prevented man from partaking of eternal life.

Jesus Christ, the last Adam, came to terminate the old man. The old man is the corrupted man – he had become mutated – injected by sin through disobedience. How did the last Adam deal with this mutated man? Through His death on the cross, the 'old man' was crucified and brought to an end (Rom. 6:6). In His resurrection, Christ became the Tree of Life – available for man to receive, partake of, and live by. He said, "Eat My flesh and drink My blood" to have eternal life (John 6:54). Jesus is the vine tree and the life for men (male and female) to partake of Him. This was God's purpose in eternity past, now, and into the eternal future: That man would ingest and partake of Himself so that man would become one with Him and express His attributes in their human nature. *"But we all, with unveiled face, beholding as in a mirror the glory of the Lord, are being transformed into the same image from glory to glory, just as by the Spirit of the Lord"* (2 Cor. 3:18).

Now, the result of ingesting the Tree of Life is that man produces the fruit of the Spirit. Characteristics that are truly human yet altogether divine: love, joy, peace, longsuffering, kindness, goodness, faithfulness, gentleness, and self-control that do not end or dissipate. God's desire was not simply that man would have His image and likeness, but also bear the fruit of His life and nature. Man would literally become His children, His offspring, expressing God's characteristics in every way. Man would have the inner capacity to emulate God, the physical dexterity and reflection of God, and God's divine-eternal life and nature.

Man enters this mystical, miraculous union with God by eating Jesus, the real Tree of Life. It is this oneness with God that man lives daily on earth. Additionally, Jesus is extremely accessible to man anywhere at any time. No fleshly work or effort is needed. No requirements other than an open heart to believe and receive Him.

God Clothed Adam and Eve with Skins

> And the LORD God made for Adam and for his wife garments of skins and clothed them.
>
> – Gen 3:21, ESV

> So in Christ Jesus you are all children of God through faith, 27 for all of you who were baptized into Christ have clothed yourselves with Christ.
>
> – Gal 3:26-27

God warned Adam that if he were to eat of the Tree of Good and Evil, he would surely die (Gen. 2:17). Now that Satan deceived Eve, and Adam was disobedient in that they ate of the Tree of the Knowledge of Good and Evil, resulting in death, God is (if you would) in a quandary. Why? Because, since they now face the consequence of sin's penalty – death – then God's eternal purpose would be thwarted by His enemy; but if they continue to live, then God's word ("you will surely die") would be made meaningless and He would be pronounced unrighteous. So, God devised a way to save them and maintain His righteousness. His way of salvation was also a type of Jesus Christ: He clothed them with skins, whereby blood was shed.

To have two skins for Adam and Eve, two animals had to die (assuming that one animal can cover a person). God killed these animals and He provided Adam and Eve with these skins for clothing. Now, there are two dead animal carcasses with Adam and Eve clothed in the skins of the animals. Dead animals covered their nakedness and, in that sense, took their place with Man (male and female) now living inside these dead animals. When the angels of the universe look down on Earth, they see these two slain animals, while Adam and Eve are nowhere to be found. They are gone from the face of the earth. By this deed of "covering," God fulfilled His word: "you shall surely die."

The death of these two animals and their skins covering Adam and Eve are a type of Jesus Christ, Who came to die in order for man to die in Him and live in Him. Scriptures say that when Christ died, mankind died, and when Christ was made alive, man was made alive in Him (Rom. 6:5; Gal. 2:20). Jesus Christ, as the last Adam, terminated the first Adam, which fulfilled God's promise of "you shall surely die." However, by faith, man is immersed (baptized) into Jesus Christ. Now man can be clothed with Him. He is man's clothing: man is wrapped and living inside Christ. The universe no longer sees Adam, who sinned under the pronouncement of death. Adam is gone; however, man continues to live inside Christ, the second Man. God was ready for man's salvation as soon as man sinned and was condemned to death — He prepared a way of escape for man.

Noah's Ark

> . . . to those who were disobedient long ago when God waited patiently in the days of Noah while the ark was being built. In it only a few people, eight in all, were saved through water, 21 and this water symbolizes baptism that now saves you also — not the removal of dirt from the body but the pledge of a clear conscience toward God. It saves you by the resurrection of Jesus Christ,
>
> – 1 Pet. 3:20-21, NIV

The Adamic race became intolerably wicked in God's eyes. God decided to destroy them (Gen. 6:5-7). Again, if all of man were terminated, Satan would have won. Man was to be the instrument to defeat and subdue Satan; therefore, for God's purpose to succeed, man would have to live. God's way to save humanity was for Noah to build an ark. After Noah built the ark, his entire family of eight people (four couples) plus "two of all living creatures (species)" entered the ark. Then a great flood came over the earth for 40 days and 40 nights of rain, with the "fountains of the deep" flooding the Earth. Only those in the ark were saved from the deluge.

In his epistles, Peter says that salvation in the ark was a symbol or a figure to show something else. That something else indicates that believers in Christ are raised out of the death waters of baptism and raised in newness of life in Christ, their ark of resurrection. He is the real Ark that believers have entered. He went through the judgment of God (the baptism of the death waters), and He came through in resurrection. It is in Him, in His resurrection, that His followers are saved. The ark was a symbol of the real salvation that passed through God's judgment on sinful Adam and came through in resurrection. Believers are saved in Jesus Christ, Who is their ark of salvation.

Melchizedek

> Then Melchizedek king of Salem brought out bread and wine; he [was] the priest of God Most High.
>
> – Gen 14:18

When Lot, Abraham's nephew, separated from Abraham due to conflict, Abraham let Lot choose the better portion of the land. Lot chose the lush valley of Sodom, but later, foreign kings came to conquer that land and took Lot and his family as prisoners. When Abraham (*Abram* at the time before his name was changed to *Abraham* – "father of nations") heard, he immediately took his men to rescue Lot. Abraham and his men defeated the kings who captured Lot and rescued him. Abraham returned from his victories, and on his way back, Melchizedek met him and immediately ministered to Abram bread and wine (Gen. 14:18).

Melchizedek was more than a type or prefigure of Jesus, He was the pre-incarnate Son of God since *"He is without father or mother or genealogy, having neither beginning of days nor end of life, but resembling the Son of God He continues a priest forever"* (Heb. 7:3). He ministered to Abraham just like Jesus who served bread and wine to His disciples at the last supper. After rescuing Lot, Melchizedek showed up with food and drink for Abraham. He was undefeated and unafraid, but took bold action specifically to free his "brother" from captivity.

The writer of Hebrews contrasted the priesthood of Melchizedek with that of the Aaronic priesthood. The priesthood of Aaron was for the forgiveness of sins (Heb. 5:1-5). His ministry helped those who were under the condemnation of sin and made sacrifices for sins. However, Jesus, in the order of Melchizedek, ministered bread and wine for life and living. It is a better ministry than that of Aaron. Aaron and his offerings signified Christ's death on the cross for the sins of the world. Melchizedek is Christ in resurrection ministering the indestructible life for salvation and interceding for His followers (Heb. 7:25). Jesus' ministry to rid man of sins was done once for all through His death, but His ministry of life continues forever. For the followers of Jesus today, they need nourishment from Melchizedek to be strengthened to liberate their brethren who have been captured. Furthermore, there is ministry and enjoyment from Melchizedek after the victory of rescuing our brethren.

The Son of Abraham: Isaac

> So Abraham took the wood of the burnt offering and laid [it] on Isaac his son; and he took the fire in his hand, and a knife, and the two of them went together. . . . 9 Then they came to the place of which God had told him. And Abraham built an altar there and placed the wood in order; and he bound Isaac his son and laid him on the altar, upon the wood. 10 And Abraham stretched out his hand and took the knife to slay his son. 11 But the Angel of the LORD called to him from heaven and said, "Abraham, Abraham!" So he said, "Here I am." 12 And He said, "Do not lay your hand on the lad, or do anything to him; for now I know that you fear God, since you have not withheld your son, your only [son], from Me."
>
> – Gen. 22:6, 9–12

> The book of the genealogy of Jesus Christ, the Son of David, the Son of Abraham:
>
> – Matt. 1:1

> For God so loved the world that He gave His only begotten Son, that whoever believes in Him should not perish but have everlasting life.
>
> – John 3:16

Abraham was the first one called by God to become the father of a "multitude of nations" (Gen. 17:5 – lit. the "Melo-Hagoyim" – Heb.). He had one son with Sarah (his wife): Isaac. He was Abraham's only begotten son. Abraham was to offer up His only son to be a sacrifice to God upon Mt. Moriah, near where Jesus was crucified (Gen. 22:2). Isaac had to carry the wood for the fire on his back up the hill where Abraham was going to build the altar. Issac carried the very wood that would be used for his death, just like Jesus carried His cross. Then Abraham built the altar and bound his son upon the altar to be sacrificed. However, just as Abraham was going to kill his son as an offering, God stopped him (Gen. 22:9-13). From Abraham and Isaac's point of view, he was as good as dead and was offered to God.

Abraham offered Isaac on the mountain called Mount Moriah. Likewise, this was the same site upon which Solomon's temple was built. Jesus was crucified on Golgotha, on the same geological formation where Isaac was offered. Certainly, this could not be a coincidence that out of all the places in the good land, Isaac was offered as a sacrifice in just about the same place as Jesus was crucified on the cross. Just as Issac carried the wood for the altar, Jesus bore the cross for His crucifixion (John 19:17). According to historians, Jesus would have had to carry the cross for about 1.5 miles, which is the distance from the Praetorium to Golgotha (although Simon, a man from today's Libya, helped him ([Luke 23:26]).

Abraham's offering up of Isaac was a prefigure of God the Father sacrificing His only begotten Son, Jesus Christ, to die on man's behalf. God's love is so great that He gave His only Son to be the sacrifice for our sins so that man (male and female) may live. This is not just for man to live a human life, but God's eternal life. Man's destiny was to perish, but faith in Jesus Christ gave mankind eternal life because of Jesus' crucifixion.

Joseph – The Ruler of the World

The last story in Genesis concerns Joseph, starting from chapter 37. Joseph was the son of Jacob with Rachel, who was Jacob's first love. Joseph is one of the best archetypes of Jesus Christ in the prophetic writings, spanning his being the Father's beloved son, suffering unjust persecution, and eventually becoming the ruler of the known world.

Like Jesus is God's beloved Son, Joseph was the father's beloved son (Gen. 37:3). His father sent Joseph to care for his brothers. Jesus was sent by God the Father to do God's will (John 6:38). In doing the will of his Father, Joseph was betrayed by his brothers. Though Jesus came to His own people, they rejected Him (John 1:11). As with Joseph, He was hated without reason (John 15:25), endured persecution, and was betrayed by one intimately connected to Him (Matt. 26:21).

Though Joseph was innocent, He was falsely accused and was put into prison where there were two other prisoners, one was set free and the other put to death. Jesus was the innocent and sinless Lamb of God, yet He was condemned to die on the cross (1 Pet. 2:22-24). On the cross, there were two men also being crucified. One mocked Him, but the other believed and was released from the torment of death to be in paradise with Jesus (Luke 23:39-43).

When Joseph was released from prison, he received all authority and became the ruler of the Egyptian kingdom. When Jesus came out of the prison of death in resurrection, He received all authority in heaven and earth (Matt. 28:18). Jesus was given the highest name, to Him every knee shall bow and confess Jesus is Lord (Phil. 2:9-11). Joseph was named Zaphenath-Paaneah, which means "savior of the age"

(Gesenius' Lexicon). Truly, the real savior is Jesus Christ: *"Him God has exalted to His right hand to be Prince and Savior, to give repentance to Israel and forgiveness of sins"* (Acts 5:31).

Joseph married a Gentile Egyptian woman. The Bride of Christ also included Gentiles, as Paul said that the Lord's Ekklesia (Democratic Assembly) is the wife of Christ in Ephesians 5:25. His wife includes both Jews and Gentiles (Eph. 3:6). Joseph's brothers betrayed him, but after Joseph became the ruler, he forgave them and supplied his brothers with food. Jesus forgave those who crucified Him and ministered to them in resurrection (Luke 23:34; Acts 3:15, 26). Just like Joseph's brothers recognized him, one day the Jewish brethren will also recognize Jesus the One they crucified (Rev. 1:7) and they will be saved (Rom. 11:26). Like Joseph, Jesus in fulfillment will be the true ruler over His Kingdom: *"The kingdoms of this world have become the kingdoms of our Lord and of His Christ, and He shall reign forever and ever!"* (Rev. 11:15).

The Passover

'Your lamb shall be without blemish . . . . Then the whole assembly of the congregation of Israel shall kill it at twilight. 7 'And they shall take [some] of the blood and put [it] on the two doorposts and on the lintel of the houses where they eat it. 8 'Then they shall eat the flesh on that night; roasted in fire, with unleavened bread [and] with bitter [herbs] they shall eat it. . . . 11 'And thus you shall eat it: [with] a belt on your waist, your sandals on your feet, and your staff in your hand. So you shall eat it in haste. It [is] the LORD's Passover. . . . 13 'Now the blood shall be a sign for you on the houses where you [are]. And when I see the blood, I will pass over you; and the plague shall not be on you to destroy [you] when I strike the land of Egypt.

– Exo. 12:5-8, 11

The next day John saw Jesus coming toward him, and said, "Behold! The Lamb of God who takes away the sin of the world!

– John 1:29

Therefore purge out the old leaven, that you may be a new lump, since you truly are unleavened. For indeed Christ, our Passover, was sacrificed for us.

– 1Cor. 5:7

The twelve tribes of Israel were enslaved in Egypt for over 200 years. God's people were slaves building Pharaoh's treasure cities (Deut. 5:15). Israel cried out in their distress to God, and He heard their cry. Therefore, God chose Moses to free Israel from Egypt (Ex. 3:9-10). Pharaoh would not easily let Israel leave Egypt, so Moses brought ten plagues to Egypt. The last plague was the death of all the firstborn of both man and beast in Egypt (Exod. 11:5). On a certain day, all the firstborn were to be killed.

However, God provided salvation to Israel's firstborn. It was a lamb to be slain (on Passover Preparation Day – Nisan 13) with its blood put on the doorposts and its meat eaten in haste (on Nisan 14 – Passover day) so that they would be strengthened to leave Egypt the following day. That night, when death came upon all the firstborn of Egypt, God said, *"When I see the blood, I will pass over you."* So, it happened that Israel's firstborns were saved from death due to the blood of the lamb on their doorpost.

That was a prefigure of the Lamb that was to come: Jesus Christ. He was the real Lamb of God who took away the sins of the world, and those who would believe in His saving death have His precious blood displayed to God. God's judgment of death upon sinful men will pass over them when He sees the blood of His Son, the Lamb, upon them (Rom. 5:9). The blood of Jesus redeemed man from the curse/penalty of the law. Now, through the "blood of the Lamb of God," His believers have their sins forgiven (Eph. 1:7).

While God is satisfied by the blood of the Lamb, His people are eating the "flesh" of the Lamb for strength to live (John 6:54). While the judgment of God is upon fallen men, His followers are eating and enjoying Him in faith. On one hand, the Passover has appeased God; on the other hand, His people are to ingest Him and be filled with Him. Even though God has forgiven His people, they still need to ingest Jesus as food; otherwise, they do not have the strength to move out of slavery. Christ as food enables His people to be strong in this dark world.

Jesus is the real Passover. Israel continues to observe the Passover, rooted in its origin in Egypt; likewise, followers of Jesus are to continually remember and partake of Him as their daily Passover. They are free from God's judgment and inwardly energized to live by His nourishment.

Manna in the Wilderness

> And the children of Israel ate manna forty years, until they came to an inhabited land; they ate manna until they came to the border of the land of Canaan.
>
> – Exo. 16:35

"Your fathers ate the manna in the wilderness, and are dead. 50 "This is the bread which comes down from heaven, that one may eat of it and not die. 51 "I am the living bread which came down from heaven. If anyone eats of this bread, he will live forever . . ."

– Jn. 6:49-51

After Israel left Egypt and wandered in the wilderness for forty years, God sustained them with manna. Manna came every morning for six days (with twice as much on the day before Sabbath, which was kept so they could eat it on the Sabbath or seventh day of the week). They were to gather this bread from heaven in the morning (except on the Sabbath) and eat this manna every day. Manna means "what is it" since they did not know what this white, round thing was that tasted like a wafer with honey. So, manna was this miracle bread that came down from heaven to feed Israel.

In John Chapter 6, Jesus fed 5,000 men with just two fish and five loaves of bread. The people who were fed wanted to force Jesus to be their king. They wanted a king who could perform such miracles that would provide for them. However, Jesus told them that they would still die no matter how many miracles were performed for them. He did not come to Earth to continue such supernatural feats. Rather, He came as the Bread of Life (John 6:48). He is the real manna from heaven. He wanted His people to ingest Him as the Bread of Life and not die.

Jesus' coming as the Bread from heaven was a much greater miracle than the physical manna in the wilderness, eaten by Israel for 40 years. What, God became a Man so that people could eat Him? That is amazingly awesome. It is a miracle beyond imagination; yet, the people who wanted to make Him king could not accept this. They were offended and left Him (John 6:60-66). They wanted Jesus to perform continuous miracles, but they did not desire the greatest miracle of all – to ingest Jesus and have Him within them as eternal life.

Today, Jesus is still the Bread of Life from heaven. He is here and available for man to partake of Him through faith. Many Christians would like God to care for them through miracles. God may or may not answer such prayers. However, one thing is certain: God has already performed the most awesome miracle by giving His Son as manna to man. It is now up to all men to eat of Him, the Bread of Life.

The Rock that Followed Israel

"Behold, I will stand before you there on the rock in Horeb; and you shall strike the rock, and water will come out of it, that the people may drink." And Moses did so in the sight of the elders of Israel.

– Exo. 17:6

> And in the last, the great day of the feast, Jesus stood and cried, saying, 'If any one doth thirst, let him come unto me and drink; 38 he who is believing in me, according as the Writing said, Rivers out of his belly [innermost being] shall flow of living water;' 39 and this he said of the Spirit, which those believing in him were about to receive; for not yet was the Holy Spirit, because Jesus was not yet glorified.
>
> — John 7:37-39, YLT

> And all drank the same spiritual drink. For they drank of that spiritual Rock that followed them, and that Rock was Christ.
>
> — 1 Cor. 10:4

Wandering in the desert for 40 years, water was scarce, so Israel was often thirsty. They complained, and God responded by giving them a rock. He told Moses to strike the rock with his staff or rod. Moses did so, and water came flowing out of this rock. Later, God told Moses to simply speak to the rock, and water would flow out. Moses was not supposed to strike the rock again the second time. He was only to speak to the rock for drinkable water to flow out of it.

Paul said that the Rock that followed Israel in the wilderness was Christ. Wow, a rock followed them! This imagery shows that Christ was spiritually present with them during their journey. Remarkable that Jesus cried out on the last day of the Feast of Tabernacles (Booths or Nations — John 7:1-39) for those who thirst to come to Him and drink. People feasted and drank for seven days, yet they were still thirsty. They were inwardly dried up, even though they physically and emotionally enjoyed this grand celebration together. However, their spirits, the innermost part of their being, were devoid of the Living Water of Life — only the Living God could suffice and quench their thirst. Consequently, they were still thirsty.

Those who drink of Jesus could have the source of living water in their innermost being. The source of this quenching flow, which is Jesus, was outside of them, but after drinking Him as the source of Living Water, entering their "innermost being," this Living Water would now flow out of them, quenching the thirst in others.

Jesus was speaking of the Spirit, which was not yet. Of course, the Holy Spirit within the Trinity was there in eternity, but the **drinkable Spirit** was not yet available because Jesus had not yet been glorified. Most translations of the Bible add the word "given" (not yet *given*) because it does not sound logical that the Spirit of God was not yet in existence. Nevertheless, before Jesus' death and resurrection, the Holy Spirit could readily "influence" followers of YHWH (e.g., King David declared: "Take not thy Holy Spirit from me" – Psalm 51:11), but the Holy Spirit could not enter man (i.e., "regenerate the spirit of man"). It is after His glorification that the entering of the Spirit, or, if you would, the "drinkable Spirit," became a reality (John 14:16-17). Today, when people come to Jesus, they can freely drink this living water and have their thirst quenched in the deepest part of their being. The Spirit will regenerate their human spirit by His indwelling Spirit to be the source of the Water of Life flowing to others.

Moses struck the rock with his rod. This signifies Christ being judged under God's law on the cross (Gal. 3:13). His redemption for man is once and for all. He does not need to be crucified again (Heb. 7:27). So, the water was released once Moses struck the rock just as the Spirit of God was released at Jesus' glorification. He doesn't need to be crucified again for the living water to flow. Now, mankind can simply speak to Him. Speak to the Rock, and the water flows. Today, believers must converse with Jesus throughout the day to have this Living Water flowing in and out of them to others. Wonderful is the simplicity in Christ!

The Serpent on the Pole

> Then the LORD said to Moses, "Make a fiery [serpent], and set it on a pole; and it shall be that everyone who is bitten, when he looks at it, shall live."
>
> – Num. 21:8

> "And as Moses lifted up the serpent in the wilderness, even so must the Son of Man be lifted up . . . ."
>
> – John 3:14

> For what the law could not do in that it was weak through the flesh, God [did] by sending His own Son in the likeness of sinful flesh, on account of sin: He condemned sin in the flesh,
>
> – Rom. 8:3

Israel in the wilderness murmured against God; therefore, He sent poisonous snakes among them. Many were bitten and died. They repented and cried out to God for deliverance. God's solution was for Moses to make a serpent out of bronze and put it on a pole, which was to be lifted. Anyone who would just turn to look at this serpent on the pole was healed and survived the poisonous bite. It was effortless: look and live!

Jesus referenced this event and declared that He, as the Son of Man, would be lifted on the cross (John 12:32-33). He was the bronze serpent on the pole. Just as the bronze serpent didn't have the nature of the serpent, Jesus came in the likeness of fallen man, but without the accompanying sinful nature. He looked like fallen man tempted in every way, yet He was without sin (Heb. 4:15). His death on the cross condemned and terminated the sin in man's flesh.

Likewise, man has also been bitten by the poisonous snake — Satan. Fallen man's destiny is death due to the poison of sin in man's flesh. No number of good deeds, religious behaviors, or self-sacrifices can rid man of this poison of death. Death was not from God but from Satan. Death became part of man's nature due to eating the Tree of the Knowledge of Good and Evil. There is no deliverance from the body of this death due to sin's poison. Hallelujah, Jesus came to be lifted on the cross. His death on the cross eliminated the poison of sin, and death was defeated (1 Cor. 15:54-57). Believers are freed from death to live.

The Tabernacle

> Then the cloud covered the tabernacle of meeting, and the glory of the LORD filled the tabernacle.
>
> – Exo. 40:34

> And the Word [Jesus Christ] became flesh, and did tabernacle among us, and we beheld his glory, glory as of an only begotten of a father, full of grace and truth.
>
> – John 1:14, YLT

> And he was transfigured before them, and his face shone as the sun, and his garments did become white as the light.
>
> – Matt. 17:2, YLT

The Tabernacle was a tent built while Israel wandered through the wilderness. It was a tent the size of 15'x45' and 15' tall. The outside of it was covered with a type of animal skin: maybe badgers, dolphins, manatees, or others. However, God in His glory is inside that tent. From the outside, it was nothing special but quite ordinary in appearance. Nevertheless, inside was the dwelling place of the God of glory. God spoke from within the Tabernacle (Lev. 1:1).

This is certainly an archetype of Jesus Christ. Jesus Christ is God who was clothed with flesh. From the outside, Jesus looked ordinary, a common man ("skins"). However, hidden within Him resided the God of Glory. One day, Jesus took three of His disciples up to a mountain and there He transfigured before them: He shone like the sun in His glory. In essence, Jesus peeled back the "skins" of the Tabernacle, and the disciples saw what was inside: the God of glory.

Jesus declared God; therefore, seeing Jesus was the same as seeing the Father (John 14:9). In the body of Jesus tabernacles all the fullness of the Godhead (Col. 2:9). He was the real tabernacle moving on earth. Wherever Jesus went, though in ordinary "skins," God dwelt within Him. Jesus was also the mouthpiece of God's voice. Whatever He heard from God the Father, He spoke it. Jesus was and is the walking and speaking Tabernacle (John 8:28).

The Tabernacle of old was also called the "tent of meeting." It was the place where God and man met. Jesus Christ came as such a meeting place. As the Mediator, He is the meeting place between God and man (1 Tim. 2:5). In Him is the actual union or the real meeting of God and man: divinity with humanity. Precisely because Jesus is both God and man, in Him, people can meet with God. Inside the Tabernacle is the holy of holies or the holiest of all. This is where God resides and where believers can boldly enter this holiest place through the blood of Jesus (Heb. 10:19).

Joshua and the Good Land

> Then Moses called Joshua and said to him in the sight of all Israel, "Be strong and of good courage, for you must go with this people to the land which the LORD has sworn to their fathers to give them, and you shall cause them to inherit it. 8 "And the LORD, He [is] the One who goes before you. He will be with you, He will not leave you nor forsake you; do not fear nor be dismayed."
>
> – Deut. 31:7-8

> So Joshua took the whole land, according to all that the LORD had said to Moses; and Joshua gave it as an inheritance to Israel according to their divisions by their tribes. Then the land rested from war.
>
> – Josh. 11:23

> . . . giving thanks to the Father who has qualified us to be partakers of the inheritance of the saints in the light.
>
> – Col. 1:12

> As you therefore have received Christ Jesus the Lord, so walk in Him,
>
> – Col. 2:6
>
> . . . that the blessing of Abraham might come upon the Gentiles in Christ Jesus, that we might receive the promise of the Spirit through faith.
>
> – Gal. 3:14

Joshua and *Jesus* are the same name. Both names come from the word *Yehoshua* in Hebrew, which means *Jehovah saves*. Joshua is a direct translation from Hebrew to English, and Jesus is a translation via Greek (Ἰησοῦς or transliterated to Iésous). Therefore, Joshua in the Hebrew Bible is the prefigure of Jesus Christ; thus, having the same name.

Joshua was ordained to lead Israel into the Promised Land, the "good land." Moses and Joshua came out of Egypt together, but God didn't allow Moses to enter the good land because he struck the rock the second time (Num. 20:8-12). However, Joshua was one of the two spies who believed God's word that Israel could enter the Promised Land and conquer the giants — while the other ten disbelieved. Therefore, God rewarded Joshua (and Caleb) with the entrance into the Promised Land, for he did not perish in the wilderness (Num. 14:30). After entering the good land, he, along with Caleb, led Israel to victory in their conquest of the good land. After sufficient conquest, Joshua gave each tribe their allotted inheritance of the land.

The real Joshua, Jesus, defeated all His enemies and led His followers into the Promised Land. Now all His believers have an inheritance. Jesus, as the captain of God's people, has defeated all His enemies. Today, our Joshua-Jesus is leading His followers to a glorious salvation (Eph. 1:21; Heb. 2:10). In Christ, His followers have received their inheritance. Their portion is the expanse of the Triune God. The good land represents the unsearchable riches of Christ, which believers can enjoy and partake of throughout their daily living. No matter what situation they may find themselves in, they can still partake and be in fellowship with Him. Just as Israel was to walk throughout the land in all four directions to possess the land, today the followers of the "Captain of our salvation" (Joshua-Jesus) are directed to experience and enjoy Christ throughout their daily walk.

God's promised blessing to Abraham was that he would receive a good land (Gen. 17:7). However, in the New Testament, the blessing of Abraham is the promised Spirit. Christ, as the Spirit, is the good land for His followers. The Spirit is the environment in which believers have entered and in which they live and have their being. Just as the good land has many geographical features, such as mountains, seas, hills, and valleys, the Spirit can be enjoyed whether believers are feeling up or down, encouraged or discouraged; they are in the Spirit (Rom. 8:9).

Additionally, the inheritance is shared in the saints — all who believe (Acts 26:18; Eph. 1:18). Just as the Promised Land was apportioned among the twelve tribes, so the Spirit of God dwells within all who belong to Jesus Christ. Today, the inheritance of the people of God is within all the saints; therefore, we need to fellowship with all His diverse people to receive all the inheritance. If any of God's people cut off fellowship with some of God's people, they, in essence, have cut off part of their own inheritance. All of God's people are needed for the riches of God's inheritance to be fully enjoyed.

If believers only know how to experience Christ as their Passover, they may only need Him after sinning and need forgiveness and deliverance. Some may progress and know Jesus as their daily bread, sustaining them in the "wilderness" of life. They realize they must spend some quiet time reading the Bible and praying. This may be considered enjoying Christ as the daily manna. However, God desires that believers be in constant fellowship with Him and enjoy Him throughout the day, no matter where they may walk. Their entire living should be enveloped in the Spirit. They should also reach out to fellowship with all kinds of believers around them (not just with those in the same church). This is Jesus leading them throughout the good land.

David, the Shepherd-King, a Heart for God's House

". . . The LORD also said to you [David], 'You will shepherd my people Israel, and you will be ruler over Israel.' "

– 2 Sam. 5:2, CSB

"I will not enter my house or get into my bed, 4 "I will not allow my eyes to sleep or my eyelids to slumber 5 "until I find a place for the LORD, a dwelling for the Mighty One of Jacob."

– Psa. 132:3-5, CSB

"And when He had removed him, He raised up for them David as king, to whom also He gave testimony and said, 'I have found David the [son] of Jesse, a man after My [own] heart, who will do all My will.'"

– Acts 13:22

"I am the good shepherd. The good shepherd gives His life for the sheep."

– John 10:11

His disciples remembered that it was written, "Zeal for your house will consume me."

– John 2:17, ESV

Who was King David, and what were his outstanding achievements? God appointed him as a shepherd and to be the anointed king of Israel. He united all the tribes of Israel and defeated his enemies to the extent of possessing the land promised to Abraham (2 Sam. 5:1-5; 8:1-14). God spoke of David as one after His own heart, who would do His will (Acts 13:22). God's house was both in God's heart and David's heart. God was looking for a dwelling place to rest (Isa. 66:1). The temple was His house where He longed to reside. David's pledge in Psalm 132 shows the depth of His longing to build a house for God's dwelling. David cared for both God and His people. What a wonderful archetype of Jesus Christ.

Jesus Christ came as the real Shepherd who gave His life for His sheep. He led them and fed them. Jesus, as the Shepherd, liberates His sheep from all kinds of enclosures (sheepfold) and leads them out to find green pasture (John 10:9). The Shepherd came and the Pasture is here. The sheep need to hear His voice, follow Him out of being corralled (viz., the "sheepfold"), and enjoy Him as the open pasture.

The sheepfold at the time of Jesus was embodied in the First Covenant (Heb. 8:7, 13), which became the fold of Judaism. They need to come out of the original sheepfold through the Door (Christ — John 10:1-16) and join with the Good Shepherd of the sheep with another flock which is not of that sheepfold (John 10:16) so that there will be **one flock and one Shepherd**. While the sheepfold refers to Judaism, the "other sheep" refers to the Nations (Gk. "ethnos"). They will both come together with the Good Shepherd in the Pasture. The Sheepfold separates and divides the sheep, but the Pasture is where they are liberated and united. *"Other sheep I have which are not of this fold, them also I must bring, and they will hear My voice; and there will be one flock and one shepherd"* (John 10:16). It is altogether obvious that it is in the "pasture" — not in the original fold — where the Good Shepherd is bringing all His sheep together for them to have One Shepherd and be His One Flock.

Jesus is also the real David, the conquering King. Through His death on the cross, He subdued and defeated all His enemies (Col. 2:15). Satan himself was destroyed and his weapons of death taken away (Heb. 2:14). Christ took on the curse of humanity so that people can be liberated to receive the promise of Abraham (Gal. 3:13-14). Just as King David victoriously possessed the promised land for Israel, Jesus released the blessing of Abraham, which is the promise of the Spirit to His believers. It is through

Christ (the "Seed" seen in Isaac – Galatians 3:15-18; 4:28) as the real David that His followers enjoy the riches and immeasurable vastness of the Spirit of Promise (Gal. 3:14) – the good land.

As David's heart was fixated on building a house for God, even so, Jesus was zealous for building up God's House, His dwelling place. The statement in John 2:17, "the zeal of Your house has consumed me," referred to Jesus (Psa. 69:9). He was truly devoured by the building up of God's House. He was commissioned as the Christ for the building up of His Democratic Assembly which is His House, and for which He went to the cross (Matt. 16:18-21; 1 Tim. 3:15). God's dwelling place is expressed through the oneness of His people (John 17:23). Without unity His House cannot stand (Luke 11:17). Therefore, Jesus prayed for the unity of God's people (John 17:21), and He died to gather God's scattered children into one (John 11:52).

In John 10:9, Jesus said: *"I am the door. If anyone enters by me, he will be saved and will go in and out and find pasture."* The First Covenant was God's way of salvation through the Law of Moses, which entailed the sacrifices. The Mosaic Law preserved Israel; therefore, the Law was the guardian in the Mosaic Covenant (Gal. 3:23). As part of the law in the Mosaic Covenant, sacrifices were needed to cover all their sins. God accepted all the offerings and sacrifices in the Mosaic Covenant because He foresaw the redemption of Christ as One crucified on the cross. All those offerings in the Mosaic Covenant were a token to God, and He accepted them for the forgiveness of their sins because He recognized that Jesus was to die for the sins of the whole world (Rom. 3:25). His death accomplished eternal redemption covering all people, at all times, in all places (Heb. 9:12). Therefore, Jesus was the entrance door to enter salvation in the Mosaic Covenant (viz. the original sheepfold).

Now that Jesus has come, His goal is to call the original sheep of His sheepfold and to lead these sheep out (*"To him the doorkeeper opens, and the sheep hear his voice; and he calls his own sheep by name AND LEADS THEM OUT . . . and when **he brings out his own sheep**, he goes before them; and the sheep follow him, for they know his voice"* (John 10:3-4). Alas! There are still those within the sheepfold who remain enclosed – yet the door is open. *"Shall go in and out and find pasture"* (John 10:9) is NOT a call to go into the sheepfold – that's not where the pasture is. No, it's a call to come out of the sheepfold into the pasture. Both the Shepherd and the Pasture are here; therefore, come out from the sheepfold.

Today, we who have heard the voice of the Good Shepherd, notwithstanding, have created a multitude of sheepfolds that inhibit the sheep from the other sheep of His pasture. Yet, the direction now is not to go **into any of these** sheepfolds; rather, it is to come **out** (John 10:3). In fact, it is only when God's people come out and are not isolated in their sheepfold that they can be with the Shepherd's other sheep. The Lord desires to have one flock and one Shepherd: *"And I have other sheep that are not of this fold. I must bring them also, and they will listen to my voice. So, there will be one flock, one shepherd"* (John 10:16). If believers truly hear the shepherd's voice, the result is one flock. The Lord's voice will not lead His people back to divisive sheepfolds, but to become one flock with the one Shepherd.

The one flock is the building up of God's House. Truly, Jesus, as the real David, is the Shepherd who conquered as the King, fulfilling the promise to Abraham. His heart and mission were to build God's House — God's diverse people becoming one.

Solomon Built God's House

> And David said to Solomon: "My son, as for me, it was in my mind to build a house to the name of the LORD my God; 8 "but the word of the LORD came to me, saying, 'You have shed much blood and have made great wars; you shall not build a house for My name, because you have shed much blood on the earth in My sight. 9 'Behold, a son shall be born to you, who shall be a man of rest; and I will give him rest from all his enemies all around. His name shall be Solomon, for I will give peace and quietness to Israel in his days. 10 'He shall build a house for My name, and he shall be My son, and I [will be] his Father; and I will establish the throne of his kingdom over Israel forever.'
>
> – 1 Chron. 22:7-10

> "For as Jonah was three days and three nights in the belly of the great fish, so will the Son of Man be three days and three nights in the heart of the earth. 41 "The men of Nineveh will rise up in the judgment with this generation and condemn it, because they repented at the preaching of Jonah; and indeed a greater than Jonah [is] here. 42 "The queen of the South will rise up in the judgment with this generation and condemn it, for she came from the ends of the earth to hear the wisdom of Solomon; and indeed a greater than Solomon [is] here."
>
> – Matt. 12:40-42

Solomon was a product of David's adultery and murder; yet, Solomon became the greatest king of Israel, who built God's temple. Here is the rest of the story. David saw Bathsheba bathing while her husband Uriah was fighting in a war in David's army.

David committed adultery with her, and she conceived. David wanted to conceal his sin by summoning Uriah back from the war, hoping he would sleep with his wife. However, Uriah was an honorable warrior and would not go to his wife, declaring to David that he would not enjoy being with his wife when his captain and his fellow soldiers were at war. David then devised a devious and despicable plan to have Uriah murdered by commissioning him to fight on the frontlines where he'd perish. Due to this shameful sin, God judged David. The first item of his sentence was that his child with Bathsheba would die. David deeply repented of his sin, and God graciously forgave him and gave him another son with Bathsheba – Solomon.

Solomon, whose name means "peace," inherited all that David had accomplished in his conquest of the promised land. There was no war but only peace while Solomon was king. He became the wisest and richest king in history (1 Kings 10:23). Most significantly, he built the dwelling place of God – the temple. God's glory came and filled His house (1 Kings 8). Both God and man (signified by Israel) were at rest.

Jesus compared Himself to Solomon by declaring He was "greater than Solomon." Jesus first proclaims that He is the real Jonah. Jonah went into the belly of the great fish for three days and three nights; Jesus Himself declared that the "sign of Jonah" was a prefigure of His death and resurrection. Historically, Jonah lived after Solomon, but Jesus spoke of being Jonah first, then immediately came Solomon. This shows that Jesus, being the real Solomon, reigned in peace in His resurrection (Jonah).

His power and authority over the entire universe were displayed after Christ was raised from the dead. Ephesians 1:21-23 declares that in resurrection Jesus is: *"far above all rule, and authority, and power, and dominion, and every name that is named, not only in this world, but also in that which is to come: and he put all things in subjection under his feet, and gave him to be head over all things to the church [ekklesia], which is his body, the fulness of him that fills all in all."* He is now Head of the Body, which is the fullness of Him Who fills all in all. Surely, this can only be God Himself. His corporate Body in resurrection is the dwelling place of God. God's dwelling in Solomon's temple in the Old Testament was temporary. The temple that Jesus is building is God's dwelling place for eternity (John 14:20).

Furthermore, Jesus said: Destroy this temple, and in three days I will raise it up. He was not speaking of the physical temple in Jerusalem but the temple of His body (John 2:19-21). Whether the temple was Solomon's or the rebuilt one at the time of Jesus, it foreshadowed the real temple, Jesus' body. However, it was not the physical body of the man Jesus (which was the real temple of God); rather, in resurrection (three days), the body of Jesus became mystical and corporate, composed of all His believers. His resurrection regenerated all God's people to have His life and nature, and in them, God dwells for eternity. Now the Body of Christ has many members (1 Cor. 12:12). God has truly found His eternal resting place in man. God and man dwell together in one — the Temple of God.

It is noteworthy that Jesus pointed out that Jonah, after the fish experience, went to preach to Nineveh. It was a major city of Assyria, the ruthless and preeminent Gentile empire at the time. In fact, during the time of this story, around the reign of Jeroboam II (Cir. 793-753 B.C.), Assyria was a foremost enemy of Israel and ultimately conquered the northern 10 tribes around 722 BC (i.e., the fall of the Northern Kingdom's capital, Samaria). No wonder Jonah did not want to preach to Nineveh for their salvation. Nevertheless, after spending three days and nights in the fish, he reluctantly preached to the Ninevites, and they repented to receive God's salvation. This signifies that Jesus' resurrection was not only for the Jews but included sinners from among the nations — specifically — the Assyrians.

In 1 Timothy 3:16, Paul gave a sequence of events defining the mystery of godliness: *He who was manifested in the flesh, justified in the spirit, seen of angels, preached among the nations, believed on in the world, received up in glory.* Remarkably, the sequence starts with incarnation, crucifixion, and immediately after resurrection (seen of angels), the gospel was preached to the nations (Gentiles), and their faith resulted in glory. What's more, this sequence is referring to the House of God, His Democratic Assembly as seen in 1 Timothy 3:15: *"I write so that you may know how you ought to conduct yourself in the **house of God**, which is the **ekklesia** of the living God, the pillar and ground of the truth."*

This reveals that the Temple of God, established through Christ's resurrection, was not exclusively for the Jews but also included people from every nation. The Jews at the time of Jesus thought that only they represented "the Israel of God," and the temple of God was exclusively their domain. Therefore, those from the nations (aka "Gentiles" or "goyim") could not enter the physical temple at the time of Jesus. The closest they (those from the nations) could come would be to the outermost part of the outer court called the 'court of the Gentiles' or 'court of the Nations.' However, after the resurrection of Christ, those from the Nations are now part of the entire Temple. The Temple of God is no longer merely a Jewish temple — it is comprised of all of God's people — both Jews and Gentiles (i.e., those "circumcised" and those "uncircumcised" . . . *"For in Christ Jesus neither circumcision nor uncircumcision avails anything, but a New Creation"*).

Truly, this is wisdom: It is the Temple of God, His Democratic Assembly, that manifests His multifaceted wisdom to the entire universe, and specifically to the rebellious principalities and powers (Eph. 3:10). It is here that God's glory is displayed forever and ever (Eph. 3:21). Solomon's wisdom was merely a precursor to the unfathomable wisdom of God in Christ (Rom. 11:33). Amid a wall of hatred, animosity, and jealousy between the Jews and those from the nations, Christ is now the wisdom Who makes peace between them both (1 Cor. 1:30; Eph. 2:15-16).

If King Solomon depicts Christ in resurrection, then King Solomon's predecessor, King David, can be seen as Christ's life of crucifixion. (Also note: David's firstborn with Bathsheba died, King Solomon came in "resurrection" or "second born"). While Solomon's name means *peace*, David's name means **beloved**. Certainly, Jesus is God's **beloved** Son whom God declared when Jesus started His ministry at about 30 years of age (Matt. 3:17; Luke 3:23). As God's beloved Son, He was given to the world for its salvation (John 3:16). That was the ministry journey of the Beloved: to suffer and die on the cross (Matt. 16:21). Indeed, Jesus started His ministry at 30 years old, the same age as King David who commenced his reign at age 30. (2 Sam. 5:4-5).

David lived a life full of tribulation and suffering. Though anointed as king, he was a fugitive living in caves, hiding from King Saul, who was determined to kill him (Though Jesus was anointed king, He had no place to lay His head). David suffered betrayal by his own son (2 Sam. 14-18) whom he dearly loved. So too, Jesus was betrayed by one of His twelve disciples, Judas. After David's sin of adultery and murder, his sufferings increased as prophesied. Since the fall of Adam, most of mankind's sufferings are due to their own sins. Although Jesus was sinless, He bore man's sin and suffered on mankind's behalf (1 Pet. 3:18). He didn't need to suffer yet due to man's sins, He became a Man of sorrows and acquainted with grief (Isa. 53:3). His life on earth was one of affliction and tribulation until His crucifixion.

God told David that he could not build God's house because he had been a man of war and had shed blood (1 Chron. 28:3). In a similar way, Jesus shed His blood to defeat His enemies (Heb. 2:14). His going to the cross was warfare against the enemy, Satan. In God's judgment of David's sins, the firstborn conceived by Bathsheba died. The second son, Solomon, signifies living in resurrection. The first man, Adam, had the sentence of death upon him. When Jesus died, He crucified the old man. He was the last Adam Who terminated the continuation of the first Adam. Now, He is the second man in resurrection (1 Cor. 15:47). Jesus took on the sins of the world and died to terminate the first man, Adam, under God's judgment, and He resurrected as the second man, the real Solomon. As the reigning King in peace, He built God's House, His Democratic Assembly.

Conclusion

The above items may be considered the most significant archetypes and prefigures of Jesus Christ from Adam until Solomon in the prophetic writings. Many items can be added to this list if all the books of the Hebrew Scriptures are reviewed, including the major and minor prophets. Jesus Christ is unsearchably rich with an unlimited number of facets to His person and work. Therefore, He is worthy of detailed pictorial descriptions in the archetype and figures throughout the prophetic writings.

3

THE GREAT MYSTERY: CHRIST AND HIS DEMOCRATIC ASSEMBLY

Adam and Eve

"Therefore a man shall leave his father and mother and hold fast to his wife, and the two shall become one flesh." 32 This mystery is profound, and I am saying that it refers to Christ and the church [lit. ekklesia-democratic assembly].

– Eph. 5:31-32, ESV

We have seen from previous chapters that Adam is an archetype of Christ. After God created Adam, He said: It was *not* good for him to be alone. Therefore, God brought all the animals before Adam to see what he would name them. That was God's way of letting Adam "check out" all the animals to see if he would be attracted to and mate with any of them. Adam named them all but did not find one that matched him (Gen. 2:20).

God then put Adam into a deep sleep so that He could take a rib out of Adam's side from which He made a woman who would conform to his liking. When Adam woke from sleep and saw what God had fashioned from his rib, he called and named her *woman*. The word "woman" is the feminine of the word for "man." In other words, Adam saw her as a female version of himself. They are of the same species: Adam being male and Eve being female. When Adam named all the animals on earth, he gave names to all, with none named as the same species as himself. However, when he saw the woman, he said: *"This at last is bone of my bones and flesh of my flesh; she shall be called Woman, because she was taken out of Man"* (Gen. 2:23).

Paul described this story of Adam and Eve as a foreshadowing of Christ and His Democratic Assembly (Ekklesia). Since he did so, let's consider this archetype further. Jesus Christ is the Son of the Living God — He is God. When God said it is *not* good for man to be alone, He, in essence, used Adam as His representative, that it is not good for Him to be alone. He created billions of animated items in the universe, including all the angels. Yet, none of them is of His species — with His life and nature. Therefore, Jesus Christ was put into a "deep sleep," which was death by crucifixion. Jesus gave up His life to gain His Bride (Eph. 5:25).

On the cross, a soldier pierced Jesus' side, and blood and water flowed out (John 19:34). The Lord's Democratic Assembly is composed of people. However, these people fell into sin. The fall separated man from the Tree of Life; i.e., from the Life of God. They needed redemption and forgiveness of sins to return to the Tree of Life. Therefore, Jesus shed His blood for the sins of the world and washed away the stain of sin by His blood (Rev. 1:5). By the blood of Christ, man (male and female) was essentially restored to a state of sinlessness. God declared man righteous as if he never sinned (Rom. 3:22). However, a perfect and sinless creature in God's creation still would not match Christ, the Son of God. Jesus, though divine, took on humanity through His incarnation (He became a man), but man would not match Him (be "after His kind") without divinity. Man needs to have God's eternal divine life, and therefore, he needs to partake of the Tree of Life.[5]

The second issue, water from the Lord's side, represents the outflowing of the Spirit for man's regeneration (born again/anew, from above). The water from His side signified the living water that came out of Christ, the Rock, when He was struck on the cross. Jesus in John 7:37-39 said: *"If any one doth thirst, let him come unto me and drink . . . and this he said of the Spirit, which those believing in him were about to receive; for not yet was the Holy Spirit, because Jesus was not yet glorified."* The Spirit Who was to be drinkable by man was not yet. He was not yet enterable into man. Man's thirst was unquenchable because the Water of Life (Jo. 7:38-39) was not yet. Therefore, the drinkable Spirit was not yet available until Jesus was glorified. Then the Holy Spirit could satiate the innermost part of man, his human spirit ". . . out of his innermost being will flow rivers of living water" (John 7:38 Legacy Standard Bible).

Jesus said in John 16:7: *"It is to your advantage that I go away, for if I do not go away, the Helper [Spirit] will not come to you. But if I go, I will send Him [Holy Spirit] to you."* Jesus died and came back in the resurrection to the disciples as the enterable Spirit — The Spirit that can indwell man. This is the result of regeneration or being "born again." Born again or born anew is to be born of God: to receive God's life and nature. Man (i.e., the "many who receive Him") become the very children of God through rebirth

---

5   Through the "new birth" man partakes of the Life of God—which was God's original purpose represented by the Tree of Life in the Garden of Eden. "Jesus answered, 'Most assuredly, I say to you, unless one is born of water and the Spirit, he cannot enter the kingdom of God. That which is born of the flesh is flesh, and that which is born of the Spirit is spirit" (John 3:5-6).

(John 1:12). The living water released at the Lord's death and resurrection is for man's new birth, so to become the same as He in life, nature, and expression (2 Cor. 3:18). Now the Lord can say: This is the bone of My bone and flesh of My flesh.

His believers are no longer merely created beings, but they came out of Him to be "after His kind." They are like Him in every way except that He is still the "Male," the God of the universe with His glorified humanity. As the "Spirit of Christ," He is available as the drink for humanity. And His Bride is the "female," both human and divine, depending on Him as her source. Nevertheless, they now match each other: Husband and wife. The two become one. This is the universal romance – the joining together between God and man. By His death and resurrection, He became the Life-giving Spirit to "beget us anew" from above, whereby we, once dead in our sins without the Life of God, are born again to be His Holy Bride!

Isaac and Rebekah

> Let us rejoice and exult and give him the glory, for the marriage of the Lamb has come, and his Bride has made herself ready;
>
> – Rev. 19:7, ESV

In Genesis 24, a story is told concerning Abraham desiring a wife for his son, Isaac. In this story, another archetype can be seen concerning the profound mystery of Christ and His Democratic Assembly. In the last chapter of this text, it was conclusive that Isaac was an archetype of Jesus Christ as the Only Begotten Son of God – for his father, Abraham, offered "his only son" upon the "altar of sacrifice" (Gen. 22:1-19). Therefore, it is reasonable to consider that Rebekah foreshadows the Son's Bride, His Ekklesia.

Abraham's servant, Eliezer, was responsible for finding a bride for Isaac. Since Abraham was a type of God the Father and Isaac a type of the Only Begotten Son, the Scriptures connect Eliezer to be a type of the Spirit working to prepare the Son's Bride. It is meaningful that the name "Eliezer" in Hebrew means "God of help" (Strong's) or "God is help" (BDB). In the New Testament, the Spirit of God sent after Jesus' death and resurrection is also called the "Helper." John 14:26 says: *"The Helper, the Holy Spirit, whom the Father will send in my name."* And certainly, the Holy Spirit is God; therefore, God of help or *Eliezer*.

Additionally, just as Eliezer was chronologically sent after the offering of Isaac by Abraham, the Helper Spirit was sent after the death and resurrection of Jesus Christ. John 16:7 continues: *"I tell you the truth: it is to your advantage that I go away [to death], for if I do not go away, the Helper will not come to you. But if I go, I will send him to you."* It is the Spirit as the Helper that was sent to do the work of preparing a Bride for the Son. The Father, through the Lord's death and resurrection, sends the Spirit (God) of Help to gain a Bride for the Son.

Eliezer was instructed to return to where Abraham was called out and find a wife from his kinsman. He then took 10 camels loaded with gifts representing Abraham's riches. When Eliezer found Rebekah, he put a gold ring on her nose and gold bracelets on her arms. Eliezer marked her and destined her to be Isaac's bride.

> He will glorify me, for he will take what is mine and declare it to you. 15 All that the Father has is mine; therefore I said that he will take what is mine and declare it to you.
>
> — John 16:14-15, ESV

When the Spirit was sent to the Lord's followers, He came with all the riches of the Father and the Son. All that the Father has belongs to the Son, and now the Spirit is to declare the Son with all His riches and accomplished work of grace to all His believers. The number 10 in the Bible signifies fullness and completeness[6]; therefore, the 10 camels of riches point to the unsearchable riches of Christ; the Spirit brought and made real to the believers of Jesus. The Spirit's "declaring" is His displaying and making known the riches of the Triune God to the Lord's Bride.

Not only did Rebekah receive the jewelry of gold, but also jewelry of silver and garments. All these typify riches given to the Lord's Bride as gifts of the Spirit (1 Cor. 12:4). "Gifts" mean they have been given freely. The Bride of Christ did not earn or work for even one of these gifts. They were freely given to be liberally received and enjoyed. Believers need repeated reminders that it is not their labor or behavior that can secure gifts from God. They should constantly be thankful for all the gifts: eternal life, God's divine nature, His truth, glory, power, authority, love, mercy, kindness, victory, and so much more.

Likewise, His Bride or Body — each member — ... *"having **gifts** differing according to the grace that is given to us"* (Rom. 12:6). It is abundantly clear that each one has *been given* a gift by the "same Spirit" as Paul showed in the following two portions. *"Now to **each one the manifestation of the Spirit is given** for the common good"* (1 Cor. 12:7). And *"All these are the work of one and the same Spirit, and he distributes them to each one, just as he determines"* (1 Cor. 12:11).

---

6 The number set "10" connotes both complete/fullness be it "good or bad" – the "ten horns, ten kings, ten days" in the Revelation are certainly drawing our attention to the "fullness of evil" in the latter days; whereas the "ten commandments" connotes the completeness of God's testimony and His requirements on man.

These unsearchable riches afforded to believers are the gifts and experiences of the Spirit's work in preparing the Bride for the Son (Eph. 3:8). The Spirit's first work is to convict the world concerning sin, righteousness, and judgment (John 16:8). When men are convicted of their *sin* by the Holy Spirit, they will repent and believe in the death and resurrection ("I go to the Father") of Christ which makes them *righteous* before God (John 16:9). All convicted sinners are made righteous by faith in Jesus Christ (Rom. 3:22). Additionally, while Satan is defeated and *judged*, they are liberated from his rule in this world. They are transferred from Satan's kingdom of darkness into the kingdom of the Son of His Love (Col. 1:13).

It is the work of the Spirit to give new birth to the followers of Jesus (Titus 3:5). This new birth or regeneration is of the Spirit Who transferred them into the Kingdom of God (John 3:6). This new birth is what makes believers in Jesus His kinsman (His "brethren"). Jesus' Bride has to be from His "relatives," and His bride is from the same Father — they are truly kinsmen (Heb. 2:11-12). She is qualified to be joined to the Son and be His complement, His counterpart, His very mate because she is wholly of "His kind."

The Spirit will continue transforming them until maturity — prepared as a Bride. He did not stop with regeneration but went on to renewal. This renewing and washing done by the Spirit eliminate all the wrinkles due to the oldness of the "old man" and the scars suffered from injustices and ill-treatments (Eph. 5:27). The Spirit will transform her from glory to glory and will conform her to the image of the Son (Rom. 8:29; 2 Cor. 3:18).

Interestingly, Eliezer traveled to a well to meet Rebekah just as Jesus had to go to a well to meet the Samaritan woman in John 4. Both women were out drawing water, and Eliezer and the Lord were thirsty. However, as the type of the Bride, Rebekah signifies one who had already drunk of the living water because she was like a well, providing water to the thirsty. Jesus told the Samaritan woman: *"The water that I will give him will become in him a spring of water welling up to eternal life"* (John 4:14). Rebekah represented someone full of water: she supplied not just Eliezer's company but also the 10 camels. Each camel alone can drink at least 30 gallons of water. Therefore, she provided at least 300 gallons of water to quench their thirst. She drew so much water that she was like a spring.

The Bride of Christ has become a source of living water. Since the Father, as the source of life, is in her, she has an eternal and unlimited supply of the water of life. The New Jerusalem, as the Bride of Christ, is an aquatic-city: A city gushing forth with living water. From the throne of God, at her pinnacle, issuing forth the water of life spiraling down the entire bride-city (Rev. 22:1). She is also the temple of God where God dwells. The Psalmist said: *"There is a river whose streams make glad the city of God, the holy habitation of the Most High"* (Psa. 46:4). Ezekiel 47 speaks of water flowing out of the temple of God, which became a river, and wherever the river flows, everything shall live. As this river turns salt into fresh water for life and drinking (Eze. 47:9), so a believer — when flowing with living water to quench others — is participating in the life and ministry of the Bride. No wonder at the close of the Revelation we hear: *"And the Spirit and the Bride say, 'Come!' And let him who hears say, 'Come!' And let him who thirsts come. Whoever desires, let him take the water of life freely!"* (Rev. 22:17).

Rebekah was brought to Isaac, whom she had never seen (not a video or a photo). Bridegroom unseen; yet, she took a long journey to marry him. How wonderful that believers who constitute the Bride are also taking a long journey to marry the Bridegroom Jesus, Whom they have not seen. This verse is certainly an appropriate reflection of Rebekah's story.

> Though you have not seen him, you love him. Though you do not now see him, you believe in him and rejoice with joy that is inexpressible and filled with glory,
>
> – 1 Pet. 1:8, ESV

Believers' "long journey" is often filled with trials, tribulations, and temptations; therefore, it is a journey of endurance (Heb. 12:1-2). However, since they are looking forward to the Bridegroom (see Him by faith), they are rejoicing with inexpressible joy and full of glory. Those who journey to marry the Bridegroom may suffer along the way, but they are full of rejoicing with glory and bursting with living water to quench those thirsty around them.

Finally, the last verse of chapter 24: *"Then Isaac brought her into his mother Sarah's tent; and he took Rebekah and she became his wife, and he loved her. So Isaac was comforted after his mother's death."* What a beautiful ending! Isaac and Rebekah were joined together in Sarah's tent. Paul allegorized Sarah as the Covenant of Promise, and she is the mother of the free: all those liberated from the bondage of the Mosaic law (Gal. 4:22-28). The believers, being part of the Bride, are enjoying grace in the Covenant of Promise. They had complete freedom of choice to be joined to Christ. Every step of their long journey is one of grace and liberation. None of them were forced or coerced in their pursuit to be joined to Christ; rather, they are always full of rejoicing.

Isaac was comforted by uniting with Rebekah as his wife. For many theologians, it is difficult to ascribe such an emotion to the Son of God — that He needs to be comforted. Nevertheless, the Scriptures show that God was grieved: *The Lord was sorry that He had made man on the earth, and He was grieved in His heart* (Gen. 6:6). Man (male and female), who was to join together in a union with Him, became so corrupted that there was only evil in his heart continually. God was grieved to the extent that He had to judge and send the flood to destroy man. Additionally, God was grieved by Israel due to their rebellion in the wilderness (Psa. 78:40). God sorrowed over the ultimate separation from created man and Israel's rebellion against Him. A person troubled by grief needs comforting.

No wonder God would be comforted when He finally joins Himself to a worthy Bride who exactly matches Him. His eternal purpose is to have a people who can be prepared as His bride. Not only is He comforted from all His past griefs, but He rejoices over His Bride in satisfaction. This verse highlights God's heart when the Bride has made herself ready:

> For [as] a young man marries a virgin, [So] shall your sons marry you; And [as] the bridegroom rejoices over the bride, [So] shall your God rejoice over you.
>
> – Isa 62:5

What a wonderful picture displayed in God's heart. Often God is viewed without any characteristics of vulnerability, nor desiring joy and pleasure – not human. Yes, God is full of emotion and feelings. Remember, man was made in His image and likeness; therefore, man's character (not including sin) is God's direct reflection. This last verse concerning Isaac and Rebekah represents a wonderful romance between God and man!

It is more than noteworthy concerning the consecration of the Bride (Rebekah). When Eliezer was clear that Rebekah's relatives had concurred with her departure, another "10" presented itself. *"But her brother and her mother said, 'Let the young woman stay with us a few days, at least ten; after that she may go.'"* (Gen. 24:55). This may be considered the negative side of the "10" aforementioned (i.e., the 10 camels and the "fullness of water"). Here, the "10" is designed to "compromise" Rebekah. How reasonable it would have been for her to remain "a few days, at least ten; after that, she may go." No, Eliezer (an archetype, Helper, of the Holy Spirit) replied: *"Do not hinder me, since the LORD has prospered my way; send me away so that I may go to my master"* (Gen. 24:56). Praise the Lord that the Holy Spirit is so persistent, without compromise, relentless to bring the Bride to the Bridegroom. But what of Rebekah? Will she compromise to stay, or comply with Eliezer's leading and go immediately? *"So they said, 'We will call the young woman and ask her personally.' Then they called Rebekah and said to her, 'Will you go with this man?'"* (Gen. 24:57a).

Yes, the Bride of Isaac must make a "personal decision" — either she has heard the Spirit's call and is "all in" or she is "reasonably compromised." Will she reject the offer of the "10 days" — do these 10 days not resemble ". . . the devil is about to throw some of you into prison, that you may be tested, and you will have tribulation **ten days**" (Rev. 2:10)? Finally, we hear her say: "I WILL GO!" This is the commitment — there's no compromise — she knows her calling is absolute. And so do her relatives . . . for they begin to prophesy concerning Rebekah:

"And they blessed Rebekah and said to her: 'Our sister, may you become the mother of thousands of ten thousands; and may your descendants possess the gates of those who hate them.'" (Gen. 24:60). Similarly, Isaac's mother, Sarai's name was changed to Sarah, for we read of Abraham's wife: *"As for Sarai your wife, you shall not call her name Sarai, but Sarah shall be her name. And I will bless her and also give you a son by her (Isaac); then I will bless her, and she shall be a mother of nations; kings of peoples shall be from her"* (Gen. 17:15-16). Both Sarah and Rebekah participate in what is known as the "Melo-Ha-Goyim" (i.e., the "Multitude of Nations" – Gen. 17:4).

The Bride of Christ is in an utter display as that vast multitude of nations "which no man could number" (Rev. 7:9). Yes, there indeed are the Twelve Tribes of Israel before this scene that no man could number (Rev. 7:1-8), but the "Melo-Ha-Goyim" promised to Sarah and Rebekah astounds! All are united with the Lamb, and Who is this Lamb, and those gathered before Him? *"Come, I will show you **the Woman, the Lamb's Bride**"* (Majority Text – Rev. 21:9). Sarah-Rebekah prophetically declares that the Bride of the Lamb includes all the nations. She is without compromise, without spot or blemish or any such thing (Eph. 5:27) . . . in absolute devotion to the Groom. She is of His kind: THE WOMAN . . . the Woman as the Bride of the Lamb, her Isaac.

God Took Israel as His Wife

When a man courts a woman for marriage, it is typical to reveal to her who he is: his strength, character, and financial status. Next is to determine whether she has similar compatible character traits. The most important is whether she will be faithful without having a heart for anyone else. At the time of marriage, it is common for the husband and wife to have a vow of devotion to each other. God acted similarly with Israel: attracted her with His strength, wealth, and natural character, then at the time of marriage asked reciprocally for her commitment.

> 'You have seen what I did to the Egyptians, and [how] I bore you on eagles' wings and brought you to Myself.
>
> — Exo. 19:4

"When I passed by you again and looked upon you, indeed your time [was] the time of love; so I spread My wing over you and covered your nakedness. Yes, I swore an oath to you and entered into a covenant with you, and you became Mine," says the Lord GOD.

Ezek. 16:8

Since calling Abraham, God set His sights on his offspring — the twelve tribes of Israel. God desired to join Himself to them like a husband in union with his wife. God chose Israel because He loved her above all people on earth (like a husband loves His wife). She would be a special treasure to God (Deut. 7:6-8). Therefore, God delivered Israel from Egypt as one ready for marriage. The covenant He entered into with Israel was a marriage vow (contract): He committed Himself to her and she committed herself to Him — a bilateral agreement.

After Joseph rescued Israel from famine and brought them to Egypt, they stayed in Egypt for over 200 years and multiplied to more than two million people. During that period, they had mostly forgotten the God of their forefathers; thus, Moses had to ask God His name. In Egypt, Israel may have gotten to know the river god, sun god, moon god, and many idolatrous gods, but they did not know God. So, God introduced Himself and declared that He is Yahweh (YHWH) or Jehovah, the ever-existing and self-existing One — I am Who I am (Exo. 3:14). All the idols are manmade, man created them. Only Yahweh is self-existing!

According to Exodus 6:3, this was the first time God unveiled the meaning of His name to anyone. He is the source of all creation and life. He is the I AM. Without Him, nothing exists. God made His formal introduction to Israel and unveiled Who He is. Additionally, He is the One Who brought Israel out of their slavery. He was powerful enough to carry them on eagles' wings and liberate them from Egypt. This was God's wooing and courting of Israel. He did this to attract her to Himself.

God is powerful and self-existing, but what are His nature and character traits — what is He like? People in different cultures have made their conjectures about sundry gods. To many, their god is bloodthirsty, desiring men to sacrifice their children to please him. If their gods are displeased, they will be enraged and punish them. In Greek mythology, much was written about their gods. They have traits such as jealousy, anger, revengefulness, impatience, and insecurity; their gods are avaricious. They even commit adultery and murder. Since Israel had no idea concerning God's nature and character, Yahweh wrote His testimony concerning Himself — The Ten Commandments (Exo. 31:18).

The Ten Commandments were embedded in His marriage covenant with a dual purpose. First, it is to disclose God's nature and character so Israel will know her suitor. Second, to receive from Israel a reciprocal vow of a monogamous marriage and a pledge to match her husband's nature and character. By giving His testimony, Israel would come to know the One courting them and proposing to them in marriage. Seeing the Ten Commandments as a marriage vow is much different from simply God issuing laws for humans to obey.

Since the foundation of God's throne is righteousness and justice (Psa. 89:14), God cannot break or breach any of His commandments. It would be impossible for God to make a commandment that He can then transgress. Whatever He commanded, He can keep for eternity. God does not perform as in an event to keep His commandments. Therefore, these ten commandments testify to Who He is — His nature and character traits.

Thus, the commandment to keep the Sabbath day shows God knows how to rest, and He is a God of rest. After His creation work, He rested. For the new creation, God labored together with His Son whereby through incarnation He would live and work on earth (John 5:17). After Jesus' crucifixion, resurrection, and ascension, God finished His work and He entered eternal rest (Heb. 4:9). His Bride would join Him in His rest.

The commandment to honor your father and mother testifies that God is a "family man." Not only is He the eternal Father, but there are to be generations and multiplications of life. He told Adam and Eve to be fruitful and multiply, to subdue and have dominion over the earth. God loves the multiplication of families from generation to generation; therefore, honor your father and mother. Naturally, every wife loves to have a husband who is strong for the family. This should be an enticement to Israel to accept God's marriage proposal.

God's testimony of "Do not murder" shows He loves life. He does not let hate or anger fester. He can be provoked but will calm down quickly. He is slow to anger and ready to forgive (Neh. 9:17). God does not kill with malice or lawlessly without justification. What a comfort to a wife knowing that her husband has his anger under control and is quick to forgive and forget failures.

God does not commit adultery. God is faithful to His one wife. Once He has chosen and married His wife, there is no divorce. It is amazing that even though Israel committed adultery and became like a harlot over and over, God remained faithful to love and keep her (Hos. 2:1-20). Beyond Israel, God committed and pledged His love to man (male and female). God never gave up on man, even though man forsook Him and became His enemy. He died for man so that man would finally become His wife (Eph. 5:25).

God does not steal. God is the possessor of heaven and earth (Gen. 14:19). The earth is the Lord's, and all it contains: the world and those who dwell in it (Psa. 24:1). Therefore, there is no need for Him to steal since He has the right to all things. Certainly, this shows His riches as the male suitor to Israel. God essentially said to Israel, "Become my wife, and you don't have to worry about a thing. I can provide all your needs and supply you eternally."

The ninth commandment is: You shall not bear false witness. This is God's testimony: "Whatever I say is true." His word is truth (John 17:17). His wife can rely on and be secured with all God has spoken. He will not utter anything in falsehood. Not only so, but when God put on flesh and died on the cross, everything He promised was fulfilled. They are all "yes and amen" (2 Cor. 1:20).

Finally, God testified that He does not covet. He is satisfied within Himself and in all He has accomplished in gaining an eternal Bride. In the world, no matter how much wealth a man has, they always desire more. Satan initiated covetousness. He was unsatisfied with his beauty, power, and wisdom; so, he desired to be God. Fallen man has the same covetous nature. However, God is forever satisfied and has no desire for another wife. He is eternally fulfilled in being joined to His one Wife (Rev. 21:9).

Israel's Marriage Vow

> Then he took the Book of the Covenant and read in the hearing of the people. And they said, "All that the LORD has said we will do, and be obedient."
>
> – Exo 24:7

As part of the marriage vow between God and Israel, God asked whether Israel would be faithful as His only wife and whether she would be just like Him with the same natural character traits. The first three commandments are Israel's commitment to be a faithful wife. The rest of the seven commandments are her pledge to have the same nature and characteristics as her Husband. Israel's reply to God's marriage proposal: "Yes, I do."

The first commandment: You shall have no other gods before Me (Exo. 20:3). From a marriage point of view, the first commandment is obvious: you (Israel) will not have another man or husband. God was saying, "I am your only husband. You are My only wife, and I request that you will not have another man in your life." That is a common expectation from every husband on earth.

The second commandment: You shall not make for yourself any images (Exo. 20:4). God's second request is also reasonable: "I don't want to see any pictures or images of your past lovers or any other man in your purse or anywhere else in the house." God is a jealous Husband and does not want to see His wife attracted to or thinking about other men (Exo. 20:5). God only has eyes for her and expects His wife only has eyes for Him.

The third commandment: You shall not take the name of Yahweh (Jehovah) your God in vain (Exo. 20:7). Most people may interpret this to mean: don't use God's name to swear. This, of course, people should not do. However, this command is more meaningful and applicable from a marriage perspective. It is common in many cultures on earth that when a woman marries a man, she takes on his name (family name). My wife used to be Sylvia Bramskov, but after marrying me, she became Sylvia Hon. She took my name. Doug's wife's name was Deborah Davison, and now it is Deborah Krieger.

After taking his name, a wife has access to all that belongs to her husband. If her husband is rich, the woman with his name will share ownership of his houses, cars, bank accounts, and everything else he owns. (Too bad for Sylvia and Deborah, Doug and I are not that rich.) What if a wife takes on the name of a rich husband through marriage and does not access and enjoy all that is his? She would have taken his name in vain. How vain it would be if she continued to live in a decrepit house, drive an old car, and dress like a homeless person. If she is not to take her husband's name in vain, she will employ all the riches and influences of her new name. Her life and living would reflect the abundant resources behind her husband's name, which is now hers.

God is full of resurrection power, eternal life, and love, and He is the possessor of heaven and earth. It would be vain to be His wife and remain poor, weak, depressed, and defeated. This is taking His name in vain. His wife is even called by His name: she bears His name (2 Chr. 7:14). Believers today have believed into His name (John 1:12). In and by His name, the Lord Jesus Christ, they possess all the power and authority in the universe (Eph. 1:18-23). How vain it would be for believers to live a life of weakness, depression, and defeat when they have **His name**. Let's not take His name in vain! Let's live in the riches of His love and life to glorify Him, the Husband. The Lord is glorified when His beautiful wife reflects His riches and splendor (Eph. 3:21).

Finally, Israel, as the wife of Yahweh, agreed to have the same nature and character as God. This is compatibility and is His match by agreeing to all ten commandments. Remember, marriage is only possible between a male and a female with the life and nature of the same kind or species. Thus, for Israel to be God's wife, she must have the nature and life character described by God's testimony. That is the purpose for Israel to commit to the rest of the 10 commandments so that she will display the same characteristics as her husband. However, when Israel continually broke the 10 commandments, she was exposed that her nature was not like God's. She was not faithful and did not have God's moral characteristics.

God Divorced Israel

After their wedding at Mount Sinai, with both parties agreeing to the marriage covenant, Israel was unfaithful to God, her Husband. She repeatedly committed adultery and even became a harlot, entering into relationships with many "men" other than her Husband. She was even worse than a typical harlot because she paid others to come to her instead of getting paid by them.

> "[You are] an adulterous wife, [who] takes strangers instead of her husband. 33 "Men make payment to all harlots, but you [Israel] made your payments to all your lovers, and hired them to come to you from all around for your harlotry.
>
> – Ezek. 16:32-33

Adultery for Israel is idolatry. When she worshipped other gods, she broke her vow to her Husband, God. He was to be her only lover, but she chased after many other gods from all the nations surrounding her. Although Israel made her vow to be God's wife alone in Exodus 24:7, she was already unfaithful before God inscribed the Ten Commandments onto the two tablets of stone. By the time Moses came down the mountain with the tablets, they had already made and worshiped a golden calf. From then on, Israel continued her adultery. Nevertheless, God would repeatedly forgive them as soon as they returned to Him.

Even though Israel was unfaithful, God was faithful to His vow of marriage and made Israel exceedingly rich and beautiful. She was renowned among the nations due to her beauty by the time of Solomon (Eze. 16:13-14). However, her adultery became worse and worse. Finally, due to Solomon's idolatry, God divided the Kingdom of David into two: ten tribes in the north called Israel, Ephraim, Jezreel, or Samaria, and the two tribes in the south (including some Levites) called Judah. This has been labeled as the "Breach of Jeroboam," who became king of the Ten Northern Tribes, and Rehoboam, king of the Two Southern Tribes. Even after this judgment from God, Israel continued playing the harlot.

> Then the Lord said to me in the days of Josiah the king, "Have you seen what faithless Israel did? She went up on every high hill and under every green tree, and she was a harlot there. I thought, 'After she has done all these things she will return to Me'; but she did not return, and her treacherous sister Judah saw it. And I saw that for all the adulteries of faithless Israel, I had sent her away and given her **a writ of divorce**, yet her treacherous sister Judah did not fear; but she went and was a harlot also.
>
> – Jer. 3:6-10

Since Israel (the northern 10 tribes) never returned to her Husband after more than 200 years of division from Judah, God divorced her by giving her an official "writ of divorce" and sent her away (Assyrian deportation – Cir. 720 BC). The 200 years started when Jeroboam prevented Israel from going to the "uniting center of Jerusalem" for worship by setting up two "sacred cows" at the borders of Israel (north and south) for Israel to worship. Although God was forced to divorce her due to her unrepentant harlotry, it became a huge predicament for God. First, it would mean that God was wrong for choosing Israel to be His wife. How can God be wrong? Second, God cannot simply find another wife to marry since He maintained His commitment to her even after the divorce by declaring that He would faithfully love her with an everlasting love: *I have loved you with an everlasting love; therefore, I have continued my faithfulness to you* (Jer. 31:3; Hos. 1:6, 8). How can God still be faithful and love her after divorcing her? This is mind-blowing love and faithfulness.

Then there is even a bigger problem: according to God's law, a husband cannot remarry a wife whom he has divorced and she has been defiled by marriage to another husband (Deut. 24:1-4 – her remarriage to another husband is considered adultery). So, Israel's unfaithfulness put God into a quandary. He promised to love her faithfully with everlasting love; yet, He cannot remarry her. Again, how could He give her a writ of divorce and then remarry her since she has gone after "other lovers" and played the harlot if she goes back to Him, that would be an abomination because she has been defiled.

Meanwhile, Judah did not learn from Israel and also continued her adultery by worshipping other gods. Although God did not use the language of divorce with Judah; nevertheless, she was sent away ("put away"). Thus, God sent Israel away to Assyria, and by intermarriage, she was swallowed up by the nations[7] (Hos. 8:8). About 120 years later, around 600 BC, Judah was led captive into Babylon. The wife of Yahweh was gone: divided, divorced, and sent away.

God's heart's desire for a people as a wife seems to be ill-conceived, and His choice is a failure. All the angels, especially His rebellious angels, could mock Him for His foolish love and marriage. Nevertheless, God did not give up. In the same chapter in Jeremiah 31 where God declared His everlasting love and faithfulness, He spoke of a **new marriage covenant**. This New Covenant is with **both** Israel and Judah. They will be brought back together, and God will have a new marriage covenant with her. This New Covenant will solve God's remarriage dilemma, and this marriage will last for eternity.

---

7   Assyrian Deportation and Resettlement: The Story of Samaria - TheTorah.com

"Behold, the days are coming, declares the LORD, when I will **make a new covenant with the house of Israel and the house of Judah,** 32 not like the covenant that I made with their fathers on the day when I took them by the hand to bring them out of the land of Egypt, my covenant that they broke, though **I was their husband,** declares the LORD.

— Jer. 31:31-32, ESV

And likewise the cup after they had eaten, saying, "This cup that is poured out for you is **the new covenant in my blood.**"

— Luk. 22:20, ESV

It is remarkable that after Israel had been scattered and swallowed up by the nations, the Lord prophesied to bring them back to the good land. There they will: *come and sing aloud on the height of Zion, and they shall be radiant over the goodness of the LORD, over the grain, the wine, and the oil, and over the young of the flock and the herd; their life shall be like a watered garden, and they shall languish no more* (Jer. 31:12). When will this happen? Then out of nowhere, the Lord said: *"A voice is heard in Ramah, lamentation and bitter weeping. Rachel is weeping for her children; she refuses to be comforted for her children, because they are no more"* (Jer. 31:15). This was spoken completely out of context. Conjecture: this was spoken so it could be quoted when Jesus was born, and King Herod had all the babies 2 years and younger killed. This verse can be cited as a fulfillment of prophecy (Matt. 2:18). In essence, Jeremiah pointed to the time when Israel would be restored to the good land as a wife — at the coming of the Messiah!

This prophecy in Jeremiah 31 explicitly references Jesus Christ, Who would receive back Israel as sons and a bride, though they would have intermingled with the nations due to the divorce. Jesus came to reunite Israel with God, her Husband. In the same chapter, the New Covenant was prophesied in contrast to the first one, where God became Israel's Husband (Jer. 31:32). The New Covenant was established by blood, by death — this New Covenant was not bilateral as the Mosaic Covenant — it was unilateral . . . He alone would make and fulfill the agreement! The Person who died was God in Christ. God shed His blood for the sins of His people. God was Israel's first Husband, and Israel's divorce was under the law of the first Husband. The first Husband, according to the law, could NOT remarry Israel — for it would be an abomination as long as the first Husband lived. **However, the first Husband died**; therefore, Israel could not remarry Him (the first Husband) even if she wanted to. God shed His blood to redeem Israel from the judgment of the law (Acts 20:28). Good news: that is not the end of the story. He was resurrected as "another man." God in Christ resurrected to be the new Husband Whom Israel can now marry without breaking God's law (Rom. 7:3-4) . . . *"Therefore, my brethren, you also have become dead to the law through the body of Christ, that you may be married to another — to Him who was raised from the dead, that we should bear fruit to God."*

God's love and wisdom brought Israel back to Himself. The same God Who chose Israel as His wife did not give up on her. Though He divorced her due to her harlotry, He came in the flesh to die for her. The same God in resurrection became the new Husband to receive her back as His wife. This union in Christ will last throughout all eternity. There will be no more going astray to idols. They will be "married and live happily ever after."

In this portion of the text, the question of why this new marriage can last for eternity will not be discussed since it will be covered in a later chapter. What was considered here is how God can remarry Israel legally without breaking His laws. Rabbinical authorities have pondered for centuries how God could keep His vows after divorcing Israel — Romans 7:1-4 resolves this dilemma.

This story of God being the Husband and Israel being the bride was not just a type or a figure of the great mystery described by Paul in Ephesians 5; it is the great mystery itself. If students of the Hebrew Scriptures miss this marriage, they would have missed the central point of the entire narrative. Praise God that the apostle Paul did not miss it, but saw the mystery unveiled. Do you see it? The mystery of the Bride of Messiah is unveiled in such a manner: *"Now to Him who is able to establish you according to my gospel and the preaching of Jesus Christ, according to the revelation of the mystery kept secret since the world began but now made manifest, and by the prophetic Scripture made known to all nations . . ."* (Rom. 16:25-26a).

Solomon Is a Type of Christ Marrying a Diverse People

Many scholars consider that Psalm 45 was written concerning King Solomon's wedding; nevertheless, it is also prophetic concerning the coming Christ and His Bride.

> You are fairer than the sons of men; Grace is poured upon Your lips; Therefore God has blessed You forever. 3 Gird Your sword upon [Your] thigh, O Mighty One, With Your glory and Your majesty. . . . 6 Your throne, O God, [is] forever and ever; A scepter of righteousness [is] the scepter of Your kingdom. 7 You love righteousness and hate wickedness; Therefore God, Your God, has anointed You with the oil of gladness more than Your companions.
>
> — Psa. 45:2-3, 6-7

It was shown in the previous chapter that Solomon was a prefigure or an archetype of Jesus Christ. Here Solomon was praised as an extraordinarily handsome man who was "fairer" than all others. He is also a warrior with his enemies defeated before him: full of glory and majesty. Then, in verse 6, this poetic psalm became a prophecy concerning the coming Messiah, Jesus. This handsome, glorious, victorious king is God on the throne. Verses 6-7 were directly quoted in Hebrews 1:8-9 concerning Jesus Christ.

"Your throne, O God, is forever and ever." Certainly, King Solomon was not God. His throne was not God's throne. Only Jesus, as the Son of God, is on the throne. However, the incarnated God who put on flesh as a Man, also has God as His God: *"God, Your God, has anointed You."* At this point, there is no doubt that this Psalm was prophetic concerning the Messiah. Jesus Christ is both God and man. Indeed: *"The queen of the South will rise up in the judgment with this generation and condemn it, for she came from the ends of the earth to hear the wisdom of Solomon; and indeed a greater than Solomon is here"* (Matt. 12:42).

The God-man is having a wedding. He has His Bride by His side, and many other women are included in this wedding. This poem concerning Solomon also alludes to the many other women surrounding Solomon. There was the queen, but there were also the many daughters of kings and a company of virgins following. History tells us that Solomon had 700 wives and 300 concubines (1 Kings 11:3). Since this psalm is also a prophecy concerning Jesus Christ, this poetic writing points out that Solomon's many wives typify that the Bride of Christ is not one single person, but it is a corporate person.

From a moral standpoint and according to God's ordination, Solomon should have had only one wife. Negatively, these foreign wives turned his heart to idols. However, when positively seen as an archetype of Jesus Christ, the many wives are a prefigure of Christ's Bride composed of myriads of people. Additionally, these women being from all the nations round about, show that Christ's Bride is composed of people from every nation, tribe, and tongue (Rev. 5:9; 7:9). The Bride of Christ is a corporate person composed of both Jews (i.e., Judah) and people from all the nations and together they constitute the Israel of God (Gal. 6:16).

From a typology point of view, it was wonderful that Solomon first married an Egyptian princess. Likewise, he also married an Ammonite woman from whom came his heir, Rehoboam, who succeeded him as king. Egypt, under the Pharaoh, serves as a type of the world under the rule of the evil one. The Ammonites were a people produced by incest between Lot and his daughter, and they were antagonists to Israel throughout their history. As an allegory, this is a powerful message that Christ's Bride does not just include the 12 tribes of Israel, but His previous enemies — the nations whom He has cursed and condemned. What a wonderful story of redemption: The Bride of Christ includes redeemed sinners and enemies whom God condemned.

The Fulfillment in Revelation

"Come, I will show you the Bride, the wife of the Lamb." [or as in a majority of manuscripts: "Come, I will show you the Woman, the Lamb's Bride"] 10 And he carried me away in the Spirit to a great, high mountain, and showed me the holy city Jerusalem coming down out of heaven from God,

– Rev 21:9-10, ESV

The Spirit and the Bride say, "Come." And let the one who hears say, "Come." And let the one who is thirsty come; let the one who desires take the water of life without price.

– Rev 22:17, ESV

At the end of the Bible, the romantic story between God and man has a happy ending. The Bride is prepared for her husband. The Bride is the city, New Jerusalem, and her husband is the Lamb, the God-man Jesus Christ. The Lamb has only one Bride, and the one Bride only has one Husband. The Bride is a composition of God's redeemed lovers from Adam through the New Testament believers as depicted by the New Jerusalem.

The New Jerusalem is the ultimate symbol of God united in one with His people. This is the meaning of marriage: two shall become one. Although the city is one, the distinctiveness of both the twelve tribes of Israel and the nations is clearly expressed. The twelve gates of the City are inscribed with the names of the twelve tribes of Israel, and the foundations of the City are the names of the twelve apostles of the Lamb. It was through the apostles' teaching, Gentile believers (Note: "Gentile" or "goyim" literally means "those from the nations") were brought into the participation of the Commonwealth of Israel (Eph. 2:12). These "twelve gates" and "twelve foundations" comprise His Glorious Bride, the Holy City.

The Lamb and His Bride are completely intertwined in perfect union. The throne is clearly described as the pinnacle and center of the Bride-City.

And he showed me a pure river of water of life, clear as crystal, proceeding from the throne of God and of the Lamb. In the middle of its street, and on either side of the river, was the tree of life, which bore twelve fruits, each tree yielding its fruit every month. The leaves of the tree were for the healing of the nations.

– Rev. 22:1–2

At the top of this mountain is the Husband King, Who is on the throne of God and the Lamb. Flowing out of the throne is the River of Life that spirals down the mountain until the base is encompassed. The Tree of Life, laden with fruit, originates from the throne, grows like a vine from the middle of the river, and courses down along both sides of the banks. What a wonderful sight of life is this Bride-City.[8]

The throne of God and the Lamb symbolize the Father and the Son within each other. For eternity, the Son is the Lamb, the Redeemer, with divinity (Son of God) and humanity (the glorified Son of Man). The River of Life is the Spirit flowing from God, becoming an integral part of the city. The Tree of Life, which is just God Himself, is the continual supply for His Bride, for eternity. The Triune God (Father, Son, and Spirit) is completely intertwined, dispersed, and everywhere with His people — the Bride.

Even though the Bride is one with God in life, sharing and partaking of His divine nature (2 Peter 1:4), and expression (and will be for eternity), God is still the Husband on the throne to be worshiped by all and the Source for all in perpetuity. What a marvelous ending to this divine romance between God and man. The Bible starts with a marriage between Adam and Eve; it ends with the real marriage between God and man.

---

8   This Bride-City is described as follows: "But you have come to Mount Zion and to the city of the living God, the heavenly Jerusalem." On the one hand, it is triangular like a Mountain, but on the other hand, it is described as "four squares" or as a cube. It is both—"She, the New-Heavenly Jerusalem, is multi-dimensional."

4

SOLOMON'S SONG OF SONGS

Song of Songs is about a king falling in love with a field worker, a country girl, who eventually becomes compatible, matching him as queen and his bride. Since Jesus Himself declared that He is the fulfillment of King Solomon by referring to Himself as "the greater than Solomon is here," the Song of Solomon can be allegorized to show a romance between Christ and His Bride. Considering this song under the inspiration of the Spirit, it shows a wonderful transformative journey of a believer becoming a member of the Bride of Christ. It is a romantic story between God, as the King, and man, as a lowly servant. Man (male and female) was not qualified to marry Christ, the King. Nevertheless, after a journey of seeking the Lord through various trials and renewals, she arrived at becoming a glorious queen. Eventually, she led the King, and He followed her and worked with her according to His eternal purpose.

As in all allegories, many reflections are up for individual interpretations. None can be 100% correct; however, given that caveat, we shall present our interpretation, which we feel brings honor to our Lord. The interpretation in the following text is based on these principles: 1) It is a romantic interaction between the God-man, Jesus Christ, and His lovers as His Bride. 2) It must be supported by the revelation in the rest of the Scriptures. 3) It can be experiential for seekers and lovers of Jesus. Although the Bride of Christ is corporate (aka the Body of Christ), she is, nevertheless, constituted by individuals who comprise her (Rom. 12:27). The goal of this interpretation is that the readers can receive new insights that would encourage and motivate them to seek the Lord, enter into progressive experiences, and mature into being a part of His Bride.

Transformative Journey Starts

[She] Let him kiss me with the kisses of his mouth — For your love [is] better than wine. 3 Because of the fragrance of your good ointments, Your name [is] ointment poured forth; Therefore the virgins love you. 4 Draw me away! [Others] We will run after you. [She] The king has brought me into his chambers. [Others] We will be glad and rejoice in you. We will remember your love more than wine. [She] Rightly do they love you.

— SS. 1:2-4

Every believer's journey begins when they fall in love with Jesus. Yes, one may know God's love and receive faith concerning Jesus' death and resurrection; however, their transformative journey starts when they proclaim their love for Jesus. It is one thing to learn about Jesus; it is another to know and feel His love. Once a believer falls in love with Jesus and pursues Him, it will persist for the rest of their lives. This spiritual journey of love continues until one is taken to meet the Lord, or He comes the second time to meet them. If the love of the Lord is missing, believers are stalled in their transformative progression. This could be the reason the Lord chastised the saints in Ephesus for leaving their first love (Rev. 2:4).

If you want to become a part of the Bride of Christ, it starts with *"Let Him kiss me."* He would be considered better, more intoxicating, and more enjoyable than anything the world can offer. You know you are in love when the name of Jesus sounds so sweet and your heart flutters with joy at the sound of His name. You must repeat His name and enjoy the pleasing fragrance of His name throughout the day. Without personally enjoying His love and reciprocating love for Him, your transformative journey has not started, or it will not continue.

"Draw Me" shows the intimate and personal relationship between the Lord and His lover. A lover of Jesus cannot be just one who is simply going along in a crowd. To seek the Lord, each person must directly interact with the Lord. However, when one person is drawn to the Lord, those around the lover of the Lord are affected to run after the Lord. Whenever one is in love with the Lord, others will be influenced and sense the Lord's beauty, causing them to run after Him. Eventually, the entire group will enjoy and love the Lord together. One flame of love will start a fire among a group of believers.

A lover of the Lord is never selfish with her love. She is eager to share and infect others with the love of the Lord. She is happy that more and more people are in love with the same Lord as hers. She confirms: *"Rightly do they love You."*

> [She] I am dark, but lovely, O daughters of Jerusalem, Like the tents of Kedar, Like the curtains of Solomon. 6 Do not look upon me, because I [am] dark, because the sun has tanned me. My mother's sons were angry with me; They made me the keeper of the vineyards, but my own vineyard I have not kept.
>
> – SS. 1:5-6

The "field maiden" realizes that her complexion is unattractive; therefore, she esteems herself lowly. She is a "nobody" working in the field. She was ashamed of herself—

"Do not look upon me." Every seeker of the Lord needs to come to such a reflection of themselves: That they are not worthy. Their daily toiling under the heat of this world has degraded and sullied them. Later in this Song, she was transformed into a queen and was praised by the King for her perfection; however, even then, she retained her humility. In her weakness, she leaned on the Lord, needing to be a seal embedded in the Lord's strong arm (SS. 8:5-6). It is essential to maintain a state of humility when seeking the Lord. *God resists the proud but gives grace to the humble* (1 Pet. 5:5).

> [She] Tell me, O you whom I love, where you feed [your flock], Where you make [it] rest at noon. For why should I be as one who veils herself by the flocks of your companions? 8 [He] If you do not know, O fairest among women, follow in the footsteps of the flock, and feed your little goats beside the shepherds' tents. 9 I have compared you, my love, To my filly [mare] among Pharaoh's chariots . . . .
>
> *– SS. 1:7-9*

King Solomon did not approach this field maiden as the king but as a shepherd. He came to her at a similar social status: she, a field worker, and he, a shepherd. Both are servants working in the open fields. If Solomon came to her with all his splendor and majesty as the most powerful king, and he went with his royal guards, she would be frozen with fear. If the king says, "I want you," there would be no choice but to go with him. Love cannot be genuine without free will. How can a field worker at the lowest social stratum dare to fall in love with the king? Therefore, the king went to her as a shepherd. She fell in love with someone similar to her status with comparable struggles. This shepherd, being alike with her, understands her, her daily toil, and her challenges. Because they share a mutual understanding, they can communicate effectively and empathize with one another.

This is a wonderful allegory of God, Who became Man to woo man (male and female), to attract man to Himself. If God came to man in all His glory and majesty, man would hide from Him in fear. It would not be possible to fall in love with God when there is such a huge gap of differences in status. God, the creator, and man, a lowly creature, are incompatible. How wonderful that God became a lowly man (Phil. 2:6-7). He came not even as a kingly man but as a slave. He was approachable, harmless, and non-threatening. People from the lowest estate can approach Him without fear. It is this God-man that His seekers fall in love with.

The field maiden seeking her beloved asked where to find and be close to her beloved. He responded: *"Follow the tracks of the flock."* The Lord, as the Shepherd, is pastoring a flock. Those seeking the Lord will find Him if they follow His flock. One may individually love the Lord and desire to seek Him. However, the way to the Lord is to find other believers shepherded by Him. Find and follow those fed by the Lord, and you will find Him there. This is a wonderful instruction by the Lord to all His lovers: He is with the other seekers. Do not seek Him in isolation; rather, be with other lovers of Jesus to find Him. Individually, one may have those precious, contemplative times with the "Lover of your soul," but know this: Follow the footsteps of the flock, for with His flock you will find His fullness!

At the beginning stage of this country girl's journey, the first thing that she was compared to was *a mare among Pharaoh's chariots.* As her journey continues, she will be transformed from being likened to a horse to a queen. A horse pulling Pharaoh's chariot shows she is strong-willed and wild, starting her journey as one transporting God's enemy. Pharaoh has generally been negatively portrayed as the enslaver of God's people and as Israel's enemy. This means she is freshly out of Egypt, from slavery. This is the beginning stage for all those who fall in love with the Lord. Nevertheless, the Lord still sees His lover as the *most beautiful among women.* Even though His seekers are wild, rebellious, and worldly, as long as they seek and love the Lord, they are the most beautiful to Him.

> A bundle of myrrh [is] my beloved to me, that lies 'all night between my breasts. 14 My beloved [is] to me a cluster of henna [blooms] in the vineyards of En Gedi. 15 [He] Behold, you [are] fair, my love! Behold, you [are] fair! you [have] dove's eyes.
>
> ~ SS. 1:13-15

> [He] Like a lily among thorns, so is my love among the daughters.
>
> ~ SS. 2:2

The field maiden continues to enjoy a loving and intimate relationship with the Lord. She was undeterred by her inward condition of being a rebellious horse. Due to this singleness to pursue and love the Lord, He appreciated her eyes as *dove's eyes.* Doves in the Scripture represent peace and purity. The first time a dove was mentioned was in Genesis 8, when Noah released a dove to test whether the flood had subsided. It was a dove carrying an olive branch in its beak — a sign that judgment had passed and peace with God had begun. When Jesus was baptized, the Holy Spirit came as a dove (Matt. 3:16). So, while she started as a wild horse, her transformation began with her eyes. She only had eyes to see the Lord in all things. She saw the Lord in whatever environment she found herself because she loved Him.

As she continues to enjoy being intimate with the Lord and admiring His beauty (SS. 1:16), the Lord declares that she is like a *lily among thorns*. In Matthew 6, Jesus taught people not to worry and not to be anxious. He said, *"Why do you worry? Consider the lilies of the field, how they grow: they neither toil nor spin and yet I say to you that even Solomon in all his glory was not arrayed like one of these"* (Matt. 6:28-29). Being likened to a lily means that the lover of Jesus lives a life free from anxiety. She trusts in God for food, clothing, and shelter. Additionally, Jesus said in Matthew 16:22 that *"thorns"* are *the cares of this world and the deceitfulness of riches*. These thorns choke the word of life so that it will not grow and bear fruit. The world today is driven by anxiety and the pursuit of riches. People lose their joy and health over worries. However, for a lover of Jesus, she is living a life liberated from the anxiety of this world. God takes good care of her as she pursues the Lord in love.

Living in Resurrection

[She] Like an apple tree among the trees of the woods, So [is] my beloved among the sons. I sat down in his shade with great delight, and his fruit [was] sweet to my taste. 4 He brought me to the banqueting house, and his banner over me [was] love. . . . 6 His left hand [is] under my head, and his right hand embraces me. . . . 8 [She] The voice of my beloved! Behold, he comes leaping upon the mountains, skipping upon the hills. 9 My beloved is like a gazelle or a young stag. Behold, he stands behind our wall; He is looking through the windows, gazing through the lattice. 10 My beloved spoke, and said to me: "Rise up, my love, my fair one, and come away. 11 For lo, the winter is past, the rain is over [and] gone.

– SS. 2:3-4, 6, 8-11

Song of Songs 2:3-7 describes a scene where she thoroughly enjoys being with the Lord because of all the things the Lord provided her. She describes all the various items from the Lord: tasting His sweet fruit, being shaded from the sun's heat, feasting in the banqueting house, and being sustained by raisin cakes. She experiences complete joy, free from anxiety, because she has been captivated by the Lord's love — His banner of love. Any lovers of the Lord would desire to remain in this environment of joy and love forever. There is no need to go anywhere or do anything else.

Suddenly, the Lord is outside calling her. While she would love to remain in that state, the Lord is outside skipping and leaping like a gazelle. He is calling her *to arise and come away*. The Lord is moving in resurrection: the *winter is past and the rain is over*. What beautiful imagery of resurrection life! The lover may be satisfied with all the things the Lord provided her, but the Lord is unsatisfied. He still has His purpose to fulfill, and her transformation journey is not over. She is not ready for marriage, so she needs to continue and follow the Lord into His resurrection.

> [He] "O my dove, in the clefts of the rock, In the secret [places] of the cliff, let me see your face, Let me hear your voice; For your voice [is] sweet, And your face [is] lovely." . . . 16 [She] My beloved [is] mine, and I [am] his. He feeds [his flock] among the lilies.
>
> *– SS*. 2:14, 16

Being with the Lord in His resurrection, she is now called *"my dove"* by the Lord. As written before, a dove is a symbol of the Holy Spirit. She is now joined to the Spirit. She can fly and soar high to the *"clefts of the rock and the secret places of the cliff"* in the Spirit of His resurrection. While there are many challenges, trials, and sufferings through a life of pursuing her beloved, she is protected in the heavens, high above all. A person in resurrection is constantly in a secret place with the Lord. Others observing her would not understand how she can endure trials and challenges with joy, grace, and love. It is because she is covertly living in resurrection without any fanfare or conceit. She is consumed with the Lord, realizing that the Lord is hers and she belongs to the Lord.

Enjoying Christ and His Provisions

> [She] By night on my bed I sought the one I love; I sought him, but I did not find him. 2 "I will rise now," [I said], "And go about the city; In the streets and in the squares I will seek the one I love." I sought him, but I did not find him. 3 The watchmen who go about the city found me; [I said], "Have you seen the one I love?" 4 Scarcely had I passed by them, when I found the one I love. I held him and would not let him go, Until I had brought him to the house of my mother, and into the chamber of her who conceived me. . . .
>
> *– SS*. 3:1-4

This is the second time in her journey that her beloved seemingly disappeared, and she is alone. The Lord is constantly moving for His purpose, and she cannot stay in her comfort zone. After declaring that the Lord is hers for her possession, He left. Again, He is gone! She has to arise to seek Him. He was not easy to find; therefore, she needed help from the watchmen. Watchmen can be likened to those who provide safety and oversight. Often, during a period of seeking, those with more experience in watching can help direct a seeker to where the Lord may be found. It is not certain if this is the case here, but, anyhow, immediately after encountering the watchmen, she found the Lord.

This seems to be a spiritual cycle: She is enjoying the Lord, He disappears, she seeks Him again and finds Him, then she arrives at a further stage of transformation. She enters into a deeper relationship with the Lord and a greater expression of Him. This is 2 Corinthians 3:18 in experience: *And we all, beholding the glory of the Lord, are being transformed into the same image from one degree of glory to another.* To be transformed from glory to glory, the seeker of the Lord cannot remain satisfied with their spiritual attainments. They need to keep going.

> Who [is] this coming out of the wilderness like pillars of smoke, Perfumed with myrrh and frankincense, With all the merchant's fragrant powders? 7 Behold, it [is] Solomon's couch, [With] sixty valiant men around it, Of the valiant of Israel. 8 They all hold swords, [being] expert in war. Every man [has] his sword on his thigh because of fear in the night. 9 Of the wood of Lebanon Solomon the King made himself a palanquin: . . . 11 Go forth, O daughters of Zion, and see King Solomon with the crown with which his mother crowned him on the day of his wedding, The day of the gladness of his heart.
>
> – SS. 3:6-9, 11

Now, the field maiden is observed to be likened to *pillars of smoke coming out of the wilderness.* When Israel went through 40 years of testing in the wilderness, God provided a pillar of cloud to guide them. This cloud signifies God's presence and glory in His dwelling place: it was at the tabernacle and in the temple (Exo. 40:38; 1 Kings 8:10). The Shulamite, as pillars of smoke, is similar to God's pillar of cloud; however, smoke is generated from the earth, and clouds are from above. Smoke from the earth is associated with the various offerings as an aroma for God's satisfaction (Lev. 1:9; 6:15). She became an offering soothing and pleasing to God. While the "wilderness" is a place of trial and suffering; nevertheless, she came out of it with no bitterness or complaints. It was not a putrid smoke to suffocate or blind, but it was perfumed with myrrh and frankincense for a pleasant and aromatic environment. Myrrh, associated with Jesus, symbolizes His suffering and death, whereas frankincense is for His divinity and resurrection[9]. In her intimacy with the Lord, while she went through trials in her journey, she came out pleasing and comforting God and man.

A pillar of smoke has a characteristic that is compliant and accommodating in the sense that a little wind or breath can move and change its direction. What a contrast when she started her journey like a mare (horse): strong-willed, difficult to tame and control. She is now like Paul, so flexible and adaptable: *I have become all things to all people, so that by all means I may save some"* (1 Cor. 9:19-22). She adapts to any situation and provides God and man with a soothing and pleasing aroma.

She also became Solomon's couch. In those days, a couch symbolized authority for meals and rest. She has become a place of relaxation and nourishment for the Lord. Additionally, she is the Lord's palanquin: she is transporting the Lord within her. She started as a mare moving Pharaoh in his chariot, but now she is the enclosure for the Lord's move. What a transformation from transporting God's enemy to transporting God Himself. Wherever she is and wherever she goes, the Lord is resting within her. Where she goes, He is there. She has become what the Lord promised: *I am with you always, to the end of the age* (Matt. 28:20).

Finally, she has become the crown on the Lord's head. She became His glory and majesty. When a king wears his crown, he is recognized immediately for His glory and authority. What a glory to the Lord to progressively transform her from a field worker to the Bride of Christ. The universe sees her beauty and gives glory and praise to God (Eph. 3:20). It is the Lord working in His lovers, transforming them to one who pleases God (Heb. 13:21). She is the Lord's crown!

Finality of Her Progress

> [He] Behold, you are fair, my love! Behold, you are fair! You have dove's eyes behind your veil. Your hair is like a flock of goats, going down from Mount Gilead. . . . 2 Your teeth . . . 3 Your lips . . . your mouth . . . Your cheeks . . . 4 Your neck . . . 5 Your two breasts . . . 7 You are altogether beautiful, my love; there is no flaw in you. . . . . 9 You have ravished my heart, My sister, [my] spouse; You have ravished my heart with one [look] of your eyes, With one link of your necklace. 10 How fair is your love, My sister, [my] spouse! How much better than wine is your love, and the scent of your perfumes than all spices!
>
> – SS. 4:1-5, 7-10

---

9   What Is Frankincense In The Bible? - Christian Website

Now, it is the Lord's turn to describe His Bride's beauty. Amazingly, the Lord describes and praises her with captivating and exhaustive language. The God-man Messiah, symbolized by Solomon, is enamored by His lover's beauty. He appraised her beauty with flowing poetic language, describing her hair, her two breasts, and more (read descriptions in the Bible). When His lover began this journey, she said to the Lord, *"Your love is better than wine."* Now, the Lord says to her: "Better is your love than wine." He is truly smitten with love for His Bride.

The Lord declares she is His sister and bride. This poetic writing calls the field maiden the Lord's sister and bride, which can be confusing from an incestual viewpoint. However, from a spiritual perspective, "sister" means she is the same kind as the Lord. She is born of the same Father and partaking of the same life and divine nature. The Lord and she are of the same species, the "same kind" (Heb. 2:11; 1 John 3:2). This is consistent with the story of Adam and Eve, and Isaac and Rebekah: The Lord and His Bride are not from different species or different people. It is precisely because she is His "sister" that she can also be His Bride. The two can be joined because they have the same life, nature, and expression.

The Lord appraised her as perfect, without flaw. This certainly should be the last stage of her spiritual journey. Where can she go any further than that of a flawless Bride of Christ? Can there be more spiritual advancement than such a stage of perfection? This is similar to Romans 1-8, where a believer has gone through the stages of justification, sanctification, and arriving at glorification. That should be the final stage of spiritual growth: glorified. A person cannot exceed salvation beyond having the same image as the Lord in glorification (Rom. 8:29-30). Nevertheless, just as Romans 8 is only half of the Romans' epistle, now the seeker's "glorification" in her perfection as the Bride of Christ is only half of this Song. There is more to come.

In the physical world, believers go through various experiences in a timeline; it is not so with God. He is not limited, and that which Christ accomplished by His death, resurrection, and ascension is eternal, transcending time and space. To Him, His purpose is eternally completed and finished. This is confirmed by passages such as these: *"... these [believers] He also glorified"* (Rom. 8:30); *"raised us up together [with Christ], and made us sit together in the heavenly places in Christ Jesus"* (Eph. 2:6). The translator used the past tense, showing that they are accomplished. Both glorification and sitting in the heavenly places in the timeline are in the future, but in God's eyes, they are already performed. Therefore, at this stage, while she continues to pursue Christ in this world, it may not necessarily mean that she is perfect with no flaws. Nevertheless, since she is living in Christ, she identifies with His perfection. She has put on Christ, and Christ's perfection is her testimony before the Lord.

Appreciating Christ Himself

> [She] I sleep, but my heart is awake; [It is] the voice of my beloved! He knocks, [saying], "Open for me, my sister, my love, my dove, my perfect one; For my head is covered with dew, My locks with the drops of the night." 3 I have taken off my robe; How can I put it on [again]? I have washed my feet; How can I defile them?
>
> – SS. 5:2-3

The bride has reached perfection. She wants to stay in that state of glory. Nevertheless, the Lord is gone again. Why would the Lord leave someone who has arrived at being His bride in this stage of holiness? The Lord is outside, but unlike her past experiences, this time she is not happy to go to the Lord outside. Now that she is clean and perfect, she does not want to go out and get dirty. She would rather stay in the comfort of her holiness.

This is a warning to all seekers of the Lord: it is possible and prophetic to arrive at a spiritual stage where you would want to stay put in your exalted condition even though the Lord is no longer there. You are content to dwell in your spiritual achievements and holiness, even though He is gone.

> I opened for my beloved, but my beloved had turned away [and] was gone. My heart leaped up when he spoke. I sought him, but I could not find him; I called him, but he gave me no answer. 7 The watchmen who went about the city found me. They struck me, they wounded me; The keepers of the walls took my veil away from me.
>
> – SS. 5:6-7

Eventually, the field maiden got up and opened the door to the Lord's knocking, but it was too late. He is already gone and not to be found. She sought Him, but He did not answer. She met the watchmen again; however, this time, instead of being a help to her, they abused her. They took away her veil, putting her to shame. In deeper stages of seeking the Lord, those who once offered help may become sources of resistance and obstacles. They may not understand why someone who has arrived at a mature status is out wandering. These may be overseers in a church or a "discipler" in a ministry where you have been a respected member, but now you want to seek the Lord outside the "house" where you have been kept holy. She is on her own with no one able to help.

At some point, a lover of the Lord will have to seek Him individually, isolated from others. Can she find the Lord on her own, even when facing ridicule and opposition from those she once admired? This can test whether she is seeking to please men or God. And unlike when she first started seeking the Lord, where she could follow the Lord's flock, now there is no group to follow. She has no one to trust but the Lord Himself.

While she sought her Beloved, she met a group of women. They were curious as to why she was so desperate to find Him. They asked: *"What is your beloved more than another beloved, O fairest among women?"* (Song 5:9). When believers are seeking and loving the Lord, it causes others around them to become curious to know about the Lord. Why is she still loving the Lord in the face of opposition? Who is He?

> [She] My beloved is white [radiant] and ruddy, chief among ten thousand. 11 His head . . . his locks . . . . 12 His eyes . . . . 13 His cheeks . . . His lips . . . . 14 His arms . . . His body . . . . 15 His legs . . . His appearance . . . . 16 His mouth is most sweet, Yes, he is altogether lovely. This is my beloved, and this is my friend, O daughters of Jerusalem!
>
> – SS. 5:10-16
>
> [Others] Where has your beloved gone, O fairest among women? Where has your beloved turned aside, that we may seek him with you?
>
> – SS. 6:1

The seeker started describing the Lord to them in detailed poetic imagery. She portrays Him from the head down to His legs. She has been intimately gazing at His every part. Previously, she spoke lovingly about what the Lord has done or given her. She appreciated the Lord (in chapter 2) bringing her to the banqueting house and providing raisin cakes, apples, and shade from the sun. Now, she is just describing the Lord Himself. It is not what He has done or given, but He is altogether desirable. Even if He does not do anything for her, she loves Him.

At this stage of her journey, even though she missed the Lord's presence, yet, due to her past loving experiences with the Lord, she can speak of Him in a glowing portrayal. There is a need to store up experiences of Christ so that there is a readiness to speak of Him in intimate detail, even when His presence is gone. Her explanation of the beauty of the Lord caused those listening also to desire and seek Him with her. This is a wonderful illustration of "preaching the gospel." It was not about being saved from hell and going to heaven. Rather, it is about portraying Jesus to attract others to seek the Lord because of His wonder and beauty.[10]

When the Lord Jesus put on flesh, there is a strong indication that the form He took was not physically attractive. Concerning the coming Messiah, Isaiah prophesied: *"Like a root out of dry ground; he had no form or majesty that we should look at him, and no beauty that we should desire him. He was despised and rejected by men, a man of sorrow and acquainted with grief; and as one from whom men hide their faces he was despised, and we esteemed him not"* (Isa. 53:2-3). From this portion, the Messiah was not attractive because He was not handsome.

Therefore, this wonderful and detailed poetic portrayal should be allegorized to reflect the Lord's character and nature. For example: *"My beloved is radiant and ruddy."* This can refer to the Lord's shining with His glory; He is strong and full of life. *"His mouth is most sweet"* can be understood as His words and voice are comforting and strengthening. His lovers can hear Him day and night without being tired of Him. Each description of Him can be allegorized according to how His seekers have experienced Him.

In the New Testament, there is no description of Jesus Christ's physical appearance since that was not His attractiveness. People were attracted to Him due to His character: His love, kindness, patience, suffering, gentleness, boldness, humility, authority, and power. When many of His disciples left Him because He said to "eat my flesh and drink my blood," the twelve disciples said *"Lord, to whom shall we go? You have the words of eternal life"* (John 6:68). They remained with Him, not because of His physical attractiveness, but they had tasted — *"His mouth is most sweet."*

There is only one other portion of Scripture describing Jesus from His hair to His feet, which is in Revelation chapter 1. Again, He was spoken of in a way of symbolism:

> and in the midst of the seven lampstands [One] like the Son of Man, clothed with a garment down to the feet and girded about the chest with a golden band. 14 His head and hair [were] white like wool, as white as snow, and His eyes like a flame of fire; 15 His feet [were] like fine brass, as if refined in a furnace, and His voice as the sound of many waters; 16 He had in His right hand seven stars, out of His mouth went a sharp two-edged sword, and His countenance [was] like the sun shining in its strength.
>
> – Rev 1:13-16

---

10   Henry Hon's testimony: When considering this portion of Scripture, I was convicted that I am short of describing the Lord in my experiences in such flowing detail that listeners will desire Him. I recognized that when I teach the Scriptures, I have not spoken enough about the beauty of the Lord. I determined that I need to spend some time to portray the Person of Jesus before I teach anything else.

This does not sound like the "mild-mannered" servant — Jesus portrayed in the gospels, but One in the power of resurrection. His seekers and lovers need to know and experience Him from head to toe. Perhaps *His head and His hair are white like wool, as white as snow*" means to know Him as the pure and sinless Lamb of God and experience His redemptive forgiveness freshly every day. When people gaze into His eyes, they are consumed with fire — either negatively or positively. For those disobedient, He is a consuming fire — a devastating loss. For His lovers, they will catch the zeal of His fire for God's House and receive fire in the shape of tongues to preach the good news of Jesus Christ. His words out of His mouth are a "two-edged sword" with one edge for His enemy and the other to slay the fallen man within His lovers.

The point is that at this advanced stage of her journey, the lover of Jesus is not reciting any doctrines concerning salvation, justification, or holiness. She is not looking at herself or people's opinions of her. Her entire focus is on the beauty and sweetness of Jesus. Every seeker must arrive at this stage where they have lost the taste and desire for any spiritual attainment; they are done with doctrinal debates, their degree of holiness, measuring and judging others, or assessing their success in ministries. Their focus is entirely on the many lovable aspects of Jesus' character.

Interestingly, the vivid description of Christ in Revelation is where He is amid His Ekklesias ("seven churches"). True to His mission in Matthew 16:18 — "I will build My Ekklesia" — Christ continues to build and care for His democratic assemblies. This is consistent in that after a loving, detailed portrayal of Christ in Song of Songs chapter 5, she became a peacemaker of God's people in the next chapter. In other words, in the only two portions of the Bible where Jesus Christ is described from head to feet, it is related to God's eternal purpose. This indicates that the way to continue this next phase of her journey to be a builder of unity among diverse people is to have a singular focus on the Lord Himself.

Jerusalem—A Peacemaker

> [She] My beloved has gone to his garden, To the beds of spices, To feed [his flock] in the gardens, and to gather lilies. 3 I [am] my beloved's, and my beloved [is] mine. He feeds [his flock] among the lilies.
>
> *— SS. 6:2-3*

After describing the lovely Messiah, the queen found her beloved. She knows where the Lord is: He is in His garden, His field for growing and maturing His people. God's people are His garden or farm (1 Cor. 3:9), and He is gathering lilies. As previously written, lilies are those trusting in Him. He is caring for the growth of His people like a gardener and a shepherd, and He is gathering His scattered people together into one (John 11:52). He left His bride to take care of His people. His eternal desire is not just for transformed individuals, but for a corporate people. He is the King of a Kingdom! The seeker recognized that her King was not just for her alone. He is with His people.

Appreciating that the Lord is after something more than her selfish enjoyment, she reversed her priority and said: *"I am my beloved's and my beloved is mine."* Previously, in chapter 2, she said: *"My beloved is mine and I am his."* Now, she realizes that she first belonged to the Lord rather than the Lord being hers. She prioritizes the Lord's purpose ahead of her private enjoyment of the Lord. She is now ready for the second part of her journey. No wonder, even though as an individual seeker she was transformed to become perfect, a sister and bride, she needs to continue with the Lord and partner with Him to fulfill His heart's eternal desire.

> [He] O my love, you [are as] beautiful as Tirzah, Lovely as Jerusalem, Awesome as [an army] with banners! 5 Turn your eyes away from me, for they have overcome me. Your hair [is] like a flock of goats Going down from Gilead. . . . 10 Who is she who looks forth as the morning, Fair as the moon, Clear as the sun, Awesome as [an army] with banners? . . . 13 [Others] Return, return, O Shulamite; Return, return, that we may look upon you! [The Shulamite] What would you see in the Shulamite — As it were, the dance of the two camps?
>
> — SS. 6:4-5, 10, 13

The seeker, who started as a horse pulling Pharaoh's chariot, is now likened to Jerusalem. The temple was built in Jerusalem, where all twelve diverse tribes gathered in unity to feast and worship God. There is a unique place for Israel to worship God, and the place is Jerusalem (Deut. 12:5-7). Israel was forbidden to worship God within their tribal territories. They needed to bring the produce from their territories and assemble to share in a 7-day feast. That is the time when God receives worship and glory.

Jerusalem is a compound word from "teach" and "peace" (BLB). Its meaning can be "foundation of peace" or "possession of peace" (BDB). That is certainly an appropriate name and place for the twelve diverse tribes to gather as one. They are in a place of peace, and where peace is learned. Jerusalem is the foreshadowing of the Lord's Ekklesia, which Jesus Christ came to build in the New Testament (Matt. 16:18). It is the assembly where diverse believers with differing perspectives are gathered to fellowship, and God is glorified with one mind and mouth (1 Cor. 11:19; Rom. 15:6).

Even when she was a perfected bride of Christ, it was an individual experience. It was just her and the Lord. She sought the Lord for her own spiritual progress and relationship. From Chapter 5 on, she became corporate – she became Jerusalem. She is now a peacemaker and a place for diverse and even opposing tribes to assemble for feasting and worshipping. She cares for God's people and God's purpose.

This is similar to the first half of Romans (chapters 1-8), where individual believers experienced personal spiritual progress until glorification. The second half starting from chapter 9 brings the two divided groups of believers (Jews and Gentiles [those from "the nations"]) together as one Body (Rom. 12). This joining together, without judging each other, is God's Kingdom where He is glorified (Rom. 14-15:7). It was the gospel of peace in Romans 10 that brought them together. Together in "Jerusalem," they glorified God in one accord (Rom. 15:6) and finally crushed Satan under the feet of those who are in peace (Rom. 16:20).

After being likened to Jerusalem, she became *"awesome as an army with banners."* The seeker became Jerusalem to unite diverse people in peace to defeat God's enemy. This is similar to Romans 16, where Satan is crushed under the feet of those believers who are together in peace. Satan's strategy is to divide God's people – His Kingdom (Luke 11:17). Conversely, the way to defeat Satan is to unite as one. Therefore, she progresses from Jerusalem into an awesome army.

God's eternal purpose is twofold: To be glorified and have victory over His rebellious angel, Satan. Both are fulfilled by the seeker becoming Jerusalem and an army. She became one who took care of God's Ekklesia, where God receives glory: *to him be glory in the church* [lit. ekklesia] (Eph. 3:21). And *"that through the church [lit. ekklesia] the manifold wisdom of God might now be made known to the rulers and authorities in the heavenly places . . . according to the eternal purpose [of God]* (Eph. 3:10). This is truly a leap in transformation as she journeyed: from seeking individual spirituality to becoming a place of tribal unity as one Bride of Christ (Gal. 6:14-16).

At this stage, she is called Shulamite for the first time. Shulamite is the feminine name from the same root word as Solomon, which is masculine. In other words, just as the woman is the female version of the man, Shulamite is the female name for Solomon, which means peace. Both names are derived from "Salam," which means "to be safe," "to be completed," "make amends," "be at peace," and "make prosperous" (Strong's). Therefore, peace is more than having "no conflicts," it includes positive traits of prosperity, safety, and provision. The Lord's lover arrived at having the same name as the Messiah: a peacemaker. Jesus made peace between enemies, and His lovers are also peacemakers (Eph. 2:11-18; Matt. 5:9). The bride is now the same as the groom: one is the reflection and counterpart of the other.

Shulamite is likened to the *dance of two armies*. This is prophetic: two warring armies will make peace and dance together. This happened after Solomon, during the time of his son, Rehoboam, when Jeroboam became the king of the ten northern tribes and seceded from Rehoboam, the king of Judah. They became two warring armies fighting each other for almost 200 years. However, as the Shulamite, she brought them together to fight as one and become victorious. They are no longer fighting; they are dancing and celebrating their victory. She acted upon the work of Christ on the cross in bringing these two previous enemies together in victory (more on this in a later chapter).

Leading the Lord for His Desire

> How beautiful are your feet in sandals, O prince's daughter! The curve of your thighs . . . 2 Your navel . . . Your waist . . . 3 Your two breasts . . . 4 Your neck . . . Your eyes . . . Your nose . . . 5 Your head . . . your hair . . . 6 How fair and pleasant you are, O love, with your delights! 7 Your stature . . . your breasts 8 . . . your breath . . . 9 and roof of your mouth . . .
>
> *— SS. 7:1-9*

It is surprising and wonderful that the Lord appreciates His Bride so intimately and lovingly. He is, after all, the creator God and the Lord of lords with all things under His feet. Yet, this poetic portrayal of His love for her sounds profoundly human. Astonishingly, He is human! God has become human to engage with His Bride in the most loving and intimate relationship as between two lovers. This is mysterious yet true!

Remember that she started as a field maiden, darkened by the sun from field labor. She was a horse pulling Pharaoh's chariot, really nothing for the Lord to describe appreciatively. Look at her now at this stage of maturity. The Lord is in love with every part of her. His eyes are set on His Bride since she has captivated Him.

This is the picture of Christ and His Democratic Assembly. His diverse people have become the Bride of Christ. Since His Bride is also His Body, He appreciates every part of her. Every member of the Bride, like His Body, is needed to make the whole beautiful. The chapters found in 1 Corinthians 12 and Romans 12 are filled with the diversity and beauty of all the members of the Bride. Every part is wonderful and needed. If believers realize how much Christ appreciates every member of His Bride, they would also have the same esteem for all the members. They would refrain from judging and criticizing one another. Instead, they would appreciate each believer with honor and love.

> [She] Come, my beloved, let us go forth to the field; Let us lodge in the villages. 12 Let us get up early to the vineyards; Let us see if the vine has budded, [whether] the grape blossoms are open, [And] the pomegranates are in bloom. There I will give you my love.
>
> – *SS*. 7:11-12

As a true partner to her beloved and one who understands His eternal purpose, she led with conviction. She makes the decision and asks Him to follow. She is leading Him to where He wanted to go and what He wanted to do in the first place. She went to stay with His people in the villages and care for His vineyards. In John 15, Jesus said: *I am the vine and you are the branches.* This is exactly akin to what Paul said: *For just as the body is one and has many members, and all the members of the body, though many, are one body, so it is with Christ* (1 Cor. 12:12). Just as the many branches constitute a vine, the many members of His Body are Christ. Not just members of His Body, but members of Christ.

Her focus is now on God's people and the corporate Christ, which is His Democratic Assembly. Although the Lord is transforming individually His seekers and lovers, his eternal purpose is not with many individuals. He is not marrying many individuals; He is marrying one corporate Bride. His Bride is composed of every people, tribe, nation, and tongue. They are many and diverse; nevertheless, they are one. His people in oneness fulfill His prayer in John 17. While division is the symptom of immaturity (1 Cor. 3:1-4), diversity in unity (not uniformity) is His Bride making herself ready for marriage (Rev. 19:7). The Shulamite has joined this quest to help make ready the Lord's eternal Bride.

"There, I will give you my love." The Shulamite tells the Lord to come and work with her if He wants her love. Wow, what audacity! She knows the Lord is in love with her; He has to follow her to receive her love. However, this is a profoundly romantic stage between two lovers. She bids Him to work together with her for His purpose, and it is in that service that she loves Him. This is similar to what the Lord in John 21 said to Simon: *"Do you love me?" He said to him, "Yes, Lord; you know that I love you."* Jesus said to him, *"Feed my lambs."* Those who are caring for God's people are loving the Lord.

The apostle Paul was a good example of taking the initiative to do the Lord's work. Once he got converted and knew God's purpose, he was off running the race to build the Lord's Ekklesia. He traveled and went to many places on his own initiative. While he was taking the lead to go to the "villages" and care for the "vineyards," only once in Acts 16 did the Spirit tell him not to go further into Asia Minor but to go to Macedonia.

He knew the Lord's heart, so he led, and the Lord followed. All who love the Lord must reach the stage of understanding His purpose in building His Democratic Assembly and intentionally take action to fulfill it. In so doing, the Lord receives love.

Actively Waiting for Glorification

> Oh, that you were like my brother, who nursed at my mother's breasts! [If] I should find you outside, I would kiss you; I would not be despised. 2 I would lead you [and] bring you into the house of my mother, she [who] used to instruct me. I would cause you to drink of spiced wine, of the juice of my pomegranate.
>
> – SS. 8:1-2

In the days of Solomon, culturally, it was not acceptable to show affection in public between lovers. However, it was an acceptable norm to display affection between siblings. She desires to be open in her intimacy and affection with the Lord. Today, there is an aversion from the people of the world toward lovers of Jesus. They are often despised by the world. The world does not understand why a person would want to "waste" their lives on pursuing Jesus. Therefore, lovers of the Lord frequently do not publicly show their love and intimacy with Jesus.

Therefore, she desires the time when Jesus returns in glory and she is glorified. Referencing the believers' glorification, Paul said: *"In order that he might be the firstborn among many brothers"* (Rom. 8:29-30). Paul addresses the Lord as the Firstborn among many brethren. This is consistent with the Shulamite's sentiment. At that time of glorification with the Lord's return, the affection between His lovers and Him will be open and trumpeted. Christ and His ekklesia (Democratic Assembly) will display their union for all to see (Rev. 22:17).

Additionally, Paul said that the mother of all Christ's followers is the Jerusalem above (Gal. 4:26). The New Jerusalem is the eternal dwelling place for both God and His people. The *"house of my mother"* is the New Jerusalem — the place of the Bride with the Bridegroom. They are together in the same place. Therefore, while she serves the Lord for His purpose in the villages and vineyards, she longs for the Lord's second advent, where she can openly express her love for the Lord to the entire world. The world will witness the marriage of the Lamb with His Bride (Rev. 21:2). The universe will observe the God-man Creator-Redeemer enjoying the sweetness and open affection from His Bride as the New Jerusalem.

[She] Set me as a seal upon your heart, as a seal upon your arm; For love [is as] strong as death, Jealousy [as] cruel as the grave; Its flames [are] flames of fire, A most vehement flame. 7 Many waters cannot quench love, nor can the floods drown it. If a man would give for love all the wealth of his house, it would be utterly despised.

– SS. 8:6-7

Even though the Shulamite is mature in the Lord, spiritually a "perfect" bride, and works together with the Lord for His purpose, she continues to realize that she is weak. She cannot depend on herself, her attainments, experiences, and maturity. She wants to be permanently stamped as a seal on the Lord's heart and arm. She perpetually depends on the Lord's heart of love and arm of strength. Concerning the Lord's arm, a psalmist said in 118:16: The strong right arm of the LORD is raised in triumph. *The strong right arm of the LORD has done glorious things!*

Even more than His strength, she relies on His love. At the end of Romans 8, even though believers are at the stage of glorification, they still rely on God's love. Paul said that though believers go through various trials and tribulations: *"No, in all these things we are more than conquerors through him who loved us"* (Rom. 8:37). It is not their seeking, pursuit, diligence, spirituality, holiness, or service; God's love has brought them through. Nothing can separate them from the love of God; They are eternally sealed in His love (Rom. 8:38-39).

She compares the Lord's love to that of death, and His passion or jealousy compares to the grave. When death comes calling, no one can resist; it is fierce and cruel. Poetically, God's love can only be compared to the most negative force since it is the strongest imagery people can understand. From a man's point of view, human love can be resisted and rejected; therefore, it is not so strong. However, no man can reject or refuse death and the grave. Sooner or later, one must submit to it. Death is cruel: it does not matter if you just got married or are the father of many young children; when death calls, you must leave what's precious behind.

This is the love of God the Shulamite desires because His love conquered her. She cannot resist and requests that His love and passion will not stop. Even if she loses everything in the world – she welcomes His love. A love that is as strong as death and passion as cruel as the grave.

John Newton, who wrote the famous song "Amazing Grace," was a slave trader before he became a follower of Jesus. He was a hardened man who became the captain of a slave ship. In another song, he wrote: "Lord, Thou hast won, at length I yield / My heart by mighty grace compelled / Surrenders all to Thee; / Against Thy terrors long I strove, / But who can stand against Thy love? / Love conquers even me." That is the love of God expressed by the Shulamite.

> [The Shulamite's Brothers] We have a little sister, and she has no breasts. What shall we do for our sister in the day when she is spoken for? . . . 10 [She] I [am] a wall, and my breasts like towers; Then I became in his eyes as one who found [brings out] peace. 11 Solomon had a vineyard at Baal Hamon; He leased the vineyard to keepers; Everyone was to bring for its fruit A thousand silver [coins]. . . . 13 [He] You who dwell in the gardens, The companions listen for your voice — Let me hear it! 14 [She] Make haste, my beloved, and be like a gazelle or a young stag on the mountains of spices.
>
> – SS. 8:8, 10–11, 13–14

At the beginning of this chapter, we see the Shulamite desiring to be glorified so that in the coming Kingdom, she and the Lord can have an open, intimate relationship without being despised. In the meantime, she is not passively waiting with nothing to do. Rather, she continues to care for those believers (her siblings) who are immature. They still need to grow and develop by partaking of the divine nature and becoming mature like her. The breast can be allegorized to be beauty, comfort, and nourishment. At this stage, the Shulamite is a wall signifying protection; yet, she has two towering breasts. She lavishly cherishes and nourishes those around her.

Often, believers who have developed separation in the world (holiness), like walls, are not easily approachable or accessible. They keep their distance from those whom they consider worldly sinners or immature. For the Shulamite, while being holy, is open and available to provide comfort and nourishment. Consider the Lord Jesus, the most holy and uniquely qualified to be called the Holy One. He is a high and thick wall against His enemy. Nevertheless, He was a friend of sinners and accessible to the vilest of them all. He healed, comforted, and fed them. His holiness was not an outward show of separation; it was of the heart (Rom. 2:29). His heart was not attached to anything common or of this world. His heart was uniquely for God and one with Him alone. Nevertheless, He desired to be with those broken reprobates to heal and to save them (Matt. 9:12).

Additionally, she realized that the vineyards belong to the Lord, and He expects to receive profit from those tending them. This is similar to John 15, where the Lord demanded fruit from all His branches. Believers, as part of the Lord's vine, are the Father's vineyard. Each branch is to bear fruit or be subjected to judgment. They are obligated and accountable, rendering regular payment to the Lord. This shows that while believers await glorification and the coming kingdom, they are busy caring for the immature and sinners. This is to bear fruit as a payment to God.

In the eyes of the Lord, the Shulamite with such functions is a person who brings out peace — a peacemaker. According to Paul, immature believers are divisive (1 Cor. 3:1-4). They struggle with jealousy against each other concerning Bible teachings, spiritual practices, and personalities among various teachers. She does not contend with the immature; instead, she cherishes and nourishes them until they grow into unity with all believers in maturity (Eph. 4:13). In this way, she fosters peace among the saints.

Peace becomes a central theme starting in Chapter Five, as it is the primary characteristic essential for building up the Lord's Body. His Body is the joining together of His diverse people who were, in many cases, antagonists toward each other with contrary perspectives. Therefore, peacemakers are needed. The meaning of peace is not just the absence of conflicts, but that everyone would be comfortable and secure while enjoying a bountiful supply.

Although the Shulamite is actively serving toward the Lord's satisfaction, she is resting and enjoying in a garden. She is not exhausted and sweaty from laboring for the Lord's purpose. She is in a lush garden with companions. Hebrews says: *"For whoever has entered God's rest has also rested from his works as God did from his. Let us therefore strive to enter that rest"* (Heb. 4:10-11). She has entered and is enjoying God's rest. God rested after Jesus' crucifixion, resurrection, and ascension. His work is completed, and He rested. The Shulamite is serving and laboring in a state of rest. It is not just a Sabbath day rest once a week; she entered eternal rest 24/7. This is the way to labor in the New Testament — while resting in Christ's completed work. If a believer is complaining and discouraged with their ministry, they are not in the garden.

The Shulamite is enjoying the garden with companions. At the end of chapter 4, she is perfect yet alone in her house. Now, she is not alone but has others serving and enjoying with her. In a survey of American pastors, 65% feel loneliness and isolation.[11] That is an unhealthy state of ministry. It is no wonder that, according to the same survey, 38% of the pastors want to quit. This is a symptom of laboring outside the garden, without rest, enjoyment, and the support of companions. The Shulamite can serve and labor continually her entire life, awaiting glorification because she has entered His rest with other like-minded seekers.

The last verse of this Song is a cry for the Lord to come. She is ready to receive and be joined to Him in glory. This is similar to the end of Revelation, where there

---

11   7-Year Trends: Pastors Feel More Loneliness & Less Support - Barna Group

was a similar cry: *Come, Lord Jesus* (Rev. 22:20)! She has completed her transformative journey and is now prepared as a member of the Lord's Bride. Many Christians may view the Lord's second coming as a way to escape their problems in this troubled world. However, at the Lord's second advent, there is also the judgment seat of Christ for His believers (2 Cor. 5:10). Would you rather meet a judge or your bridegroom? It is doubtful whether anyone will call his judge to come quickly, but a bride will yearn for the groom — *quickly come*. Those desirous to meet the Bridegroom should consider pursuing the Lord in the pattern of the Shulamite. Her journey provides a good road map for preparation to become a member of His Bride.

The Lord's Bride is the corporate New Jerusalem composed of all His people. He is not marrying many individuals. However, it takes mature individuals to prepare the Bride for marriage. In the letters to the seven Ekklesias ("churches") in Revelation 2-3, to each Ekklesia, there is a call for individuals to overcome: *"He who has an ear, let him hear what the Spirit says to the churches [ekklesias]. To him who overcomes . . . ."* It does not matter whether that particular "church" is good or bad; the call went out to every believer to arise and overcome. In other words, one cannot be passive and be satisfied with his/her condition, even if they are a member of the best "church" or Ekklesia. Each is to overcome individually and pursue the Lord. Therefore, the Song of Songs is best understood as an allegory of the believer's journey of growth, transformation, and maturity — learning to partner with the Lord for His eternal purpose while still on earth.

5

THE MYSTERY OF GODLINESS—GOD MANIFESTED IN THE FLESH

But if I am delayed, [I write] so that you may know how you ought to conduct yourself in the house of God, which is the church [ekklesia] of the living God, the pillar and ground of the truth. 16 And without controversy great is the mystery of godliness: God was manifested in the flesh, Justified in the Spirit, Seen by angels, Preached among the Gentiles, Believed on in the world, Received up in [Gk. into] glory.

—1 Tim. 3:15-16

Paul Defined the Great Mystery of Godliness

Paul emphasizes the significance of the Household of God, which is the Ekklesia (Democratic Assembly) of the living God. How to conduct oneself in God's Household is a serious matter, and godliness is tightly intertwined with the conduct needed in His democratic assembly, the pillar and base of the truth. "Godliness" to most people relates to proper and holy behavior. Endeavoring to improve behavior and conduct in God's Household can be easily taught and accepted. However, Paul declares that godliness is a great mystery. It is not as apparent as most people would assume. A great mystery requires enlightenment and revelation to be seen and understood. The mystery of godliness is more awesome than what either the moral, philosophical, or religious minds can conjure up. Without the working of this mysterious godliness, no amount of behavioral improvement can be acceptable in God's Household.

Paul clearly defined the mystery of godliness, presenting it not as a single moment or focused on just one aspect of Christ's life, but as a series of profound, interconnected events. This mystery encompasses multiple phases, revealing the divine plan through the person and work of Jesus Christ.

Most Christians promptly agree with the statement: *"God was manifested in the flesh"* — a reference to the incarnation, when God became man (John 1:14). Every follower of Christ must believe that God took on human form, born of a woman, with a genealogy that traces back to Adam (Luke 3:38) or in Matthew 1:1-17, the genealogical record of Jesus from Abraham to Mary. The spirit of the antichrist denies that God has come in the flesh (2 John 1:7). Yet at the heart of the Christian faith lies this foundational truth: Jesus Christ is both fully God and fully man — **God manifested in the flesh**.

Paul did not stop with this first declaration of godliness. He continued, describing the next phase: *"justified in the Spirit."* This refers to Christ's death and resurrection. Jesus did not merely become human; He also suffered through crucifixion, died, and was raised to life by the power of the Spirit (Rom. 8:11). His resurrection is the ultimate testimony that God justified Him — declaring the Son's sacrifice as wholly righteous — acceptable to satisfy the wrath of God upon sin. Had Jesus been unrighteous, like other men, He would have remained in the grave. His resurrection proves that though He took on the sins of the whole world, God accepted His death as a sacrifice for sins (Heb. 9:26). Jesus was justified and His believers were also justified by His resurrection (Rom. 4:25). His household, family members, are all justified together with Him — **justified in Spirit**.

The third phase of the mystery of godliness is that Christ was *"seen by angels."* This phase describes His ascension to heaven when two angels appeared as witnesses (Acts 1:9-11). Upon ascending, He was exalted to the throne and was made Lord and Christ (Acts 2:36). What is even more stunning is that at the Lord's death, resurrection, and ascension He *"disarmed principalities and powers, He made a public spectacle of them, triumphing over them in it"* (Col. 2:15). The "principalities and powers" refers to rebellious angelic beings who followed Satan. They were disarmed — defeated — by the ascended Christ. Though this victory was not visible in the physical world, Christ's triumph must have been a spectacular victory. Satan and his treacherous angelic host were publicly humiliated in the unseen realm — a victory **seen by angels**.

The fourth phase of the mystery of godliness is *"preached among the Gentiles."* After the Lord's ascension, He poured out His Spirit like a rushing mighty wind (Acts 2:4, 33). The 120 emerged from the upper room proclaiming the gospel of Jesus Christ (Acts 2:4, 33). They brought salvation to the Jews on the day of Pentecost. Soon after, in Acts 10, the gospel reached the Gentiles at Cornelius's house. They believed in the Lord Jesus, and the entire household received the Spirit.

In Acts 11, as persecution scattered believers, some went to Antioch and preached the gospel to the Greeks. Later, in Acts 13:2, the Holy Spirit commissioned Paul and

Barnabas to preach the gospel to the Gentiles (i.e., "the nations" or "ethnos"). Since then, the gospel of Jesus Christ has reached Gentiles in every continent and just about every nation on earth — **preached among the Gentiles**.

The fifth phase is "*believed on in the world.*" For nearly 2000 years, the gospel has endured, reaching "*every tribe and tongue and people and nation.*" God's desire, as stated in 1 Timothy 2:4, is for all people — not just the Jews — to be saved. Salvation extends to both the Jew and the Gentile, who are now united as one Household under God — **believed on in the world**.

It is essential to remember that 1 Timothy 3 speaks of the Lord's House — His Ekklesia, or democratic assembly. Jesus died not only to save individuals but to reconcile former enemies into one unified family. This is the heart of the gospel message — "the gospel of peace" (Eph. 2:17), through which God establishes His dwelling place among His people. Ephesians 2: Jesus died to break down the wall of hatred between divided people, making them one temple — a dwelling for God by the Spirit (Eph. 2:21-22). Thus, the ultimate goal of the gospel is not simply to get individuals to heaven, but to build a diverse, yet united people, among whom God dwells — His Household, His Temple, His Ekklesia.

The final phase is "*received up in glory.*" This is the destiny of all who follow Him — glory. The consummate expression of the Lord's Ekklesia is the New Jerusalem, described as the Bride of the Lamb, to which all believers have come (Heb. 12:22). The New Jerusalem descends from heaven to earth, radiant with the glory of God (Rev. 21:10-11). It is the eternal dwelling of God among a people made one in Christ — **received up into glory**.

Each Believer Is Responsible to Act, Overcome

Being received into glory is intrinsically tied to rising up and building God's temple — His dwelling place on earth today. Believers cannot passively wait to be received into glory; rather, they are called to overcome the divisions that are tearing down God's Temple.

In Revelation 3:7-13, the Spirit speaks to the Ekklesia ("church") in Philadelphia. Out of the seven Ekklesias mentioned in Revelation 2-3, only the Ekklesia in Philadelphia received praise from the Lord. But why were they appreciated? The text offers no explicit explanation except for the meaning of their name. The word "Philadelphia" means "brotherly love" (BLB). The one Democratic Assembly in that city must have had an assortment of people consisting of Jews, Gentiles, the rich, the poor, and believers from many different backgrounds. Yet, despite their differences, they loved one another and were not divided. They kept the Lord's new commandment: "*Love one another as I have loved you*" (John 13:34).

The Lord didn't praise them for their strength. In fact, He said that they had *"little strength"* (Rev. 3:8). Yet, with their limited strength, they kept the Lord's Word and did not deny His name (Rev. 3:8). These two elements were in the Lord's prayer in John 17, in which He asked the Father for His people to be one in unity. The Lord's word is truth (John 17:17). The believers in Philadelphia did not use the Scriptures for argument, debate, and division; instead, they cherished the truth — Jesus Himself, who is the Word of God throughout the Scripture.

Unity also requires the Father's name: *"Keep through Your name those whom You have given Me, that they may be one as We are"* (John 17:11). Unlike the Corinthians — who divided over the names of Paul, Apollos, and Cephas — the believers in Philadelphia stayed centered on one name — The Lord's. Their simplicity in keeping His Word and His name enabled them to love one another in unity.

Although the Lord praised them, the Spirit still issued a call to those with an ear to hear to overcome. The call is for anyone to "hold fast what you have" (Rev. 3:11). One cannot afford to be passive, as if they have already arrived. No — until the Bride is made ready, believers must continue running the race. Those who drift risk spiritual decline or backsliding. Therefore, holding fast to love and unity remains an ongoing pursuit.

> He who overcomes, I will make him a pillar in the temple of My God, and he shall go out no more. I will write on him the name of My God and the name of the city of My God, the New Jerusalem, which comes down out of heaven from My God. And [I will write on him] My new name.
>
> – Rev 3:12

It is conclusive that loving one another builds up God's temple, and this building up occurs through each person. When someone faithfully overcomes, they not only become a fitting part of the temple themselves but also influence others to do the same. Such an overcomer becomes an indispensable pillar in God's Temple and bears the name: New Jerusalem. They have matured into peacemakers (since *Jerusalem* means "foundation of peace"). Such people are glorified together with the city of God.

Therefore, those who have received the gospel and matured to participate in the glory of the New Jerusalem are the final phase of God manifested in the flesh.

According to Paul's definition, God manifested in the flesh is not just the singular person of Jesus Christ, but Jesus united with His followers. He is the Head, and they are His Body. Together, they form the Household of God on earth. Although Jesus is physically in heaven, God's Household — His democratic assembly — is God manifested in the flesh on earth. It is awe-inspiring to realize that God is manifested in the flesh of His followers today, those who are building His Household in unity.

This is supported by 2 John 1:7, where John said that the deceivers and antichrists are those who do not acknowledge Jesus Christ as coming in the flesh. The verb "coming" is present tense. If this referred only to Jesus of Nazareth, it would be in the past tense: *"He came in the flesh."* The present tense indicates that Jesus Christ is still coming in the flesh — through His Body, the Household of God.

In Scripture, "flesh" typically refers to fallen, sinful humanity — a term often used negatively. For example:

- *"I am of the flesh, sold under sin" (Rom. 7:14);*
- *"Nothing good dwells . . . in my flesh" (Rom. 8:18);*
- *"Those who are in the flesh cannot please God" (Rom. 8:8).*

This makes it even more significant that God is manifested in the flesh. God took what Satan had utterly corrupted and used it to manifest Himself. This is the magnificent work of God's redemption and transformation: God is manifested in the flesh of a diverse people. This is the mystery of godliness, God's Ekklesia (Democratic Assembly) on earth.

The Calling of Abraham

In the New Testament, God's House or Household is His Ekklesia — His democratic assembly, the body of His people. This is the same "house" in Matthew 21:13, where Jesus said: *"My house shall be called a house of prayer."* At the time, He was referring to the physical temple in Jerusalem. In the Old Testament, the house of God was a physical structure. However, Acts 17:24 affirms that God does not dwell in temples made with hands. Thus, the physical temple symbolized God dwelling with His people. As He said: *"I will dwell among the sons of Israel and will be their God"* (Exod. 29:45; 1 Kings 6:13).

In this chapter, it will be shown that the "sons of Israel" were not a pure race of people. They were diverse and mixed. Furthermore, they were fallen people of the flesh. Nevertheless, the Mosaic covenant transformed these previously enslaved people in Egypt to their zenith at the time of Solomon's temple. A diverse people were united under David and Solomon, culminating in God's glory descending at the dedication of His temple. That temple, filled with God's glory, testified that His diverse people were united and had become His dwelling place.

In other words, the people of Israel were not united because of a shared genetic heritage, nor did God dwell with them because they were more righteous than the surrounding nations. Rather, these mixed and assorted people, fallen in the flesh, became one as God's dwelling place through God's covenant given by Moses.

God's eternal desire is to dwell among His people. He created Adam and Eve for this very purpose. However, they were seduced by Satan and fell into sin. The sin and death nature was injected into the Adamic race, and their human nature was transmuted to a nature more akin to rebellious Satan. Eventually, God saw man (male and female) and said: *"the wickedness of man was great in the earth, and that every intent of the thoughts of his heart was only evil continually"* (Gen. 6:5).

God did not create "flesh." Adam and Eve were living souls with physical bodies. However, by the time of Noah, humanity had become flesh (Gen. 6:3). God repented that He had created man and judged the earth with a flood. Yet, through Noah's ark, He preserved a remnant — Noah and his family of eight souls.

Those eight people started multiplying again, but the sin and death nature remained in their flesh. As they grew and multiplied, their rebellion against God also flourished. Four hundred years later, a mighty warrior against the Lord, named Nimrod, arose and led an uprising against God by building the Tower of Babel, designed to reach heaven and challenge God. In response to this unified rebellion, God called Abram (aka Abraham) out of this land of idolatry. Now the LORD said to Abram, *"Go from your country and your kindred and your father's house to the land that I will show you"* (Gen. 12:1).

When calling Abram to the promised land, God declared, *"For all the land that you see I will give to you and to your offspring [seed] forever"* (Gen. 13:15). This blessing of the promised land was intended for Abram's seed. However, Abram was childless; so, he asked God whether his faithful servant could be his heir. God rejected that idea and said, *"Look toward heaven, and number the stars, if you are able to number them."* Then he said to him, *"So shall your offspring [seed] be. And he believed the LORD, and He counted it to him as righteousness"* (Gen 15:5-6). Though old and childless, Abram believed God's promise that he would have a child, and that faith made him righteous before God.

This is truly remarkable! An unrighteous man of fallen flesh can become righteous in God's eyes simply by believing in God's promised seed. Based on this profound fact, the apostle Paul reasonably argued in Romans 4 that all people — regardless of lineage — are justified by faith in God's promised Seed. Abraham became the father of all people of faith, regardless of whether they have a specific genetic heritage or religion (e.g., circumcision). Abraham not only became the father of the Jewish nation, but he also became the father of many nations (Rom. 4:16-17).

Paul also made it clear that the promised seed was not ultimately Isaac. Isaac was a foreshadowing of someone greater yet to come.

Now to Abraham and his Seed were the promises made. He does not say, "And to seeds," as of many, but as of one, "And to your Seed," who is Christ.

– Gal 3:16

The Seed God promised Abraham was Jesus Christ, who came approximately 2000 years later. Although God did provide a physical child (seed) to Abraham, in God's eyes, Jesus Christ is the true Seed of Abraham. This one Seed was not just Jesus but included all His diverse believers. Nevertheless, Isaac was necessary so that Jesus Christ could be conceived in the flesh as a descendant of Abraham's lineage.

> There is neither Jew nor Greek, there is neither slave nor free, there is neither male nor female; for you are all one in Christ Jesus. 29 And if you [are] Christ's, then you are Abraham's seed, and heirs according to the promise.
>
> – Gal 3:28-29

This reveals that from the beginning, when God called Abram, He never abandoned the rest of mankind. His original purpose – that man (both male and female) would bear His image, express Him, and exercise dominion over the earth – remained fully intact. Satan's role in causing humanity to rebel did not derail God's plan. His calling of Abraham was not God playing favoritism to one person or one race, since His heart is that *all people* would be included through Abraham.

Let's consider the prophecies given not only to Abraham, but also to Isaac, Jacob, and Jacob's grandson Ephraim. They conclusively show God's heart being for all mankind, regardless of their differences. He worked through the patriarchs for the sake of all nations.

God's promise to Abraham:

> "Behold, my covenant is with you, and you shall be the father of a multitude of nations (*Heb. Melo Ha-Goyim*)–(Note: "multitude of nations" literally means: "Fullness of the Gentiles" or "Fullness of the Nations")
>
> – Genesis 17:4

God's promise to Isaac:

> "I will make your offspring as numerous as the stars of the sky, I will give your offspring all these lands, and all the nations of the earth will be blessed by your offspring,"
>
> – Genesis 26:4, CSB

God's promise to Israel (Jacob) when He changed his name:

> "And God said to him, 'I am God Almighty; be fruitful and increase in number. A nation and a community of nations [literally "fullness of the nations"] will come from you, and kings will be among your descendants."
>
> – Genesis 35:11

Jacob's Prophecy over Ephraim:

> Jacob (Israel) purposely crossed his hands, putting his right hand upon Ephraim as he prophesied: "He [Manasseh] too will become great. Nevertheless, his younger brother [Ephraim] will be greater than he, and his descendants will become *a group of nations* (NIV—but most translations render this as **"a multitude of nations"**) . . . So he put Ephraim ahead of Manasseh."
>
> – Genesis 48:19-20

These prophecies demonstrate that God's desire for all humanity is to be part of His original plan, which never changed. Despite Adam's fall and the corruption of mankind by the time of Noah, God's plan remained: all of mankind would express Him and overcome His enemy.

Nevertheless, God promised Abraham a Seed, and through this Seed, all the nations would be blessed. To bring forth this Seed, God needed a people directly descended from Abraham. Therefore, He called Abraham's descendants out of slavery in Egypt to make them a nation. To preserve them and maintain a clear genetic line to the coming of the Seed, God gave the Mosaic Covenant, also known as the Old Covenant (2 Cor. 3:14) or the First Covenant (Heb. 8:7). Through this First Covenant, God prepared the way to bring all of mankind to the Seed, Jesus Christ.

> Therefore the law was our tutor [to bring us] to Christ, that we might be justified by faith.
>
> – Gal. 3:24

Calling the People from Egypt and into the Promised Land

In God's plan, the Promised Seed, through whom people from all the nations would be brought to faith, would not come until 2000 years after Abraham. To bring forth this

Promised Seed, God needed to preserve a people descended from Abraham. Abraham begat Isaac, Isaac begat Jacob, and Jacob's twelve sons eventually settled in Egypt after Joseph became Egypt's prime minister.

At the beginning of their settlement in Egypt, the Israelites were treated well due to Joseph's favor with Pharaoh. However, after Joseph passed, a new Pharaoh, who did not know Joseph, arose in Egypt, who enslaved the Israelites (Exod. 1:8-11). They remained enslaved in Egypt for 200 years, amassing a population of two to three million. They lost much of their cultural heritage, especially their knowledge of God. Circumcision alone did not separate them from the nations since the Egyptians also had such practices during that time.[12] Nevertheless, tribal identities must have remained strong enough for the Egyptians to recognize and enslave them as a distinct people.

God heard the cries of the Israelites in their suffering and did not forget His covenant with Abraham, Isaac, and Jacob. He used Moses to deliver Israel from Egypt, so instead of serving Pharaoh, they would serve and worship Yahweh (Exo. 8:1). He had to start from scratch with Israel, so to speak, because after more than 200 years, and at least 2 million people later, they did not know God. So, God had to start by introducing His name: Yahweh — I AM (Exo. 3:14). With Abraham, God called one person, but with Moses, He called more than 2 million people.

These people were not better, holier, or more righteous than other nations. After more than two centuries in Egypt, they had adopted Egyptian ways, both in character and desires. In the beginning and even near the end of their 40-year journey through the wilderness, the Israelites longed to return to Egypt (Exo. 16:3; Num. 14:2-4). Yet out of these people — much like the surrounding nations — God would make His dwelling. The ultimate manifestation of God dwelling among them occurred about 500 years later when the Solomonic Temple was built. What a transformation! If God can do it with them, He can do it with all people on the earth, just as He originally intended. Israel became a precursor, a living example of what God will accomplish for all humanity.

The instrument of Israel's transformation was the Law, given through Moses. The Mosaic Covenant took a sinful, diverse, and scattered people of the flesh and made them a dwelling place of God. United, they conquered their enemies and manifested God's glory. They temporarily fulfilled what God intended at creation: Expressing God's image and subduing His enemies. This was made possible because the Mosaic Covenant united them around the prefigures of Jesus Christ. Likewise, His people, seen in these prophetic Scriptures, revealed the congregation, the Ekklesia that He always intended.

---

12 Circumcision in the Ancient World - EARLY CHURCH HISTORY

There were four main features of the Mosaic Covenant:

1. **The Ten Commandments** — Representing God's character and nature
2. **The Ark of the Covenant and the Tabernacle** — Foreshadowing the Incarnate Christ
3. **The offerings** — Pointing to the redeeming and nourishing Christ
4. **One Place of Worship, Zion** — Symbolizing unity in Christ

Through the commandments and these four elements, He accomplished His purpose: to manifest Himself in human flesh. These four components will be explored in detail later in this chapter.

A Diverse and Mixed People

Even though the 12 tribes of Israel descended from their patriarchs: Abraham, Isaac, and Jacob — it is easy to assume that Israel, in which God's glory was manifested during the time of David and Solomon, was a single race from one genetic origin. According to Biblical records, Abraham, Sarah, Isaac, and Rebecca belonged to the same ethnic group. However, Jacob's twelve sons were born from four different women. While Leah and Rachel (not Rebecca, who was Isaac's wife) came from the same family line, the other two, Bilhah and Zilpah, were handmaids or slaves. In those times, slaves were typically taken from conquered people. Therefore, it is likely that Bilhah and Zilpah were of different ethnic origins.

Joseph, one of the twelve sons, married an Egyptian woman and had two sons: Manasseh and Ephraim. Later, during Israel's time in the wilderness, when the tribe of Levi was chosen to be priests, the tribes of Manasseh and Ephraim were counted among the 12 tribes of Israel. These two tribes, therefore, contained genetic material from Egyptian ancestry.

Additionally, when Israel escaped Egypt, the Bible states that a *"mixed multitude also went up with them"* (Exo. 12:38). This mixed multitude could have been Egyptians, other slaves, and people of various ethnic backgrounds. In any case, they were not native Israelites.

In His mercy, God made a provision for all foreigners to participate in His Mosaic covenant.

> Also the sons of the foreigner Who join themselves to the LORD, to serve Him, And to love the name of the LORD, to be His servants — Everyone who keeps from defiling the Sabbath, And holds fast My covenant — 7 Even them I will bring to My holy mountain, And make them joyful in My house of prayer. Their burnt offerings and their sacrifices [Will be] accepted on My altar; For My house shall be called a house of prayer for all nations.
>
> — Isaiah 56:6-7

This passage demonstrates that God's choice for fulfilling His purpose was not limited to a single ethnic group. His purpose was being fulfilled through the Mosaic Covenant, which was open to all people. God is not a respecter of persons (Acts 10:34). His goal was to manifest His purpose through diverse people in the flesh, and the Mosaic Covenant made that possible.

This is significant: all should be mindful that God has opened a wide door for all foreigners (Gentiles, Heb. *goyim*) to be included in His Household — His Kingdom. On one hand, Israel was God's chosen people (Deut. 7:6); on the other hand, God welcomed anyone with a heart to join themselves to Him as part of Israel, whether or not their lineage could be traced to native Israelites of the 12 tribes.

Let's consider a few prominent people who were included in "Israel." They came from people groups not only foreigners to the 12 tribes but, in some cases, from lineage historically condemned by God. These examples show that Israel was not particularly righteous compared to the rest of fallen humankind. Rather, the way Israel manifested God was due entirely to God's covenant. Israel had no grounds for boasting, for all the glory belongs to God. It was God's Mosaic Covenant that made them — and all foreigners — special.

Moses and Zipporah

Moses, the undisputed leader of Israel and a member of the tribe of Levi, married Zipporah, the daughter of a Midianite priest (Exo. 2:21). They had two sons: Gershom and Eliezer. Both sons played prominent roles in Levitical service related to the Tabernacle and Temple. Shebuel, a descendant of Gershom, served as a chief officer in King David's administration. Rehabiah, a descendant of Eliezer, was a leader among the Levites during David's reign (1 Chron. 23:16-17). Thus, within the priestly tribe of Levi, genetics from among the nations were included.

Joshua and Caleb

While Moses led Israel into the wilderness, Joshua and Caleb led them into the Promised Land. These two men were the only adults from the Exodus generation allowed to enter the land of promise, due to their resolute faith in God's word. Both are the most prominent figures in the journey into the good land. They were the only two men over 20 years of age who did not die in the wilderness. After coming out of Egypt, Moses sent 12 men into the Promised Land to spy it out. Two of the twelve, Joshua (from the tribe of Ephraim) and Caleb (from the tribe of Judah), gave an encouraging report telling Israel that they could be victorious over their enemies and possess the Land (Num. 13:26-33). However, the other 10 spies gave a discouraging report, leading to

Israel's unbelief and God's judgment: the nation would wander in the wilderness for 40 years until everyone over 20 years, except for Joshua and Caleb, died.

Joshua's name is especially significant, as it is the Hebrew equivalent of "Jesus" in the New Testament. Even more notable is that this son of Joseph was born of an Egyptian woman. That means his genetic roots are as much from Egypt as from Israel. Yet, he was the chief leader of Israel going into the Good Land.

Caleb was even more ethnically blended. He was the son of Jephunneh the Kenizzite (Numbers 32:12), not one of the twelve tribes. There are two possible origins for the Kenizzites: They were most likely inhabitants of Canaan (Genesis 15:19), or descendants of Kenaz, a grandson of Esau (Genesis 36:11). If Caleb's ancestry traces to a Canaanite tribe, then God called Israel to drive them out. If his ancestry is from Esau, then he was an Edomite — historically an enemy of Israel. Either way, Caleb's background was not originally Israelite. Caleb was likely absorbed into the tribe of Judah through his mother, and from thence he rose to become a leader within the tribe of Judah.

Joshua and Caleb were exemplary in their faith, courage, and leadership, but were not of full Israelite descent. They belonged, at least partially, to ethnic groups historically opposed to Israel. Yet they became central figures in God's plan to lead His people into the Promised Land.

Moreover, the solidarity of purpose expressed in these two displays the initial unity between what became the Two Tribes of the South (Judah — seen in Caleb) and the Ten Tribes of the North (Ephraim/Israel/Jezreel/Samaria, seen in Joshua).

Lastly, it is significant that the Ark of the Covenant, containing the Glory of God, entered the Good Land under Joshua's (Ephraim's) jurisdiction (at Shiloh in Ephraim) for approximately 396 years and then under Caleb (Judah's) jurisdiction (in Jerusalem) for another 396 years (with 27 years with King David in the City of David at the Tabernacle of David), before its disappearance during the Babylonian Captivity (1405-586 B.C.).[13]

David and Solomon's Ancestry

David and Solomon's lineage holds great significance, since they were ancestors of Jesus Christ. They represent the pinnacle of God's presence and manifestation among Israel in the Hebrew Scriptures, culminating in the building of God's temple. Both were of

---

13   Doug Krieger has done a meticulous series of calculations from Scripture related to this topic in his text, *Signs in the Heavens & On The Earth, Man's Days are Numbered and He is Measured* whereby he discovered that these two sets of numbers (396 + 396 = 792) are fractals of the 12,000 furlongs (660 ft. X 12,000 = 7,920,000 linear feet or 792) of the edges of the New Jerusalem and the "27" as the 27 books of the New Testament, the full revelation of the Messiah (Ref. Rev. 21:16). Thus, the Messiah's plan has always been to unify God's people to express His glory—through the centrality of Christ, their Messiah.

the tribe of Judah, the royal line, from which Jesus, the King of kings, would eventually descend. Their family history is rich in meaning and worthy of reflection.

Judah and Tamar

Judah, the patriarch of the tribe of Judah, fathered a child in a scandalous event. His heir was conceived through an encounter with his daughter-in-law, Tamar, who had disguised herself as a prostitute (Gen. 38). From the outset, the lineage of David, Solomon, and ultimately Jesus included people marked by fleshly weakness and scandal.

Tamar, a Canaanite woman, was first married to Judah's eldest son. According to local custom, Judah's second son was to produce an heir for his deceased brother, but he also died. He passed away before having a son. Judah should have given Tamar to his youngest son, but he failed to do so. Therefore, Tamar disguised herself as a harlot to entice Judah. She was successful, and he went into her, and she conceived. When Judah discovered that Tamar had become a prostitute and conceived, his immediate reaction was to burn her to death. After she showed proof that the conception came from him, he admitted his wrongdoing and that she was more righteous. Her firstborn son, Perez, became part of the ancestral line of David, Solomon, and Jesus.

Rahab the Harlot in Jericho

Jericho was the first city Israel was to conquer in the Promised Land. Joshua sent spies into Jericho to observe the city. They found Rahab, a harlot in the city, to shelter them (Joshua 2). When the king of Jericho heard of spies in his city, soldiers went to Rahab's house to search for them. Since she recognized that God was with Israel, she protected the spies in exchange for her family being spared when Jericho fell to Israel.

Rahab, a sinful woman from a condemned people, eventually became the wife of Salmon. They bore Boaz, the great-grandfather of King David. Once again, the line of David, Solomon, and Jesus includes a foreigner redeemed by faith, testifying to the inclusiveness of God's infinite grace and mercy (Hebrews 11:31).

Boaz and Ruth

Ruth's story is one of love, loyalty, and redemption — so much so that an entire book of the Bible bears her name. A Moabite woman, Ruth, married into a family from Bethlehem in Judah. Moabites were cursed by God and excluded from God's assembly (Deut. 23:3-6), and they remained enemies of Israel for generations. Yet Ruth chose to leave her Moabite people and cling to Naomi, her Israelite mother-in-law, who was also a widow. Naomi wanted to return Ruth to her Moabite people since Naomi was leaving Moab's land to return to Bethlehem. Ruth famously declared to Naomi:

> For where you go I will go, and where you lodge I will lodge. Your people shall be my people, and your God my God.
>
> – Ruth 1:16

Naomi and Ruth returned to the land of Judah as impoverished widows. Elimelech, Naomi's deceased husband, possessed land in Bethlehem, but with no male heir, his family line was at risk of ending. Naomi needed a kinsman-redeemer to purchase the land and provide for her and Ruth. Without a male heir, selling the land would end Elimelech's family line. Boaz, a wealthy relative of Elimelech, took notice of Ruth due to her loyalty to Naomi and showed kindness towards her. Following the custom of levirate marriage, Boaz agreed to purchase Elimelech's land and marry Ruth to maintain Elimelech's family line. The union of Boaz and Ruth produced a son, Obed, who became the father of Jesse, and Jesse was the father of King David. Boaz's actions led to two significant outcomes:

1. He preserved Elimelech's family line.
2. His lineage ultimately led to King David, and through him, to Jesus, the Messiah.

In this way, Boaz serves as a type of Christ, and Elimelech, Naomi, and Ruth represent fallen humanity – poor, needy, and on the brink of extinction. Boaz, a "kinsman-redeemer," parallels Christ, who, as a near relative, joined humanity in the flesh. His marriage to Ruth symbolizes Christ's incarnation, joining Himself to humanity. Through His incarnation and redemptive death, he ensured humanity's restoration and future. In Christ's resurrection, the divine lineage – culminating in David, Solomon, and Jesus – was fulfilled. God's enemies were defeated, and His house was established among men.

David and Bathsheba

The story of David and Bathsheba, leading to the birth of Solomon, stands as one of the darkest accounts in the Old Testament (2 Samuel 11-12). It illustrates the depths of human sin: David broke all the moral commandments – he coveted, committed adultery, lied, and arranged the murder of Bathsheba's husband, Uriah. One day, David was relaxing at his house while his army was at war. He saw a beautiful woman bathing, and he **coveted** her. She was the wife of one of David's loyal "thirty mighty men", Uriah the Hittite. David **stole** her anyway and slept with her. She conceived a child due to David's **adultery**. To cover up the conception of this child, David called Uriah back from the war and encouraged him to sleep with his wife. Uriah, loyal, disciplined, and an ultimate selfless "team player," would not sleep with his wife. He declared to David: *"The ark and Israel and Judah are staying in tents, and my commander Joab and my lord's men are camped in the open country. How could I go to my house to eat and drink and make love to my wife? As surely as you live, I will not do such a thing!"* (2 Sam. 11:11). David even got him drunk, and he still would not go home to his wife but rather slept with the servants.

David then came up with a despicable plan to murder Uriah most treacherously. He told his general, Joab, to send Uriah to the front line, and when the fighting was at its fiercest, Joab withdrew the army at King David's injunction, allowing Uriah to fight and die alone. Thus, King David **murdered** a loyal and brave soldier. When word came to David that Uriah died, he spoke a deceptive word, saying: In war, people die, so do not be discouraged and move on. He knew the truth but spoke **false words** cloaked in a true saying (2 Sam. 11:25). David then took Bathsheba for his wife.

God judged David's actions harshly. The child from that initial union died. However, due to David's repentance, God showed mercy to him, and he had a second son with Bethsheba, Solomon. Solomon became the builder of God's temple. Ironically, from this moral collapse came one of the greatest manifestations of God's glory. This is the most remarkable display of God's mercy, forgiveness, and grace. Out of this momentous failure came the utmost in "**God manifested in the flesh.**" Certainly, it was not Israel's righteous acts or their holy nature, but the keeping and working of the Mosaic covenant that brought forth the temple displaying God's glory.

Conclusion about King David

Therefore, it is surprising that King David, Israel's foremost monarch, is not a pure Israelite. From what is known of his ancestry based on Rahab and Ruth, his great-grandfather, Obed, was overwhelmingly 75% Gentile by blood. Including Tamar, a Canaanite, David's heritage was less than 78% Israelite. This does not account for potential foreign marriages in the seven generations from Judah and Tamar to Ruth and Boaz. The point is striking: King David, the symbol of Israel's golden age, was over 21% of "Gentile" origin, descended from peoples once cursed or condemned. Yet, he was chosen by God to be the foundation of Israel's monarchy and a forefather of the Messiah.

The greatest warrior-king of Israel was deeply flawed and substantially foreign. Yet through him, God manifested His presence in Israel like never before. The building of God's house, the establishment of divine kingship, and the fulfillment of covenant promises all flowed through this mixed, fallen, yet divinely chosen lineage. It is a stunning display of the power of the Mosaic Covenant and the grace of God — that He would use the weak, one of sinful flesh, and the outsider to bring forth His glory.

Other Significant Gentiles Used by God

King David had a group of mighty and loyal warriors who remained with him from the time he escaped Saul's wrath until he became king of Israel. This is a group of misfits.

> David left Gath and escaped to the cave of Adullam. When his brothers and his father's household heard about it, they went down to him there. All those who were in distress or in debt or discontented gathered around him, and he became their commander. About four hundred men were with him.
>
> – 1 Sam. 22:1-2, NIV

They were not regarded as upright or "holy" individuals. They were the kind of people typically found on the outskirts of society. At the time, David was considered an outlaw, pursued by King Saul for Capital Punishment. Those gathered around him may have considered David one of them, also fleeing Saul's authority. They, in essence, would exemplify men of flesh. Among them were Gentiles – foreigners – who supported David during his time of distress. Though the exact number is not recorded, four notable and faithful foreign warriors are chronicled in Scripture.

Uriah the Hittite

Uriah is another example of one who escaped judgment by joining himself to the Mosaic law and was ultimately used by God to make King David's lineage, through Solomon, align with the Messiah. Uriah was Bathsheba's husband – the same man who refused to sleep in his own house while his fellow soldiers were at war, out of his loyalty to David's army. The Hittites were Canaanites who occupied the Promised Land when Joshua led Israel into it (Joshua 11:3). God told Israel to destroy all its inhabitants because of their idolatry, which included child sacrifices by fire (Deut. 12:31). Additionally, giants known as Nephilim – offspring of angels ("sons of God") and human women – were there. These beings contributed to the wickedness that led to the judgment and destruction of humanity during Noah's time (Gen. 6:2-7).

Despite this background, Uriah – a Hittite – became one of David's most trusted warriors, and was listed among his "Thirty Mighty Men" (2 Sam. 23:39). Repeatedly, the Bible shows how God pronounces judgment on sin, yet always provides a path to redemption. This principle began with Adam and Eve, although God said they would surely die if they ate of the forbidden tree. Nevertheless, after they ate, God provided a way of redemption for them and said their life would continue with an offspring.

Ittai the Gittite

He is from Gath, a Philistine city. The Philistines were notorious enemies of Israel for prolonged periods. Gath is the Philistine city from where the infamous giant, Goliath, hailed (1 Sam. 17:4). So, in a way, Ittai has two strikes against him: He is a Philistine, and he is from Gath. When David was fleeing from Absalom, his son, who was trying to kill him, he took his people and fled Jerusalem. David was surprised that Ittai wanted to take his family and fellow Gittites to follow David (2 Sam. 15:18-22). Ittai was like Ruth in her declaration to follow Naomi: Ittai said, *"As the LORD lives, and as my lord the king lives, surely in whatever place my lord the king shall be, whether in death or life, even there also your servant will be."* This is a good picture of how believers who were previously enemies of God can be received to follow King Jesus due to His redemptive work (Rom. 5:10).

Zelek the Ammonite

Ammonites are descendants of Lot's younger daughter through incest with Father Lot. The older daughter, through incest with Lot, gave birth to the Moabites. Moabites and the Ammonites were specifically excluded from the Lord's assembly unto the 10th generation. Not only were they descended from incest, these Ammonites became fierce enemies to Israel. The specific reason for their exclusion was that they would not provide food and water when Israel was in the wilderness after leaving Egypt. They also hired the prophet Balaam to curse Israel (Deut. 23:3-6). While Ruth was a Moabite, Zelek is an Ammonite named as one of David's mighty men of valor.

These and many other foreigners were part of the misfits that supported David when he was an outlaw hunted down by Saul. These men valiantly fought for David against all his enemies, both before and after he was crowned king over all Israel's 12 Tribes. They were specifically mentioned, and many exploits of valor and heroism were described. Significantly, foreigners were enormously involved in David's successful journey from outlaw to king over all Israel.

King Hiram of Tyre

Solomon's temple, God's house, is the apex of mankind's journey with God, which started from Adam and Eve. Abraham's descendants through Isaac and Jacob and the 12 tribes ultimately arrive at God's glory, which filled the House of the Lord. This is the manifestation of His dwelling among the people who were united under the Mosaic Covenant.

We find that in 1 Kings 5, a description of how Solomon engaged the king of Tyre to accomplish several significant contributions relative to God's temple.

1. King Hiram contributed a large quantity of cedar and cypress wood from Lebanon.
2. King Hiram transported a large quantity of these woods by sea.
3. King Hiram provided one highly skilled craftsman and many other skilled workmen who directly built the temple.
4. Significantly, the building of the temple relied on Gentiles or foreigners.
5. The material that King Hiram of Tyre provided was used as the main frame and roofing of the temple structure, along with the paneling and the flooring. The cedar and cypress wood were the key materials for framing the temple. The importance of the material supplied by a Gentile king is remarkable.
6. The chief builder provided by the King was Hiram-Abi (aka Hiram Abiff), whose father was from Tyre and whose mother was from the tribe of Dan. He was an experienced craftsman in various materials, such as gold, silver, bronze, iron, stone, wood, yarn of purple, blue, crimson, and fine linen. He supervised all the intricate work in the temple. He completed all the intricate designs given to him (2 Chron. 2:13-14). There were many other craftsmen King Hiram provided to King Solomon who worked side-by-side with Israelite workers (1 Kings 5:6). So, the temple was crafted and supervised by a person who was considered a Gentile.

God considered Tyre as part of Canaan, which Israel was to conquer (Josh. 19:24-30), meaning they were enemies of Israel. Furthermore, this is the same Tyre that during Ezekiel's time, God condemned. This is the city that produced the Prince of Tyre, who was filled with pride. He considered himself a god with beauty and wisdom, making himself rich and powerful. In the same chapter of Ezekiel 28, using the Prince of Tyre as a springboard, God starts in verse 11 to prophesy against the King of Tyre, whose identity is directly associated with God's rebellious angel, Lucifer (Eze 28:14-16).

Therefore, how amazing it is that God used people from the enemy's territory, inspired and ruled by Satan (no less), to contribute material and labor for the building of God's temple. Scores of souls who once were "hell's angels" have been delivered from the Kingdom of Darkness into the Kingdom of His Dear Son (Col. 1:13). God can use anyone for His purpose – anyone with a heart to serve Him is welcomed and accepted. This shows again that God is not a respecter of any one race or nationality. He delights to take the worst of the worst from among the nations to build His Temple in that "to whom much is forgiven, loves much" (Luke 7:47).

The Mosaic Covenant: Fulfilling God's Purpose

The mystery of godliness is fully unveiled in the Hebrew prophetic scriptures as shown above. It is astounding that God manifested Himself in the flesh, with the pinnacle being the building of God's temple. The men of flesh that dwelt among the Israelites were not just of one ethnicity or race, but a diverse people representative of all mankind. How did the righteous and holy God accomplish such an audacious feat, and this among divided peoples who were His enemies? They were not just God's enemies, but enemies among themselves. Yet, God united them together to be His dwelling place on earth.

The Mosaic law accomplished what was impossible. What God did through the Mosaic law was greater than His power of creation. Most readers may be in awe of the various supernatural feats God performed in the Hebrew Scriptures. Notwithstanding, they may not appreciate this wonderful mystery hidden in the prophetic Scriptures. Most Christians have a negative view of the Old (aka First) Covenant—the Mosaic Law. They may consider it God's unreasonable demands with harsh judgments for the lawbreakers. This is why many Christians have a negative view of the God of the Old Testament, assuming that the God of the New Testament is different from the God of the Old.

What God accomplished with the Mosaic Covenant was exactly what He planned to do with the New Covenant of Jesus Christ. The Mosaic Covenant was temporary, showing an archetype of the New Covenant, which is permanent and eternal. Let's review the primary items of the Mosaic Covenant in more detail.

1. The Ten Commandments — God's character and nature (which never changes)
2. The Ark of the Covenant and the Tabernacle — The incarnate Christ
3. The various offerings (sacrifices) — redemption and nourishment
4. The three annual feasts which are celebrated at God's chosen unique place (Zion/Jerusalem) — wherein God's glory is manifested in the unity of His people

The Ten Commandments – God's Testimony

As discussed in an earlier chapter, this was a testimony of God's nature and character. This is the first item to establish: Who God is. The purpose of the Ten Commandments was not primarily a demand for man to behave righteously, but a testimony of who God is. This was spoken by God to Moses on Mount Sinai in Exodus 20.

The Ark of the Covenant and the Tabernacle – Christ's Incarnation

In Exodus chapter 25 through 40, Moses gave initial instructions concerning the building of the Ark of the Covenant, then the Tabernacle, including all the furniture and priestly garments. The Ark is the most important item since it houses the Glory of God (1 Sam. 4:21). God's presence was domiciled in the Ark — He spoke from it (Exo. 25:22). The Ark is where God met with man (the High Priest). It was during this time of the Mosaic Covenant that God and man came together. Within the Ark were three items: The two tablets of God's testimony (the 10 Commandments), a pot of manna, and Aaron's rod that budded. This is an astonishing picture of the Trinity — the "three-one God."

The Ark is the most important article in the Tabernacle or Tent of Testimony. Without the Ark, the Tabernacle is just an empty tent with various utensils and objects. The Tabernacle was made specifically to house the Ark. The tablets were called God's testimony (Exo. 25:16, 21). Their primary function was not to regulate man's behavior; rather, it was His testimony concerning His nature and character. God's glory and the Father's righteous and holy nature are inseparable.

The second item in the Ark was a pot of manna (Exo. 16:33-34). This no doubt referred to the Son since Jesus declared He is the true bread (manna) of life from heaven (John 6:33-35). The manna from heaven in the wilderness sustained Israel physically for 40 years. However, that was not the true bread since they eventually died in the wilderness. Jesus is the real manna from heaven. He is the Bread of Life for ingesting so that whoever eats of Him will have eternal life.

God's desire through the Son was to bring humanity into the eternal fellowship shared between the Father and the Son. Jesus spoke of Himself as the true manna, saying that whoever eats of it will live and never die. In John 6, Jesus declares three times, "I will raise him up at the last day," each revealing a key step in receiving eternal life:

- John 6:40 – *"Everyone who sees the Son and believes in Him may have everlasting life."* → **SEE** the Son.
- John 6:44 – *"No one can come to Me unless the Father who sent Me draws him."* → **DRAWN** by the Father.
- John 6:54 – *"Whoever eats My flesh and drinks My blood has eternal life."* → **EAT and DRINK** of Jesus, becoming one with the Bread sent from Heaven.

These three steps — seeing the Son, being drawn by the Father, and becoming intimately one with the Son — reflect the journey into eternal life, where we are sustained and nourished by Christ Himself.

The third item (Aaron's rod) can represent the Spirit of resurrection (Rom. 8:11). When Israel rebelled against Moses in Numbers 17, God requested that the head of each tribe bring their rod or staff with their names written on it. Aaron's name was written on the rod representing Levi. All 12 rods were then placed inside the Tabernacle. The next day, Moses brought out the 12 rods to display a sign to the whole congregation. Out of these 12 dead cut-down sticks of wood, Aaron's rod *"had sprouted and put forth buds, had produced blossoms and yielded ripe almonds"* (Num. 17:8). This is resurrection life! Life and fruit sprang up from a dead stick, representing the work of the Spirit of Resurrection. It is the Spirit that gives life (John 6:63). This is the resurrection Life Jesus spoke of when He said: "I will raise him up at the last day" (John 6:40, 44, 54).

The Ark with these three items was an archetype of God in His Tri-unity (aka triune nature). The one Ark manifesting God's glory has three items inside representing the Father, Son, and Holy Spirit. The two tablets reveal the Father's nature; the hidden manna reveals the Son's Person and Work; and Aaron's rod, which budded the Spirit's resurrection fruit. The Ark resided in the innermost part of the Tabernacle. The Tabernacle consists of the Outer Court, where the sacrifices were offered. Within the tent is the Holy Place with a lampstand (menorah), a table for bread (shewbread), and an altar of incense. Finally, there is the holiest of all, where the Ark of the Covenant was placed. The Ark was separated from the Holy Place by a thick curtain. As discussed in a previous chapter, the Tabernacle is an archetype of the incarnated Jesus Christ.

> In the beginning was the Word, and the Word was with God, and the Word was God; . . . 14 And the Word became flesh, and did tabernacle among us, and we beheld his glory, glory as of an only begotten of a father, full of grace and truth.
>
> – John 1:1, 14, YLT

> For in Him [Jesus Christ] dwells all the fullness of the Godhead bodily;
>
> – Col. 2:9

Jesus Christ is the Tabernacle of God in the New Testament. He is the true Tabernacle indwelt by God and manifested as the Triune God. It was not just one-third or two-thirds of God who came in the flesh, but the fullness of God dwelt in Him ("All the fullness of the very substance of God dwells in Christ bodily" Col. 2:9). Jesus Christ looked like an ordinary man of flesh from His birth to His crucifixion. He worked. He was tired, hungry, and thirsty like all men born of the flesh. Nevertheless, hidden within Him was and is the fullness of God. Just as the Tabernacle of old was the way to

God within the Holy of Holies, where God resides, Jesus Christ is the way to God (John 14:6). By the end of the book of Exodus, the Ark and the Tabernacle were constructed and erected. *"And the glory of the LORD filled the Tabernacle"* (Exo. 40:34), just as ". . . the glory of the LORD filled the temple" (Solomon's Temple in 2 Chron. 7).

The offerings – Redemption and Nourishment

On the one hand, the law declares God's character and nature; on the other hand, it exposes humanity's deficiencies and sins. Paul wrote: *"Therefore by the deeds of the law no flesh will be justified in His sight, for by the law is the knowledge of sin"* (Rom. 3:20). Humanity falls far short of God's character and glory (Rom. 3:23). Due to sin, humanity needed atonement to be made right with God — to escape God's wrath upon sin. The offerings in the Mosaic Covenant are sacrifices made to God for atonement, restoring the relationship between the offerer and God.

Starting in Leviticus, the Mosaic law continued with the description of all the various offerings. All these offerings point to the many aspects of what Jesus Christ (the perfect sacrifice for sin) accomplished in His crucifixion, resurrection, and ascension.

> And walk in love, as Christ also has loved us and given Himself for us, an offering and a sacrifice to God for a sweet-smelling aroma.
>
> – Eph. 5:2

> The next day John saw Jesus coming toward him, and said, "Behold! The Lamb of God who takes away the sin of the world!
>
> Jn. 1:29

Let's examine these various offerings:

1. The Burnt Offering

The first offering was described in Leviticus 1: the Burnt Offering. This sacrifice involves the entire animal being completely offered up to God on the altar. This sacrifice signifies complete obedience to God and a life wholly lived out for God's purpose and satisfaction. The offerer would place his hand on the head of the bull or goat, showing he is identifying with the sacrifice. The animal took the offerer's place to be 100% for God's satisfaction. This offering speaks of Jesus Christ, whose entire life, existence, and death were for God's purpose and satisfaction. Jesus Christ was 100% obedient and submissive to God — He is and was the perfect sacrifice to appease the wrath of God upon sin's consequences.

2. The Grain or Meal Offering

In Leviticus 2, the grain offering is described. The grain offering consists of fine flour, oil, frankincense, salt, and without leaven. The fine flour speaks of Christ in His pure and unadulterated (fine) humanity. He was 100% genuinely human. Yet, He was mingled or wholly in union with the Holy Spirit (oil). The frankincense given to Jesus at His birth signifies His purity and divinity. His life and living were one with the salt, signifying that He is the One who kills corruption. Though He put on flesh as a man, He was without sin (unleavened). The fine, pure, and genuine humanity of Jesus qualifies Him to be an offering to God on behalf of man. The offerer of Christ as the Grain Offering appreciates and is thankful for His wonderful incarnation and humanity.

3. The Peace Offering

Leviticus 3 describes the Peace Offering. Christ as the Peace Offering made peace between God and man: *"We have peace with God through our Lord Jesus Christ"* (Rom. 5:1). Additionally, Christ made peace between peoples who were enemies: *"He might reconcile both (Jews and Gentiles) to God in one body through the cross by which he put the hostility to death. He came to proclaim the good news of peace"* (Eph. 2:16-17). The peace offering was shared between all the parties: the inner parts and fat were burnt and offered up to God; the breast and thighs were for the priests to eat, and the rest of the meat for the offerer. This shows that there is sharing and fellowship between God and man, as well as between men. When Christ is enjoyed as the Peace Offering, there is fellowship between those who were previously divided (Jew and Gentile), and He is our Peace Offering among brethren with contrary perspectives today.

4. The Sin Offering

The sin offering, described in Leviticus 4, is offered for "unintentional" sins. This speaks of man's sinful nature, which causes man to sin, though he has no intention of doing so. For example, the 10th commandment: You shall not covet. The coveting in man naturally occurs when he sees or considers items desirable, usually held by another person(s). It is unintentional and unavoidable. This is the indwelling sin within man, which Romans 7 speaks of. When Christ was crucified, the sinful "old man" died with Him. Believers are identified with Him as one who is the sin offering. Through enjoying and experiencing Christ, the sinful nature of man in the flesh is dead. Through the Sin Offering, believers are freed from the slavery demanded by sin (Rom. 6:6-7).

5. Guilt or Trespass Offering

This offering, described in Leviticus 5, is for specific trespasses that have caused damage and need restitution. Jesus Christ is the sacrifice that took away the sins of the world (John 1:29). When believers fall into sin and have a guilty conscience, they can confess their sins and be cleansed and forgiven (1 John 1:9). This is possible because Jesus is the Guilt Offering who is now the advocate before God for all believers in Christ (1 John 2:1). How wonderful to have a guilt-free conscience! There is boldness before God because of the blood of Jesus (Heb. 10:19, 22). However, there is still a requirement to make restitution to have peace with those wronged or damaged. This "Trespass Offering" alluded to in 1 John speaks of "walking in the Light" with one another for mutual fellowship. Once a trespass or sin against another person is exposed in the light, it must be confessed. Not only confessed to the Lord but also to the person wronged, and restitution may be needed to amend their loss. Indeed, we "deceive ourselves" if we say we do not have this type of sin with one another. Therefore, when we confess this divisive sin of trespassing against one another, then the blood of Jesus Christ, His Son, keeps on cleansing us from all such divisive and "trespassing" sin.

6. Wave Offering and Heave Offering

When making a Wave Offering, the priest moves the offering back and forth horizontally. When the priest makes a Heave Offering, he uses the vertical up and down motion. Let's consider how the Wave Offering signifies Christ's resurrection, and the Heave Offering signifies His ascension. The offerings do not just foreshadow the death of Christ, but also His resurrection and ascension. Here is how the Wave and Heave Offerings at the time of the Feast of Firstfruits are revealed as an archetype of the resurrection and ascension of Christ (Lev. 23:10-11).

The **Wave Offering** was a sheaf of barley waved before God. Barley is the first crop to ripen in Israel, just before the Passover. The first fruits of the initial harvest symbolize resurrection, as seeds are buried in death, and new life emerges, manifesting in their fruit. Christ's resurrection is the first fruit of all His followers who will be resurrected (1 Cor. 15:20). Significantly, Jesus' resurrection occurred on the same day as the Feast of Firstfruits, celebrated during Passover week (Nisan 16 or 17, with Passover on Nisan 14). Passover commemorates Christ's death, while the Feast of Firstfruits celebrates His resurrection.

The **Heave Offering** was when the priests lifted the offering toward heaven, which symbolizes the ascension of the offering. After Jesus' resurrection, He ascended to the throne and was made Lord of lords with everything under His feet (Eph. 1:20-22). He is now seated at "the right hand of God," signifying that He is God's authority in the universe. There was another celebration of the Feast of Firstfruits during the Feast of Weeks, which is 50 days after the Passover — Pentecost (Lev. 23:17). The Heave Offering was conducted after the Wave Offering during the second Feast of Firstfruits (Num. 18:26-28). Significantly, only the Wave Offering was made at the first Feast of Firstfruits during the Passover. At the second Feast of Firstfruits, on the day of Pentecost, both the Wave and Heave Offerings were made.

The fulfillment of the firstfruits is related to the Spirit. Therefore, Paul says that followers of Christ have "the firstfruits of the Spirit" (Rom. 8:23). When the Lord was resurrected, He became the Life-Giving Spirit to live within His followers. After He ascended, He poured out His Spirit upon His disciples to give them power and authority for the building up of His One Body. When His followers offer Christ as these offerings, they are identified with Him, joined to Him, and are one with Him in His death, resurrection, ascension, and anointing. They can work together with Christ to carry out His mission of building His Democratic Assembly. Christ, as these offerings, can be richly experienced by His followers today.

These two Feasts of Firstfruits, one at Passover and the other at Pentecost, typify two aspects of the Spirit. One aspect is His resurrection for indwelling His believers for life, and the other at the outpouring of the Spirit for clothing His believers with power — the one within and the other upon His people. This corresponds to the two promises of the Spirit and two fulfillments of the Spirit.

In John 7:37-39 and 14:16-17, the Lord Jesus promised that after His glorification (death and resurrection), the Spirit would indwell His disciples. This aspect of the Spirit within them was to be their eternal life, their very Life Source. This was fulfilled when Jesus met with His disciples after His resurrection and *"He breathed on (lit. into) them, and said to them, 'Receive the Holy Spirit'"* (or "Holy Breath" - John 20:22). Breath is for living. The Lord breathed into His disciples the Spirit of Life, thereby indwelling them. How could the 120 in the Upper Room pray for 10 days without the Spirit of Life in them before Pentecost? (Ref. Acts 1 and 2)

Then in Luke 24:49, the Lord promised another aspect: *"And behold, I am sending the promise of my Father upon you. But stay in the city until you are clothed with power from on high."* This clothing was for power to work with the Lord. This was fulfilled on the day of Pentecost. The Spirit came as a violent wind and caused the disciples to speak forth the gospel. In contrast to breath, a strong wind can do much work, such as moving a ship or generating electricity. This clothing of the Spirit gave His followers power and authority to serve and minister to others. When they came before the people gathered in Jerusalem on Pentecost, they were clothed with the Spirit. They started boldly preaching the gospel of Jesus Christ — thousands believed. All believers today, being one with the Lord in His Spirit of power, can continue the Lord's ministry on earth. This is the fulfillment of the Lord saying: All authority is given to Me, go and make disciples (Matt. 28:18).

The Day of Atonement

Once a year is the Day of Atonement, where offerings are made on behalf of all Israel — it is one of the three festival days whereupon all male Israelites were to come to Zion/Jerusalem to celebrate (Passover, Pentecost, and Day of Atonement — Deuteronomy 16:16).

A blanket forgiveness for the sins of all the people under the Mosaic Covenant resulted in a continual peaceful relationship with God. A bull was offered as a whole Burnt Offering to God. In addition to the bull, two goats were chosen — one was sacrificed as a Sin Offering and the other was let loose to run freely. The one that ran freely was called the "scapegoat," which means the "escape goat." The goat that was sacrificed foreshadowed Jesus Christ being crucified for man's sins. The goat that ran freely carried all of man's sins away into the wilderness (outside the gate of Jerusalem, the holy city).

However, another interpretation can be that the goat that was let loose represents God's people who are set free by the death of Christ (Gal. 5:1). Interestingly, over time, the meaning of the word "scapegoat" changed. Now it more likely refers to the person who took the blame or punishment for someone else's action, and not to the person who escaped. This modern definition also fits how Jesus Christ is the "scapegoat" since He knew no sin but took the punishment and died on man's behalf so that man may escape death (2 Cor. 5:21; John 11:50).

How wonderful that Jesus Christ is the fulfillment of the offerings made on the Day of Atonement. Hebrews 10:1 states that the law concerning the atonement sacrifice is: *"A shadow of the good things to come."* Hebrews 10:4 continues: *"For it is not possible that the blood of bulls and goats could take away sins."* Instead of making offerings yearly, which could not take away sins, Jesus came to be the real sacrifice to sanctify His people *"through the offering of the body of Jesus Christ once for all"* (Heb. 10:10).

God Chose a Unique Place to Worship – Unity of His Diverse People

> But you shall seek the place that the LORD your God will choose out of all your tribes to put his name and make his habitation there. There you shall go, 6 and there you shall bring your burnt offerings and your sacrifices, your tithes and the contribution that you present, your vow offerings, your

freewill offerings, and the firstborn of your herd and of your flock. 7 And there you shall eat before the LORD your God, and you shall rejoice, you and your households, in all that you undertake, in which the LORD your God has blessed you. 8 "You shall not do according to all that we are doing here today, everyone doing whatever is right in his own eyes, . . . 17 You may not eat within your towns the tithe of your grain or of your wine or of your oil, or the firstborn of your herd or of your flock, or any of your vow offerings that you vow, or your freewill offerings or the contribution that you present, 18 but you shall eat them before the LORD your God in the place that the LORD your God will choose. . ..

– Deut. 12:5–8, 17–18, ESV

"Three times a year all your males shall appear before the LORD your God in the place which He chooses: at the Feast of Unleavened Bread, at the Feast of Weeks, and at the Feast of Tabernacles; and they shall not appear before the LORD empty-handed.

– Deut. 16:15–16

According to the Mosaic Covenant, there is only one place to make offerings: That is the place where the Ark of the Covenant resides (first in Shiloh, Ephraim, in a "tent" or Jerusalem, Judah, in the Tabernacle of David, or finally Solomon's Temple). The Tabernacle (tent) was movable, but the temple in Jerusalem became permanent. All the offerings were to be presented at the altar of the Lord. It was unlawful to make an offering at any other place. On a few special occasions, God permitted sacrifices at a different place, such as with Gideon or Samuel at Mizpah. Nevertheless, the Mosaic law was clear: there was only one place to sacrifice to God.

This requirement certainly seems overly restrictive. Israel's 12 tribes are spread out in the Promised Land. So, it is inconvenient and arduous to travel long distances to make an offering to worship God. If God had only been interested in worship from His people, He could have allowed them to worship throughout the Promised Land among the 12 tribes. However, **the worship of God comes from the unity of His people**. True worship comes out of His purpose being fulfilled. This purpose is entirely centered on the unity of His people. Only in unity is His glory expressed and His enemy subdued.

Additionally, unity and worship take place before the Ark of the Testimony. The Ark was in movable tents/tabernacles and later permanently resided in the temple built by Solomon. God's glory and testimony were first revealed in the incarnate Jesus. After His death and resurrection, that same glory and testimony came to dwell in His people — His Ekklesia, the participatory democratic assembly. Therefore, to worship before the God who resides on earth, it must be at the one place of His choosing — and that place of unity is the very Ekklesia being built by Christ Himself.

Furthermore, three times a year, all the men (usually with their families) from all 12 tribes were required to appear at the place where God chose to feast for seven days — these are known as the "Festivals or Feasts of the Lord." It was a time of feasting and celebrating God's blessings upon Israel. Everyone was obligated to bring the top portion of what was produced in their inheritance from the land. The northern part of the land may be growing apples, those in the south grew mangos, those on the plains may have grown wheat and raised cattle, and those by the sea may have fish. When all Israel came together to feast, by bringing their top portions, all 12 tribes could feast on the riches of the entire Promised Land. By sharing what was produced with each other, all of Israel feasted on the entire good land — they all shared the bounty of the Promised Land before the Lord. There was equity between the rich and the poor because it was a time of sharing and thanksgiving. Like the gathering of manna, *"those who gather much have none left over and those who gather little had no lack."* These annual feasts (Moedim, the Lord's Appointed Feast Days) were their worship of God — for it was before the Lord in unity they feasted.

Due to this commandment of the unique place for the diverse tribes to worship God, His people with variances would become one and remain in unity wherever the Ark of the Covenant did abide, be it in Ephraim or Judah. . . in a tent or the temple. This was God's way and wisdom. This was an unmistakable requirement in the Mosaic Covenant. Disobeying this commandment to come to the place of God's choosing was condemned by God as *"everyone doing whatever is right in his own eyes."*

Most Christians apply the above phrase as a general disobedience to God's 10 commandments. However, significantly, this phrase was used specifically in relation to neglecting the unity of the 12 tribes in the place where God chooses. When believers offer worship to God but neglect coming together for fellowship in unity with those from other "tribes," that is condemned by God as *"everyone doing whatever is right in his own eyes."*

During Moses and Joshua

During the time of Israel's 40 years in the wilderness, they followed the Mosaic Covenant to make offerings at the Tent of Testimony/The Tabernacle. Likewise, they gathered for their annual feasts. They observed the Passover Feast, but could not fully celebrate the Feasts of Weeks or Tabernacles without harvests — harvests that could only come from the Promised Land. Even though two and a half tribes had an inheritance of land east of the Jordan River, all 12 tribes united as one to cross the Jordan to possess the Promised Land (Jos. 3:17, 4:12-13). After Joshua and Caleb led Israel into the Promised Land, they continued their worship at the one place where the Ark and Tabernacle were — Shiloh in Ephraim's portion. That singular place of worship kept Israel's diverse tribes united; therefore, they defeated their enemies and possessed a major portion of the Promised Land.

By the end of the book of Joshua, it was recorded that each of the 12 tribes received their inheritance of the land. Nine and a half tribes received land west of the Jordan River, and two and a half tribes received land east of the river. The Levites also received their cities and pasturelands, located and scattered among all 12 tribes on both sides of the Jordan River. Now that every tribe had received their inheritance, *"So Joshua sent the people away, every man to his inheritance"* (Jos. 24:28).

During the period of the Judges

After the tribes went to their tribal inheritance, there was no record of the 12 tribes uniting to fight their enemies. More significantly, there was no record of the 12 tribes keeping the annual feasts. Indeed, they forsook the Feast Days of the Mosaic Covenant. The period of the judges would span almost 450 years (Ref. Acts 13:20 — "until Samuel the prophet"). This time frame can be described as a long duration of moral decline, and a cycle of sin, coupled with God's merciful deliverance. Israel, satisfied with their selfish inheritance of the land, did not work together anymore to defeat the rest of their Canaanite enemies. Since not all the Canaanites were driven away, they enticed Israel to worship their idolatrous gods. Therefore, Israel faced continual warfare internally and externally. If God had not raised up various judges during this period, Israel would have been annihilated or assimilated, thereby becoming just like the Canaanites in their midst.

This period can be summed up by the last verse in Judges: *"In those days there was no king in Israel. Everyone did what was right in his own eyes"* (Judges 21:25). God, as the King, was the ruler through the Mosaic Covenant. Israel did not need a human monarch because they had already agreed to the Mosaic Covenant with God. The Lord God considered this a "marriage contract" whereby at Sinai Israel declared "I will" to His proposal (Ref. Exodus 19:5, 17; Isaiah 54:5 (Niv); Jer. 3:14). However, when Israel forsook the Mosaic Covenant, in essence, they forsook their husband, God's rule.

By quoting *"everyone did what was right in his own eyes,"* God specifically judged them for forsaking God's chosen place for the 12 tribes to assemble for feasting and worshipping in unity. Their division by staying in their own inheritance and not sharing in God's ordained feasts was their lawlessness. Since it was a diverse people, without practicing this specific command in the Mosaic laws, Israel was divided and scattered. There was nothing to hold them together.

The last story in Judges was a heinous crime committed by some of the tribe of Benjamin, who raped and murdered the wife of a Levite. The Levite then cut her body into 12 pieces and sent a piece to each of the 12 tribes. This abomination stirred up the 11 tribes to almost annihilate the tribe of Benjamin. This body, being cut into 12 pieces, may represent how divided and fallen Israel had become. Therefore, the Judges ended with every man returning to His inheritance. And the last verse ending the Judges with *"Everyone did what was right in his own eyes"* (Jud. 21:25), affirms their rejection of unity, which is expressed in God's requirement for the centralized worship and feasting of all 12 tribes.

The priestly corruption described at the outset of 1 Samuel signals a decisive rupture in Israel's faithfulness to the Mosaic Covenant. The priesthood became completely corrupt. They treated the people's offerings as their "piggy bank" by taking the best portions; thus, stealing from God. The sons of the high priest were even sleeping with the women who came to the temple. Although by then Israel had broken their covenant with God, they wanted to use God superstitiously by bringing the Ark into battle against their enemies. It seems that God did not want to be used in such a way; therefore, Israel was defeated, and He allowed the Ark to be captured by the Philistines. The Ark was no longer needed since Israel forsook God and His covenant.

This was the sad result of some 450 years of neglecting the Mosaic Covenant. The first abandonment of the Mosaic Covenant was that Israel forsook the centralized place of feasting and worshipping God. As mentioned previously, there was no record of all 12 tribes coming together for feasting as required by God. With the rejection of centralized worship before the Ark, the remaining pillars of the Mosaic Law gradually declined. Although the last item to depart was the most crucial, it was the Ark of God's glory and testimony (1 Sam. 4:22; Exo. 25:16). Nevertheless, degradation began with the forsaking of the assembly of God's diverse people in unity expressed before the Ark.

David A Man After God's Own Heart

> "Surely I will not go into the chamber of my house, Or go up to the comfort of my bed; 4 I will not give sleep to my eyes [Or] slumber to my eyelids, 5 Until I find a place for the LORD, A dwelling place for the Mighty One of Jacob." . . . 13 For the LORD has chosen Zion; He has desired [it] for His dwelling place:
>
> – Psalm 132:3-5, 13

In 2 Samuel 5, David was anointed king over all of Israel. All the tribes of Israel came to David at Hebron and said, *"Behold, we are your bone and flesh. In times past, when Saul was king over us, it was you who led out and brought in Israel. And the LORD said to you, 'You shall be shepherd of my people Israel, and you shall be prince over Israel'"* (2 Sam. 5:1-2 ESV). Significantly, the beginning of recovering the adherence to the Mosaic Covenant started with the unity of God's diverse people. From this beginning, God was able to gain the place He chose by bringing back the Ark of His glory and testimony, wherein He could be served by a holy priesthood, making offerings, and establishing the annual feasts. This is the Mosaic Covenant, which brought down God's glory. The unity of all the tribes was a major milestone in the beginning of God recovering His glory with the Mosaic Covenant.

The first thing David did as king was to capture Jerusalem. The Jebusites occupied Jerusalem at the time, but the city had a long history in the Bible dating back to the time of Abraham. After Abraham rescued Lot, his nephew, by defeating 5 kings, he was met by Melchizedek, the king of Salem and the priest of the Most High God (Gen. 14:18). Melchizedek was the pre-incarnated Son of God who ministered bread and wine to Abraham (Heb. 7:3). He was the king of Salem (peace). Salem is the same city as Jeru**salem,** where God's dwelling place, Zion, was located (Psa. 76:2). Remarkably, the first record of the appearance of the pre-incarnated Son of God was called the King of Salem. The first mention of Salem (Jerusalem) was a city directly connected to God.

After Abraham and Sarah finally gave birth to their only son, Isaac, God asked him to offer Isaac as a sacrifice. The place where he built an altar to perform this sacrifice was on the geological formation of Mt. Moriah (Gen. 22:2). Again, Moriah is also where Jerusalem is located (2 Chron. 3:1). Therefore, from its first mention, Jerusalem was a significant city in Moses' writings (Torah).

What possessed David to capture Jerusalem as the first act of being king of all 12 tribes? The most spiritual reason would be that he understood from the law of Moses (Torah) concerning Jerusalem and its significance as stated above. According to the law of Moses, David would also know that God had chosen a place to put His name for His habitation (Deut. 12). God's heart was for a dwelling place to rest. God said: *"The heaven is my throne and the earth is my footstool, but where is the place of my rest?"* (Acts 7:49; Isa. 61:1-2). Yes, God does not dwell in a house made by hands; nevertheless, the Mosaic Covenant required a physical symbol of God resting in His house. The tabernacle represented God dwelling with His diverse people in unity. Nevertheless, God desired a permanent dwelling place rather than a tent, yet He never revealed what was in His heart to anyone (2 Sam. 7:5-7). There was no record that God told David to capture Jerusalem. David, being a man after God's heart, instinctively and intuitively defeated and occupied Jerusalem for his kingdom and the place for God's dwelling.

In the next chapter of 2 Samuel 6, after the conquest of Jerusalem, David brought back the Ark of God. This was another action manifesting a man after God's heart. He desired and cared for God's glory and testimony. David brought the Ark to Jerusalem and placed it inside a newly erected tent. This was his heart for the renewal of the Mosaic Covenant. When the ark came into Jerusalem, David shamelessly leaped and danced in worship to God. That event, with all the offerings made to God, was a blessing for all the people of Israel.

In the next chapter, David said: *"See now, I dwell in a house of cedar, but the ark of God dwells in a tent"* (2 Sam. 7:2). By this word, God knew David wanted to build a house for Him (1 King 8:18). However, God said that David would not be the one to build His house because David was a man of war and had shed much blood (1 Chron. 22:8). Although David did not build God's house, the temple, he prepared abundantly the material and labor needed. He spoke to Solomon these words: *"With great pains I have provided for the house of the LORD 100,000 talents of gold, a million talents of silver, and bronze and iron beyond weighing, for there is so much of it; timber and stone, too, I have provided. To these you must add. You have an abundance of workmen: stonecutters, masons, carpenters, and all kinds of craftsmen without number, skilled in working gold, silver, bronze, and iron. Arise and work! The LORD be with you!"* (1 Chron. 22:14-16). Other records indicate that he gave far more than the items previously mentioned.

Psalms 132 expresses David's zeal for the Lord's house — truly inspiring. His entire motivation for living was for God's dwelling place. He was possessed by His desire to build God's house. His heart for God was absolute without wavering. He gave himself wholly to satisfy God with a house according to God's purpose. As seen at the beginning of this chapter, God's House in the New Testament age is His Democratic Assembly (Ekklesia). Today, believers need the same determination to build God's House.

However, even with such a heart for God, David was still a sinful man, susceptible to temptation. As mentioned previously, David committed adultery with Bathsheba, had her husband, Uriah, murdered in battle, and broke all of God's moral commandments.

Now, after David had won all his battles externally and internally, Satan enticed David to number the people of Israel (1 Chr. 21:1). Scriptures did not say for what reason, but it can be surmised that it was out of pride or lack of trust in God. After numbering the people, David knew in his heart that he had sinned greatly against God (2 Sam. 24:10). God came to judge David and gave him three options: 3 years of famine, 3 months defeated by enemies, or 3 days of the sword of the Lord (1 Chr. 21:11-12). David picked the 3 days to be judged directly by God's hand. So, a plague came through the land, and 70,000 men died.

To stop the plague, God, through His prophet, told David to go and set up an altar on the threshing floor owned by Araunah, a Jebusite (2 Sam. 24:18). Araunah wanted to give the site to David for free, but in verse 24 David said, *"No, but I will buy it from you for a price. I will not offer burnt offerings to the LORD my God that cost me nothing."* So, David bought the site for the full price and built an altar for his burnt offering and peace offering to the Lord, and the plague ended.

Sovereignly, this threshing floor was on Mount Moriah, and it became the site for Solomon to build God's temple. *"Then Solomon began to build the house of the LORD in Jerusalem on Mount Moriah, where the LORD had appeared to David his father, at the place that David had appointed, on the threshing floor of Ornan (aka Araunah) the Jebusite"* (2 Chron. 3:1 ESV). Certainly, this is the place God chose to put His name. This was the place where Melchizedek was king and the place where Abraham offered his son, Isaac.

Eventually, Solomon built God's house, the temple. When the temple was finished, *"the priests could not stand to minister because of the cloud, for the glory of the LORD filled the house of the LORD"* (1 Kings 8:11). God obtained a house on earth for His dwelling. How magnificent! The God of heaven, without a dwelling place, found His home on earth. Even though His glory filled the temple, His dwelling place was His people. Emphasizing again: The temple symbolically confirms that He dwells in His diverse people in unity.

Indeed, after the Father revealed to Peter who Jesus was: *"You are the Messiah (Christ), the Son of the Living God,"* Jesus said to Peter, *"I will build my ekklesia (democratic assembly)."* It was from that day forward that *"Jesus began to show to His disciples that He must go to Jerusalem, and suffer many things from the elders and chief priests and scribes, and be killed, and be raised the third day"* (Matt. 16:16-21). Just as David paid a full price for the site of the temple, the Messiah paid the full price for our redemption and for the building up of His Ekklesia. He is our "Whole Burnt Offering." It was and is upon this place of sacrifice that God's people are united as His Ekklesia (Democratic Assembly)!

In Solomon's dedication prayer, he said repeatedly seven times to pray toward the temple and God will answer (1 Kings 8). These prayers include defeating Israel's enemies, forgiveness of sins, food supply, dedications to God, and peace among brethren. All these prayers will be answered as prayers are offered to God toward the temple. This shows that God desires His people to constantly remember that His dwelling place is among the unity of His people. When the people's hearts are for the oneness of His people, God will answer.

The fulfillment of this "prayer toward the temple" is when Jesus said that His Democratic Assembly has the authority to bind or loose on earth and heaven will answer (Matt. 18:18). Then He continues speaking to the 2 or 3 that were in His Ekklesia, *"if two of you agree [symphony or harmony] together on earth concerning anything that they ask, it will be done for them by My Father in heaven."* These two or three in Matthew 18 were in harmonious accord with the entire Ekklesia. Therefore, they have the same authority to bind and to loose on earth as the Lord's Ekklesia. Being in harmonious unity with the Ekklesia makes them representatives of the Lord's authority on earth. This is the reality of praying toward the temple in the Old Testament. The Father answers the prayers of those whose hearts are in **symphony**, in harmony with the unity of His diverse people.

When the temple was completed, the priests were overwhelmed by God's glory. This must be similar to being "taken up in glory" when godliness is defined in 1 Timothy 3:16. Here is the finality of God manifested in the flesh — taken up in glory. God receives glory, and His people are glorified.

Truly, this was the period of the glorification of God's diverse people. There was no war but only peace and tranquility during the reign of Solomon. There were riches abounding to the extent that the queen of Sheba said, *"I did not believe the words until I came and saw with my own eyes; and indeed the half was not told me. Your wisdom and prosperity exceed the fame of which I heard"* (1 Kings 10:7). The glory displayed was beyond imagination. The reality of this glorification of Israel was and still is the glory found in the unity of His diverse people, as Paul declares: "To Him be glory in the ekklesia [democratic assembly] by Christ Jesus to all generations, forever and ever. Amen" (Eph. 3:21).

What a wonderful story of God's mercy, forgiveness, grace, and God being manifest in the flesh. Solomon, the temple builder, was born out of David's sin with Bathsheba. The site of God's temple was established as a result of David's sin in numbering Israel. On one hand, man's flesh was displayed, on the other hand, God gained His dwelling place and His glory manifested on earth. David's story testifies that *"all things work together for good to those who love God, to those who are the called according to His purpose"* (Rom. 8:28). Since David loved God and was called for God's purpose, David's failures, though he was judged and punished for them, were used to fulfill God's purpose for His house — God manifested in the flesh. Truly, as Paul declared at the close of Romans 11: *"For God has committed them all to disobedience, that He might have mercy on all. Oh, the depth of the riches both of the wisdom and knowledge of God! How unsearchable are His judgments and His ways past finding out . . . for of Him and through Him and to Him are all things, to whom be glory forever, Amen"* (Rom. 11:32-36, excerpts).

Conclusion

Back to 1 Timothy 3 concerning the proper conduct in the Household of God, the Ekklesia of the living God, which is the pillar and base of the truth. The appropriate conduct in God's Household is essentially dependent on the mystery of godliness which covers a sequence of events starting with Christ's incarnation, followed by His crucifixion, resurrection, ascension, outpouring of the Spirit anointing His followers with power and authority, the preaching of the gospel, a growing body of believers in the world, and finally His built-up and mature people as His one Temple is taken up in glory.

This mystery of godliness, unveiled in the prophetic writings, starts with Abraham's journey concerning Israel, to whom God promised that he would be a father of many nations, and God's desire to be manifested on earth. At the pinnacle of this journey, Israel stands united—a nation woven and united together from a rich tapestry of diverse people. God dwelt among them with the glory of God manifested in God's temple. God found a dwelling place among the people of the flesh in unity.

They were not united because of a singular racial or genetic identity. Rather, it was a mixed multitude replete with foreigners (Gentiles) in its top leadership. King David himself was genetically more than 21% of non-Jewish descent. Foreigners played a significant role in the construction of the temple. Additionally, they were not a people more righteous or holier than others. They were of the flesh just like people of other nations. They wrestled with the weakness of their sinful nature, succumbing to various temptations until David and Solomon built the Temple. So, their conduct was not what would be expected and normally judged as righteous or holy by any standard. What could have made these diverse people of flesh become God's united dwelling place? The Mosaic Covenant transformed these people of flesh and united them to be God's habitation on earth — to house His glory.

The Mosaic Covenant unveiled God's nature and character. The Ark in the Tabernacle depicted God's incarnation in Jesus Christ. The offerings performed by the priests proclaimed the fullness of Christ's work: His crucifixion for atonement, His resurrection as divine nourishment, and His ascension with the Spirit's outpouring — so that His people might share in His authority and be equipped for ministry. Finally, God chose one place for His people to assemble and feast three times a year to build His diverse people in unity — bringing down His glory. The Mosaic Covenant was the gospel proclaimed in the Hebrew Scriptures for all mankind — both Israel and Gentiles — since anyone could come to God through it. Through this gospel, God manifested Himself in the flesh of those who believed and practiced the entirety of the Mosaic Covenant. He did so among both Israel and those from the nations. This is the mystery of godliness revealed in the prophetic writings.

Therefore, the unique way for them to conduct themselves was to enjoy and practice the entirety of the Mosaic Covenant. Without revelation, most people have a warped concept of the Mosaic Law. Their view is one of unfulfillable demands followed by judgment and condemnation. Contrarily, the whole of God's law given by Moses is full of freedom, love, mercy, and peace. It was only by conducting themselves according to the entire law that Israel, with all the foreigners, could become God's united dwelling place on earth.

The Mosaic Covenant was not perfect since it did not give God's eternal life to His people (Gal. 3:21). It was not faultless (Heb. 8:7) in that the Almighty found "fault with them." Yes, the Law was and will always be spiritual (Rom 7:14) because it clearly defines the very nature of God Almighty. However, they who said "I will" to His proposal under Mt. Sinai — the Mosaic Covenant — could not adhere to this bilateral agreement. They desperately needed another accord, a unilateral promise, another mountain, Mt. Moriah. Therefore, a new covenant was needed in Jesus Christ (Heb. 8:8-13). Now, as He declares: *"I will put My laws in their mind and write them on their hearts; and I will be their God, and they shall be My people . . . In that He says, 'A New Covenant,' He has made the first obsolete. Now what is becoming obsolete and growing old is ready to vanish away."*

Because of the Mosaic Covenant's temporary nature, Israel's decline began at the height of King Solomon's reign. They never recovered until the advent of Jesus Christ, who established the New Covenant. This will be considered in later chapters of this text. Nevertheless, the Mosaic Covenant was a wonderful archetype, unveiling the mystery that the New Covenant would eternally accomplish. The mystery of godliness is truly fulfilled in Jesus Christ with the diverse members of God's Household.

6

THE MYSTERY OF GOD'S OIKONOMIA (ECONOMY)

God's *oikonomia* (anglicized: "economy") was not spoken of directly as a mystery. However, it is closely associated with God's mysteries since Paul used the phrase *"the oikonomia (plan) of the mystery hidden for ages."* It is a critical matter that without God's *oikonomia*, God's mysterious purpose is occluded. Therefore, Paul says that he must bring this matter of God's *oikonomia* to light for all to see (Eph. 3:9). The Greek word in that verse for "plan" (DBY: "administration", ASV: "dispensation") is *oikonomia*.

> To me, though I am the very least of all the saints, this grace was given, to preach to the Gentiles the unsearchable riches of Christ, 9 and to bring to light for everyone what is the plan [oikonomia] of the mystery hidden for ages in God, who created all things . . .
>
> – Eph. 3:8-9, ESV

The Greek word for *economy* is *oikonomia*. It was prominently used in the New Testament when describing the mystery relating to God's will, pleasure, and eternal purpose. Without a full understanding of this word and the concept of *oikonomia*, it would be difficult to comprehend what God is doing to fulfill His purpose. The apostle Paul was determined to bring this work of *oikonomia* to light. All believers should not only participate in the *oikonomia* of grace but should take active responsibility for carrying out and furthering God's *oikonomia*.

Oikonomia and the Mystery of God's Eternal Purpose

Understanding *oikonomia* is critical to understanding the mystery of God's eternal purpose. The definition of this Greek word is "management of a household" (Vine's). *Oikonomia* is a word rich in meaning. Yes, translators have used various English words for *oikonomia* in the New Testament, depending on context: administration, dispensation, plan, stewardship, and economy.

In biblical times, "household management" referred to the intentional and skillful administration required to guide a household toward maturity. The following scenario uses the various translated words (underlined) for oikonomia to explain different facets of how this Greek word is used.

> A rich father who desired to build up his family would have an <u>administration</u> to <u>dispense</u> food to multiple generations of his children scattered across his vast land. The purpose is for them to be fed and grow to increase his household. The <u>steward</u> would be the one dispensing food — he would be responsible for carrying out this <u>plan</u> to grow his family.

Contemporary usage of the word, economy, is the production, distribution, and consumption of goods. If any part of this chain is weak, the entire economy suffers. A growing economy equals a strong nation. *Oikonomia* is composed of two words: *oiko*, which means "house," and *nomia*, which is derived from the Greek root word *nomos*, which means "law; Therefore, *oikonomia* means "house-law."

Law (nomos) comes from the primary word *nemo*, which means, *"To parcel out, especially food or grazing to animals"*.[14] It seems counterintuitive that the law, which seems so demanding and condemning, comes from a word meaning the parceling out of food. In God's view, His laws have an underlying purpose: ***to feed***.

God's original intention in establishing the law was not something for His children to keep, but rather to give them food. Interestingly, the very first command from God was to eat: *"Of every tree of the garden you may freely eat"* (Gen. 1:26). Food was given through the law, which included not just the Ten Commandments but also offerings — and the eating of those offerings. When a commandment was broken, to fulfill the law, an offering had to be made, accompanied by the consumption of the offering. According to the law, righteousness was made possible by these offerings. When the offerings were made for peace, sins, and trespasses (guilt), a portion was eaten. In the New Testament, Jesus Christ is revealed as our real offering; thus, believers partake and eat of Him as the Lamb of God.

God's Economy Is How He Accomplishes His Will and Eternal Purpose

God makes known to His children His mysterious will, to head up all things in Christ. This is accomplished by His oikonomia (economy).

---

14 (www.biblestudytools.com/lexicons/greek/nas/nomos)

> Making known unto us the mystery of his will, according to his good pleasure which he purposed in him 10 unto a dispensation of the fulness of the times, to sum up all things in Christ, the things in the heavens, and the things upon the earth; in him.
>
> –Eph. 1:9-10, ASV

God has a will — a purpose — according to His good pleasure. Likewise, humans tend to orient their goals and purposes around what gratifies them, reflecting the desires that most deeply move their hearts. God's ultimate purpose, however, is to head up all things in Christ. Everything in the universe will be summed up in Christ as the head. Christ, from His resurrection and ascension, is eternally both God and man. God's purpose is designed to bring everything under the headship of Jesus Christ. Believers will not be able to grasp the depth and height of what this means until eternity.

While this won't happen in totality until the future, God's economy (*oikonomia*) is needed during this *age of time* before eternity. Therefore, before time is filled up (or over with — "when time shall be no more" — Rev. 10:6-9), God's economy "in time" is needed. Today, it is God's economy that accomplishes what He desires. It fulfills His purpose whereby all things are headed up in Christ. Therefore, God's economy is God's way (method or plan) to accomplish His ultimate will.

These verses clearly show the prominence of God's economy (*oikonomia*) in relationship to His will, purpose, and pleasure. Consequently, understanding God's economy is critical in realizing God's ultimate purpose. Believers who do not understand the concept of God's economy may easily become entangled with non-essential doctrines or Christian practices, thereby becoming subservient to outward religious regulations or hypes. Alas! How tragic it is to miss the mark of God's eternal purpose.

Stewards Dispensing Grace—the Riches of Christ

Stewards in God's economy should be dispensing grace (the riches of Christ for every believer's enjoyment) with a vision of building up God's household. An example of a steward in the New Testament is the Apostle Paul. Paul received the *oikonomia* (stewardship, dispensation, administration) of the grace of God, so he could then dispense this grace to believers.

> . . . (if indeed ye have heard of the administration [oikonomia] of the grace of God which has been given to me towards [Greek: into] you, that by revelation the mystery has been made known to me . . .)
>
> – Ephesians 3:2-3, DBY

Paul wrote about God's economy given to him — the economy of grace. He understood he was a steward administering and dispensing this grace to people. Again, here the *oikonomia* is closely connected to "mystery." The word "grace" (Gk. *charis*) means "that which affords joy, pleasure, delight, sweetness, charm, loveliness" (Thayer's). The "grace of God" or the "grace of the Lord Jesus" means the joy, pleasure, and delight that can only come from God and the Lord Jesus. They are special and heavenly, unlike any joy or pleasure of the earth.

Grace is the spiritual food believers need for sustenance and spiritual growth. Grace was given to Paul so he could be a "dispenser of grace" to humanity. God's entire economy is an economy of grace. Grace is the "product" that became available through Jesus Christ (John 1:17). Grace is to be distributed to all believers so they can enjoy all the riches of Christ, thereby growing up into maturity. The entire chain of God's economy is grace — its supply is unlimited because its eternal source is Jesus Christ.

All humanity demands and seeks grace (pleasure and enjoyment). Therefore, stewards are needed to distribute grace to all men. Physical food is not just a necessity — there is true enjoyment and pleasure in partaking (eating). The grace of the Lord is not just spiritual food and supply for the Christian journey; it is also their joy, pleasure, and delight as they travel toward fulfilling God's eternal purpose — maturity within God's Household.

Dispensing the Unsearchable Riches of Christ for All Men

> . . . of which I am become minister according to the gift of the grace of God given to me, according to the working of His power. To me, less than the least of all saints, has this grace been given, to announce among the nations the glad tidings of the unsearchable riches of the Christ.
>
> – Ephesians 3:7–8, DBY

A minister is like a waiter serving food. The "food" that Paul served was grace. The gospel (glad tidings, or the good news) makes available or unveils Christ's unsearchable riches. The gospel is much more than going to "heaven" and not going to "hell." Let's consider an item of the good news: the Lord's love. How *unsearchably* rich is His love! For eternity, believers will not be able to fathom its depth. He loved His people even when they were His enemies. Love, then, is ministered as part of this grace wherein the believer enjoys the unsearchable riches found in Christ alone. Additionally, there is no need to go to heaven to enjoy God's love. His love is richly available today amid this darkened world.

The Scriptures describe Jesus' person, character, and function using many different symbolic images: He is the rock, shepherd, door, cornerstone, top stone, morning star, first fruit, bridegroom, captain, bread of life . . . and much more. Each one of these items will take an eternity to appreciate. All of these are His riches for dispensing.

His work on the cross, resurrection, ascension, and enthronement to be both Lord and Christ is also *unsearchably* rich. Believers can appreciate the inexhaustible riches of Jesus Christ. This is the gospel (glad tidings) for dispensing to all who would hear. Enjoying the unsearchable riches of Christ declares His abundant grace. He plans to distribute or dispense His grace – this is God's *oikonomia* (economy).

God Desires All Men to See and Participate in His Economy

God desires all men to see and participate in this economy or dispensation; therefore, Paul was charged to enlighten everyone to see the *oikonomia* of the mystery.

> . . . and to enlighten all with the knowledge of what is the administration [oikonomia] of the mystery hidden throughout the ages in God, who has created all things.
>
> – Eph. 3:9, DBY

As one who had received God's *oikonomia*, Paul enlightened others to understand this *oikonomia*, revealing its mystery. It is interesting to note that God's *oikonomia* is a concept that needs enlightenment, akin to the enlightenment needed for believers to receive Jesus Christ at the time of salvation. Every believer needs to see and understand God's economy as soon as they believe in Jesus Christ.

Believers who have been enlightened concerning God's economy, like Paul, will want all to understand and participate in God's economy. However, unlike Paul's heavy burden for this, the amount of teaching and speaking among believers today concerning this knowledge of God's *oikonomia* is minuscule, even minimized, or deprecated. Readers should ask themselves how often they have heard of God's *oikonomia* taught or preached. Yes, most well-meaning ministers emphasize sundry programs/teachings in an effort to "disciple" either people or even "nations" to be true followers of Christ. However, rarely included in such "programs" is an emphasis upon what God is really after for each believer, encapsulated in how He desires to dispense His grace. How distant and remote is this understanding of God's *oikonomia* among God's ministers! Such knowledge is critical for believers to stay the course – living out His divine life and being equipped to serve God and humanity. Though this topic is essential for God's eternal purpose, why has it been hidden from most Christians with little emphasis in general Christian discourse today?

Resulting in Ekklesia: Glorify God and Shame His Enemies

God's eternal purpose in having a built-up Democratic Assembly (Ekklesia) is designed to bring glory to God and shame to His enemies.

> To the intent that now the manifold wisdom of God might be made known by the church [ekklesia] to the principalities and powers in the heavenly [places], 11 according to the eternal purpose which He accomplished in Christ Jesus our Lord, . . . 21 to Him [be] glory in the church [ekklesia] by Christ Jesus to all generations, forever and ever. Amen.
>
> – Eph. 3:10–11, 21

The result or the outcome of God's economy is the building up of His Household — the Ekklesia — through which the multifaceted wisdom of God will be made known to all heavenly beings. True "discipleship" is not designed to ingratiate one's individual spirituality, per se. Administering God's eternal plan and purpose for the ages brings about "glory to God" — that "glory" is manifested in the way of the manifestation of His Democratic Assembly — then, and then only does God receive glory!

This "glory" is especially true vis-à-vis Satan and all the angels who have followed His rebellion. God could not manifest His manifold wisdom (or "glory") without an adversary also full of wisdom (Eze. 28:12). The more complex the problem, the more wisdom is needed to solve the problem. The loftier the purpose or goal, the more profound wisdom (or "glory") will be displayed when it is accomplished.

After the creation of man (male and female), Satan entered the scene to fully corrupt man by injecting man with sin and death. This manifestation of satanic life and nature resulted in the corruption of the image of God — man. All of humanity became God's enemy. Man was condemned under the righteous judgment of God — awaiting the ultimate wrath of God upon sin. Humanity (His offspring), once loved and desired by God, was contaminated to the core of its DNA. In this dismal and seemingly hopeless state, God intervened to restore His image, man. God's recovery work through Jesus Christ did not just rescue man back to his created state, but it went far beyond that originality. Man was to be born anew with divine life — to become a partaker of the divine nature. It was God's pleasure to have many sons — a family — and ultimately with man as the Household of God. This Household, known as His Ekklesia (democratic assembly), is the culmination of His manifold and extensive wisdom at its zenith.

Creation was easy for God: He spoke and it was. It displays His glory in His creative power. However, not much wisdom was manifested since wisdom is best expressed when there is a problem to solve. The greater the problem, the more wisdom is needed. When Satan rebelled against God and corrupted man, the entire universe was watching what God would do and how He would react. God had never faced such an enormous challenge, so how would He solve this universal crisis? How would He change what had become through Adam's fall, a corrupt "old man" and create "One New Man," thereby not only restoring His original creation, man, but revealing through His multifaceted wisdom, the "New Creation," one far superior to the original.

His wisdom includes sending His Only Begotten Son, Jesus Christ, to be incarnate as a man. It was wisdom wherein He lived a sinless life and was crucified to accomplish redemption for all men. In His death, He terminated the "old man" which describes the sinful, fallen part of man (Rom. 6:6), and took away Satan's ultimate weapon — death (Heb. 2:14). Wisdom was manifested when Jesus resurrected; God's people regenerated in His resurrection (1 Pet. 1:3; 2 Tim. 2:11). Tremendous wisdom was displayed to make a man both Lord and Christ sitting on God's throne. The very man that Satan seduced and became his partner in rebellion and disobedience would become the one who would defeat and crush the serpent's head (Rom. 16:20). It must have amazed and awestruck all the angelic hosts. In His wisdom, God poured out the Spirit, so that the men under Satan's control who divide and fight each other could now love each other, being united as God's family and, more so, to become the Bride of Christ. They have become the receptors of God's dispensing — His (*oikonomia*) of grace and stewards (*oikonomia*) themselves, dispensing grace to others. Each of these diverse individuals has a unique journey displaying distinctive facets of God's incredible, multifaceted wisdom.

When these unique facets come together, they manifest God's Ekklesia (Democratic Assembly). This truly is the culmination of all His wisdom. She is the ultimate result of God's amazing and intricate solution to the problem of the universe. Additionally, she is God's eternal purpose and heart's desire. No wonder His Ekklesia, His Family and Bride, manifests God's multifaceted wisdom to and in the entire universe, especially to the rebellious angels. It is this same democratic assembly that gives glory to God. Without His Ekklesia, His glory is obstructed or partially demonstrated. The universe expresses to God its loftiest and greatest opinion of His majesty and splendor at the manifestation of His Ekklesia. God's glory is seen when His Household (family) shines in the universe. She is the product of God's *oikonomia!*

God's Oikonomia Unveiled in the Prophetic Writings

Eating the fruit of the Tree of Life

> Then God said, "Let Us make man in Our image, according to Our likeness; let them have dominion over the fish of the sea, over the birds of the air, and over the cattle, over all the earth and over every creeping thing that creeps on the earth."
>
> – Gen, 1:26

> And out of the ground the LORD God made every tree grow that is pleasant to the sight and good for food. The tree of life [was] also in the midst of the garden, and the tree of the knowledge of good and evil.
>
> – Gen, 2:9

> Then the LORD God said, "Behold, the man has become like one of Us, to know good and evil. And now, lest he put out his hand and take also of the tree of life, and eat, and live forever" – . . . 24 So He drove out the man; and He placed cherubim at the east of the garden of Eden, and a flaming sword which turned every way, to guard the way to the tree of life.
>
> – Gen. 3:22, 24

When God created all sea, air, and land creatures, He spoke and they were. They were all created according to their *kind*. Each was according to its own kind. However, when man (male and female) was fashioned, he was not created according to his kind, but according to God's image and likeness. He was according to *God's kind*. Unlike all the other creatures, God created man in a special and specific way,

"*And Jehovah God formed man of the dust of the ground, and breathed into his nostrils the breath of life, and man became a living soul*" (Gen 2:7 ASV). Man's body was from the earth, and God breathed into him the breath of life. Man became a living soul. The breath of God into man was unique since He didn't do that with any other creature. This "breath of life" in man formed his spirit. Therefore, Zechariah spoke concerning God's creation: He "*stretches out the heavens, lays the foundation of the earth, and forms the spirit of man within him*" (Zech 12:1). God considers man's spirit to be the most sacred part of man – wholly designed to fulfill His ultimate purpose.

The totality of man consists of three parts: spirit, soul, and body (1 Thes. 5:23). This is shown in Genesis when God made the body using the dust of the earth, then

God's breath entered man, forming his human spirit, and together this man became a living soul. The body is for interacting with the physical world. The soul in Greek is *"psyche,"* the origin of the English word "psychology." The soul is the psychological being of man, interacting in thinking (mind), feeling (emotion), and deciding (will). However, in God's eyes, the most essential part of man is his human spirit. God's breath created man's spirit; both have, if you would, similar substance or essence. As shown later, this substance at creation did not include God's eternal life. Nevertheless, the spirit of man, likened to God's Spirit, can receive or contain the very Life of God and unite with Him. This is the part of man that can be born of God (John 3:6). Therefore, if man only lives in the physical and psychological world and ignores God, his spirit is inactive or deadened. Man's spirit was created so that man could receive God and have His eternal life joined and integrated into man.

Man's spirit is the secret to receiving God's light (Prov. 20:27). God's Spirit and man's spirit are joined with the same testimony (Rom. 8:16). God is seeking worshippers who use their spirits to commune with Him. These are true worshippers (John 4:24). When men believe and receive Jesus Christ as Lord and Savior, He enters their spirits and becomes united with them (2 Tim. 4:22). Their regenerated and renewed spirits become dominant over their whole person: *"For God has not given us a spirit of fear, but of power and of love and of a sound mind"* (2 Tim. 1:7). Men's souls flounder in fear without an anchor because of their unregenerated spirits. Now men, having Christ in their spirits, have a will of power, a loving emotion as Christ loves, and a renewed and keen mind.

God's grand plan of having a family with many offspring was unveiled with the creation of man. God created man (male and female) in His own image and likeness, so that humanity could express and represent God on earth (Gen. 1:26). Man possesses internal faculties such as emotion, cognition, discernment, and intention, which are similar to those of God. Man loves and hates, he thinks logically and gains knowledge, and he has a will to purpose. These characteristics mirror God's so that when the universe looks at man, it sees a multiplication of the expression of God.

Likewise, man has the physical likeness of God. When God (Yahweh) met Abraham in Genesis 18, Abraham described Him as a man. This verse may be the most striking: *"I see four men loose, walking amid the fire; and they are not hurt, and the form of the fourth is like the Son of God"* (Dan. 3:25). There were four men in the furnace, and one of them was like the Son of God. This man was like the Son of God! So, man took on God's likeness. God also appeared in the likeness of man when He wrestled with Jacob. These examples show that God's physical makeup looks like man since man was created in God's likeness.

When God created man, He said, *"Let us make man in our image and after our likeness."* It was only with man that His plurality was manifested. God is uniquely one; yet, He is also distinctly Father, Son, and Holy Spirit. His image and likeness include the reality that the one God has a plurality. So, when God made man (singular), He said let them (plural) have dominion. The singular man that God created is also plural. God did not make a woman independent from man; rather, woman came out of man. From these two — male and female expressions of one man — came generations, multiplying to approximately 8.2 billion people by 2025. In God's eyes, the multitude of humanity is in one man, Adam. Therefore, just as the three of God are one and in one fellowship, to express the image and likeness of God, humanity should also be *a multitude in one.*

God's purpose was not only that man would have His image and likeness, but that man would have His life and nature — indeed, man was made to be inhabited by God! That was the purpose of the Tree of Life. If man partook and ate of it, he would have the eternal life of God. Genesis 3:22 shows that man never partook of the Tree of Life in the garden. He was made to partake of the Tree of Life, but man did not do so. God drove man away from the Tree of Life so that man would not live with the sinful nature for eternity. He ate of the Tree of the Knowledge of Good and Evil first, and from then on, God prevented man from partaking of the Tree of Life.

In a previous chapter, it was clear that the Tree of Life typified Jesus Christ as the vine tree of life in the New Testament. Jesus is the real Tree of Life for man to partake of and enjoy. Man receives eternal life by ingesting Jesus (John 6:54). From the beginning of the creation of man, feeding man with the real food of Jesus Christ (Tree of Life) was God's ultimate plan. God's *oikonomia* was alluded to at the time of man's creation: they would have His life by eating and partaking of Him.

If man had eaten the Tree of Life, he would not merely have had the image and likeness of God, but would have had His life and nature within him. That would make man in every way God's offspring. Without God's life and nature, man would only be a facsimile, a resemblance, of God, similar to what an artificially intelligent humanoid is to man. That is not what God is after according to His eternal purpose. He wanted a family of His sons and daughters born of Him, sharing in His life and nature.

This is why the human spirit is so essential, since this is the part of man created to receive and ingest God as the Tree of Life. God's economy is God's plan to dispense Himself into man, specifically man's spirit. Man is made to eat of the Tree of Life. God plans to inject His life and nature into His created humanity so that humanity would not just be "creatures" on the planet bearing His image and likeness, but His offspring with His life and nature. This plan is His *oikonomia*: to feed His chosen people with His life and nature so that they become His family. *"He destined us in love to be his sons through Jesus Christ, according to the purpose of his will"* (Eph 1:5 RSV).

Through the shed blood of the Lord Jesus, man, once again, is placed before the Tree of Life. He is not only forgiven and repositioned, but now can partake of Jesus Christ, the Tree of Life. The preaching of repentance and forgiveness of sin is necessary, but it should not stop there. Forgiveness is so that man can partake of Christ, AND bear fruit unto God.

Joseph, Being the Steward

> And Pharaoh said to his servants, "Can we find [such a one] as this, a man in whom [is] the Spirit of God?" . . . 40 "You shall be over my house, and all my people shall be ruled according to your word; only in regard to the throne will I be greater than you." 41 And Pharaoh said to Joseph, "See, I have set you over all the land of Egypt."
>
> – Gen. 41:38, 40-41

> Then Joseph provided his father, his brothers, and all his father's household with bread, according to the number in [their] families.
>
> – Gen. 47:12

Joseph was a wonderful example of God's steward, one who feeds God's people so that they may grow. Joseph was a man of God. He was an archetype of Jesus Christ. Joseph became what would be called the prime minister of Egypt. He was the chief administrator of the entire country, specifically of its economy. Pharaoh was more of a figurehead as king on the throne, but Joseph was the practical ruler of Egypt. It is noteworthy that Joseph was in prison for many years. It was like a death sentence with no hope of getting out. However, when he successfully interpreted Pharaoh's dream, he was immediately made the ruler of Egypt. This is a wonderful archetype of the resurrection of Jesus from the dead; He was made both Lord and Christ (Acts 2:36).

When Israel went down to Egypt, there were 70 people (Gen. 46:27). It was during a famine that they went with nothing to be ministered to by Joseph, and he provided for them. Joseph provided land for dwelling and bread for sustenance. Joseph fed them per God's stewardship. These 70 people, some 200 years later, grew into over 2 million people. They became a mighty people while being fed in Egypt. This is a good example of a minister of God (a steward) providing food to God's people, so that they grow to become mature. God spoke concerning Israel when they were to come out of Egypt: *"I made you thrive like a plant in the field; and you grew, matured, and became very beautiful"* (Eze. 16:7).

Israel's journey in Egypt started with Joseph being a steward feeding them. After receiving nourishment for 200 years, they multiplied until they were as countless as the stars in heaven (Deut. 1:10). From a mere 70 individuals — hardly a nation — they grew into a mature people numbering over 2 million. Israel became an army of 600,000 men (Exo. 7:4). This is the work of God's *oikonomia* as seen through the stewardship of Joseph.

The Passover Lamb

"Speak to all the congregation of Israel, saying: 'On the tenth of this month every man shall take for himself a lamb, according to the house of [his] father, a lamb for a household. . . . 7 'And they shall take [some] of the blood and put [it] on the two doorposts and on the lintel of the houses where they eat it. 8 'Then they shall eat the flesh on that night; roasted in fire, with unleavened bread [and] with bitter [herbs] they shall eat it.

– Exo 12:3, 7–8

Chapter 2 of this book describes the Passover Lamb as a type of Christ. Here again is the matter of dispensing food. With the eating of the lamb, Israel was to eat unleavened bread and bitter herbs, which are included in the Passover meal. Unleavened bread in this context signifies the sinless life of Christ. Leaven in the Bible often denotes something negative. 1 Corinthians 5:8 says: *"Therefore let us keep the feast, not with old leaven, nor with the leaven of malice and wickedness, but with the unleavened bread of sincerity and truth."* This verse, in which the word *"feast"* refers to Christ as the Passover, thus shows the negativity and exclusion of leaven. Jesus Christ is the only sinless person who defines sincerity and truth. "Bread" made of produce from the earth points to His humanity. Christ's humanity is pure and sinless. He is the bread of truth.

Bitter Herbs being "bitter" can have multiple interpretations. A common one is that "bitter herbs" can be a reminder of the bitterness of slavery in Egypt, from which God delivered them, in that the Egyptians made Israel's lives bitter with hard bondage (Exo. 1:14). All those partaking of Christ as the Passover should remember their liberty from slavery. Previously, they served Pharaoh building His treasure cities, but now they are liberated to enjoy God, to worship and serve God. They were slaves for over 200 years, but the Passover feast is a release from slavery. Egypt under the rule of Pharaoh can be an archetype of the secular world, where all people are enslaved for the purpose of building the kingdom of darkness. Through Christ, God's people are freed from the anxiety and slavery of this world.

However, believers can be under another kind of slavery, which is God's law according to the Old Covenant (Gal. 4:21-31). The negative context of Galatians was that Peter, including most of the Jewish believers, divided and separated themselves from Gentile believers. For this action of division, Peter was rebuked by Paul in Galatians 2 for not walking according to the "truth of the gospel." These Jewish believers segregated themselves. They went back to fulfill the law in separating themselves from Gentile sinners (Acts 10:28). Yes, this was biblical under the Mosaic Covenant; however, this practice, divinely inspired, separated them from Gentile believers. In doing so, they had violated the tenets of the New Covenant whereby Gentiles were wholly, through the blood of His cross, welcomed to the table. The Law had become a bondage to these Judaizers. So, Galatians 5:13 declares: *"For you, brethren, have been called to liberty; only do not use liberty as an opportunity for the flesh, but through love serve one another."*

The evidence of liberation is serving one another in love: Jewish believers serving Gentile believers and vice versa. They were enemies full of hostility, but now they love to serve one another. Wow, what liberation! Therefore, when believers have communion to remember the Lord (the reality of the Passover meal), they need to discern that they are partaking of the one Body of Christ (1 Cor. 11:29). There cannot be division in the Body. The Lord's one Body is constituted of believers who used to be contrary and envious of each other. Now they are liberated to love and serve one another in their distinctiveness. Distinctiveness, yes — Separation, no!

The Bible also says that death is bitter (Ecc. 7:26). Therefore, the "bitter herb" for the Passover can also be interpreted as partaking of Christ's death on the cross. Christ died on the cross for man's redemption and forgiveness of sins. He is uniquely qualified to accomplish this since He is God's sinless and unblemished Lamb (1 Pet. 1:19; 1 John 3:5). No one else can participate in His death for redemption. Since that is the case, why did Jesus say that those who desire to follow Him must carry their cross (Matt. 16:24)? What is the purpose of His believers partaking in the "bitter herb" of the cross?

Certainly, Jesus died for man's sins, but that is not all. He also died to gather His scattered children into one (John 11:52). He was crucified to break down the wall of enmity dividing Jews and Gentiles to make them one new man (Eph. 2:15-16). The oneness of God's people is His ekklesia (Democratic Assembly) that He was to build by going to the cross (Matt. 16:21; Eph. 5:25). He died to bring peace and unite His divided people (Jew and Gentile). When Jesus said to "come after me" in Matthew 16:24, He was going to build up His Ekklesia through His death and resurrection. The goal of believers bearing the cross is to build up the Lord's one Body. Those who earnestly pursue true spirituality and discipleship cannot attain their goal apart from the maturity required to foster unity within the Body of Christ. The testing of being a "disciple" is whether one can love and fellowship with those contrary to oneself. The maturity of the Christian life can only be measured by offering our bodies to His One Body (Romans 12) — a corporate sacrifice, well pleasing, which is our reasonable service.

> I now rejoice in my sufferings for you, and fill up in my flesh what is lacking in the afflictions of Christ, for the sake of His body, which is the church [ekklesia],
>
> – Col. 1:24

Here, the apostle Paul says that the afflictions of Christ were lacking, and Paul's sufferings were to fill up that lack. These afflictions were not for redemption, the forgiveness of sins, but for the Lord's Body, His Democratic Assembly. The journey of Paul's sufferings by carrying the cross is the way a disciple can truly follow the Lord. Paul endured many hardships and persecutions during his travels ministering to the saints. His going to many places and laboring in ministry was the Lord's going. If he had stayed home and done nothing, his many tribulations for the gospel would have been avoided. Therefore, his suffering continued the affliction of Christ for His Body.

Those caring for other believers, especially those with a contrary perspective, often will bear some suffering. The more believers serve one another, the greater the possibility of afflictions, misunderstandings, and loss they will encounter. Anyone desiring to avoid suffering for the Body of Christ should be passive and not serve anyone. Go to church on Sundays (or Saturdays), then stay home for the rest of the week. However, the more you minister to others, especially those different than you, such as in a democratic environment, the sufferings of Christ will fill up — even in your body. This "filling up the afflictions of Christ" to the brim will issue in the Lord's Bride making herself ready for His second advent.

Most Christians consider taking up the cross or experiencing the cross to be a matter of personal holiness. From that perspective, the focus of the cross is to deliver them from their sins or worldliness. For example, if a Christian dresses according to modern fashion or is attracted to alcoholic beverages, they need to take up the cross. Those who know the cross will have self-control, they will have overcome sins, and they will live a holy life. However, according to Scriptures, that was not the primary focus of the cross. Further supported by Paul in 2 Corinthians chapter 3, bearing the cross is for giving life to others. His experience of the dying of Jesus is so that the life of Jesus may work in others. He said: *"So then death is working in us, but life in you"* (2 Cor. 4:12).

Therefore, partaking of these "bitter herbs" during the Passover is to receive the crucified and resurrected Christ, with whom believers will know the cross in their service to others. This is the Lord's *oikonomia*, the dispensing of food, for the building up of His family, His corporate Body. This is how God gained a people for Himself (Exo. 6:7).

When believers observe the communion in the New Testament, it is the reality of the Passover feast of the Old Covenant. Christ is remembered and enjoyed; simultaneously, it celebrates the oneness of God's people, the Body of Christ. Believers, through partaking of Christ, are bearing the cross to have peace with all kinds of people, especially those different from themselves. They are free from the slavery of the law, which under the Mosaic Covenant required separation between peoples, but now they serve not only one another but others outside their nation, the Gentiles or other "ethnos" (ethnic peoples). This communal celebration is a testimony of peace with all God's people in their daily lives.

Offerings for Distributing Food

Not only was the Passover Lamb for sustenance or consumption, but virtually all the offerings were designed for eating. The previous chapter showed that after offering an animal for a Peace Offering, both the offeror and the priests received a portion for consumption. It was an offering of fellowship. In the other offerings: meal, sin, and guilt offerings, a portion was given to the priests to eat. Since the priests belonging to the tribe of Levi did not have an allotment of land, their portion would be from the offerings of all the other tribes.

One aspect of the Mosaic Covenant (aka the Law) was to expose the failures of the Israelites. When an Israelite failed to adhere to the Ten Commandments, he must make an offering of peace, sin, or guilt. The offering was an archetype of Christ as the One judged and condemned on the offeror's behalf. However, the offeror and/or the priest who conducted the offering were to eat of it—they were, in essence, to eat of Christ. As with the Passover Lamb, the blood satisfied God's judgment or wrath upon sin, and the meat they ate nourished God's people. The blood of the sacrifice was for God to see (the blood was brushed outside on the doorpost and lintels of the house). When He saw the blood, His wrath through the Angel of Death would pass over them. What Israel directly enjoyed was eating the lamb inside their homes because the blood of the sacrifice allowed them to eat the Lamb.

Most Christians appreciate the reality that Jesus died for them to forgive their sins. While this is certainly good news, they readily disregard the eating of Jesus for enjoyment and strength. Preaching the forgiveness of sins is wonderful, but shouldn't the gospel also point the repentant to eating the Lamb? The eating of the sacrifices is an archetype of consuming Jesus whenever believers have fallen short of God's requirements. Without the shedding of blood, there is no forgiveness/remission of sin (Heb. 9:22); but the shedding of blood for the remission of sin(s) provides access to eating of the Lamb!

God's original intention was that Israel would be a kingdom of priests. Each Israelite was to be a priest to have a direct relationship with Him. However, when they nationally failed to keep their side of this conditional accord/betrothal at Mount Sinai (for He longed to be their Husband — Jer. 31:31-34), God singled out the tribe of Levi to be the priests of Israel. The priest under the Mosaic Covenant was to bring man to God, to conduct the sacrifices on the offeror's behalf.

In the New Testament, all the followers of Jesus are made priests (1 Pet. 2:5). They do not need anyone to be an intermediary between them and God. Each one can now come to God directly through Jesus Christ. However, newer or weaker believers may need help coming to and seeking God. When any believer notices that another needs help, the person helping can participate to assist the weaker believer turn to Jesus (Gal. 6:1). The one helping and ministering in this way would be considered as one functioning as a priest. This can be anyone, not only the "clergy" or professional pastors, ministers, or so-called "ordained" members of the congregation.

Today, when a believer brings another person to Christ in fellowship and prayer, both have a portion of Christ as food. For example, a brother is downcast due to his recent failures. Another brother comes alongside to fellowship with him, pointing out that he is forgiven because of Christ's death, and Christ is still working in him. After a short time, they pray together, and the downcast brother recovers in the joy of the Lord. When this happens, the stronger brother who functions as a priest also partakes of Christ as his offering. Often, the person who helped the other person turn back to God may enjoy Christ even more as a participating priest. Therefore, all believers should endeavor to function as priests to bring others to God through Jesus Christ. This is how priests and the offerors partake of Jesus Christ as the sacrifice to God.

When many believers notice other Christians who are in need, they may consider their own inadequacies and decline to help. They may think that only a pastor is qualified to help those in need. Since they are not a pastor, they are incapable of assisting. Others may feel that since they are also weak and struggling with failures, they are unqualified to strengthen anyone else. These considerations are a tactic of Satan to disable Christians from their priestly functions. The priests under the Mosaic Covenant, though marked by weakness and sin (Heb. 5:2), still fulfilled their role in drawing others to God. Likewise, those who, through deception or neglect, fail to assist others in coming to Christ will miss the joy of sharing in Christ as priests.

The Mystery of God's Oikonomia (Economy)   141

Under the Mosaic Covenant, various offerings were made depending on the situation or failure of the offeror. One could offer a burnt offering and another a guilt offering based on various circumstances. An Israelite could choose which offering matched his situation. Under the New Covenant, Jesus Christ is the all-in-one offering. Offering Himself to God through death, He is the Burnt Offering – God's wrath upon sin is 100% satisfied. Christ is also the Grain (meal) Offering – through His fine and perfect humanity united with God's Spirit. Furthermore, He is the Peace Offering (including Wave and Heave offerings) – through Christ, we have peace between God and man, and also peace among men. He is the Sin Offering – He put to death the sinful nature in man and nailed it to His cross. Finally, He is the Guilt or Trespass Offering – He is the one who recompensed God all of man's trespasses and guilt. When believers offer these sacrifices, then they enjoy Christ today; it is superfluous to differentiate what type of offering He is, since He is all of them. Whenever there is a problem with God or with men, Christ is the solution. The essential part of the solution is that He is consumed, ingested, and enjoyed. In this way, believers are strengthened by Christ as our singular, yet multifaceted, offering.

Therefore, from the viewpoint of distributing food, the more the Ten Commandments were broken, the more offerings were needed, resulting in enjoying and consuming the offerings. This understanding can readily be applied to believers living under the New Covenant. Every time there is conviction of sin or failure, believers should turn to Jesus Christ to enjoy Him as their redemption and food for strengthening in their weaknesses. Therefore, Paul could say in Romans 5:20, *"Where sin abounded, grace abounded much more."* The offerings show *oikonomia*, or *house-law*. This has everything to do with the distribution of food for the maturity of God's Household.

Manna

> So they gathered it every morning, every man according to his need. And when the sun became hot, it melted. . . . 31 And the house of Israel called its name Manna [lit. "what is it"]. And it [was] like white coriander seed, and the taste of it [was] like wafers [made] with honey.
>
> – Exo. 16:21, 31

> "We remember the fish which we ate freely in Egypt, the cucumbers, the melons, the leeks, the onions, and the garlic; 6 "but now our whole being [is] dried up; [there is] nothing at all except this manna [before] our eyes!"
>
> – Num. 11:5-6

"As the living Father sent Me, and I live because of the Father, so he who feeds on Me will live because of Me." 58 "This is the bread which came down from heaven — not as your fathers ate the manna, and are dead. He who eats this bread will live forever."

– John 6:57-58

God cared for the feeding of His people. While Israel wandered in the wilderness for 40 years, God prepared heavenly bread for them six days a week (On the Sixth day, they were to gather twice as much, so they did not work on the sabbath day — if they gathered too much on any day, the surplus would spoil, but on the sixth day the surplus did not spoil). Again, this shows God's *oikonomia* or dispensation. He desired to feed and nourish them with special food to prepare them for entrance into the Promised Land. They needed a change in diet. They were not ready to be God's people because they needed a transformation in their nature or being.

Even though the Israelites came out of Egypt, they retained the taste and nature of Egypt. They were longing for the food of Egypt. How true is this adage: "You are what you eat." Having eaten Egyptian food for over 200 years, they had, in many ways, become Egyptian themselves. This is like many followers of Christ. They may be saved and regenerated, but their hearts are still inclined to things of this dark world. The apostle John defines the world as *"the lust of the flesh, the lust of the eyes, and the pride of life"* (1 John 2:16). While believers have experienced salvation through Christ as the Passover, their hearts and tastes are still inclined toward the world. They may not yet be mature enough to manifest God's glory as His people.

Manna was small, round, and like thin flakes lying on the ground in the morning hours before the sun got hot (Exo. 16:14). Under the hot sun, manna would melt away. It looks like a coriander seed, signifying that it is something of resurrection life. Every seed is full of life. It presents a picture of death and resurrection. Its taste is akin to a wafer with honey: sweet and nourishing. Everyone was required to gather every morning (except for the Sabbath day), even though some may gather more and others less (Exo. 16:16-17). However, everyone had enough to be filled when they brought it together.

In John 6, manna is presented as Jesus Christ, the bread from heaven. Practically, the Scripture says: *"Man shall not live on bread alone, but by every word that comes from the mouth of God"* (Matt. 4:4). Therefore, for believers today, Manna signifies spending time in God's Word to see and receive Christ — His person and work. Jesus Christ and God's eternal purpose are unveiled in the Scriptures; therefore, Christians should spend time in the Scriptures to see Jesus while turning their hearts to Christ (John 5:39). We really need our understanding reconfigured when coming to the Word of God—this is not "brain food"—it is "Spirit and life" which feeds our human spirit which then provides "the overcoming energy of the Spirit" to transform the soul!

Manna, being small like dew on the ground, meant it was easy work, but to pick up about two quarts of this every day had to be quite tedious. This is similar to reading and studying the Bible. The Bible is easy to read; it does not take a high school degree to understand. However, one needs to devote time to studying and looking for Christ and His mysteries revealed in it (aka "a deep dive"). The food is not the Bible per se, but the Word of God hidden in the pages of the Bible. Many can read the Bible and walk away with laws and ethics, which far too often lead to condemning themselves and judging others. That is not manna. The real food for the spirit and soul is when Jesus Christ and His work are revealed in the Bible. It is best to read His Word with prayer and meditation—don't eat too fast lest you get a stomachache or worse, a headache; in sum: "Taste AND SEE that the Lord is good!" (Psa. 34:8)

Manna, like a seed, is God's word with resurrection and regeneration power. *"For you have been born again, not of perishable seed, but of imperishable, through the living and enduring word of God"* (1 Pet. 1:23). Here, God's word is likened to a seed. The Seed of God, being His Word, has the power to regenerate. God created man with a human spirit. However, man's spirit is inactive until it is "born again." This is the new birth with God's life and nature. When man (male and female) is brought into fellowship with the Word of God, the new birth is experienced. This birth does not perish but is eternal because the Word is living and eternally enduring.

Manna, which is sweet to the taste, signifies that whenever Jesus is seen and encountered in God's Word, one can taste sweetness in fellowship with Him. *"Then I took the little book out of the angel's hand and ate it, and it was as sweet as honey in my mouth. But when I had eaten it, my stomach became bitter* (Rev. 10:10). This scroll is the Word of God. It is sweet when eaten like Manna. Those who see Christ and His eternal purpose in God's Word enjoy this nourishment. As the disciples said to Jesus, *"Lord, to whom shall we go, You have words of eternal life"* (John 6:68). However, after the sweet taste, it becomes bitter in the stomach. This can refer to the operation of the cross of Christ, healing and liberating those tasting the sweetness of Christ. Believers, like the Israelites who had become Egyptians with love for this darkened world in their constitution, needed the transforming power of the cross. Even as they partook of the sweet taste of manna, the death and resurrection of Christ were at work transforming their inner constitution. Cough medicines are a good example: generally, they are sweet to the taste, then after ingesting, the active ingredients commence their mysterious or healing work in the body.

"As newborn babes desire earnestly the pure mental milk of the word, that by it you may grow up to salvation, if indeed you have tasted that the Lord is good" (1 Pet. 2:2-3 DBY). Yes, the Word of God is spiritual; however, spiritual nourishment comes through a mental or logical understanding of His Word. The Greek word for "word" in this verse is *"logikos,"* anglicized to "logical." It is a derivative of the Greek word *Logos,* which is used for Jesus as the eternal Word (John 1:1). To receive milk or food from God's Word, the mind needs to understand the logical thoughts conveyed in the Scripture. Simultaneously, the spirit of faith is activated to have the fellowship of the Spirit through prayer.

If one has received nourishment from this "milk" to grow by reading and studying the Scriptures, there would be an inward response and taste that "the Lord is good." If there is a feeling of guilt, burden, or judging others after studying the Scriptures, that is a sign of missing the nourishment of the Word. The sweet taste of the goodness of the Lord should be present whenever God's Word is understood. It is by the sweet taste of the Lord in the Bible that there is nourishment and growth. A person may know many biblical facts, yet still lack spiritual growth — evidenced by bondage to worldly desires or divisiveness toward believers who differ from them.

Manna was to be gathered before the sun got hot. The hot sun can refer to the hustle and bustle of the day. When problems or demands arise during work or family life, people heat up with anxiety or anger. That would no longer be the time to get into the Word and receive nourishment from the Lord. The best time to read and study Scriptures with prayers for receiving nourishment is before challenges or demands that psychologically fire up a person. Therefore, it is a good practice to set aside a "quiet" time for the Lord before "the sun became hot, it [manna] melted." Jesus as manna will not melt, but the ability to gather for feeding is gone if one casually approaches his portion, thinking it doesn't matter when they should gather. Better get the "early bird special" before they're all gone!

As believers eat Jesus (as bread from heaven), they will live as Jesus lived, depending on the Father (John 6:57). Jesus lived by the Father. The Father was His source while He lived on earth. The Father's love, mind, and will were also Jesus' as He lived on earth. This is the dependency and transformation of all His people feeding on Jesus. The more believers feed on Jesus sweetly and intimately as they gain the knowledge of Him, the more they are transformed by the renewing of the mind (Rom. 12:2). This is God's way of changing His people who were constituted with a satanic nature, transforming them into a people with God's nature. They can now represent God as His people or Household. This is God's *oikonomia* (economy) unveiled by Israel eating manna.

The Riches in the Promised Land

> And they ate of the produce of the land on the day after the Passover, unleavened bread and parched grain, on the very same day. 12 Then the manna ceased on the day after they had eaten the produce of the land, and the children of Israel no longer had manna, but they ate the food of the land of Canaan that year.
>
> *– Josh. 5:11-12*

> For the LORD your God is bringing you into a good land, a land of brooks of water, of fountains and springs, that flow out of valleys and hills; 8 a land of wheat and barley, of vines and fig trees and pomegranates, a land of olive oil and honey; 9 a land in which you will eat bread without scarcity, in which you will lack nothing; . . . 10 When you have eaten and are full, then you shall bless the LORD your God for the good land which He has given you.
>
> *– Deut. 8:7-10*

> "So Moses swore on that day, saying, 'Surely the land where your foot has trodden shall be your inheritance and your children's forever, because you have wholly followed the LORD my God.'"
>
> *– Josh. 14:9*

Many Christians consider the Promised Land prefigures heaven. It means crossing the Jordan River is passing away from this earth and entering heaven, the "good land." If that is the case, then believers will not have the opportunity to consider what can be learned from Israel's journey into the Promised Land. A clear sign that entering the Promised Land is for today, while they are on earth, is that the eating of manna continued for 4-5 days after crossing the Jordan into the Promised Land. Scriptures say that manna did not cease until a day after they started eating the produce of the Good Land. That shows an overlap between manna and the produce of the land for a continuation of feeding. This indicates that the Promised Land should not be interpreted as heaven since manna continued and overlapped while in the Promised Land. This signifies that God cares for the continual dispensing and ingesting of food (*oikonomia*) by His people from the wilderness into the Promised Land, from one environment into the next. Also, Hebrews 3 confirms that believers are to enter into the rest of the Promised Land today: *"Today, if you will hear His voice, do not harden your hearts as in the rebellion"* (Heb. 3:15). Believers are encouraged to go into the rest while on earth.

What was the produce of the land that Israel ate? A diversity of food: Wheat, barley, vines, figs, pomegranates, olive oil, honey, cattle, sheep, fish, and more. There, Israel ate without scarcity. When they were filled, they would bless the Lord for such a good land. Israel went from eating one kind of bread[15] for 40 years to eating a wide variety of food. Since manna represented Christ as bread for food, the overlap with eating the produce of the Land should also signify Christ as food in its variety. This diverse food in the Promised Land represents the unsearchable riches of Christ (Eph. 3:8). In the Good Land, Christ can be enjoyed in a wide range of food, everywhere, anytime, and all the time. While manna had its limitations, the food in the Good Land was unlimited.

Joshua told Israel, *"Every place that the sole of your foot will tread upon I have given you"* (Josh. 1:3). They were to walk throughout the land with hills, valleys, plains, fountains, rivers, and the sea. They were to explore this land, and wherever they found themselves, there was a particular food for them to consume. Jesus Christ as food can be ingested no matter what the environment is — whether high in the hills, low in the valleys, by the sea, or by rivers . . . Christ can be enjoyed. The assortment of food depends on the geography of the land. For example, in the hills there may be vineyards, on the plains there would be wheat, in the middle part of the land, most likely figs and olives, in the southern part there would be dates, by the sea there would be fish, etc. The point is that wherever they tread as they explore and possess the land, they will inevitably discover another kind of food supply. Their diet changed depending on their location and movement at various times.

Often, believers devote their "quiet time" to nourishing themselves in the Word, but as they start their day under the "hot sun," they might neglect being nourished in fellowship with the Lord. They may be unaware that, as they live, depending on the landscape of their lives, they can experience various aspects of Christ. Christ can — and should — be experienced and enjoyed in any environment and at any time of day. Their journey through their day may cause them to be busy, anxious, angry, disheartened, boastful, or simply uneventful. Believers need to explore knowing Christ throughout the landscape of their lives. This matches the experience of the Israelites eating of the produce of the Promised Land: the unsearchable riches of Christ made available to be enjoyed in all environments found in the Good Land.

Examples of Eating the Various Produce of Christ

Let's consider a few examples of how Christ can be experienced and enjoyed as one journeys through the day and encounters various environments and conditions.

---

15   They also ate quail at night, but that was due to their complaining against eating just manna. Numbers 11 describes the story of God giving them so much meat to eat that it came out of their nose, and while they were eating a plague came upon them.

Having successes in life. When life is smooth and there are blessings in a believer's journey, thanksgiving can be offered to God for Christ being the land "flowing with milk and honey." Let's consider when things went well with Jesus. He was at the height of His popularity, having just magnificently raised Lazarus from the dead. He entered Jerusalem with the multitude praising and adoring Him. At that time of fame, He spoke of Himself as a grain of wheat that would produce much fruit. He said: *"Unless a grain of wheat falls into the ground and dies, it remains alone; but if it dies, it produces much grain"* (John 12:24). Likewise, for believers when everything is fine, they should partake of Jesus as their real wheat, which signifies believers need to ingest and experience Christ amid the successes in their lives. Often, when things are going well, Christians can become boastful and neglect the Lord. However, that is the time for eating "wheat," whereby Christ needs to be enjoyed in not loving their successes in life but would rather suffer as a grain of wheat falling into the ground to bear fruit to God (John 12:25). That is the time to appreciate Christ's death not for redemption but for bearing fruit. "Lord Jesus, thank you for your blessings on my life, but I want to experience your death so that You may have more fruit in my life." As Christ is partaken in this way, there may be an inward moaning due to spiritual poverty in the world, resulting in the bearing of comforting fruit (Matt. 5:4).

Anxieties of life. Many Christians may experience various anxieties of life. These challenges open opportunities to explore how Christ can be enjoyed in such times. Eating Christ as barley can be just the food needed. Barley is the first grain to be harvested in the Promised Land. Following the Passover Preparation day when Christ was crucified (13th of Nisan — the Lamb was slain), then on Passover Day, 14 Nisan, the Lamb was eaten. Christ was 3 days and 3 nights in the "grave" (Passover night/day, Nisan 14; Feast of Unleavened Bread night/day, Nisan 15; and the weekly Sabbath day night/day. Nisan 16; and then on Nisan 17 (Saturday eve/Sunday commencement at 6:00 p.m.) the Wave Offering began (He was resurrected — aka Feast of Firstfruits — Lev. 23:9-14: ". . . on the day after the Sabbath the priest shall wave it) — representing the first fruits of the barley harvest. This is the day of the resurrection of Christ (Nisan 16/17), showing that the barley was a symbol of Christ's resurrection.[16]

---

16   It is noteworthy that Noah's Ark landed on the Mountains of Ararat (land) on Nisan 17, showing us that, arising from the waters of death, the land came up out of the water in support of Noah's Ark (Gen. 8:4, the 7th Month in Noah's Era was the month of Nisan, which at the first Passover changed to the First Month on the Hebrew Calendar—Exo. 12:2; Deut. 16:1-2 wherein Abib later became Nisan on the Hebrew Festival Calendar). In summary:

Nisan 13 – Wednesday – Passover Preparation Day - Christ was crucified/cut off (the Lamb was slain) – Exo. 12:3-6 and 6 days before Passover Day (John 12:1; Friday, Nisan 8 through Nisan 13, inclusive)

Nisan 14 – Thursday – Passover Day – Christ was Buried (the Lamb was eaten) – Exo. 12:8 (the evening of the 13th and 14th of Nisan – constituting Day 1, evening and morning)

Nisan 15 – Friday – Feast of Unleavened Bread – Christ is our sinless offering – Exo. 18-19 (the evening of the 14th and commencement of the 15 of Nisan in the "evening" – constituting Day 2, evening and morning

Nisan 16 – Saturday – Feast of First Fruits or Wave Offering—the Resurrection of Christ on 16/17 Nisan – constituting Day 3, evening and morning – Gen. 8:4; Matt. 12:38-42

Nisan 17 – Sunday – Resurrection of Christ (after fulfilling Jonah's Sign, 3 days and 3 nights or Nisan 14, 15, 16 and then on Nisan 17 (6 p.m. – end of Nisan 16) He arose from the grave!

There is a story in John 6:6-13 where 5000 men were hungry and the Lord told His disciples to give them food to eat. They certainly would be anxious and frustrated about how they could feed so many people. This is akin to when many of His followers in their daily living find themselves short of resources to take care of their responsibilities. Jesus asked them what they had, and a lad came up with only five barley loaves and two small fish. The Lord offered thanks, distributed the food, fed all the people, and 12 baskets full were leftover. These 5 barley loaves are symbolic of the resurrection life of Christ. Often, shortages of resources test whether believers will become anxious or will they take the opportunity to ingest Christ as the resurrection power. If they become child-like and partake of Christ's resurrection life, they will find God taking care of their needs. They will have plenty to feed others as well — "Gather up the fragments that remain, so that nothing is lost" (John 6:12). The resurrection life of Christ liberates believers from anxiety and supplies them with spiritual food with enough to nourish the hungry around them — nothing is lost!

Disappointments in life. What if the daily journey takes one to a place of disappointment or disheartened setbacks? Believers should be those who can keep their joy under any circumstance because they *"rejoice in the Lord always"* (Phil. 4:4). They know that partaking of Christ as the vine produces wine. Jesus is the vine that produces wine to cheer both God and man (Judges 9:13). Wine symbolizes joy and celebration. If wine were to run out at a wedding, there's no need to be disappointed: Jesus simply turns the water into the best wine (Jn. 2:9). The followers of Jesus always keep their joy. No frustration can depress them because they partake of Jesus as their joyful wine. When frustration comes, they know it's time to drink spiritual wine — they are driven to drink! Any discouragement only drives them to more wine. What a wonderful Jesus we have as the vine in the Promised Land, continually causing His people to rejoice!

Conflict with others. As believers journey throughout life, conflict will arise with others, including fellow Christians. This can happen at work, school, or even within the family. In such discord or dispute, one should avail oneself of Christ as olive oil. The olive branch is a symbol of peace in the Scriptures. After Noah's flood, to show that conflict and judgment were over, a dove brought back an olive branch (Gen. 8:11). Olive oil in the Bible often represents the Spirit of God as the anointing oil. Olive oil was the main ingredient for the anointing oil, being that of the Spirit upon those anointed (1 Sam. 16:3; Isa. 61:1). In Psalm 133, unity is very much connected to this anointing oil: *"Behold, how good and how pleasant it is for brethren to dwell together in unity! It is like the precious oil upon the head . . ."* Ephesians 4:3 says, *"endeavoring to keep the **unity of the Spirit** in the bond of **peace.**"* Unity and peace are of the Spirit. When there is division and discord, at least one of the parties needs to be a peacemaker by experiencing the unity of the Spirit. When one participates in the fellowship of the Spirit, they can maintain unity because they have *"all lowliness and gentleness, with longsuffering, bearing with one another in love"* (Eph. 4:2). Forgiveness is a natural result of such characteristics. Without forgiveness given to those who offend, it is impossible to have peace and unity.

A conflict can be in the form of persecution from the enemy upon the followers of the Lord for righteousness' sake (Matt. 5:10-11). Believers who journey through life seeking to live godly as a testimony for Jesus will suffer persecution (2 Tim. 3:12). Just as oil results from the heavy pressing on olives, persecution is a kind of pressure on His followers to squeeze out the oil of the Spirit. When those who are persecuted maintain the joy of the Lord under such pressure, the Spirit is released. While they are being pressed, others around them are receiving life (2 Cor. 4:12). Those outside the enjoyment of Christ as the Good Land, when under persecution or pressure, will be downcast, complaining, or lash out. However, those in fellowship with Christ as olive oil will not simply be sustained, but will release and feed others as the Lord did: *"The Spirit of the LORD is upon Me, Because He has anointed Me to preach the gospel to the poor; He has sent Me to heal the brokenhearted, to proclaim liberty to the captives and recovery of sight to the blind, To set at liberty those who are oppressed"* (Luke 4:18). Therefore, believers enjoying the produce of the Good Land are not afraid of any type of challenge or tribulation.

The Mundane and Ordinary can often be a believer's journey through life with nothing special — few highs or lows. That is also an environment to enjoy Christ. Maybe that is the time to enjoy Christ as the pomegranate and fig. A pomegranate chock-full of red juicy seeds is a symbol of the beauty in the life of Christ. Figs denote well-being and security (Micah 4:4). Life may seem mundane, but when Christ, as pomegranates and figs, is eaten, the beauty and security of life are enjoyed and appreciated in ordinary life. Those in fellowship with Christ in their mundaneness store up Christ as the life-giving seed and nourishment for others when ministry opportunities arise.

The point is that eating the produce of the Promised Land is very different from eating manna. While eating manna is in an environment of quietness without distractions, eating the produce of the land is one of exploring and finding Christ in all the various landscapes of life. Every environment throughout a Christian life can be another opportunity for partaking of Christ as food for growth and enjoyment. Historically, Israel ate the Passover first, then manna, and then the produce in the Promised Land; it is not so for New Covenant believers. As soon as a person is "born from above" (regenerated by the Spirit of God), all three types of Christ as food are immediately available. Christ as the Passover is always available for the forgiveness of sins and deliverance; Christ as manna can be eaten immediately in God's Word. Christ, throughout all the landscapes of life, is constantly available to be enjoyed. This is God's *oikonomia* to dispense food to His people.

The Annual Feasts

> And you shall rejoice in your feast, you and your son and your daughter, your male servant and your female servant and the Levite, the stranger and the fatherless and the widow, who [are] within your gates. 15 Seven days you shall keep a sacred feast to the LORD your God in the place which the LORD chooses, because the LORD your God will bless you in all your produce and in all the work of your hands, so that you surely rejoice. 16 **Three times a year** all your males shall appear before the LORD your God in the place which He chooses: at the Feast of Unleavened Bread, at the Feast of Weeks, and at the Feast of Tabernacles; and they shall not appear before the LORD empty-handed. 17 Every man [shall give] as he is able, according to the blessing of the LORD your God which He has given you.
>
> – Deut. 16:14-17

> Then he said to them, "Go your way, eat the fat, drink the sweet, and send portions to those for whom nothing is prepared; for [this] day [is] holy to our Lord. Do not sorrow, for the joy of the LORD is your strength."
>
> – Neh. 8:10

After Joshua led the Israelites to possess the Promised Land, he distributed the inheritance of the land to each tribe (Josh. 13-19). The 12 tribes were scattered throughout the land, including two and a half tribes east of the Jordan River and nine and a half tribes to its west. Some were up north in the mountainous region, some were by the sea, others were in the hills and plains, yet others were in the southern desert region. Each tribe received its inheritance (Josh. 19:49). God desired to keep these 12 tribes as one people to express and represent Him. Therefore, He commanded that all the tribes must come to the place He chose (Jerusalem) to feast and worship three times a year. Even though they had their land, they were to gather as one nation to celebrate and glorify God in Zion/Jerusalem.

Once a tribe settled in the land of their inheritance, they would commence to partake of the food produced in that portion of the land. For example, the tribe in the north, which is mountainous, likely produced apples and could raise goats. The tribes by the sea undoubtedly would have fish, and those in the low hills and plains could readily have figs, vineyards, olives, and cattle. The southernmost tribe probably specialized in dates, or even mangoes. The point is that depending on the geography of the land, the food produced by each tribe would have been quite different.

If each tribe stayed to itself in its inheritance of the land, its diet would be rather limited. They would have missed the riches of the entire land. One of the purposes of God's command for them was to go to the unique place of worship to feast there so that all of Israel could share and partake of the variety of food throughout the land. When each family from every tribe went to the feasts, they were to bring their produce to share with all the tribes. It is at such a time that those southern tribes could enjoy the apples from the north; those from the north could partake of dates and coconuts from the south; those by the sea would share their fish and partake of the grains and cattle from other regions. During the feasts, all the tribes of Israel enjoyed and ate of the fullness of the land they inherited.

Without feasting three times a year, Israel would have missed out on the fruit of their entire inheritance. This was God's dispensing of the riches of the fullness of the Promised Land to His people. If the tribe from the north decided that they would only share (fellowship) with those tribes surrounding them and not with the southern tribes, they would miss out on a large assortment of riches, such as dates and coconuts. The point is that to enjoy the entire land, each tribe must share and fellowship with every one of the 12 tribes throughout the land.

The three corporate feasts were (1) the Feast of Unleavened Bread in the first month of Israel's calendar (Nisan - spring); (2) the Feast of Weeks at Pentecost (50 days after Passover); and (3) the Feast of Tabernacles in the seventh month (Tishrei - fall). It is significant that the Hebrew Scriptures only recorded two Feasts of Tabernacles after leaving Egypt until after their return from the Babylonian captivity, a period of approximately 1000 years (1445-537 BC). The first one was when Solomon finished building the temple. The second time was after the return from Babylon to the rebuilding of the temple and the walls of Jerusalem. Both times were related to God's temple and Jerusalem. The last feast of the year (Tabernacles) has everything to do with the building of God's house, an archetype of God's Democratic Assembly in the New Testament. This Feast of Tabernacles was an abundant time of "fellowship" where all the Israelite families gathered in literally thousands of "open tents" to share the abundance of the Promised Land with one another — from "booth to booth." What a wondrous picture of the fellowship of God's People under the New Covenant "from house to house."

The Feast of Unleavened Bread, associated with the Passover, represents the beginning of Israel's journey with their deliverance from Egypt. The Feast of Tabernacles marks the culmination of Israel's harvest cycle and symbolizes the destination of their journey — a place where the unity of God's people is visibly expressed in Jerusalem. God's temple is built to house God's glory on earth. Historically, the Feast of Tabernacles is the most joyous of all the feasts. Compared to the Feast of Unleavened Bread in the Spring, the Feast of Tabernacles has the most assortment of produce to share since it is at the end of harvest season. It embodies the land's riches for all the inhabitants to enjoy and partake. Significantly, an Israelite can only have this pleasure by going to Jerusalem for this abundant feast.

The Feast of Tabernacles, the concluding feast, is where God's joyous people find strength. The "joy of the Lord is your strength" is a popular saying among Christians for encouragement. In context, this was spoken during the Feast of Tabernacles when Israel came together in unity (Neh. 8:10). This joy of the Lord was not spoken of in the state of their division or their captivity in Babylon. This strengthening joy is among those who were once scattered and came back in unity for God's purpose. Therefore, when believers lack joy or strength, they should be reminded to be in the Feast of Tabernacles — come together with diverse believers and share the Lord in unity.

The first time the idea of blessing the Lord came up in the Hebrew Scriptures was a prophecy: *"When you have eaten and are full, then you shall bless the LORD"* (Deut. 8:10). This prophecy was fulfilled at the Feast of Tabernacles. When all Israel came together to feast on the riches of the entire land and were full, then they blessed the Lord. The Lord first ensured that His people were richly fed, which resulted in God being blessed by His people. This again is the principle of His *oikonomia*. For the Father to be glorified by His family, His family should be fed and grow to maturity. Israel's maturation was exhibited by the building of God's temple, where God was glorified. The Lord was truly blessed by His dwelling place on earth, and His glory filled the house during the Solomonic dedication (2 Chron. 7:1-3). Israel gathered to feast on the rich assortment of the land, and God was blessed with a House where He was glorified. The temple was the result of God's dispensing His riches to Israel (*oikonomia*): A diverse people (including strangers or foreigners) in unity, glorifying God.

Inheriting God, the Holy Spirit

> . . . that the blessing of Abraham might come upon the Gentiles ["ethnos" or "nations"] in Christ Jesus, that we might receive the promise of the Spirit through faith.
>
> – Gal. 3:14

In Him you also [trusted], after you heard the word of truth, the gospel of your salvation; in whom also, having believed, you were sealed with the Holy Spirit of promise, 14 who is the guarantee [foretaste] of our **inheritance** until the redemption of the purchased possession, to the praise of His glory.

– Eph. 1:13-14

. . . to open their eyes, [in order] to turn [them] from darkness to light, and [from] the power of Satan to God, that they may receive forgiveness of sins and an inheritance among [in] those who are sanctified by faith in Me.

– Acts 26:18

. . . the eyes of your understanding being enlightened; that you may know what is the hope of His calling, what are the riches of the glory of His inheritance **in** the saints,

– Eph. 1:18

. . . that Christ may dwell in your hearts through faith; that you, being rooted and grounded in love, 18 may be able to comprehend with all the saints what [is] the width and length and depth and height — 19 to know the love of Christ which passes knowledge; that you may be filled with all the fullness of God.

– Eph. 3:17-19

Israel's inheritance was the Promised Land — the entire land as far as the eyes could see east, west, north, and south as God told Abraham (Gen. 13:14-15). The 12 tribes were spread out, each settling in a specific part of the land. To enjoy the riches of the entire land, all 12 tribes must come to Jerusalem to share and eat the produce of the land produced by each tribe. This was God's desire: that through these feasts, Israel would be united, whereby God would be glorified. Under the New Covenant (Testament), the reality of this principle was at the very heart of Paul's calling and prayer. The **inheritance** for the followers of Jesus is akin to the earthly inheritance of the Israelites within the Promised Land. Praise the Lord — it is the Spirit of Christ Himself within the believers.

According to Galatians 3:14, the Holy Spirit is the promise to Abraham that has come upon the believers of Christ. The entire promise of the Spirit came into and upon all of His people by faith in Jesus. God made an inheritance for His people through the Holy Spirit. Ephesians 1:14 supports this reality: at the moment of faith when hearing the gospel, a believer is sealed by the Holy Spirit of promise. What was promised by God was immediately sealed upon a believer at the moment of regeneration ("born again"). Waiting was not necessary, nor was any effort or work needed; faith only sealed a believer of Jesus Christ. A seal in those days fused the wax onto the paper and included a signet, a mark of ownership. A seal upon a believer means the Spirit is now permanently placed upon the inner being of a believer, and the ownership belongs to God alone. When the angels in the universe see this person, they know this person belongs to God — their destiny is bound to eternal glory.

The Holy Spirit is also a guarantee, which in Greek means a "foretaste of the fullness to come" (Thayer's). This means the believer receives the Holy Spirit as the guarantee of the coming full taste or portion. If believers enjoy the Holy Spirit today, they can be certain that much more of God is awaiting them for their full enjoyment. Additionally, the fullness of the Holy Spirit is more of the same Spirit believers received when they were initially sealed. The more a believer enjoys the riches of the Spirit today, the more they look forward to the fullness yet to come. Conversely, if a believer does not enjoy the Spirit today, they will likely be disappointed in the coming kingdom, which is centered on God in the fullness of His riches. For example, if one's focus on the future kingdom is on a physical celestial palace, it may not meet their expectations.

Paul said that His calling was to make known the *"inheritance in those who are sanctified."* Most Christian teachers focus on the first part: *"to turn [them] from darkness to light, and [from] the power of Satan to God, that they may receive forgiveness of sins."* However, Paul also desired to open people's eyes to see the **inheritance** afforded to each believer. However, this inheritance is **in** the saints: all those sanctified by faith in the Lord Jesus. Every believer is set apart or "sanctified." They all have been sealed by the Holy Spirit. They are unique and not common like unbelievers. God has placed Himself as the **inheritance** in each believer. God's people need their eyes opened to see this wonderful reality.

Some translators use the word "among" those sanctified instead of "in." However, the Greek word *"en"* primarily means "in" (Strong's). It is more accurate to say that the believer's inheritance is **in** those sanctified by faith. In other words, the believer's inheritance is in all the other believers. The Spirit is needed to open the inner eyes to see this: "My inheritance of God is in all the other believers of Christ." God, as the Spirit, is in all His people, and if I want my entire inheritance, I need to seek and know the Spirit within the other believers.

Ephesians 1:18 supports this same revelation. Paul prayed that the eyes of a believer's understanding be opened so that each one may know *"the riches of the glory of His inheritance in the saints."* God's people need a revelation to have this understanding:

the riches of their inheritance, being God, are in the saints. God has placed Himself within His people; therefore, if you want all His riches, you need all His people. If you cut off and disregard some of His people, you are cheating yourself and will miss a portion of your inheritance. If you want all your inheritance, you can only receive it from all the other saints.

For example, a rich father has 10 children. In his will, he distributes his $10 million estate to them. However, to ensure his children have a good relationship with each other and continue as a family, he decides to distribute his inheritance to them in a way that they need to be open and responsive to each other. He leaves each sibling one million dollars, but only $100,000.00 is given directly to each one. The other $900,000 is given to each sibling, earmarked for the other 9 siblings – $100,000 each. That way, for each sibling to truly receive the $1 million, they would each have to collect $100,000 from their 9 siblings. In other words, if anyone cuts off a sibling, that one would lose $100,000. He would lose another $100,000 for each additional sibling alienated. Therefore, for any of the father's children to receive their total $1 million, they would have to stay in good standing with the other 9 siblings. If they did not have good relations with, let's say, four other siblings, then $400,000.00 would be deducted from their $1,000,000.00 estate; therefore, they would only receive $600,000.00.

The inheritance of God is spread out among and in the saints. When believers are divided and do not receive fellowship from those they disagree with over doctrinal, political, or social issues, they, in essence, cut off some of their inheritance. The more diverse believers they alienate, the smaller their inheritance. Most may end up only having a spiritual relationship with their own tribe (Baptists, Pentecostals, Catholics, rich, or poor, etc.). If so, their inheritance has been reduced!

One may wonder, "If I have God, don't I have the entire God? How can God be in pieces, spread among different kinds of believers? If I have God, why do I need other believers to have all the riches of my inheritance?" Yes, you have the entire God when you receive Jesus Christ as Savior and Lord; however, you do not know how rich God is in all the ways He can be enjoyed and experienced. Your experience of God is limited to your circumstances. There is no way for you to know how God can be enjoyed in an environment foreign to you. For example, if you are a man, there is no way you can know how to experience His riches as a woman. The only way to know God's riches experienced by this woman is to be in fellowship with this sister by hearing how she enjoys and experiences the riches of Christ.

God's inheritance is spread out among His people, which includes Jews, Gentiles, rich, poor, blacks, whites, Asians, men, women, old, young, educated, uneducated, conservative, liberal, Catholics, Baptists, Pentecostals, orthodox, etc. The inheritance of God is within all these different kinds of people. The more one fellowships with God's diverse people, the more there is an appreciation of the riches of God who can fit into all the various circumstances and be enjoyed. How can a master know how a slave enjoys the riches of Christ and vice versa? How can an Evangelical identify how a Catholic believer enjoys Christ without fellowship and vice versa?

> . . . that Christ may dwell in your hearts through faith; that you, being rooted and grounded in love, 18 may be able to comprehend with all the saints what [is] the width and length and depth and height — 19 to know the love of Christ which passes knowledge; that you may be filled with all the fullness of God.
>
> – Eph. 3:17-19

This was a portion of Paul's prayer to the Father. In this prayer, Paul seems to have the Old Testament Promised Land in view since he illustrated that believers should be rooted and grounded. Rooting and grounding are on land. Then he speaks of knowing the dimensions of Christ, which can be an allusion to the four directions of the Good Land (Gen. 13:15). The "all" in "all the saints" does not refer to all as in quantity, such as: Comprehend with a million saints. The "all" in verse 18 is "all kinds" or "all types" (Thayer's) of saints. It is among diverse believers that we find the empowerment to know the dimensions of Christ and the love of God, which surpasses our natural understanding.

If a person only fellowships with one kind of believer, those like him, then he may only know one dimension of Christ. Even if he gathers with 1 million believers, since they are all the same kind, they are essentially the same tribe experiencing the same portion of the Promised Land. However, even if he gathers with only 15 or so people, yet there is a variety of rich, poor, socially liberal, and conservative, Catholic, Baptists, Pentecostal, white, black, and Asian, each with different experiences of Christ due to their distinct journey, then the dimensions of Christ with His love are comprehended. The word "comprehend" in Greek means "seize, possess, apprehend, attain" (Strong's). The multi-dimensionality of Christ and His love can only be known or possessed in a fellowship with various believers.

This is the environment of the Lord's Ekklesia (Democratic Assembly) where it is necessary to have believers from different perspectives and experiences (1 Cor. 11:19). This is where each can appreciate the riches of Christ experienced in a wide assortment of environments. It is unsearchable how rich Christ is as believers explore the love of Christ operating in all these diverse believers.

In the early gatherings (Ekklesia), without fellowshipping with Gentile believers, the Jewish believers would not understand how someone from the Nations could experience Christ while eating unclean food or having no special "Sabbath" day. Today, a Christian in the Reformed tradition can only know how Christ can be experienced in the Pentecostal gifts by fellowshipping with believers in that "tribe."

In this kind of *"ekklesia"* fellowship, the participants are *"filled with the fullness of God."* Back in Ephesians 1:23, the fullness of God is the Body of Christ, His Democratic Assembly (Ekklesia). It is important to recognize that understanding Christ and His love requires connecting with all types of believers. The more this fellowship is experienced among a variety of believers, the more they will be filled — the result is the fullness of God. By relating to all the different kinds of believers, the ability to know the unsearchable dimensions of Christ is realized.

In conclusion, God's *oikonomia* of dispensing food to His Household comes not just from Him directly through His apostles (ministers), but through all the members of the Body of Christ. By receiving and dispensing the unsearchable riches of Christ among diverse believers, God's Household, His Ekklesia, is built up and manifested to the glory of God.

7

THE HIDDEN MYSTERY, CHRIST IN YOU, THE HOPE OF GLORY

After David's conquest of the Promised Land and Solomon built the temple, then God's glory filled the temple. This glory was God expressed in the unity of His people. God gained a kingdom on earth that expressed and represented Him. Israel achieved the height of its triumph due to the keeping of the Mosaic Covenant. This outcome was not due to Israel's righteousness or holiness but their eventual faithful practice of God's covenant (initiated at Mt. Sinai).

However, the Mosaic Covenant was not permanent or infallible, since it was an imperfect archetype of what God intended. Therefore, after a short period of glory with the Solomonic Temple, Israel started degrading — even during Solomon's reign. He began to worship idols and turned his back on God. Israel's decline continued for some 242 years (Solomon's Temple Dedication in 954 B.C. until 712 B.C., the final date of Israel's Northern Ten Tribes deportation into Assyria) and an additional 126 years (712-586 B.C.) when Judah's two southern tribes were brought into Babylonian Captivity with the Temple's destruction under King Nebuchadnezzar. During this period of devastation, the major and minor prophetic books were written, beginning with Obediah. There were 10 prophetic books written to Israel and Judah for over 200 years, warning them of imminent destruction if they did not repent from their sinful ways. God was very patient with them.

Simultaneously, within these prophetic warnings, there were encouraging words focused on the coming of a New Covenant and the re-gathering of all 12 tribes of Israel (Ephraim and Judah) for the renewal and fulfillment of God's eternal purpose. This chapter will first detail the implications of the New Covenant, which is essentially Christ's Spirit in His people, and the following chapter will focus on what should be impossible by any stretch of the imagination: how can there be the restoration of **all Israel? (i.e., ALL 12 tribes)**

For if that first [covenant] had been faultless, then no place would have been sought for a second. 8 Because finding fault with them, He says: "Behold, the days are coming, says the LORD, when I will make a **new covenant** with **the house of Israel** and with the **house of Judah**. [Note: Both houses are considered all Israel.]

– Heb. 8:7-8

[Is] the law then against the promises of God? Certainly not! For if there had been a law given which could have given life, truly righteousness would have been by the law.

– Gal. 3:21

The Mosaic ("first") covenant was flawed because it could not transmit God's eternal life into His people – it was "spiritual" but without divine empowerment (Rom. 7:14). No matter one's faithful adherence to the Law, the inward being and nature of the Israelites and the foreigners who kept the Mosaic Covenant did not change. Their nature continued as one fallen in sin: *"For it is not possible that the blood of bulls and goats could take away sins"* (Heb. 10:4). Their sins were only covered over by the blood of the animal sacrifices, waiting for the real sacrificial blood of Jesus Christ (Rom. 3:25-26). Additionally, the life of God needs to be received to express and represent God's reality. As shown by the manna, offerings, and produce of the Promised Land, Israel only received God's life as an archetype of Christ, the reality. They were a shadow of receiving the coming of the real Person Who is the reality – Jesus Christ (Col. 2:16-17).

The New Covenant has everything to do with the hidden mystery of *"Christ in you, the hope of glory."* The prophet Ezekiel spoke of the coming New Covenant in this way: *"I will put My Spirit within you and cause you to walk in My statutes, and you will keep My judgments and do them"* (Ezek. 36:26-27). This prophecy was impossible to fulfill until the coming of Jesus Christ. This phrase concerning the Spirit being within His people was never described in this way concerning any of His people in the Hebrew Scriptures. Jesus confirmed this when He said the Spirit, so received, was not yet because Jesus was not yet glorified" (John 7:39). This was something mysterious and unique that God was to do: Put His Spirit within them. How could the holy God reside within His people?

So, let's jump into the hidden mystery unveiled in the New Testament, for it is here we find the New Covenant's "empowerment."

Christ in You, the Hope of Glory

> ... of which [His Body, the ekklesia] I became a minister according to the stewardship from God, which was given to me for you, to fulfill the word of God, 26 **the mystery which has been hidden from ages and from generations, but now has been revealed to His saints.** 27 To them God willed to make known what are the riches of the glory of this mystery among the Gentiles: which is **Christ in you, the hope of glory**.
>
> – Col. 1:25-27

It is indeed a hidden mystery: **Christ in you, Jews and Gentiles**. The Gentiles were outcasts; therefore, Apostle Paul said concerning them as *"afar off . . . without Christ, being aliens from the commonwealth of Israel and strangers from the covenants of promise, having no hope and without God in the world"* (Eph. 2:17, 12). Nevertheless, for Paul to complete or fulfill the Word of God, he was chosen to make known this mystery hidden from both angels and men — **Christ in the Nations is the hope of glory**. Even now, when the Hebrew Scriptures are read, it is not easy to see this mystery revealed. The Gentiles were not God's people. God gave laws to separate His chosen people, Israel, from the Gentiles (Acts 10:28). Yet, Paul said this was a mystery and that the word of God would not be complete until he made known — Christ in the Gentiles!

Therefore, without Paul writing this bold and definitive declaration, this matter may have stayed hidden in the Hebrew Scriptures. With Paul's stewardship (*oikonomia*) for the building up of the Lord's Body, "Christ in you" was the focus of His message. He labored to preach and teach with all wisdom this reality of Christ within the believers (both Jews and Gentiles). Spiritual maturity for Christians is when they live the life of **Christ-in-you**, no matter the circumstances or challenges they face. What an awesome reality and mystery to have Christ, the God-man in resurrection, within every believer.

It boggles the mind to ponder this: Christ in you. Is Christ really in His followers, or is it simply a metaphor? People may say that Christ is not actually in you; rather, it just means you think about Christ so much that he is "in you." It would be like saying, "Football is in him." Football is not actually in that person. It means he loves football so much that it is in him. Scripture reveals that Christ is actually in people, like the food they eat is literally in them. Many other scriptures show that Jesus Christ is truly in His believers. Here are a few:

> Examine yourselves [as to] whether you are in the faith. Test yourselves. Do you not know yourselves, that Jesus Christ is in you?
>
> –2 Cor. 13:5

> . . . that Christ may dwell in your hearts through faith; that you, being rooted and grounded in love,
>
> – Eph. 3:17

> I have been crucified with Christ; it is no longer I who live, but Christ lives in me; and the [life] which I now live in the flesh I live by faith in the Son of God, who loved me and gave Himself for me.
>
> – Gal. 2:20

With Christ dwelling in believers, their positive character and attributes become indistinguishable, whether it is Christ or them. They become two living as one. They have their original God-created personality and characteristics, but they also have the new divine eternal life of Christ in them. When they live out "Christ-in-you," then who is living — them or Christ? It is hard to describe such mysterious life and living. Theologians have used different words to describe this reality of living together with Christ as one: Union, joined, grafted, mingled, co-inherent, the "crucified life," the "inner life," and other expressions. There is no separation between believers and Christ living as one; there abides distinction, but Christ and the believer are inseparable!

Consider Galatians 2:20: Paul declares he is crucified with Christ and no longer lives, but Christ lives in him. The next sentence, he says, ". . . the life which I now live in the flesh," which he clearly says he lives. So, is Paul living or not? First, he says, "It is no longer I who live," then immediately afterward he says, "I live by the faith of the Son of God." This is the mystery of two lives living as one. Paul was not "replaced." He was very much there. When Paul lived by faith, Christ was the one living in him. When he said, "It is no longer I who live," this referred to the man without Christ. That man without Christ has been crucified. Now, he is a new man forever with Christ living in him.

The physical illustration that can be used for two becoming one is eating and drinking. The food eaten starts outside the person as a separate item. The person eating and the food are two. However, after eating and digesting, the food and the person become one. They become inseparable and, frankly, indistinguishable. Where does food in his body begin, and where does it end? His entire body is made up of the food he eats. Additionally, the ingested food is the fuel that **empowers** him to live daily. He is uniquely dependent on food to live. Simultaneously, food is living in and through him.

> Whoever eats My flesh and drinks My blood has eternal life, and I will raise him up at the last day. 55 "For My flesh is food indeed, and My blood is drink indeed. 56 "He who eats My flesh and drinks My blood abides in Me, and I in him. 57 "As the living Father sent Me, and I live because of the Father, so he who feeds on Me will live because of Me.
>
> – John 6:54-57

Jesus' words are shocking: eat Him and drink Him. He used a physical illustration to show the relationship between Him and His believers: ". . . abides in Me and I in him." They are still two but are also one. They exist and live within each other — co-inherence. Just as the Father and the Son are two, they are absolutely one. They existed within each other. Therefore, by ingesting Jesus, believers live by or because of Him just as Jesus lives because of the Father. The Father was the source of life in Jesus as the incarnated Man. He could not live without or outside the Father. Similarly, by ingesting Jesus, believers are **empowered** to live as Jesus lived. This is the hidden mystery of "Christ in you, the hope of glory."

What does this look like in the Christian life? Consider these verses.

> But the fruit of the Spirit is love, joy, peace, longsuffering, kindness, goodness, faithfulness, 23 gentleness, self-control . . .
>
> – Gal. 5:22-23

Surprisingly, the fruit of the Spirit does not include any characteristics that are supernatural or miraculous. Rather, they are very human. Every person can claim to have such characteristics. Every parent and bridegroom can truly declare they have love. What joy the bridegroom shares with his loving bride. There is peace experienced by a mother watching her healthy baby asleep. Every person can testify to possessing other similar characteristics. Even the most sinful person can claim they have shown kindness, faithfulness, and gentleness to others at one time or another. These items are part of human nature. So why is it called the fruit of the Spirit? Do people need the Spirit if they already possess these attributes? There must be something more.

The "something more" is when these characteristics run out due to the limitations and deficiencies of human life. Yes, human nature does have these characteristics since they are created in God's image and likeness, but they are finite and discretionary. Love can run out if the person they love becomes too difficult. Joy and peace can disappear easily when there are obstacles. A person can suffer for a limited period before they lash out at people around them or fall into despair. Forgiveness may only be extended to those still providing value, but cannot be extended to the one who is offending — this individual can be discarded. People are generally very selective about whom they want to show favor and to whom they show aversion.

Since Christ is in them, believers bearing the fruit of the Spirit are very different in their conduct and inner being. Their nature is no longer purely human, but also eternally divine. The same human characteristics are now empowered and enhanced by the Spirit of Christ. The "I" who has a joint union with Christ displays these characteristics in embattled environments. In other words, the harsher and the more challenging the circumstances, the more love, joy, peace, kindness, etc. are experienced and manifested. The "Christ-in-you life" is most evident in adversity — precisely when, by human logic and expectation, these qualities can no longer persist. How can one love an enemy? How can there be joy when the surroundings are dismal? How can one be disrespected and insulted yet still show gentleness and kindness toward the offenders? How can one suffer for a long period and not be in despair, but have remaining peace? The unique answer is the mystery unveiled: *"Christ in you, the hope of glory."*

The *Christ-in-you life* includes the effectiveness of His crucifixion, resurrection, and ascension. Jesus said, *"I am the resurrection and the life"* (John 11:25). Knowing the *Christ-in-you life* includes experiencing His resurrection. There is nothing more terminal and cruel than death. Nevertheless, Jesus Christ conquered death and the grave in His resurrection. Remarkably, there is no experience and manifestation of resurrection without death. The most powerful negative force in the universe has been made of no effect by the beauty and glory of resurrection. Christ's resurrected and ascended life operates in His people because He lives in them.

Jesus Christ's human-divine resurrection life in His followers shines amid challenges, oppositions, and devastations. Therefore, His followers are not fearful of whatever may come. The "hope of glory" is not only in the future resurrection but also today. Against all odds, glory is manifested in a person's life who lives "Christ-in-you."

> Therefore, as [the] elect of God, holy and beloved, put on tender mercies, kindness, humility, meekness, longsuffering; 13 bearing with one another, and forgiving one another, if anyone has a complaint against another; even as Christ forgave you, so you also [must do]. 14 But above all these things put on love, which is the bond of perfection.
>
> – Col. 3:12-14

> . . . with all lowliness and gentleness, with longsuffering, bearing with one another in love, 3 endeavoring to keep the unity of the Spirit in the bond of peace.
>
> – Eph. 4:2-3

Additionally, the "you" in "Christ in you" is a collective you (plural), not an individual "you." Jesus Christ is in a corporate group of people who are His Body, His Democratic Assembly (Ekklesia). This requires the oneness of His diverse people. Individuals need His Body to experience and display the fullness of the reality of Christ-in-you. An individual outside the experience of the Body of Christ, where there are contradictory views, would miss the testing of whether they are living "Christ-in-you." It is in God's Ekklesia that the Christ-in-you life can grow and mature.

The context of Colossians 3 is that in the new man, where Christ is all and in all, all kinds of diverse people are at odds with one another: Greek and Jew, circumcised and uncircumcised, barbarian, Scythian, slave and free (Col. 3:11). These people groups could be polar opposites to each other and might even consider each other as enemies. Nevertheless, through faith, they all have come into the same community of Christ. It is impossible not to have conflict, debate, criticism, and division. It would be much easier to have segregated communities instead of fellowshipping as one in Christ's Body. However, the *Christ-in-you life* is not meant to be lived by individuals outside the fellowship of the Body of Christ. It is Christ in **you, His Body**.

In His Body, the New Man, the various characteristics are listed: *tender mercies, kindness, humility, meekness, longsuffering; bearing with one another, forgiving one another, and above all putting on love* (Col. 3:12-14). These qualities are tested in situations of tension and potential conflict. It is normal and widespread among Christians to segregate themselves into groups, whether it is ethnically, doctrinally, demographically, or according to spiritual/holiness practices. There is a feeling of comfort and like-mindedness when they are with their kind. However, the glory of God is displayed in the oneness of His diverse people. It is Christ in the **plural you**, the hope of glory. "Christ-in-you" is displayed when diverse and often contrarian believers forgive and love one another.

Again, Ephesians 4 supports this need to live Christ-in-you among believers who might be antagonistic toward each other (such as Jews and Greeks, or masters and slaves). These characteristics are similar to the fruit of the Spirit, which are pronounced: lowliness and gentleness, with longsuffering, bearing with one another in love. The purpose of these divine-human traits is to keep the unity of the Spirit. The unity of the Lord's Body needs Christ-in-you. How believers interact with polar-opposite Christians manifests their maturity in living a life of "Christ-in-you." The glory of God is displayed in this oneness of His people as seen in the archetype of the Solomonic Temple.

The Mosaic Covenant is Obsolete, Christ in You Is the New Covenant

> In that He says, "A new [covenant]," He has made the first obsolete. Now what is becoming obsolete and growing old is ready to vanish away.
>
> – Heb. 8:13
>
> Then He took the cup, and gave thanks, and gave [it] to them, saying, "Drink from it, all of you." 28 "For this is My blood of the new covenant, which is shed for many for the remission of sins."
>
> – Matt. 26:27-28

The New Covenant is the fulfillment of the Mosaic Covenant. The Mosaic Covenant pointed to the coming Christ and His Democratic Assembly. The Mosaic Covenant was a mere shadow of Christ (Col. 2:16-17). Since the Mosaic Covenant was only a shadow, it could not fulfill God's purpose for eternity. It could only fulfill God's purpose temporarily with David and Solomon's temple. God's eternal purpose needs the New Covenant, which Jesus Christ enacted by His blood. With the coming of the New, the Mosaic (old) is obsolete and ready to disappear.

Here is the ordination of the New Covenant: Christ shed His blood, and in resurrection, His followers partake of Him, and He dwells **in** them. The symbol of living by Christ in faith is eating and drinking the bread and the cup at His table. The weekly or daily participation in the Lord's Supper declares His *oikonomia*: ingesting Christ as the living Spirit whereby He lives in His people. Since His death and resurrection enacted the New Covenant, believers are commanded to eat and drink Him (Matt. 26:26-27). Through Jesus Christ, the New Covenant promised in the Hebrew Scriptures has arrived in fullness (Jer. 31:31).

Historical Review at the Time of Prophecy concerning the New Covenant.

The portion of history amid the prophetic writings concerning the New Covenant is critical to its understanding, since the Mosaic Covenant could not give life. Although it was spiritual, it was flawed, because its standards (which described the very nature of God) could not be sustained by Israel. She fell and quickly degraded from her zenith. Solomon, in his sinful nature, had 700 wives and 300 concubines. His heart was turned away from the Lord to the idols of his wives (1 Kings 11:3-4). God was angry with Solomon and said his kingdom would be taken away during his son, Rehoboam's reign.

Thus, the kingdom of David would be divided, with ten of the twelve tribes going to his servant Jeroboam. Solomon's son, Rehoboam, would remain with 2 tribes (1 Kings 11:11-37). So it happened that after Solomon's death, Jeroboam, with the ten tribes of Israel, came to Rehoboam asking for tax and labor relief. Rehoboam not only refused but demanded more to make their burden even greater. Due to this unbearable *yoke*, Jeroboam led away the ten northern tribes and became their king as prophesied by the Lord (1 Kings 12:1-24).

Although God divided the administration or kingdom to be governed into two different kings or ministers, He never intended the 12 tribes to stop their united worship of Him. God didn't forsake His choice of a singular place for all 12 tribes to worship in unity. Jerusalem, with the temple, remained the place for all His people to gather for worship and feasting. Worship to God can only transpire when His diverse people come together as one in the place He has chosen.

God made Jeroboam king of Israel's Ten Northern Tribes, but Jeroboam was insecure. He did not want Israel to go to Jerusalem to worship Yahweh as commanded. Instead, he reasoned that if Israel (also known as Ephraim, Jezreel, Samaria) went to the temple to worship, their hearts and loyalty would return to Judah. Therefore, he systematized division between God's people by setting up two golden calves in two worship centers with his non-Levitical priests and a new time of the feast (1 Kings 12:26-33). This golden calf worship was institutionalized, whereupon a wall of separation between God's people took place. God never intended this separation in worship to take place.

Jeroboam's scheme and action in systematizing a permanent division among the 12 tribes were so abhorrent that God repeatedly remembered and condemned the "breach of Jeroboam." Throughout the history of the 18 kings of Israel after Jeroboam (a total of 19), all continued in the ways of Jeroboam — all were "evil." God used the phrase "sins (ways) of Jeroboam" 21 times to emphasize that Jeroboam's division resulted in Israel's apostasy. Due to Jeroboam's division, Israel-Ephraim and Judah were in continual conflict, with five outbreaks of war between them. It was so terrible that in one war between brothers against brothers, 500,000 Israelites died in battle (2 Chron. 13:17).

Israel never did come back to God. All the kings of Israel (ten tribes) worshipped idols and were evil in God's eyes. They departed from God, the temple, the priesthood, and the law of Moses. They became like the nations around them by worshipping every kind of idol. Israel never repented and was designated as "Lo-Ruhamah" (no mercy) and "Lo-Ammi" (not my people) by Yahweh (Hosea 1:6, 9). Therefore, God divorced Ephraim-Israel and put them away (Jer. 3:8).

God used Assyria to judge and defeat the Ten Tribes (Israel-Ephraim) and deported them to Assyria (circa BC 745-712). The Assyrian Empire occupied about 120 nations at the time. When the Assyrians conquered a tribe or nation, their strategy was to swap out the population, scatter the conquered people, and assimilate them among the Assyrians' vast empire. Assyria did so to Israel's Ten Northern Tribes. The Assyrians assimilated them — *"Israel is swallowed up; now they are **among the Nations"*** (Hosea 8:7-8). Ephraim became synonymous with the *Nations* (Gen. 48:19; Hosea 1:10; 2:23; 8:7-8; Acts 15:14, 17). They did not just get lost to be found one day. They disappeared as identifiable tribes. Since Israel was already worshipping idols like the nations around them, it was reasonable that they easily integrated into the nations through generations of intermarriage — in essence and substance, they became utterly identified with the "nations." The Samaritans, mentioned in the New Testament and who had no dealings with the Jews, were typical of such a mixed race.

On the other hand, Judah (with Benjamin), despite a few evil kings among 20 kings, generally kept the things of God's Mosaic covenant intact; furthermore, Jacob had prophesied that *". . . the scepter shall not depart from Judah, nor a lawgiver from between his feet, until Shiloh comes; and to Him shall be the obedience of the people"* (Gen. 49: 10). This "Shiloh" refers to the "Prince of Peace" and preserves the Messianic line of Judah wherein the Son of David (through King David of Judah) preserved the linage unto the birth of Jesus, the Messiah. Judah remained married to God. However, they eventually also forsook God to the point where God had to discipline them by sending the Babylonians to defeat and exile them to Babylon. Indeed, Judah was described as more "treacherous" than her sister, Israel (Jer. 3:10-11); however, Israel was given a "certificate of divorce" by Yahweh (Jer. 3:8). Nevertheless, there were still those from Judah, like Daniel and many others, who worshipped and prayed to Yahweh in captivity. They remained distinct and separate in the land of captivity (aka, the Seventy Years of Babylonian Captivity — CIR. 608-537 BC).

Isaiah – The Coming Messiah Restoring His People by His Oikonomia

Traditionally, the Hebrew Scriptures are divided into 4 sections: the Pentateuch or the Torah, the historical books, the poetic books, and the prophetic books. The prophets started their ministries in the 8th century BCE and lasted until Malachi during the 5th century BCE. Isaiah is the first of the "prophetic books." His ministry was contemporary during the defeat of Israel (the Ten Northern Tribes) and their deportation. He was fully aware of God's judgment on Israel-Ephraim and prophesied to Judah in the hope of their repentance because they, too, were forsaking God as their northern brethren.

Most theologians consider the book of Isaiah to span three distinct periods: Before Judah's defeat, 70 years of captivity, and their return to Judea after the 70 years. The three periods are divided by Isaiah chapters 1-39, 40-55, and 56-66.

This section of the text will focus on Christ and His restoration work to bring Christ into His people in the first two periods, from chapters 1 through 55. Amid the apostasy and subsequent judgment of God's people, hope was delivered by the prophet Isaiah. It is not the end. There will be a new beginning with the coming of the Messiah!

> Therefore the Lord Himself will give you a sign: Behold, the virgin shall conceive and bear a Son, and shall call His name Immanuel.
>
> — Isa. 7:14

> For unto us a Child is born, Unto us a Son is given; And the government will be upon His shoulder. And His name will be called Wonderful, Counselor, Mighty God, Everlasting Father, Prince of Peace. 7 Of the increase of [His] government and peace [There will be] no end.
>
> — Isa. 9:6-7

What clear prophecies concerning the coming of Jesus, the Messiah! Jesus was born of the virgin Mary and was called Immanuel — God with us (Matt. 1:23). He brought God to man. This baby was the Son of God, and His name is called Mighty God and the Everlasting Father. He and His Father are one (John 10:30). He is Wonderful! He is the Prince of Peace, our Shiloh, and His kingdom will be one of eternal peace. These verses speak of His person being the God-man

> And in that day there shall be a Root of Jesse, Who shall stand as a banner to the people; For the Gentiles [aka "the Nations"] shall seek Him, And His resting place shall be glorious.
>
> — Isa. 11:10

> Therefore thus says the Lord GOD: "Behold, I lay in Zion a stone for a foundation, A tried stone, a precious cornerstone, a sure foundation; Whoever believes will not act hastily."
>
> — Isa. 28:16

These two portions speak of His work as the Messiah. Remember, the Gentiles/Nations assimilated/absorbed the Ten Northern Tribes. Ephraim (Israel) became synonymous with the Nations (aka Gentiles); therefore, in God's wisdom and love, to take care of the Nations is to care for Israel. Christ came to draw not just the Jews but also the Gentiles back to God. The nations will seek Him, and He will be the resting place for both the Jews and the Nations.

The Messiah's work is to build up God's real temple since He is the foundation stone and a precious cornerstone. God's temple under the New Covenant is His Ekklesia (Democratic Assembly) where He is the foundation for God's building (Matt. 16:18; 1 Cor. 3:11). He is also the Cornerstone joining the walls of the Temple — Jews and Gentiles who were enemies (Eph. 2:20). The building up of God's dwelling place as a rest for both God and man consists of both the Jews of Judah and those called out from the Nations — this is the fulfillment of the prophets. The Messiah will build His temple — the eternal rest for God and man.

Paul quoted Isaiah 28:16 in Romans 10:11 in the section concerning the preaching of the gospel of peace (Rom. 10:15).[17] However, Paul changed the phrase from "will not act in haste" to "will not be put to shame." The gospel of peace in that chapter was not preached to unbelievers but to Jewish and Gentile believers who were divided.[18] Members of each group were ashamed of being seen with members of those seen as inferior. This was the case with Jewish believers in Antioch when they divided and separated themselves from their Gentile counterparts since they didn't want to be seen eating with "sinners" (Gal. 2:12-15). They were ashamed to be seen fellowshipping with Gentile sinners. Jesus, as the Cornerstone, desired to save them from shame, so that they could be in one fellowship as His One Body. The Jews and the Gentiles would be saved from their shame of association with each other through the gospel of peace.

The Coming of the Messiah and the New Covenant

Chapter 40 of Isaiah marks the beginning of the second period, during which Judah was exiled to Babylon. It seems that all hope was lost for all 12 tribes. Ten of them were scattered and assimilated by Assyria, and Judah, with Benjamin and the Levites, went into Babylonian captivity. The great kingdom of David and Solomon's temple was no more. Nothing of value relating to the twelve tribes of Israel was left in the Promised Land. It seemed that God's work with His chosen Israel had come to nothing. Under

---

17   The NU-Text (manuscript) omits the "gospel of peace." However, that quote came from Isa. 52:7, and in the Hebrew text it reads, ". . . Are the feet of him who brings good news, who proclaims peace . . ." Therefore, the TR-Text is more accurate here.

18   See exposition on Romans in *The Completion Gospel* (2 chapters in *One Truth*) and the *Gospel of the Kingdom* (2 chapters in *God's Kind*) by Henry Hon.

these dismal circumstances, Chapter 40 starts with a prophetic word announcing John the Baptist, who introduced Jesus Christ in the New Testament. Sovereignly, Chapter 40 can represent the beginning of the New Covenant, as the Hebrew Scriptures have 39 books, and the 40th book could be considered the book of Matthew's Gospel, the first book of the New Testament (or New Covenant).

> "Comfort, yes, comfort My people!" Says your God. 2 "Speak comfort to Jerusalem, and cry out to her, That her warfare is ended, That her iniquity is pardoned; For she has received from the LORD's hand Double for all her sins." 3 The voice of one crying in the wilderness: "Prepare the way of the LORD; Make straight in the desert A highway for our God. . . . 8 The grass withers, the flower fades, But the word of our God stands forever." . . . 11 He will feed His flock like a shepherd; He will gather the lambs with His arm, And carry [them] in His bosom, [And] gently lead those who are with young. . . . 13 Who has directed the Spirit of the LORD, Or [as] His counselor has taught Him?"
>
> – Isa. 40:1-3, 8, 11, 13

While there are Hebrew Scriptures alluding to a plurality within the singular God, here is an emphatic portion describing God as distinctly three. God in His Trinity came to comfort Judah, who had been punished for their iniquity. God (the Father) is ready to forgive and move on with the coming of the Son. *"Prepare the way of the Lord"* was John the Baptist's proclamation introducing the coming of Jesus Christ in the New Testament (Matt. 3:1-3). Jesus Christ came as the eternal Word of God (John 1:1), the great Shepherd who feeds, gathers, and leads His people (John 10:11; 11:52). Finally, the Spirit was revealed as the One actively working on earth. Significantly, the introduction to God's work in the New Testament starts with a clear reference to God who is distinctly Father, Son, and Holy Spirit, yet inseparably one. He, in His Trinity, was fully unveiled throughout the New Testament Scriptures.

> "Behold! **My Servant** whom I uphold, **My Elect One** [in whom] My soul delights! I have put **My Spirit** upon **Him**; He will bring forth justice to the Gentiles. . . . 6 "I, **the LORD**, have called You in righteousness, And will hold Your hand; I will keep You and give You as a covenant to the people, As a light to the Gentiles, 7 To open blind eyes, To bring out prisoners from the prison, Those who sit in darkness from the prison house.
>
> – Isa. 42:1, 6-7

> The **Spirit of the LORD** [is] upon Me, Because **He** has anointed **Me** to preach the gospel to [the] poor; **He** has sent **Me** to heal the brokenhearted, To proclaim liberty to [the] captives And recovery of sight to [the] blind, To set at liberty those who are oppressed. . .
>
> – Luke 4:18

The Son of God was incarnated to be a man and received a ministry for those scattered in captivity. He was sent to preach the gospel, to heal, to give sight to the blind, and to liberate the oppressed captives. For this ministry, He was anointed by the Spirit of God. Again, this was spoken during the captivity in Babylon and the scattering among the Gentiles. What a hope in the coming of the Messiah! This speaks of Jesus being a covenant. Without Jesus, there cannot be a New Covenant. While the Mosaic Covenant was on stone tablets, the New Covenant is the person of Jesus Christ: **"Give You as a covenant to the People."** While the ten northern tribes were assimilated by the nations, God sent forth Jesus as the light to them in the darkness. What Jesus was anointed to accomplish was completed through His work of crucifixion, resurrection, ascension, and the outpouring of the Spirit.

> And now the LORD says, Who formed Me from the womb [to be] His Servant, To bring Jacob back to Him, So that Israel is gathered to Him . . . 6 Indeed He says, "It is too small a thing that You should be My Servant to raise up the tribes of Jacob, And to restore the preserved ones of Israel; I will also give You as a light to the Gentiles, that You should be My salvation to the ends of the earth."
>
> – Isa. 49:5-6

This refers to Christ in His incarnation. He was in the womb of a human virgin and came as God's Servant. The emphasis here concerning His coming is not for redemption due to man's sins, but for gathering Israel. He came to gather all the tribes of Jacob. By the time of this writing by Isaiah, the Northern Ten Tribes, called Israel or Ephraim, were already assimilated by Assyria. Ephraim had been swallowed up among the Gentiles (Hos. 8:8). This was what God did to Israel: *"So I scattered them among the nations, and they were dispersed throughout the countries"* (Eze 36:19).[19]

---

19   Today, their DNA is utterly assimilated among the Nations throughout the globe. The so-called "Lost Tribes of Israel," insofar as discovering their DNA among the tribes of the earth, is a rather mindless pursuit full of conjecture and ambiguity. Today, believers in Yeshuah/Jesus are accorded the title of "sons of Promise" because, as Paul clearly says: "For you are all sons of God through faith in Christ Jesus" (Gal. 3:26). Christ, as was Isaac, is the Son/Seed of Promise; therefore, since we who believe are IN Christ, we are, consequently, all sons of God through faith in Christ. "And if you are Christ's, then you are Abraham's seed, and heirs according to the promise" (Gal. 3:29).

The prophecy of Jesus coming to gather His people from among the nations is supported by what John said in His gospel concerning the death of Jesus Christ: *"He* [Caiaphas, the High Priest] *did not say on his own authority; but being high priest that year he prophesied that Jesus would die for the [Jewish] nation, and not for that nation only, but also that He would gather together in one the children of God who were scattered abroad"* (John 11:51-52). In gathering His dispersed people, Jesus Christ is the light to the Nations/Gentiles. What did the Gentiles have to do with the tribes of Jacob? Much, in every way. Because 10 of those tribes were assimilated and have become Gentiles. Therefore, being the light to the Gentiles is needed to awaken the swallowed-up Ten Tribes to be gathered. His salvation is not just for Judah (the Jewish Nation), but to the ends of the earth.

John, in his gospel, immediately makes mention — after the prophetic statements delivered by the High Priest, Caiaphas, almost in the most obscure fashion, wherein he states *"…from that day on, they plotted to put Him to death, the following: "Therefore Jesus no longer walked openly among the Jews, but went from there into the country near the wilderness, to a city called **Ephraim*** (Heb. "fruitful"), and there remained with His disciples" (John 11:53-54). Is this coincidental or purposefully inserted by John to bring attention to Ephraim before our Lord's crucifixion in Jerusalem (John 12 onward)? Why insert this into the text if it is simply miscellaneous information? No! "... and not only for that nation but also for the scattered children of God, to bring them [both Judah and Ephraim – Jew and Gentile] AND **make them one**" (John 11:52 – NIV). At stake before and through His crucifixion, He had but one consuming passion: The oneness of the "children of God" who Caiaphas "prophesied that Jesus would die for the nation [Judah], and not for that nation only" [He would die for Ephraim/Gentiles].

All of mankind is included in His salvation while maintaining His faithfulness and promise to Abraham through Isaac, and the gathering of the 12 Tribes of Jacob.

> So the ransomed of the LORD shall return, and come to Zion with singing, With everlasting joy on their heads. They shall obtain joy and gladness; Sorrow and sighing shall flee away.
>
> — Isa. 51:11

> Awake, awake! Put on your strength, O Zion; Put on your beautiful garments, O Jerusalem, the holy city! . . . 2 Shake yourself from the dust, arise; Sit down, O Jerusalem! Loose yourself from the bonds of your neck, O captive daughter of Zion! . . . 7 How beautiful upon the mountains Are the feet of him who brings good news, who proclaims peace, who brings glad tidings of good [things], Who proclaims salvation, who says to Zion, "Your God reigns!"
>
> — Isa. 52:1-2, 7

The coming together of His diverse people is Zion. God ransomed or redeemed His people for Zion, the place of unity. The oneness of God's people is God's habitation (Psa. 132-133). God chose a unique place for His people to worship. He never gave up on this place even after the devastation and scattering of His people. However, to God, Zion was not just a place; it was His people. His people in unity are called Zion: *"And say to Zion, 'You are My people'"* (Isa. 51:16). The physical Zion symbolizes God's diverse people in unity. Without the unity of His people, there is no Zion.

Many Christians may think that Zion for Christians is heaven, a place of celestial Home. Therefore, they believe Christians cannot be united until the heavenly kingdom. However, Jesus prayed specifically that His people would become one here on earth for this dark world to see (John 17:21). So, when God's people are one on earth, that is Zion. Christians do not need to wait for the heavenly kingdom since the oneness of God's people is the reality of Zion. Hebrews 12:22 says, *"You have come to mount Zion . . . "* declaring that believers, followers of Christ, are in Zion already. Zion is on earth, and the oneness among the faithful makes Zion a reality here and now, not in the sweet by-and-by.

What joy for God's people to return to Zion from captivity! Come to Zion with singing and gladness. There is no sorrow and sighing in the place of unity. When God's people are unified, it is the time of restoration and renewal. Jeroboam created a systematized division among God's people, which caused the eventual disintegration of the tribes. Now there are the preachers of peace on the mountains of Jerusalem proclaiming salvation in the place of unity.

Isaiah 52:7 was quoted by Paul in Romans 10:15 for preaching the gospel of peace. In Rome, there was a wall of division between the Jewish and the Gentile believers, where each had their reasons to boast of their superiority over the other. The simple gospel of Christ's incarnation, death, resurrection, and Lordship breaks down these walls of division and brings them salvation through their common faith. This is the gospel presented in four verses (Rom. 10:6-9). They are saved when the two previously divided people are joined by Jesus, the chief cornerstone for building God's temple in Zion (Rom. 10:11-13).[20] The oneness of God's diverse people returning to unity is where God reigns. His glory returns, and His majesty manifests.

> He grew up before him like a tender shoot, and like a root out of dry ground.
> He had no beauty or majesty to attract us to him, nothing in his appearance
> that we should desire him. 3 He was despised and rejected by mankind, a man

---

20   See the complete exposition of Romans chapters 9-16 by Henry Hon in the *Completion Gospel* chapters in His book *One Truth* or the chapters on the *Gospel of the Kingdom* in his book *God's Kind.*

of suffering, and familiar with pain. Like one from whom people hide their faces he was despised, and we held him in low esteem. 4 Surely he took up our pain and bore our suffering, yet we considered him punished by God, stricken by him, and afflicted. 5 But he was pierced for our transgressions, he was crushed for our iniquities; the punishment that brought us peace was on him, and by his wounds we are healed. 6 We all, like sheep, have gone astray, each of us has turned to our own way; and the LORD has laid on him the iniquity of us all. 7 He was oppressed and afflicted, yet he did not open his mouth; he was led like a lamb to the slaughter, and as a sheep before its shearers is silent, so he did not open his mouth. 8 By oppression and judgment he was taken away. Yet who of his generation protested? For he was cut off from the land of the living; for the transgression of my people he was punished. 9 He was assigned a grave with the wicked, and with the rich in his death, though he had done no violence, nor was any deceit in his mouth.

— Isa. 53:2-9, NIV

Isaiah 53 is one of the best-known prophecies detailing the crucifixion and resurrection of Jesus Christ. In this portion of the Scriptures, His appearance, suffering, and death for the sins of the world are clearly described. This touching and in-depth description of the Lord's crucifixion immediately after speaking of Zion, the unity of God's people, parallels the Lord's prayer in John 17. In that chapter, Jesus prayed earnestly and desperately three times for the oneness of His people. This oneness includes both His Jewish believers and the Gentile believers who were to follow (John 17:20). After that prayer for oneness, He was betrayed and judged that night and crucified in the morning. The Lord went to the cross to build up His Ekklesia (Democratic Assembly), which gathers His scattered children into one (Matt. 16:18-21; John 11:51-52).

These verses above describe how Jesus was led to be crucified as a lamb led to the slaughter. He died for man's transgressions. Though He was sinless, He was crucified with two criminals who deserved death. However, He was buried in a new tomb of a rich person. This prophecy accurately described Jesus Christ's death and burial some 700+ years later. Now, the prophecy continues with His resurrection.

Yet it was the LORD's will to crush him and cause him to suffer, and though the LORD makes his life an offering for sin, he will see his offspring and prolong his days, and the will of the LORD will prosper in his hand. 11 After he has suffered, he will see the light of life and be satisfied; by his knowledge my righteous servant will justify many, and he will bear their iniquities.

— Isa. 53:10-11

Though Jesus died as an offering for man's sin, *"he will see his offspring and prolong his days."* This speaks of the Lord's resurrection with His many followers. If He had not resurrected, how could He have seen His offspring? His days were prolonged even to eternity. The "offspring" or "seed" here is a singular noun; however, it is a corporate seed including many diverse people. Galatians 3 says this singular seed includes Jew, Greek, slave, free, male, and female (Gal. 3:28-29). Jesus died as one grain; when He resurrected, He bore much fruit (Jn. 12:24). Yes, He was exceedingly "fruitful" (Ephraim's meaning).

In His resurrection, Jesus saw *"the light of life,"* and He was satisfied with the multiplication of Himself in many children — for in proclaiming that He was the Light of the world (John 8:12), He had set before Him an unspeakable joy: *"Believe in the Light, that you may become **sons of Light"*** (John 12:36). He fulfilled His mission as the anointed One. He rejoiced to see the wall of hostility between His people broken down so that they may be gathered into one (Eph. 2:14-15). God was satisfied that Christ had fulfilled His eternal purpose through His death and resurrection. A multitude of His diverse people are justified, regenerated, and unified by the work of Christ to become His "sons of Light." And as will be seen in the next chapter of Isaiah, Christ in His resurrection shall be fully satisfied by gaining His bride, His wife.

> For your Maker [is] your husband, The LORD of hosts [is] His name; And your Redeemer [is] the Holy One of Israel; He is called the God of the whole earth. . . . 7 "For a mere moment I have forsaken you, But with great mercies I will gather you. 8 With a little wrath I hid My face from you for a moment; But with everlasting kindness I will have mercy on you," Says the LORD, your Redeemer. . . . 10 For the mountains shall depart And the hills be removed, But My kindness shall not depart from you, Nor shall My covenant of peace be removed," Says the LORD, who has mercy on you.
>
> – Isa. 54:5, 7-8, 10

How romantic and faithful is God, the Husband! Both Israel-Ephraim and Israel-Judah were unfaithful, so they were chastised and driven away to foreign lands. God hid His face from her with a little wrath. Now is the time of mercies. He came as the Redeemer to bring His wife back to Himself. The Redeemer gave His life to die for His wife. This happened in the previous chapter, Isaiah 53. God made a great sacrifice at the cost of death to bring her back. This is like Ephesians 5:25 where Paul said: *"Husbands, love your wives, just as Christ also loved the ekklesia (aka "church") and gave (lit. "gave up") Himself for her."*

God's work of redemption and regeneration to bring His wife back to Himself is forever. His kindness shall not depart. There will not be another falling away as with Israel and Judah. The unique way for this marriage of God and man to last into eternity without any more separation is due to the new and eternal covenant of peace. This covenant of peace cannot refer to the Mosaic Covenant since the Spirit said in Hebrews 8:13: *"In that He says, 'A new covenant,' He has made the first [Mosaic] obsolete. Now what is becoming obsolete and growing old is ready to vanish away."* The Mosaic Covenant was not meant to last forever. Since the Mosaic Covenant was only an archetype of God's New Covenant, eventually the marriage between God and the 12 Tribes of Israel ended in divorce and separation. The eternal covenant is the New Covenant enacted by the death and resurrection of Jesus Christ. The New Covenant enables the eternal marriage between God and His people.

> "Ho! Everyone who thirsts, come to the waters; And you who have no money, come, buy and eat. Yes, come, buy wine and milk without money and without price. 2 Why do you spend money for [what is] not bread, and your wages for [what] does not satisfy? Listen carefully to Me, and eat [what is] good, and let your soul delight itself in abundance. 3 Incline your ear, and come to Me. Hear, and your soul shall live; And I will make an **everlasting covenant** with you — The sure mercies of David.
>
> — Isa. 55:1-3

God has done everything through the work of Jesus Christ by implementing a New Covenant: Redemption, regeneration, peace between enemies, bringing back His wife, and everything else according to His eternal purpose. Christ, as the Anointed One, finished His work. So, what is the part that His people play in all this? What are His people to do?

Just come to eat and drink without money or price. What!? That's it? Yes, come freely to the table to eat and drink what God has prepared. We described God's *oikonomia* in a previous chapter. This is God's dispensing or administering in the New Covenant. Reconsider what Jesus said: *As the living Father sent Me, and I live because of the Father, so he who feeds on Me will live because of Me* (John 6:57). The way to live as Jesus lived is to feed on Him. Christians are desirous to live as Jesus lived, and they would ask, "What would Jesus do?" before acting or moving. However, according to Jesus, the way is not to mimic Him, but to eat and drink of Him, then living as He lived becomes spontaneous.

Many Christians think that ingesting Jesus is only at the time of faith. Eating and drinking Jesus is only needed once when they first repent and believe in Jesus. No, it needs to continue just like eating and drinking physically; believers also need to feed on Jesus daily. In letters written to the seven "churches" in Revelation, the Spirit called for believers to overcome any form of degradation in the "churches." To those in Ephesus, the result of overcoming, is to eat of the Tree of Life (Rev. 2:7). To believers in Pergamos, the result of overcoming is to eat of the hidden manna (Rev. 2:17). Finally, the Lord is knocking on the door of the "church" in Laodicea because He was outside of that "church." Overcomers are those who respond to Christ's knock, opening the door so that He may come in and share a feast of fellowship with them. These cases show that eating and drinking are prominent and essential for believers throughout their journey, from the beginning to the end. Even in eternity, the main features of the eternal Jerusalem are eating of the tree of life and drinking the river of life.

The symbol of remembering Jesus is eating and drinking Him as the bread and the cup. This is the symbol that the New Covenant believers practiced daily or weekly. Their entire Democratic Assembly was centered around the Lord's Supper — declaring that eating and drinking of Him was their shared reality (1 Cor. 11:17–26). Receiving Jesus as food and drink is the first and the last thing we are called to do now that the New Covenant is in effect. This is the believers' privilege and responsibility in fulfilling God's eternal purpose.

After speaking of eating His flesh and drinking His blood in John 6, Jesus said that His flesh profits nothing. His words are spirit and life (John 6:63). The way to receive and ingest Jesus is through His words. Here in Isaiah 55, the same was spoken: *"Listen carefully to Me, and eat what is good, and let your soul delight itself in abundance. Incline your ear, and come to Me. Hear, and your soul shall live."* This food is His words. As believers read and study the Bible, conveying God's Word, the words of Jesus will speak throughout the day, and those living words feed and give life to every believer.

When considering the Scriptures, His Words, believers need to *"come to Me."* Those were the exact words of Jesus when He chastised the Pharisees for searching the Scriptures and *"not willing to come to Me that you may have life."* The Scriptures testify concerning Jesus Christ; therefore, a person missing the knowledge and understanding of Jesus Christ would have missed the entire point of the Scriptures.

> ". . . all things must be fulfilled which were written in the Law of Moses and [the] Prophets and [the] Psalms concerning Me." 45 And He opened their understanding, that they might comprehend the Scriptures.
>
> – Luke 24:44-45

The focus of the entire Hebrew Scriptures is to unveil Jesus Christ — His person and work. If the understanding of Jesus Christ is missed when reading the Scriptures, it is not yet comprehended. The only way to understand the Scriptures is to see Jesus throughout. That is exactly the attempt of the authors of this book: to unveil Jesus Christ and His accomplishments hidden in the Hebrew Scriptures.

Jeremiah — The New Covenant Unilateral and Unconditional

Jeremiah began His ministry in Judah after the Northern Ten Tribes were deported. He continued speaking for God after Judah's first defeat by the Babylonian king, Nebuchadnezzar. Jeremiah prophesied that Judah's captivity in Babylon would last 70 years (Jer. 29:10; 607-537 BC).

In Jeremiah Chapter 30, God spoke to both Israel (Ephraim's Ten Northern Tribes) and Judah (Israel's Two Southern Tribes and the Levites) that they would return to the Promised Land (Jer. 30:2-3). It seems impossible for Israel to be gathered back since they have already been scattered, and in Ephraim's case, swallowed up/assimilated, among the nations (Jer. 30:11). Nevertheless, God remembered His love for all Israel: He has loved her with an everlasting love, and He will draw her to Himself again (Jer. 31:3). God's speaking in Jeremiah 31 was focused mainly on Israel (Ephraim). For approximately 200 years from the day of King Jeroboam until their deportation to Assyria (cir. 919-721 BC), Ephraim did not gather to feast and worship at Zion; yet, one day, they will desire Zion (Jer. 31:6). The Lord will gather His scattered people from all over the nations of the earth and gather them again to the Promised Land (Jer. 31:8). They shall come and sing in the height of Zion, streaming into the goodness of the LORD. Their souls shall be like a well-watered garden, and they shall not sorrow anymore (Jer. 31:12). What a faithful and wonderful Husband!

When will all this take place? It undoubtedly commences at the inauguration of the New Covenant. Jeremiah explicitly itemizes the details of the New Covenant; although Ezekiel highlights aspects of the New Covenant as well (Ezek. 11:16-20; 36; especially vss. 26-27 and Ezek. 34:25; 37:26). All the tribes of Jacob returning to Zion in the Promised Land will commence effective at the enactment of the New Covenant. The Mosaic Covenant took a multitude of chapters to itemize all its promises and requirements. The Mosaic Covenant was a bilateral, conditional agreement: Israel, as the wife of Jehovah, was required to fulfill her part, while the Almighty, as the faithful husband, would certainly uphold His (Exo. 19:5). If Israel remained faithful, she would be blessed; if she disobeyed, she would be cursed (Deut. 28:15). In contrast, the New Covenant presents four promises without stipulations. It is unilateral and unconditional — God will accomplish what He has pledged, independent of human performance. There are no demands from God. He will do it by Himself. All His people need to do is receive what He has accomplished for them. This is truly good news!

1. The Imparting of the Law of Life

> "Behold, the days are coming, says the LORD, when I will make a **new covenant** with the house of Israel and with the house of Judah — 32 "not according to the covenant that I made with their fathers in the day [that] I took them by the hand to lead them out of the land of Egypt, My covenant which they broke, though I was a **husband** to them, says the LORD. 33 "But this [is] the covenant that I will make with the house of Israel after those days, says the LORD: I will put My law in their minds, and write it on their hearts; and I will be their God, and they shall be My people. 34 "No more shall every man teach his neighbor, and every man his brother, saying, 'Know the LORD,' for they all shall know Me, from the least of them to the greatest of them, says the LORD. For I will forgive their iniquity, and their sin I will remember no more."
>
> — Jer. 31:31-34

> "I will give you a new heart and put a new spirit within you; I will take the heart of stone out of your flesh and give you a heart of flesh. 27 "I will put My Spirit within you and cause you to walk in My statutes, and you will keep My judgments and do [them].
>
> — Eze. 36:26-27

Amazingly, the New Covenant is for both Israel-Ephraim and Israel-Judah. One has been scattered and absorbed among the nations (Ephraim), and the other (Judah) was taken into captivity in Babylon. The first blessing of His New Covenant is: *"I will put My law in their minds, and write it on their hearts."* The Law in the Mosaic Covenant was on a tablet outside of man, but the Law in the New Covenant became an integral part of man and his character. This first item is the most crucial since this "law" is the very Christ in them — the essence of the New Covenant.

The heart signifies man's being: nature, character, and personality. The word "write" indicates inscribing something. The Law inscribed in man's heart means the Law of God is now part of man's nature and character, just as it is part of God's nature and character. Previously, man had a fallen nature, so he needed to work at following God's Law, which was foreign to him. He had to work at it with much effort because the Law was alien to him. This is like a monkey trying to act like a man! As hard as a monkey tries, it will eventually fail, because it is still a monkey. In the New Covenant, man does not have to try to follow God's Law because the nature of God's written law is now written upon man's nature, his heart.

How does this happen? The New Covenant is the Spirit of God Who comes into and becomes an integral part of man: **Christ-in-you**. The Spirit of God is no longer outside (or simply "upon") man, but within man, joined in perfect union with man. The fact of the Spirit of God coming into man is the vital difference between the Mosaic Covenant and the New Covenant. The union between divinity and humanity as seen in the God-Man, Jesus Christ (as "fully God" and "fully man") — this was a hidden mystery, most certainly, and all the more a hidden mystery (now revealed) as the New Covenant is the very Spirit of Christ indwelling His people!

Notice that the Spirit is the One causing man to walk according to His Law. It is no longer man's effort working to keep God's Law; rather, the Spirit of God with His life and nature causes (empowers and energizes) man to live by God's Law. With the Spirit within man, God has given His people this promise: *"You shall"* keep my Law (Ezek. 36:27). The word *"shall"* means that keeping God's Law is inevitable. Due to the Spirit of God in man, man shall keep and live out God's laws. Sooner or later, man shall, without a doubt, predictably, express the very life and nature of God.

This is akin to the Lord Jesus saying, *"You shall be perfect as your heavenly Father is perfect"* (Matt. 5:48). In the same chapter, Jesus elevated the definition of adultery to include looking at a woman with lust in the heart, murder to include being angry, and real love is when one loves their enemy. These requirements are humanly impossible to keep and laughable to suggest one can fulfill them. Nevertheless, He promised they would be perfect or complete as their heavenly Father. Why? Because they are born of God. Now, God is their Father. Like father, like son. God's characteristics will be in His sons. This is like an earthly father telling his newborn son, "You shall grow up and be like me — able to run, play ball, talk, and work with me." Even though the baby is completely helpless at that point, the father knows that because the baby was born of him and possesses his life, one day the baby will grow up to be a man like him. This is the essence of the New Covenant: God's Spirit coming into man.

> Therefore, no condemnation now exists for those in Christ Jesus, because the Spirit's Law of life in Christ Jesus has set you free from the law of sin and of death. What the law could not do since it was limited by the flesh, God did. He condemned sin in the flesh by sending His own Son in flesh like ours under sin's domain, and as a sin offering, in order that the Law's requirement would be accomplished in us who do not walk according to the flesh but according to the Spirit.
>
> – Romans 8:1–4, HCSB

The entrance of the Spirit into man brings the Law of divine life into man. This is the Spirit's Law of Life. Every life has a law. This law is not outside of life; rather, life itself is the law. An apple's "life" will bear apples. It will never bear oranges or bananas. That is the law of the apple's life. It is completely dependable and predictable. A dog's "law of life" will cause this dog to run, bark, wag its tail, and grow hair like a dog. When human beings produce offspring, it is predictable that, based on the law of life, the child will grow with human characteristics. No prayer is needed — "Lord, please make certain that my baby is human!" That would be a ridiculous prayer.

The Spirit of God, with His life, is also a law. This law is not the same as the Ten Commandments outside of man requiring man to act and behave like God. Rather, when the Spirit enters man and joins man with God's life and nature, this law of divine, eternal life enters as well. This is the Law that frees believers from the law of sin and death and fulfills God's requirement in every believer. It is no longer man's effort to fulfill the requirements of God's Law, but the Spirit's Law is their law of life. What freedom from condemnation when a person realizes it is God's Law of life, which shall inevitably fulfill the highest requirements of God's character in every believer!

What the external Law could not do since man's flesh is sinful, God terminated that flesh (viz., the "flesh of sin") on the cross. He then entered man with His Spirit, and His Law of life caused His character to be fully expressed in man; thus, God and man together fulfill God's external Law. How wonderful is this New Covenant! God *will* do it, and He is doing it! Man's part is simply to enjoy God as life and cooperate with the growth and maturing of God's life.

2. He Is Our God, and We Are His people

> But you are a chosen race, a royal priesthood, a holy nation, a people for His possession, so that you may proclaim the praises of the One who called you out of darkness into His marvelous light.
>
> *– 1 Peter 2:9, HCSB*

The second item is *"I will be their God, and they shall be My people."* To be God's people is much more than just a group of human beings acquired by Him. The Greek word for "people" in Hebrews 8:10 and 1 Peter 2:9 is *laos*, which means, "A people, tribe, nation, all those who are of the same stock and language" (Thayer's). The word "stock" means "the descendants of one individual," which is a group having unity of descent (Merriam-Webster). So, when God says, "They shall be My people," it is very significant indeed.

In the New Covenant, believers are not just a mass of human beings belonging to God as the Creator. Instead, their ancestry is *God*; They descended from God. They are the same "kind" as God. They are no different intrinsically in their life and nature. They are His people, His relatives, and they communicate using the same language.

When God said, *"They shall be my people,"* this did not have the same meaning as the owner of some puppies saying, "These are my puppies." Rather, it would be like Jacob in the Hebrew Scriptures looking at his twelve tribes (sons) and saying, "These are my people," since they are his offspring. See the difference? A human and a puppy are two different species with different languages; however, Israel's ancestry is literally from Jacob.

How can believers be God's people and from His lineage? The reason is that God's Spirit is in them — Christ in them. Since believers are born of God and are now inextricably joined to Him with His life and nature, they are God's people.

Israel under the Mosaic Covenant did not have God's life and nature within them. They were God's people pre-regeneration. Although they had God's image and likeness as in creation, they were not God's species in life or nature. Therefore, they were not a match for God in a lasting marriage; they were not **God's kind**. Remember, marriage can only be between a male and a female of the same species. The marriage between God and His people under the Mosaic Covenant was merely a shadow of the future reality. It was bound to fail, and it spectacularly did so. Israel at the time did not possess God's life and nature. However, the New Covenant made God's people the same as He in life, nature, and expression. They are now the same kind as God; therefore, the marriage in the New Covenant between God and man is eternal. Astounding divine truth — God Almighty knew this marriage of Himself with Israel seemingly would not hold because, if you would, it was not, as the expression goes, "a match made in heaven." Yet, He declared that He, as her Husband, had married Israel forever. To accomplish this, as we have already explained (Rom. 7:1-4), the "first husband" had to die, so that she (his first wife), could be married to another, even to Him Who is raised from the dead!

Yet, God is still their God. God is still the distinct One to be uniquely worshipped and adored for eternity. The uplifting of human beings becoming God's people in the way of birth does not diminish in any way God's status, glory, and uniqueness; rather, His people can express Him and proclaim His praise at the highest level above all creation. This proclamation is not just in words but also in His people. God's very life and nature are multiplied, and His glory is magnified. Therefore, being God's people, His Bride, is wonderful and glorious to God.[21]

---

21   Scripture highlighting "You shall be my people, and I will be your God" alluding to the New Covenant include Gen. 17:7; Exo. 6:7; Lev. 26:11-12; Jer. 7:23; Jer. 30:18-22; Ezek. 34:24, 36:28; Hos. 2:23; Zech. 13:9; Joel 2:27; Rev. 21:3.

3. Knowing God

> Nevertheless you have an anointing from the Holy One, and you all know. I have not written to you that you do not know the truth, but that you do know it, and that no lie is of the truth . . . Now as for you, the anointing that you received from him resides in you, and you have no need for anyone to teach you. But as his anointing teaches you about all things, it is true and is not a lie. Just as it has taught you, you reside in him.
>
> – 1 John 2:20-21, 27, NET

The third blessing of the New Covenant reveals that *"no one needs to teach God's people to know God; all shall know Him from the least to the greatest."* There are two different Greek words for the word "know" in Hebrews 8:11 and 1 John 2:20-21. The first "know" is from the Greek word *ginosko*, and the second "know" is from the Greek word *oida* (or its verb form, *eido*). According to Vine's New Testament Expository Dictionary, *ginosko* frequently suggests inception or "progress" in knowledge, while *oida* suggests "fullness" of knowledge. According to J.N. Darby, *ginosko* signifies objective knowledge — what a man has learned or acquired. *Oida* conveys the thought of what is inward — the inward consciousness in the mind or intuitive knowledge not immediately derived from what is external. Based on these definitions, the third blessing says believers in the New Covenant do not need man to teach them an external, objective knowledge of God, because each one has an inward, intuitive knowing of God in fullness.

Knowing God in the way of *oida* for believers is the same way Jesus knows (*oida*) the Father. In John 8:55, Jesus said to the Jews concerning God: *"You do not know (ginosko) Him, but I know (oida) Him."* Unbelieving Jews at the time did not have a concept of knowing God externally, but Jesus, as the Son, knew God in full, inwardly, and intuitively. It is very significant for believers to know (*oida*) God in the New Covenant the same way as Jesus knows (*oida*) God, the Father. How is this possible? It is only because of the first blessing of the New Covenant, namely, Christ in them, the Spirit of God residing in the believer, becoming part of their inward being. Therefore, they can intuitively and inwardly know God in full, just as Jesus did while on earth.

We find support for this thought in 1 John 2:20. God, the Holy One, anoints believers. This anointing is the Spirit (Acts 10:38), and because of this anointing, all believers know (*oida*) the truth. They do not need men to teach them because the anointing Spirit within them teaches all things related to the truth. This teaching causes them to reside or remain in Jesus Christ. This does not mean believers do not need any external teachers to instruct them from the Bible concerning the truth. It does mean that if they pay attention to the anointing within them, the Spirit will witness in them, and they will intuitively know what is and is not the truth as they listen to Bible teachers. It is the Spirit in them Who discerns what is healthy, acceptable truth, and what to reject and avoid.

The goal of the Anointing's teaching is for believers to remain and reside in Jesus Christ and for Christ to abide in them. The focus of the anointing Spirit is not for teaching believers which car to buy, where to invest, or what career to choose, but to always live in Jesus Christ — to remain in Him. As believers live through the day, the anointing is constantly moving. This "moving" is a witness to the reality that they are in union with each other. The anointing Spirit's work continuously brings believers back to Jesus Christ when they are experientially distracted. This is the third blessing of the New Covenant: believers know (*oida*) God as the truth, making them unmovable as they reside in the indwelling Jesus Christ.

> Little children, it is the last hour; and as you have heard that the Antichrist is coming, even now many antichrists have come, by which we know that it is the last hour. 19 They went out from us, but they were not of us . . . 20 But you have an anointing from the Holy One, and you know all things. . . . 27 But the anointing which you have received from Him abides in you, and you do not need that anyone teach you; but as the same anointing teaches you concerning all things, and is true, and is not a lie, and just as it has taught you, you will abide in Him.
>
> – 1 John 2:18–20, 27

Under the Mosaic Covenant, God related to and spoke to His people through intermediaries: priests and prophets. However, God desires all His children to know Him directly, from the least to the greatest. 1 John 2 speaks of many Antichrists, who are already operating among God's children. These Antichrists worked and traveled together with the apostles for a time. These are Christian workers who may have been well respected, but then something shifted: they no longer pointed people to Christ, but subtly redirected dependence toward themselves.

The word "anti" means "against" or "in place of." While most people are thinking of the "Antichrist" as the devil during the end times with the number 666, these Antichrists among Christians now are already deviously and massively influencing God's people. Instead of each believer learning to follow the teaching of the anointing within, these Antichrists have taken the place of the anointing Spirit to guide and retain the loyalty of those under their influence.

Immediately after the warning concerning Antichrists, John said that the anointing is within all Christ's followers, and they know all things. The word "anointing" in Greek is from the same root word for "Christ." Therefore, the Antichrists in practice were the anti-anointing within the believers. Jesus Christ, as the "anointed One," is the anointer. Each one of His followers is joined to the Anointed One and has received the same anointing from God (2 Cor. 1:21). However, these Antichrists' goal is to replace the anointing with themselves as the intermediary person. This teaching and practice would cut off God's people from the New Covenant and revert them to the practices of the Mosaic Covenant.

While the true apostles' goal, as with all genuine ministers of Christ, is to mature the saints so they can live and serve directly under the anointing Spirit abiding in them, the antichrists work to retain believers' dependence on their "pastoring" or "discipling." This would cause saints to doubt the anointing Spirit within them and instead listen to and obey an intermediary person. These antichrists are "wolves" when Paul declared that even among the elders of the "church" in Ephesus, some will arise *"speaking perverse things, to draw away the disciples after themselves"* (Acts 20:30). Under their tutelage, believers are *"always learning and never able to come to the knowledge of the truth"* (2 Tim. 3:7).

Believers need to be aware of the prevalence of the spirit of the Antichrist working to detach them from the direct guidance and teaching of the anointing Spirit. This is the third blessing of the New Covenant, which believers should pursue and not neglect.

4. Sins Are Forgiven and No Longer Remembered

> Therefore, let it be known to you, brothers, that through this one forgiveness of sins is proclaimed to you, and by this one everyone who believes is justified from everything from which the Law of Moses could not justify you.
>
> – Acts 13:38–39, NET

The last blessing of the New Covenant is, *"I will forgive their iniquity, and their sin I will remember no more."* This certainly is wonderful news for all humankind, for all are sinners. This forgiveness is accomplished only through Jesus Christ.

Faith in Jesus Christ is the sole necessity for justification . . . to be made righteous in God's sight. God has an amazing memory. On one hand, God can never forget man's sins, no matter how hard men try to please God by the works of the Law. On the other hand, once a person believes *into* Jesus Christ, God forgets all of his sins. To God, it is as if man never sinned. When Satan tries to accuse a believer before God, God will say to Satan, in effect: "What are you talking about? I do not have any record of this person's sins. This one is sinless and righteous in My judgment."

To most believers, being forgiven by God is the first and most important blessing. But to God, although significant, it is the least important! This is the last item of the New Covenant. God's eternal purpose was not to forgive man's sins but to be joined with him in eternal union.

Sin came into the picture in Genesis 3 and put a stop to God's plan; therefore, God had to clean up sin in man before continuing with His eternal plan. After man was cleansed from sin through the cross of Jesus Christ, God continued His plan of coming into man and becoming one with man. The first three blessings of the New Covenant were part of God's eternal plan. The last item relating to sin was a temporary setback, which God rectified and thereby revealed to the entire universe His character, His love — *for God so loved the world that He gave His only begotten Son*" (John 3:16).

Therefore, Christians should not fill their thoughts with the issue of sin and the forgiveness of sin. Once forgiven, they need to focus on enjoying God in Jesus Christ with the working of the Spirit's Law of life. Believers are of the same tribe and language as God, and today, fully know God inwardly and intuitively.

Ezekiel – The New Covenant Made Two People One

"Therefore say, 'Thus says the Lord GOD: "Although I have cast them far off among the Gentiles, and although I have scattered them among the countries, yet I shall be a little sanctuary for them in the countries where they have gone." ' 17 "Therefore say, 'Thus says the Lord GOD: "I will gather you from the peoples, assemble you from the countries where you have been scattered, and I will give you the land of Israel." ' 18 "And they will go there, and they will take away all its detestable things and all its abominations from there. 19 "Then I will give them one heart, and I will put a new spirit within them, and take the stony heart out of their flesh, and give them a heart of flesh, 20 "that they may walk in My statutes and keep My judgments and do them; and they shall be My people, and I will be their God.

– Ezek. 11:16-20

"For I will take you from among the nations, gather you out of all countries, and bring you into your own land. 25 "Then I will sprinkle clean water on you, and you shall be clean; I will cleanse you from all your filthiness and from all your idols. 26 "I will give you a new heart and put a new spirit within you; I will take the heart of stone out of your flesh and give you a heart of flesh. 27 "I will put My Spirit within you and cause you to walk in My statutes, and you will keep My judgments and do [them].

– Ezek. 36:24-27

Ezekiel's ministry was primarily going into the Babylonian Captivity. He was among the first wave of deportation to Babylon and was a contemporary of Jeremiah and Daniel. While Isaiah prophesied eloquently concerning the coming Messiah and spoke of a covenant of peace, Jeremiah itemized the New Covenant. However, Ezekiel described the performance and result of the New Covenant by the indwelling Holy Spirit.

Without the indwelling Spirit, the New Covenant does not have a way to operate within God's people. The eating and drinking in Isaiah 55 are the receiving of the Holy Spirit. The Mosaic Covenant set the framework for God's relationship with man. The New Covenant is the reality of that framework, and the indwelling Spirit is the life, nature, and power enabling the eternal relationship between God and man. Without the indwelling Spirit, man would be stuck with an inferior covenant (Mosaic), which cannot fulfill God's eternal purpose.

The promise of the indwelling and transforming Spirit is directly and tightly connected with the New Covenant. In Ezekiel 36:27, *"I will put my Spirit within you"* speaks of the Spirit's indwelling His people. Then in Ezekiel 36:26, *"take [out] the heart of stone . . . and give you a heart of flesh"* speaks of the Spirit·transforming the inner being of His people. Continuing this discourse is the unveiling of the New Covenant, the next chapter after Ezekiel 36 says, *"Moreover I will make a covenant of peace with them, and it shall be an everlasting covenant with them"* (Ezekiel 37:26). This shows conclusively that the indwelling Spirit (Christ-in-you) is essentially integrated into the New Covenant.

> On the last day, that great [day] of the feast, Jesus stood and cried out, saying, "If anyone thirsts, let him come to Me and drink. 38 "He who believes in Me, as the Scripture has said, out of his heart will flow rivers of living water." 39 But this He spoke concerning the Spirit, whom those believing in Him would receive; for the Holy Spirit was not yet [given], because Jesus was not yet glorified.
>
> – John 7:37-39

The great feast spoken of here refers to the Feast of Tabernacles, which is the last of the 3 annual feasts in Jerusalem according to the Mosaic Law. It should be a time of rejoicing and national unity. However, the joy is gone, and what is left is an empty shell taking place at a religious feast. Instead of joy and rejoicing, the leaders of the Jews are angry, judgmental, and desire to kill Jesus. Instead of worshipping God, they are trying to kill the God who became man (John 7:25) on their behalf.

Although the Jews came to Jerusalem for this feast, the glory of God had left the temple (first and second temples) long ago. The unity of the 12 tribes had already been broken; Ephraim-Israel had been deported, and the first wave of Judah's captivity was still in Babylon. Then Ezekiel, while in Babylon, saw in a vision the glory of God leaving Solomon's Temple (Eze. 10:18). The Ark of the Testimony was also gone. When the Babylonians came to destroy the temple, it had disappeared . . . it was altogether missing in the second temple. In the second temple, rebuilt during Haggai's time, the Holy of Holies was empty. The Ark of the Covenant was gone, and the glory of God didn't come back to fill it. Even though King Herod expanded the second temple to a magnificent structure much bigger than Solomon's, without God's glory, it was a mere symbol of a religion of law without God's presence.

Remember that the glory of God filled the first temple due to the unity of all the tribes of Israel. Since the physical unity was permanently destroyed by the scattering of the Ten Northern Tribes (Ephraim) and the captivity of the Two Southern Tribes (Judah), the glory of God could not return to the temple, no matter its grandeur and magnificence. God does not dwell in a building of stones but among the unity of His people.

During Haggai's time, he encouraged the returning Jews to finish rebuilding the second temple; however, what he described in his prophecy did not come to pass with the Second Temple. He said, *"The glory of this latter temple shall be greater than the former,' says the LORD of hosts. 'And in this place I will give peace,' says the LORD of hosts"* (Hag. 2:9). The glory of God never did fill the second temple as His glory filled the first. And there was no peace: The Jews continued to be an occupied people, and up until the year 2025, they continued to wage war with their neighbors. Therefore, Haggai's prophecy must be speaking about another temple to come.

Certainly, there was no glory or peace at the time of Jesus when the Jewish religious leaders were trying to kill Him. On the last day of such a "great" 7-day feast, Jesus stood and screamed out for those thirsty to come to Him and drink. Although they were doing their religious duties, He knew they were thirsty — thirsty for God and reality. Whoever drinks from Him will have the water source in him, and out of the drinker's inner being would flow rivers of living water. God, as the living water, is no longer in the physical temple; He wants to inhabit the temple of His believers.

Jesus was speaking of the imminent possibility of receiving the Spirit as prophesied by Ezekiel. He said that the drinkable Spirit was not yet because He had not yet been glorified (crucified and resurrected). Notwithstanding, the Holy Spirit had existed with the Father and the Son in eternity past. Therefore, many translators (as quoted above) add the word "given" since they reasoned that the Holy Spirit had always been, just not yet *given*. Nevertheless, that was an interpretation and not what Jesus said. The drinkable or receivable Holy Spirit needs Jesus to be glorified. He needed to go through the process of glorification before the Holy Spirit could be received.

About His glorification, Jesus said in John 12:24, *"Unless a grain of wheat falls into the ground and dies, it remains alone; but if it dies, it produces much grain."* This verse speaks of His death and resurrection as His glorification.

> Nevertheless I tell you the truth. It is to your advantage that I go away [to death]; for if I do not go away, the Helper [Holy Spirit] will not come to you; but if I depart, I will send Him to you.
>
> – John 16:7

> The Spirit of truth, whom the world cannot receive, because it neither sees Him nor knows Him; but you know Him, for He dwells with you and will be in you. 18 I will not leave you orphans; I will come to you.
>
> – John 14:17-18

John further clarified the reality and fulfillment of Ezekiel's prophecy concerning the indwelling Spirit. Jesus said that it is to the advantage or profit of the disciples that He goes into death. It is through death and resurrection that the Holy Spirit can be imparted to His followers. Even though the Holy Spirit has existed in eternity past, the One who can be within His people can only be sent after the Lord's death and resurrection. The Holy Spirit is the indwelling Christ — "the Spirit of Christ." Jesus said, *"He will be in you,"* and *"I will come to you."* The Spirit and the Son are two, but also one.

All four items of the New Covenant are now real. All that people must do is believe in what He has accomplished. Believing is receiving by faith that Jesus Christ has enacted and made the New Covenant completely effective, experiential. There are no requirements to be fulfilled. Simply tell the Lord, "Thank You for all that You have done for me; I turn (repent) to You and believe all You have accomplished." This kind of prayer is needed when first coming to faith and throughout one's daily journey — "Christ in me, the hope of glory."

This is the New Covenant: Christ-in-you as prophesied by Ezekiel. Christ-in-you will fulfill all that God promised in His unilateral and unconditional New Covenant. What was prophesied by the prophetic writings is realized and accomplished by Jesus Christ. The New Covenant is also called the **covenant of peace**, as previously spoken of in this chapter, but will be expanded upon in the next chapter.

8

THE MYSTERY OF CHRIST: GENTILES AND JEWS ARE A JOINT BODY

If indeed ye have heard of the administration [*oikonomia*] of the grace of God which has been given to me towards you, 3 that by revelation the mystery has been made known to me, (according as I have written before briefly, 4 by which, in reading it, ye can understand my intelligence in the **mystery of the Christ**,) 5 which in other generations has not been made known to the sons of men, as it has now been revealed to his holy apostles and prophets in [the power of the] Spirit, 6 **that [they who are of] the nations should be joint heirs, and a joint body, and joint partakers of [his] promise in Christ Jesus by the glad tidings;**

– Eph. 3:2-6, DBY

Jesus Christ is a mystery: What was His ultimate mission as the Messiah, what has He accomplished, what is He doing now, and can His accomplishments be physically seen on earth? According to Paul, these questions can be answered before His second advent at the end of this age. Paul saw this mystery by revelation and wrote it down so that all his readers could also understand the mystery of Christ — namely, the unity between Jews and Gentiles. This mystery was not revealed before the writings in the New Testament. Nevertheless, upon examining the New Testament, James in Acts 15 made a direct connection between the prophetic Scriptures (Old Testament) and the unity between Jews and Gentiles that occurred under the New Covenant. As we will see in detail later in this chapter and the next, James declared this challenging and complex phenomenon a fulfillment of prophecy.

Before considering the prophetic writings, let's first clearly understand the mystery of Christ from Paul's letter to the Ekklesia in Ephesus. The mystery of Christ is that *"the Gentiles should be joint heirs, joint body, and joint partakers of God's promise."* These two divided people, who were enemies for almost 1,000 years (since the "breach of

Jeroboam"), would come together and be united in their distinctiveness. Though remaining Jews and Gentiles, they would unite as one. The mystery of Christ is that through Him these two peoples would become one — viz. that those called out from the Nations would now be joint heirs, included in the "joint body" and be joint partakers of God's promise with the Jewish nation, yet maintaining their distinctiveness, while inseparable as His One People.

Joint Inheritance

Being a **joint heir** can refer to the inheritance first given to Israel. This inheritance was given to Abraham, Isaac, Jacob, and then the 12 tribes of Israel. The Gentiles were excluded from this inheritance, but now the Gentiles are joint heirs. They now participate in the same inheritance as the Jews. However, the real inheritance promised to Abraham was not a piece of physical land, but the Holy Spirit. *"That the blessing of Abraham might come upon the Gentiles in Christ Jesus, that we might **receive the promise of the Spirit through faith**"* (Gal. 3:14). Paul stated that this promise is the inheritance (Gal. 3:18).

All that God is as the "I am," the source of life and creation, is available to the Jews and Gentiles by the Holy Spirit. The Holy Spirit, as the inheritance of Gentiles and Jews, means that it is their lot or portion for eternity. Listen to what Jesus said about this inheritance, the Holy Spirit:

> He [the Spirit of Truth] will glorify Me, for He will take of what is Mine and declare [it] to you. 15 "All things that the Father has are Mine. Therefore, I said that He will take of Mine and declare [it] to you.
>
> – John 16:14-15

All that is of the Father is the Son's, and the Spirit will declare or make known all that is of the Son to His believers. That is the entire Trinity, who He is, and what He has accomplished, now being made known to His people daily. He cannot be exhausted. His followers are never lacking. All of the Triune God is for them to enjoy and employ. What an inheritance!

Joint Body

The joint body refers to the Body of Christ in Ephesians 1:22-23: *"And has put all things under His [Christ] feet, and gave Him to be head over all things to the assembly [ekklesia], which is His body, the fullness of Him who fills all in all."* The Lord's Body, which is the Lord's Democratic Assembly (Ekklesia), shares in all the power He attained in His resurrection and ascension. Since everything is under His feet and He is the Head over all things, this same power and authority are with His democratic assembly.

How did these two enemies become one Body? *"For He Himself is our peace, who has made both* [Jews and Gentiles] *one, and has broken down the middle wall of separation, having abolished in His flesh the enmity, the law of commandments in ordinances, so as to create in Himself one new man from the two, making peace"* (Eph. 2:14-15). The Lord's cross broke down the wall of separation and hatred between these two enemies to create one new man, thus making peace. This peace is one of the fulfillments of the New Covenant. The Gentiles are no longer strangers and foreigners, but they are now being built together with Jewish believers into a temple of the Lord.

The "commandment in ordinances" generally refers to the ceremonial or lifestyle commandments in the Mosaic Covenant, such as those relating to the priesthood, offerings, dietary restrictions, keeping of days, annual feasts, etc. These have generated envy, hatred, and separation between the Jews and the Gentiles. Over time, additional ordinances were derived — many of which were created by well-meaning interpretations of the Law. For example, "a Sabbath day's journey" was determined to be 2,000 cubits or approximately 4,200 feet. This distance was derived from the Israelites, who were 2,000 cubits behind the Ark of the Covenant as they traveled around Jericho following the Ark of the Covenant (Joshua 3:3-4). Jews would keep this man-made ordinance on the Sabbath and would not be allowed to travel more than a distance of 4,200 feet from wherever they found themselves. All these dividing ordinances were abolished to create One New Man.

> having been built on the foundation of the apostles and prophets, Jesus Christ Himself being the chief corner[stone], 21 in whom the whole building, being fitted together, grows into a holy temple in the Lord, 22 in whom you [Jews and Gentiles] also **are being built together** for a dwelling place of God in the Spirit.
>
> – Eph. 2:20-22

Now the Lord's Democratic Assembly is the Temple, the dwelling place of God. Under the Mosaic Covenant, Solomon's temple was God's dwelling place. That was temporary and foreshadowed the real Temple. This is not a temple of stones, but a living and growing temple composed of two peoples: Jews and Gentiles — or said another way, "the Jewish Nation/Judah" and those Gentiles called out from among the nations, (Ephraim-Israel). Jesus Christ, being the Peacemaker, is the cornerstone joining these once-divided people into one.

Ephesians 3 now says that the joining of two peoples is God's eternal purpose, showing God's manifold wisdom to all the rebellious angels.

> to the intent that now the manifold wisdom of God might be made known by the church [ekklesia] to the principalities and powers in the heavenly [places], 11 according to the eternal purpose which He accomplished in Christ Jesus our Lord, . . . 21 to Him be glory in the church [ekklesia] by Christ Jesus to all generations, forever and ever. Amen.
>
> – Eph. 3:10-11, 21

Paul confirmed again in Chapter 3 that the joint body is His Democratic Assembly. According to God's eternal purpose, His Ekklesia will manifest God's multifaceted wisdom to the entire universe, especially to those rebellious angels who followed Satan. They cannot fathom God's wisdom until they observe His democratic assembly. It is amazing wisdom to bring together rebellious sinners who were once enemies and part of the kingdom of darkness and make them one as God's dwelling place.

In the Old Testament, the glory of God filled Solomon's temple. That temple was symbolic of the unity among God's people; it was temporary. The real and eternal temple to be filled with God's glory is His Democratic Assembly. This is God's people in oneness for eternity. This temple is what God desired from the beginning: His dwelling among His people. Without the unity of God's diverse people, His wisdom cannot be manifested. Without this unity so manifested, He would have no eternal dwelling place.

The unity of God's people is essential; therefore, Ephesians 4 continues:

> I, therefore, the prisoner of the Lord, beseech you to walk worthy of the calling with which you were called, 2 with all lowliness and gentleness, with longsuffering, bearing with one another in love, 3 endeavoring to keep the unity of the Spirit in the bond of peace.
>
> – Eph. 4:1-3

Paul made clear that all Christians have a calling, the same calling: To be united as the Lord's body. Therefore, to walk worthily of this calling, believers are to endeavor to keep the unity of the Spirit. Christians may consider that they have different callings, such as becoming a preacher, a pastor, a gospel singer, a missionary, etc. However, in the big picture, everyone has the same calling: to unite with our brothers and sisters in Christ. Peace among previous enemies is needed because we are *"called in one body"* (Col. 3:15). Keep the unity of the Spirit!

Due to differences between His people who were enemies, *"all lowliness and gentleness, with longsuffering, bearing with one another in love"* is critically needed. Remember, these are Gentiles and Jews, being the most divided and warring people for centuries. They represent every other group of people separated by animosity and hatred toward each other. There is no excuse for division between any other group of Christians, since Jews and Gentiles can be united in Christ. It is no wonder that to stay in fellowship among diverse believers, these qualities are essential: lowliness, gentleness, longsuffering, meekness, and bearing in love.

The rest of Ephesians 4 continues to highlight the need to work out a practical unity among diverse believers.

> till we all come to the unity of the faith and of the knowledge of the Son of God, to a perfect man, to the measure of the stature of the fullness of Christ; . . . 15 but, speaking the truth in love, may grow up in all things into Him who is the head — Christ — 16 from whom the whole body, joined and knit together by what every joint supplies, according to the effective working by which every part does its share, causes growth of the body for the edifying of itself in love. . . . 30 And do not grieve the Holy Spirit of God, by whom you were sealed for the day of redemption. 31 Let all bitterness, wrath, anger, clamor, and evil speaking be put away from you, with all malice. 32 And be kind to one another, tenderhearted, forgiving one another, even as God in Christ forgave you.
>
> – Eph. 4:13, 15-16, 30-32

It grieves the Holy Spirit when there are problems between believers. The items mentioned are due to offenses and infighting between believers. That is why there is a need to "forgive one another" as God in Christ forgave each person, no matter which side of the disagreement. Again, all these practical characteristics and actions are needed to keep peace among the Jews and the Gentiles, or in today's case, among every divisive identity Christians have found among themselves.

The historical practice of Christians is to segregate into various groups or churches with "like-minded" people. These silos of believers are typically discouraged and even prevented from mingling with believers who are different to showcase the oneness of God's diverse people. God needs to manifest the work of Christ on the cross by bringing previous enemies into unity. Until this unity is practically manifested for all to see, God's wisdom and glory will still be hidden from the world.

Joint Partakers

Finally, the third item of the mystery of Christ is that Gentiles and Jews are to be joint partakers in God's promises. This is related to Paul's dispensation (*oikonomia*) of grace in Ephesians 3:2. Paul's stewardship [*oikonomia*] was to dispense the grace of God. John 1:17 states: *"For the law was given through Moses,* [but] *grace and truth came through Jesus Christ."* The grace spoken of in the New Testament is simply Jesus Christ. This grace is much more than "unmerited favor" as most may understand. The grace of the Lord is the enjoyment of Jesus Himself with all He is and all He has accomplished for God's people. This grace is not mere knowledge but experiential by His people with joy, pleasure, and rejoicing, which is the Greek meaning of "grace" (Gk. *karis*). Whenever believers experience and enjoy who Jesus Christ is and what He has eternally accomplished, they have joy and rejoicing. That is the unique sign of grace: *"Rejoice in the Lord always and again I say rejoice"* (Phil. 4:4). The Greek word for "rejoice" is the root word for "grace." In other words, a lack of rejoicing is a lack of the grace of the Lord.

Paul, as a steward, dispenses grace while both Jews and Gentiles are now joint partakers of this same grace. All of God's people have access to grace for partaking, contributing, and participating. The way to build up the one Body is to partake of grace (this is God's *oikonomia* as seen in previous chapters). Only by partaking in the Lord's grace as food (nourishment) can believers grow and mature into His Temple. All the characteristics described in Ephesians 4, in arriving at unity among diverse believers, can only flourish due to partaking in grace. All of God's promises are included in the grace of the Lord Jesus. *"For all the promises of God in Him* [Christ] *are Yes, and in Him Amen, to the glory of God through us"* (2 Cor. 1:20).

This partaking of grace is through the glad tidings or the gospel. The gospel is the channel through which all His riches come. Paul said in the same chapter: *"I should preach among the Gentiles the unsearchable riches of Christ"* (Eph. 3:8). Most Christians consider the gospel to be only the initial good news extended/announced to unbelievers. However, since the riches of Christ are unsearchable, the preaching of the good news is unending. Participating in the unsearchable riches of Christ as grace for God's people is not just for unbelievers or babes in Christ. These unsearchable riches must be unveiled continually through preaching, even extending to mature believers. A major reason the Body of Christ — His Ekklesia — has not yet matured to impact the world lies in this: many believers still fall short of truly seeing and enjoying the unsearchable riches of Christ. Therefore, let all His people partake of God's promises and grow to maturity.

Jews and Gentiles being joint heirs, joint body, and joint partakers can be called the "threefold joining of Jews and Gentiles," a shortened description of the mystery of Christ.

James Declared the Fulfillment of the Mystery of Christ

James, the half-brother of Jesus, in Acts 15, stunningly declared the fulfillment of a prophetic Scripture (Amos 9:11-12) that **the tabernacle or United Kingdom of David is the fellowship and oneness between Jews and Gentiles**. Through the Spirit's unveiling, he boldly proclaimed this prophetic fulfillment amid contentions over whether to accept the Gentile believers just as they are without their conversion to the law of Moses (many Jewish believers considered them "sinners" or "unsaved" because they still had not been circumcised — Acts 15:1-5). James' interpretation and application have broadened the understanding of many other difficult prophecies concerning Israel-Ephraim and Judah.

There are many prophecies concerning reuniting the 12 tribes (Israel-Ephraim and Judah), which most Bible teachers have relegated their fulfillment to the future heavenly kingdom. They reasoned that these prophecies could not be realized during the present age on earth. So, without James' proclamation in Acts 15:13-21, it would be difficult and suspect for anyone to interpret and apply these prophecies for today. Well-meaning Christian scholars, let alone Jewish scholars, interpret and/or view Acts 15 and Amos 9 as utterly futuristic and set their fulfillment into the distant future, the Millennium, or "other worldly" timeframe. Yet, what James declared was for the "here and now" — he summarized the findings of the so-called "Jerusalem Council" and tied them to immediate prophetic fulfillment. In reality, the United Kingdom of David, wherein all 12 Tribes were administered under the governance of King David, was happening right then and there.

Let's review the Scriptural and historical records to consider the aftermath of the Assyrian conquest of Israel-Ephraim to understand the impossibility of reuniting the 12 tribes until James' declaration.

> In the ninth year of Hoshea, the king of Assyria took Samaria and carried Israel away to Assyria, and placed them in Halah and by the Habor, the River of Gozan, and in the cities of the Medes.
>
> – 2 Kings 17:6

> Ephraim [Israel] has mixed himself among the peoples [nations] . . .
>
> – Hos. 7:8

> Within sixty-five years Ephraim [Israel] will be broken [lit. "shattered"], [So that it will] not [be] a people.
>
> – Isa. 7:8

> Israel is swallowed up; already they are among the nations as a useless vessel.
>
> – Hos. 8:8

Due to Solomon's sin of idolatry, God divided David's kingdom into two during the reign of Solomon's son, Rehoboam.[22] The northern 10 tribes under King Jeroboam became Israel or Ephraim. Judah, under King Rehoboam, retained only the tribe of Benjamin (along with the Levites). Jeroboam institutionalized a separation from the Mosaic Covenant by having his own god (golden calves), places of worship (Dan and Bethel) instead of Jerusalem, and priests instead of Levites. This sin of Jeroboam continued for about 200 years until the Assyrians' conquest. During this period, none of the kings brought Israel back to God and the Mosaic Covenant. In essence, they became like all the other nations. According to the above Scriptures, when the Assyrians swapped population by migrating some from the nations to the land of Israel and deporting many Israelites to Assyria, Israel (Ephraim) was readily assimilated into the nations. Their identity as the nation of Israel, as the 10 tribes dissolved, was shattered. They became no longer identifiable as a people through generations of intermarriage. Israel-Ephraim is "broken, not a people," and they have become a "useless vessel" like the nations.

On the other hand, Judah kept the temple to worship God, had Levitical priests to make offerings, with the Levites who taught the law. Therefore, they had some good kings who would periodically return the nation to God and the Mosaic Covenant. Eventually, they also strayed; consequently, God disciplined them by the Babylonians' conquest; nevertheless, even as captives in Babylon, there were men of God who kept the law of Moses. These were people like Daniel, Ezekiel, and others who remembered Jerusalem and the eventual return to that city.

When the Jews (Judah), including Benjamin and the Levites, came back to Jerusalem to rebuild the temple and the wall surrounding the city, they considered themselves faithful to God's covenant and became the representation of all Israel. It was during this Babylonian Captivity and immediately thereafter that the term "Jews" (*Yehudi/Yehudia*) was identified with Judah-Israel but not with Ephraim-Israel.

After the Jews returned from exile in Babylon, Jews and Israelites became interchangeable (Ezra 1;3; Neh. 11:20). Through them Jesus Christ came; therefore, Paul speaking concerning specifically about the Jews, said: *"Who are Israelites, to whom pertain the adoption, the glory, the covenants, the giving of the law, the service of God, and the*

---

22   This dividing of the 12 Tribes can be traced back to Jacob's dividing his family into "two companies" or groups (Gen. 32:7) when he faced off with his brother Esau. It was highlighted in Joseph's enslavement, and later signified with Caleb (Judah) and Joshua (Ephraim) when these "two spies who gave a good report" led the children of Israel into the Promised Land; and, of course, the Ark of the Covenant remaining in Shiloh/Ephraim for nearly 400 years and then nearly 400 years in Judah/Jerusalem.

promises; of whom are the fathers and from whom, according to the flesh, Christ came, who is over all, eternally blessed God. Amen" (Rom 9:4-5).

After Pentecost, many Jews believed in Jesus as the Messiah. By Acts 4, already 5,000 men (not counting women and children) believed in Jesus Christ. By Acts 15, even many priests and Pharisees had come to faith (Acts 6:7; 15:5). Later, in Acts 21, James declares that myriads (tens of thousands) of Jews believed in Jesus and remained zealous for the law. To the Jews, Jesus the Messiah was simply an extension of the Mosaic Covenant. The Messiah belongs to the Jews who were faithful in bringing forth Jesus Christ. Believing that Jesus is the Messiah strengthened their resolve for Moses, since if not for their faithfulness to the Mosaic law, Jesus' ancestors would not be in the Promised Land to bring Him forth in Bethlehem.

It was well within God's Covenant for the Jews to demand that Gentile Christians also be converted to Moses. They could not refute that the Spirit had come upon the Gentiles just as upon the Jews (Acts 10:45). Nevertheless, they could quote: *"Also the sons of the foreigner who join themselves to the LORD, to serve Him, and to love the name of the LORD, to be His servants — everyone who keeps from defiling the Sabbath, and holds fast My covenant"* (Isa. 56:6). They could boldly declare: "Yes, the Gentiles can join and be part of God's people if they also keep God's Mosaic Covenant."

Therefore, these Jewish believers had a strong Scriptural basis to go to the Gentile Christian and tell them: *"Unless you are circumcised according to the custom of Moses, you cannot be saved"* (Acts 15:1). The Jewish believers seem to be saying: "Having faith in Jesus is not enough, there is also a requirement to follow the law of Moses." So, with a good conscience, they went to the Gentile world proclaiming *"a different gospel"* (Gal. 1:6): believing in Jesus is the beginning, now those called out from the Nations ("ethnos" or Gentiles) must also follow Moses.

The gospel of Jesus Christ is simple: Jesus, as the Son of God, died and rose from the dead. He arose as the Lord of all. By believing in His resurrection and accepting Him as Lord, a person is saved (Rom. 10:9). There are no other requirements — salvation is by grace and not by works (Eph. 2:8-9).

The Gentiles were confused. These Gentiles received and were saved by the gospel of Jesus Christ in faith. Then they heard they also needed to abide by the law of Moses — to become Jewish. The Council in Jerusalem was to clear up this confusion. Since the source of this "other gospel" came from the Jewish believers ("Judaizers") in Jerusalem (Acts 15:24), Paul, Barnabas, and a contingent of Gentiles went to have a conference with the entire Democratic Assembly in Jerusalem, together with the apostles and elders.

After much dispute among the brethren concerning whether Gentiles needed to abide by the law of Moses (become Jewish), James, half-brother of Jesus, gave a concluding word. This word is stunning and astonishing, and it can only be revealed to James through the enlightenment of the Holy Spirit.

> And with this the words of the prophets agree, just as it is written: 16 'After this I will return And will rebuild the tabernacle [kingdom] of David, which has fallen down; I will rebuild its ruins, And I will set it up; 17 So that the rest of mankind may seek the LORD, Even all the Gentiles who are called by My name, Says the LORD who does all these things.' 18 "Known to God from eternity are all His works.
>
> – Act 15:15-18

James quoted from Amos 9:11-12. That chapter started with the destruction of Israel (the northern 10 tribes), who had completely forsaken God. They did not even want to hear Amos' warning. They wanted him to leave Israel and prophesy in Judah from whence he came (Amos 7:12). However, after prophesying the destruction of Israel in verses 11 and 12, Amos spoke of the restoration of the tabernacle or dynasty (kingdom) of David. By then, David's kingdom had been shattered and divided into the northern 10 tribes and southern 2 tribes for almost 200 years (from the "breach of Jeroboam" until Amos' remarks). Amos said that the 12 tribes would be restored, the damage would be repaired, and it would be rebuilt as in the days of David. After this prophecy, things did not improve; they got much worse according to the first part of Amos 9. Israel was defeated and carried off to Assyria. As discussed previously, they were swallowed up and assimilated. They were no more a people and lost their identity as Israel. That was the end of Israel (the northern 10 tribes), with no more mention of them in the Hebrew Scriptures. They had been erased because they were now Gentiles. "Israel" is now only represented by the Jews (Judah and Benjamin).

If the northern 10 tribes disappeared, how could the United Kingdom of David be restored with all 12 tribes under his rule? The answer came with James' proclamation. It was not just one prophet, but the prophets agreed that this coming together into one body between the Jews and the Gentiles fulfilled the restoration of the United Kingdom of David. James equated the Gentiles to the 10 "lost" northern tribes and the Jews to the southern 2 tribes — Behold the restoration of all 12 tribes under King David. This is mind-blowing: James accepted the Gentiles as the tribes deported by Assyria around 722 BC when their northern Capital, Samaria, fell to the Assyrians.

Jesus is the real King David. Through Jesus Christ, the kingdom of David is restored and under His kingship. The historical King David, Judah's victorious king, foreshadowed Jesus Christ, the eternal King of the tribe of Judah. Luke's proclamation concerning Jesus: *"He will be great, and will be called the Son of the Highest, and the Lord God will give Him the throne of His father David. And He will reign over the house of Jacob forever, and of His kingdom there will be no end"* (Luke 1:32-33). For almost a thousand years, since King Rehoboam, the kingdom of David had been lost and scattered. Now the United Kingdom of David was being restored, with all 12 tribes gathered under one King — Jesus of Nazareth.

Just as the 12 tribes of old were distinct from each other, the Gentiles are even more different from the Jews. The Gentiles did not have to follow the Jewish tradition and become Jewish (Peter: ". . . by putting a yoke on the neck of the disciples which neither our fathers nor we were able to bear?" — Acts 15:10), nor do the Jews have to be Gentiles. Each tribe retains its unique identity, yet together they are united as one kingdom under King Jesus, who reigns from the eternal throne of David. What liberation in the kingdom of Jesus: there is freedom to be Gentiles (without being under the Mosaic Covenant) or to be Jewish (under the Mosaic Covenant). However, in Jesus Christ, they are united as one. . . just as in the days of old.

The oneness between Jews and Gentiles becoming one kingdom under King Jesus is the reason why Jesus died on the cross. He spoke concerning this in John 10 when He said: *"And other sheep* [Gentiles] *I have which are not of this fold [Jews]; them also I must bring, and they will hear My voice; and there will be one flock [and] one shepherd"* (John 10:16). The Gentiles are those not of "this fold" referring to those in the Jewish fold. Nevertheless, these Gentiles will hear His voice and become one flock with one Shepherd. And those sheep within the Jewish *fold*, as well, will hear the Shepherd's voice, and go out to Him through the Door of the sheepfold into the green pastures to unite with His "other sheep" (Ephraim). It is there, notwithstanding the wolves, where there is one *flock* and one Shepherd who guards them from the wolves (John 10).

At the end of the last supper, He prayed for this before His death the next day: *"I do not pray for these alone [Jews], but also for those [Gentiles] who will believe in Me through their word; that they all may be one, as You, Father, are in Me, and I in You; that they also may be one in Us, that the world may believe that You sent Me"* (John 17:20-21). "These alone" refers to the Jewish disciples, and "those" refers to the Gentile believers who will believe through the Jewish disciples' preaching. A notable example is Peter preaching at Cornelius' house in Acts 10, where this Gentile household received salvation and was baptized in the Holy Spirit.

> Now this he did not say on his own [authority]; but being high priest that
> year he prophesied that Jesus would die for the nation, 52 and not for that
> nation only, but also that He would gather together in one the children of
> God who were scattered abroad.
>
> – John 11:51-52

In John 11, the high priest, Caiaphas, prophesied that Jesus would die for the Jewish nation, but John added that Jesus' death was not just as the Jewish Messiah, but He died to gather in one God's children scattered abroad. This scattering of God's children can refer to the scattered northern 10 tribes who became Gentiles through centuries of intermarriage. Jesus died to gather them in one with the Jewish nation. The purpose of Jesus' death is abundantly clear: gather God's scattered children into one!

Application for Today

Most Christians today may not be affected by the Jewish and Gentile conflict regarding their restored unity in Christ. To most, it was just a historical event from 2000 years ago. Nevertheless, up till now and maybe resurging, there continues to be confusion among many Christians about whether it is more spiritual and Scriptural to practice Jewish traditions such as the Sabbath, dietary restrictions, or annual feasts. We should learn from the mystery of Christ that there is freedom to practice or not to practice. The oneness among believers is not based on these practices, but in Christ alone. There should be complete unity between those who practice and those who do not. Some well-intentioned brethren are resolute in their insistence that all believers in Yeshua should adhere to these aforementioned matters, or even some "Messianic Believers" who insist that Gentile believers should NOT adhere to these practices because they are not Jewish. Such insistence (and there are other contentions concerning what is and what is not practiced among sincere believers in Yeshua/Jesus) only inflicts further division within the Lord's one body. Again, "Lord, transform our minds to be your one sacrifice on your altar and not think of ourselves more highly than we ought to think."

Additionally, there is a much broader application to solving disunity among believers. Today's Christians may consider that what happened between the Jews and Gentiles in becoming one in Christ does not apply to divisions among Christians today. It is commonly accepted that there is widespread segregation, animosity, sectarianism, exclusivity, and arrogance between Christians in various groups or churches. For one, those who belong to the Catholic church have been warring with those who are Protestants over the decades, even up to the last century. Members of state churches and independent churches have also persecuted each other with violence. A huge gulf of animosity has existed between Calvinists (those believing in predestination and once-saved-always-saved) and Armenians (those who believe in losing one's salvation through free will). With the rise of Pentecostalism in the last century, a significant divide has developed between those who embrace ongoing miraculous gifts and those — often called 'cessationists' — who believe that tongues and prophetic foretelling ceased with the apostolic age. This does not include millions of other divided Christians identifying with thousands of denominations who project a superior position in holiness, orthodoxy, doctrinal accuracy, social justice, end-time prophecies, word of faith, discipleship, deliverance, universal salvation, views of eschatology/prophecy, healing, parenting, and so forth.

Even though each church or group may have its specialty and identity based on its leadership's direction, believers within every group belong to only one kingdom — the Kingdom of Christ. The most these different groups can be comparable to are the various tribes of Israel. Nevertheless, all the members of each tribe must go to Jerusalem and feast with members of other tribes three times a year. This was the only place and condition where God was worshipped and His glory displayed. Each church or group of Christians may have an identity, but that identity cannot overshadow the unique identity of the Body of Christ. Christ died and was resurrected to gather members of all the tribes together into one. While a Christian may be part of a specific 'tribe' or church, God's purpose still calls for fellowship with believers among different groups. As explored later, God designed a democratic forum — His Ekklesia — under the New Covenant, as revealed in the New Testament: a gathering place where believers from every "tribe" can feast and worship Him as one, without needing to convert to another tribe.

If the animosity and division between Jews and Gentiles can be healed and made one, then all other divisions among Christians are easy. No matter how big the gulf between the positions and doctrines of the groups, believers within these groups should be at peace with each other. The churches can be separated by their positions and labels, but the believers themselves must be liberated into the fellowship of the Body of Christ.

Ecumenism, or the Ecumenical Movement, exemplified by the World and National Council of Churches, aims to unify church organizations. Their goal is for diverse churches to work under one umbrella organization like the UN[23]. This has merits, but it is also controversial and harmful in the minds of many Evangelical Christians. They consider that compromise or watering down the truth of the Scriptures is necessary in

---

23   What is the World Council of Churches? | World Council of Churches

this organizational unity. This is not the unity as seen by the revelation of the mystery of Christ.

The diversity in unity advanced in this chapter concerning the mystery of Christ is organic among individual believers. As identifiable groups, Churches have differences and emphases in spiritual and doctrinal understandings. Nevertheless, genuine believers in these groups have the same common faith in Jesus Christ. This common faith made the New Covenant real to them — the indwelling Holy Spirit with God's life and nature. Therefore, even if the divisions among the churches are justifiably insurmountable as expected, believers within these churches should recognize that their real membership is in the Body of Christ. Their highest identity is a member of the kingdom of Christ. Therefore, despite divisions among the churches that they attend, their loyalty should be to the one fellowship of the Body of Christ. They must be in "Jerusalem" to feast and worship with all their diverse brethren in Christ.

The Rest of Mankind May Seek the Lord

In Acts 15:17, there are three groups of people. One not mentioned but inferred is the Jews, since they were part of the conflict. The second group is the Gentiles who have called or invoked the Lord's name. They referred to the *ethnic groups* who believed throughout the regions of the old Assyrian Empire or in Asia Minor (aka Gentiles), where Paul went to preach. They were troubled by the *Judaizers* (Jewish believers in Yeshua), which led to the conference/council in Jerusalem. The third group was the *rest of mankind*, which is everyone else on earth — that they would seek the Lord. The oneness between the Jews and Gentiles would cause the rest of mankind to seek the Lord. This is the end-time gospel and revival when there is unity between diverse believers. This is a wonderful prophecy: the oneness of God's people will cause the rest of mankind to seek the Lord.

This is supported by the Lord's prayer in John 17: *"that they all may be one, as You, Father, are in Me, and I in You; that they also may be one in Us, that the world may believe that You sent Me"* (John 17:21). The "they all" refers to the Gentile who believed together with the Jewish believers who preached. When these Jewish and Gentile believers are one, then the world will believe. The oneness of God's diverse people is the cause for the world, or "the rest of mankind," to believe in the reality of Jesus Christ. This is the most powerful gospel preaching, and this has to come to pass before the Lord's second advent. This is when His believers are still in this world under the rule of the "evil one" (John 17:15). Amid the worldly system of the Evil One, the diverse followers are one. This unity will cause those in the kingdom of the Evil One to believe in Jesus. Witnessing the unity of God's previously divided people is the most powerful conviction and manifestation of the reality of Jesus Christ.

The mystery of Christ unveiled by Paul is wonderful! Christians must understand this mystery. This was Paul's heart in writing Ephesians, that his readers would be able to have this understanding of the truth concerning the mystery of Christ. Without this understanding, God's people are confused or lost regarding the direction of their Christian journey. Anything less than the seeking and building up of the mystery of Christ, which is this threefold joining of Jews and Gentiles, will fall short of God's goal. Christians will be groping for direction at best, or worse, they will become divisive. It is almost inevitable that without a clear vision of the mystery of Christ, Christians will default to segregation and sectarianism.

The hope of each believer's calling is to advance and experience the unity among God's diverse people. This displays the mystery of Christ to the world.

Jesus Came to Make Peace and Conquer His Enemy

Rejoice greatly, O daughter of Zion! Shout, O daughter of Jerusalem! Behold, your King is coming to you; He [is] just and having salvation, Lowly and riding on a donkey, A colt, the foal of a donkey. 10 I will cut off the chariot from Ephraim and the horse from Jerusalem; The battle bow shall be cut off. He shall speak peace to the nations; His dominion [shall be] 'from sea to sea, And from the River to the ends of the earth.' 11 "As for you also, Because of the blood of your covenant, I will set your prisoners free from the waterless pit. . . . 13 For I have bent Judah, My [bow], Fitted the bow with Ephraim, and raised up your sons, O Zion, Against your sons, O Greece, and made you like the sword of a mighty man." 14 Then the LORD will be seen over them, and His arrow will go forth like lightning. The Lord GOD will blow the trumpet, and go with whirlwinds from the south. . . . 16 The LORD their God will save them in that day, as the flock of His people. For they [shall be like] the jewels of a crown, Lifted like a banner over His land —

– Zech. 9:9-11, 13-14, 16

Based on James' application of Amos' prophecy of Ephraim-Israel and Judah's restoration to be fulfilled by the coming together of Gentiles and Jews, other prophecies in the Hebrew Scriptures concerning the same can be similarly applied. Zechariah 9 is the prophecy concerning Jesus entering Jerusalem on a colt, the foal of a donkey (i.e., on a small "baby donkey"). Without controversy, this prophecy was fulfilled on the first day of the week (Sunday), in which His crucifixion took place in mid-week. This is when Jesus rode into Jerusalem on the colt (Matt. 21:1-11). At His death and resurrection, the New Covenant was enacted. Jesus' death is called the blood of the New Covenant (Matt. 26:28). The New Covenant came into being — it became real and activated at the shedding of His blood. All that God promised and prophesied in Jeremiah 31 was fulfilled for all His people.

This prophecy shows that the primary reason for the coming of Christ and His cross was peace between Ephraim and Jerusalem (Judah). Up to the time of Jesus, Ephraim and Judah had been at war for almost 1,000 years. Their hostility started when the kingdom of David split between the northern 10 tribes (Ephraim-Israel) and the southern 2 tribes (Judah). When Ephraim-Israel was defeated and swallowed up by the Gentiles (i.e., assimilated), these mixed-race Gentiles continued warring with Judah even after their return from the Babylonian captivity. That hatred continued between the Jews and Gentiles (Samaritans) during the time of Jesus. Then, after the day of Pentecost, the antagonism between the Jews and Gentiles followed into the "church" (ekklesia).

When Jesus died, He broke down the middle wall of hostility. He *cut off the chariot from Ephraim, and the horse from Jerusalem* (Judah); *The battle bow shall be cut off.*" This shows that the war between them ended at the cross. Remember, Ephraim-Israel is now represented by the Gentiles, while Judah continued into God's Ekklesia (democratic assembly). Their chariots and bows for warfare are cut off. They are no more. There shall be peace. This peace will spread to all the nations of the earth. In this peace, Jesus will reign over the earth. This is all due to the "blood of your covenant." This was activated at the death and resurrection of Jesus Christ.

Not only were they not fighting, but they became united and worked together in the Lord's hand to defeat His enemy. Judah became the bow, and Ephraim became the arrow used by the Lord to shoot His enemy. In their unity, the Lord used them like the sword of a mighty man. The blood of the Lord's New Covenant united their previous adversaries. Together, they have become His instruments of warfare, His bow and arrow to defeat the real enemy, Satan. No matter how long they have been opponents, God needs His people in unity so the arrow can go forth like lightning.

Again, this is not for the by and by in the future, but it is for today. Many Christians consider other Christians due to various church identities to be enemies. If not enemies, at least there is an avoidance of fellowship. However, those enjoying Christ's New Covenant will be liberated and make peace with diverse believers, no matter what church they may or may not identify with. Once the walls of division between believers are broken down with unity ensuing, then they will be His instruments for defeating God's enemy, Satan.

9

THE MYSTERY OF CHRIST IN OTHER PROPHECIES

The Four Living Creatures

> As for the likeness of their faces, [each] had the face of a man; each of the four had the face of a lion on the right side, each of the four had the face of an ox on the left side, and each of the four had the face of an eagle. 11 Thus [were] their faces. Their wings stretched upward; two [wings] of each one touched one another, and two covered their bodies. . . . 20 Wherever the spirit wanted to go, they went, [because] there the spirit went; and the wheels were lifted together with them, for the spirit of the living creatures [was] in the wheels.
>
> – Eze 1:10-11, 20

The first of Ezekiel's awesome visions began with four living creatures joined together. Apparently, it is a description of angelic cherubim. However, the first layer of unraveling this vision, just about all theologians agree, these four living creatures are an archetype of Jesus, the Messiah. He is represented by these four living creatures: man, lion, ox, and eagle. Man refers to His humanity, lion unveils Him as the King (lion of the tribe of Judah), Ox shows He lowered Himself to serve God and man as the ultimate sacrifice, and finally, He is also divine and soaring in resurrection like an eagle. He is completely directed by God the Spirit, for His human spirit and God's Spirit are one.

Another layer unveils the mystery of Christ: These four living creatures represent Christ enlarged to include all His redeemed and united people. Revelation 5:8-10 shows these four living creatures also represent creation in their worship to the Lamb, the Redeemer. Jesus Christ was glorified for making humanity kings and priests to God out of every tribe, tongue, people, and nation (Rev. 5:8-10). Through Christ's death and resurrection, He multiplied Himself to include His regenerated people as His corporate Body. Christ is now both the Head, Jesus, and the members forming His Body (1 Cor. 12:13). Therefore, the four living creatures illustrate His corporate people joined together as the mystery of Christ.

Consider the distinction and variety of these four living creatures. According to the Mosaic Law, the ox is classified as a clean animal, while the lion and eagle are considered unclean. As for man, his status can be either clean or unclean (depending on circumcision). Additionally, among these four, there are predators and prey, which can extend to warring for dominance between tribes and nations. These four living creatures naturally would not and cannot join together as one. Certainly, the clean and unclean must be separated and given the opportunity; one would devour or subjugate the other.

Nevertheless, as Christ's expression, they must be joined and move as one unit — the clean and unclean, natural enemies from diverse peoples and cultures. In Christ, they are the enlargement and extension of Him on earth. Only by joining together can Christ move on earth as God's wheel. Though joined together, there are no impediments; rather, their movements are lightning fast. In unity, they move as the Spirit moves because their spirits and God's Spirit are one.

On one hand, God's Spirit directs them to move in all six directions (including up and down). They go where the Spirit goes. On the other hand, the spirits of these creatures are in the wheels, so they can independently direct the movements of the wheels. What a wonder that God's Spirit and these individual spirits of the creatures are in perfect harmony and synchronization to be God's move on earth. Without unity, there would be no movements; they would be torn apart if each fought to go their own way. What a sight to behold — these natural enemies are joined together, no matter which direction they are seen, all four faces (man, lion, ox, and eagle) are expressed. Each kept their distinctions; yet, they are completely joined and united, moving and manifesting Christ on earth as one.

This is the mystery of Christ. The joining of clean and unclean, diversity in unity, with each part equally necessary, with no one dominating. The creatures' spirits and God's Spirit are synchronized as one, such that it is indistinguishable who is directing His move on earth. This first vision is foundational for the other visions in Ezekiel.

The Valley of Dry Bones

> Again He said to me, "Prophesy to these bones, and say to them, 'O dry bones, hear the word of the LORD! 5 'Thus says the Lord GOD to these bones: "Surely I will cause breath to enter into you, and you shall live. . . . 7 So I prophesied as I was commanded; and as I prophesied, there was a noise, and suddenly a rattling; and the bones came together, bone to bone. 8 Indeed, as I looked, the sinews and the flesh came upon them, and the skin

covered them over; but [there was] no breath in them. 9 Also He said to me, "Prophesy to the breath, prophesy, son of man, and say to the breath, 'Thus says the Lord GOD:

"Come from the four winds, O breath, and breathe on these slain, that they may live." ' " 10 So I prophesied as He commanded me, and breath came into them, and they lived, and stood upon their feet, an exceedingly great army. 11 Then He said to me, "Son of man, these bones are the whole house of Israel. They indeed say, 'Our bones are dry, our hope is lost, and we ourselves are cut off!' . . . 14 "I will put My Spirit in you, and you shall live, and I will place you in your own land. Then you shall know that I, the LORD, have spoken [it] and performed [it]," says the LORD.' "

– Ezek. 37:4-5, 7-11, 14

Since James said that the Gentiles and Jews uniting in Christ are agreed upon by the prophets (Acts 15:15), let's consider other prophetic words regarding this. In Ezekiel 37, we find a major prophecy concerning the mystery of Christ. Due to James' bold interpretation and application using Amos 9:11-12 concerning the rebuilding of the tent or dynasty of David with Jews and Gentiles, Ezekiel's prophecy can be similarly applied.

Ezekiel 36 was discussed in a previous chapter of this book as prophetic concerning the implementation of the New Covenant. The essence of the New Covenant is the indwelling Holy Spirit with God's life and nature (Ezek. 36:27). Immediately after this, in chapter 37, there was a prophecy concerning the "valley of dry bones" coming together to form the army of a united Israel. Later in the same chapter 37, the "two sticks" refer to Israel-Joseph/Ephraim joining with Israel/Judah-Benjamin to become one restored kingdom under one King. Both of these prophecies are the result of the New Covenant of Peace ("I will make a Covenant of Peace with them [Judah and Ephraim]" (Ezek. 37:26).

Ezekiel's prophetic ministry was during his captivity in Babylon. He was aware of the historical events regarding the divided kingdom that started between Jeroboam and Rehoboam, the deportation of Israel-Ephraim to Assyria, and the defeat of the southern kingdom of Judah. Therefore, his vision of the valley of dry bones signifying the dead, divided, and scattered 12 tribes of Israel was factual at the time. In such a condition, Ezekiel had no confidence when God asked whether these bones could live. Ezekiel could only faithlessly answer: "O Lord God, You know" (Eze. 37:3).

Anyhow, he obeyed God and prophesied to the bones. The response to God's word was that the bones came together — "bone to bone." This uniting of the bones was a prerequisite for all subsequent steps: sinews, flesh, skin covering the skeletons, and rising up as an army. In the New Testament, Paul likened the members of Christ's body to bones. He said that for the growth of the Body, the joints (bones) must be knit together (Col. 2:19). Before anything else can happen, members of the Body of Christ need to join together at the hearing of God's word.

God commanded Ezekiel to prophesy again. When he did, the wind of God came and filled those united with breath, and they stood up as an exceedingly great army. This army was the "whole house of Israel."[24] These dead bones, which were scattered in Assyria and Babylon, came back together to be God's great army to defeat His enemies. The divisions among Israel over the centuries resulted in the obliteration of God's army, dead and scattered bones. Nevertheless, the joining together of God's once-divided people became a great army and victoriously destroyed God's enemy.

For this army to rise again, first, there must be the preaching of Jesus Christ as envisioned in the New Covenant to give life to the dead. The hearing of Jesus Christ transmits life to the dead. *"Most assuredly, I say to you, the hour is coming, and now is, when the dead will hear the voice of the Son of God; and those who **hear** will **live**"* (John 5:25). This is the wonder of the gospel of Jesus Christ: dead people hear and by faith, they receive eternal life. These are those spiritually dead without any spiritual activities or seeking. What wonder that they hear! This transformation from death to life is easy, painless, and simple. It is the hearing of faith through the words of Christ (Rom. 10:17). The receiving of eternal life is the Holy Spirit entering and becoming one with those who respond in faith.

> We know that we have passed from death to life, because we love the brethren. He who does not love [his] brother abides in death.
>
> – 1 John 3:14

At the time of eternal life, the first and immediate transformative response is to "love the brethren." This is the joining together of the bones. Loving or joining with all other believers in Christ, including previous enemies, is the proof of eternal life. When a person is deadened, he can remain in His division and animosity with others. However, when he passes from death to life in Christ, his inward being is radically transformed from separation and hate to joining together in love. "Love the brethren" means forgiveness, fellowship, sharing, togetherness, and unity. Loving the brethren includes

---

24   Some well-meaning brethren have a concept that the "Church" (God's Ekklesia) is not in view in Ezekiel 37's Valley of Dry Bones—just the Jews. Not so. The "whole House of Israel" is in view—both Joseph, the Stick of Ephraim and the Stick of Judah.

the willingness to sacrifice for them. The eternal life expresses the love of God. The love for the brethren is with the same love God loved His people who were His enemies: He sent His Son to die for them (Rom. 5:8-10).

"Love the brethren" is not just loving those Christians in the same group or church. No, "brethren" includes all God's people regenerated in Christ. All those who have believed and received Christ are born of God, and these children of God are brethren. Loving the brethren includes loving all of God's children, no matter which group or church with which they have identified themselves. For people who are spiritually dead, their love is selective and shows disdain for those who annoy them. Passing from death to life is a momentous transformation that results in love — even love for enemies.

Christian ministries and churches have, tragically and generally, divided God's people. Those who identify under one denomination may become judgmental toward those in another. Fellowshipping with those with a contrary doctrinal or holiness understanding would be rarely welcomed. Nevertheless, those living by God's life will immediately sense love and connection with other believers, no matter which group with whom they may identify. This is the first response to speaking the Word of God, from which all the other blessings come, resulting in a great army.

For the wind of God to blow and the breath to fill the people, the requirement is to join and unite God's people. By faith, believers have individually been filled with the breath of God for their Christian journey, but that is quite different from being an awesome army to defeat God's enemy. These individual fillings of the Spirit sustained them through the trials and challenges of life. However, it is still a struggle living in the darkness of the Satanic kingdom. When will the kingdom of this world become the kingdom of Christ? When will believers defeat God's enemy to put an end to Satan's kingdom? That is the work of God's "great army." Without the victory of this great army, Christians will continue to struggle in this evil world.

The oneness of God's people will cause God's Spirit to raise His victorious army. This is when *"The kingdoms of this world have become the kingdoms of our Lord and of His Christ, and He shall reign forever and ever!"* (Rev. 11:15). In other words, divided individuals can be sustained by the Spirit, but without oneness with other believers, it is a struggle peppered with bouts of defeat. God desires a great army from which the Spirit fills those joined "bone to bone" to subdue His enemy for eternity.

God commanded Ezekiel to prophesy twice to the valley of dry bones. The first resulted in the bones joining together. The second was when the army came alive and rose up. How can these two times of prophesying be applied in the New Testament? In Ephesians 4, there were two distinct instances of speaking and both resulted in the oneness of the Body of Christ at different stages — initial and maturity.

> I, therefore, the prisoner of the Lord, beseech you to walk worthy of the calling with which you were called, 2 with all lowliness and gentleness, with longsuffering, bearing with one another in love, 3 endeavoring to keep the unity of the Spirit in the bond of peace. . . . 11 And He Himself gave some [to be] apostles, some prophets, some evangelists, and some pastors and teachers, 12 for the equipping of the saints for the work of ministry, for the edifying of the body of Christ, 13 till we all come to the unity of the faith and of the knowledge of the Son of God, to a perfect man, to the measure of the stature of the fullness of Christ;
>
> – Eph. 4:1-3, 11-13

The first speaking from God was the *"calling with which you were called."* This should be the time of faith, at hearing the gospel of Jesus Christ. All believers were called at that time, and that calling had a specific purpose — *"keep the unity of the Spirit."* To be worthy of the calling of God, believers are to join together in unity. The calling of God at the hearing of the gospel would equate to the first prophetic speaking by Ezekiel in chapter 37, and the result was the joining of *"bone to bone."* The response to God's calling is to keep or guard the unity of the Spirit. The unity of the Spirit already exists with every believer at the time of faith. Now, keep it! Hold on to it with all lowliness, gentleness, and love. A force of arrogance and offenses is at work to keep believers ("bones") apart and separated. Nevertheless, the unity of the Spirit is operating and active. Go along and cooperate with the oneness of the Spirit and forsake the natural pre-regeneration animosity between peoples.

God's calling at the time of faith was to unite. The unity of the Spirit exists within every believer at the moment of regeneration. This equates to loving the brethren when one passes from death to life. Though this is the spontaneous working of the life of God in the Spirit, baby or immature believers, without growing in the Lord's grace, will revert to their natural state of preferential identities, pridefulness, and divisiveness. This was the case with the Corinthians when they divided among themselves based on their favored ministers. Paul chastised them for being fleshly and babes in Christ (1 Cor. 3:1-4). Therefore, another "prophetic" word was needed from the five-fold ministers: apostles, prophets, evangelists, pastors, and teachers. Their equipping words were to liberate the saints from their factiousness and function within the entire Body of Christ. The result is the unity of the faith. This is a furtherance or a maturing into unity since this is described as a "perfect" or a "full-grown" man (Eph. 4:11-13).

The goal of these various gifted ministers is not to build up their personal ministries. When the goal of ministers is to build their group or church, they can easily become dividers among Christians. While the apostle did his best not to draw a following for his legacy (2 Tim. 4:16), many of today's ministers, as in history, may end up building their legacy church (denomination). The true five-fold ministers of today will have the oneness of the Body of Christ in view. Their labor is to equip believers under their ministries so that believers themselves can function not just in their ministries, but in the greater Body of Christ. They will be equipped to come to the unity of the faith with all other believers, no matter which ministry or church to which they belong. All Christians have a common faith in Jesus Christ (Titus 1:4). No matter their differences in doctrinal understandings and Christian practices, they have all been saved and have become brethren by the same faith.

The five-fold ministers help in bringing maturity to believers like Paul did. Then, like Paul, let them loose to function as the priesthood of all believers in the Body of Christ (Col. 1:28-29). The five-fold ministers cannot build the Body directly since only regular believers ministering to one another can build up the Body. The mature Body of Christ is seen in the unity of the faith between diverse believers. Those Christians who remain as babes will be tossed back and forth between polarizing and divisive teachers with a plot to trick believers into their sectarian group or church (Eph. 4:14). The differentiating factor between a minister operating under the five-fold gift or a charlatan "wolf" is whether the believers are equipped to fellowship and be one with diverse believers in the Body or not. A wolf can even be a respected elder but draw men to himself rather than letting them mingle and fellowship with all the members of Christ (Acts 20:30).

The Body of Christ in oneness is a mature man and its joints (bones) are knit together (Eph. 4:16). Like the valley of dry bones scattered about were raised up into "an army of one" — *"and they lived, and stood upon their feet, an exceedingly great army"* (Ezek. 37:10). This is the One New Man (Eph. 4:24). This new man is a corporate man consisting of both Jews and Gentiles (Eph. 2:15). This corporate man puts on the entire armor of God (Eph. 6:11). This is how Ephesians ends with a fighting warrior. Paul used many descriptive terms for God's Democratic Assembly, His diverse people in unity. Chapter 1 in Ephesians is the Body of Christ; Chapter 2 is the new man and the temple; Chapter 3 is the mystery of Christ; Chapter 4 is a mature man with the stature of the fullness of Christ; Chapter 5 is the wife of Christ; and finally, Chapter 6 is the whole armor of God.

The armor of God is not for individuals, but this armor includes all the previous descriptions of the Lord's Ekklesia. The way to put on the armor is to be in the oneness of the Body. Divided individual members of Christ are outside the protection of the armor of God. Within the unity of diverse believers is the helmet, breastplate, and shield for protection and defense. For offensive attack, there is the sword of the Spirit, and the feet shod with the gospel of peace for moving against God's enemy. In unity, believers can preach the gospel of peace to break down more walls and bring peace and fellowship between once-divided believers. This is the "exceedingly great army" prophesied in Ezekiel 37, which came from joining the bones through His Spirit breathing upon these bones that they may live!

Two Sticks Joined as One

"Say to them, 'Thus says the Lord GOD: "Surely I will take the stick of Joseph, which [is] in the hand of Ephraim, and the tribes of Israel, his companions; and I will join them with it, with the stick of Judah, and make them one stick, and they will be one in My hand." ' 20 "And the sticks on which you write will be in your hand before their eyes. 21 "Then say to them, 'Thus says the Lord GOD: "Surely I will take the children of Israel from among the nations, wherever they have gone, and will gather them from every side and bring them into their own land; 22 "and I will make them one nation in the land, on the mountains of Israel; and one king shall be king over them all; they shall no longer be two nations, nor shall they ever be divided into two kingdoms again. 23 "They shall not defile themselves anymore with their idols, nor with their detestable things, nor with any of their transgressions; but I will deliver them from all their dwelling places in which they have sinned, and will cleanse them. Then they shall be My people, and I will be their God. 24 "David My servant [shall be] king over them, and they shall all have one shepherd; they shall also walk in My judgments and observe My statutes, and do them. 25 "Then they shall dwell in the land that I have given to Jacob My servant, where your fathers dwelt; and they shall dwell there, they, their children, and their children's children, forever; and My servant David [shall be] their prince forever. 26 "Moreover I will make a covenant of peace with them, and it shall be an everlasting covenant with them; I will establish them and multiply them, and I will set My sanctuary in their midst forevermore. 27 "My tabernacle also shall be with them; indeed I will be their God, and they shall be My people.

– Ezek. 37:19-27

We repeat this most significant passage following the vision of the Valley of Dry Bones, because this second prophecy expands upon the initial vision. The mystery of Christ is the threefold joining of Gentiles and Jews into one. Again, based on James' application of Amos' prophecy to the joining together of Jews and Gentiles, this prophecy concerning the two sticks becoming one may be even more powerful and clearer than Amos' prophetic outburst. In the minds of most people, there is a sense of bias and unfairness in God choosing the 12 tribes of Israel to be His special, treasured people, holy nation. This leads to accusations of God being unjust and a different God under the Mosaic Covenant from the New Covenant implemented in the New Testament. However, from the beginning, God's heart was for the people of the entire earth — all nations. His calling of Abraham was not just for the 12 tribes but for all the people of the Earth. This deserves repeating to instill in us that from the beginning Abram's name was changed by the Almighty to "Abraham" — meaning, "Father of many nations."

> As for Me, behold, My covenant is with you, and you shall be a father of **many nations**.
>
> – Gen. 17:4

Then to Abraham's son, Isaac, God similarly promised. God spoke to Isaac thus:

> And I will make your descendants multiply as the stars of heaven; I will give to your descendants all these lands; and in your seed **all the nations of the earth** shall be blessed;
>
> – Gen. 26:4

God reaffirmed His promises of blessing all the nations through Jacob (Israel).

> Also God said to him (Israel): "I am God Almighty. Be fruitful and multiply; a nation and **a company of nations** shall proceed from you, and kings shall come from your body."
>
> – Gen 35:11

Jacob then blessed his grandson Ephraim, whose father was Joseph and his mother was a Gentile Egyptian. Jacob's two grandsons from Joseph (Ephraim and Manasseh) became sons of Jacob, thus giving Joseph a double portion of inheritance (Gen. 48:5-6).

> But his father refused and said, "I know, my son, I know. He [Manasseh] also shall become a people, and he also shall be great; but truly his younger brother [Ephraim] shall be greater than he, and his descendants shall become a **multitude of nations**."
>
> – Gen. 48:19

Here, the promise or prophecy was clear: Ephraim's descendants would become a *multitude of nations*. What a strange and wonderful prophecy that one of the 12 tribes of Israel, Ephraim, would become a multitude of nations. How can that be? Nevertheless, it was so!

It seems God got Himself into a predicament since He made clear that only the 12 tribes of Israel are His chosen people.

> For you [are] a holy people to the LORD your God; the LORD your God has chosen you to be a people for Himself, a special treasure above all the peoples on the face of the earth. 7 "The LORD did not set His love on you nor choose you because you were more in number than any other people, for you were the least of all peoples; 8 "but because the LORD loves you, and because He would keep the oath which He swore to your fathers, the LORD has brought you out with a mighty hand, and redeemed you from the house of bondage, from the hand of Pharaoh king of Egypt.
>
> – Deut. 7:6-8

> For you [Israel] are a holy people to the LORD your God, and the LORD has chosen you to be a people for Himself, a special treasure above all the peoples who [are] on the face of the earth.
>
> – Deut. 14:2

To preserve a people that would bring forth the Messiah, God specifically chose the 12 tribes of Israel to be the ancestry of Christ. How can God keep two covenants that are incompatible and oppose each other? On the one hand, God's covenant with the patriarchs promised a multitude of nations; on the other, He uniquely chose the twelve tribes of Israel to be set apart above all the nations of the earth. He can't have it both ways. If only the 12 tribes are His chosen people, then the multitude of nations cannot be His chosen people. If all the nations are selected, then the 12 tribes cannot be special above all the other nations. In God's infinite wisdom, He solved this conundrum by making use of man's rebellion and sinful failures to fulfill both promises without conflict.

After the division between the northern 10 tribes under King Jeroboam and the southern two tribes (including the Levites), the gulf between them grew worse. King Jeroboam was of the tribe of Ephraim, and Ephraim grew stronger and stronger until Ephraim became synonymous with Israel (the northern 10 tribes). Ephraim became a central hub for the other ten tribes, while Bethel was established as a worship center near its southern border with Benjamin. Ephraim's brother, Manasseh — born of the same father and mother — held territory in the heart of the northern ten tribes, directly adjacent to Ephraim to the north. Because Ephraim had a position of prominence, Manasseh did as well. Over time, Samaria — located within its territory — became the northern kingdom's capital. This is the same Samaria from which came the Samaritans in the New Testament.

It is an enormous dilemma for God when He promised and called "my people" to two opposing peoples: the Gentile nations and the 12 tribes of Israel. Ironically, the solution started when Ephraim-Israel left the worship of God for idols until they were defeated and deported to Assyria. Something wonderful was about to take place from their fall. The resolution started to formulate when a large portion of the northern 10 tribes were deported and swallowed up by the Gentiles throughout the Assyrian Empire. Then, a significant number of Assyrians were imported into Ephraim-Israel to intermingle with the 10 tribes (mainly the poor) that remained (2 Kings 17:24). Remember the Samaritans in the New Testament? They were part of this mixed race of people from the time of the Assyrian conquest. They took on the identity of Samaria, the capital of Ephraim-Israel. On one hand, these 10 tribes became Gentiles, but on the other hand, from a genetic point of view, these Gentiles also became part of Ephraim-Israel.

The Jews hated these "Samaritan" Gentiles. They were enemies of each other when Judah returned to Jerusalem from Babylon to rebuild the temple and the city (Ezra 4:10). Eventually, in the New Testament, the Jews avoided the Samaritans and their region (John 4:9). At first when the Jews heard Jesus read from Isaiah 61, *"they marveled at the gracious words which proceeded out of His mouth"* (Luke 4:22). However, when He started citing two examples of how God saved Gentiles instead of Israelites in the Hebrew Scriptures, the Jews were filled with rage and wanted to throw Him over a cliff. This shows the animosity between the Jews and these mixed-race Gentiles.

The Gentile Stick and the Judah Stick Become One Stick

The prophecy in Ezekiel 37 specifically speaks of one stick being Ephraim-Israel and the other stick being Judah. There were two sticks, but they joined into one stick. The Ephriam-Israel stick comes from many nations, and joining with Judah will become one nation with one king. *". . . And will cleanse them. Then they shall be My people, and I will be their God. David My servant shall be king over them, and they shall all have one shepherd; they shall also walk in My judgments and observe My statutes, and do them"* (Ezek. 37:23-24). These are the same items listed in the New Covenant. Here, it is called the **Covenant of Peace.**

Many Bible teachers have suggested that this prophecy will be fulfilled at the time of the second coming of Christ, when all 12 tribes will come back together in the Millennial Kingdom. Whether that is so and how it will be fulfilled is not the purview of this text. According to James in Acts 15, this "one stick" under one King took place with the crucifixion and resurrection of Jesus Christ. He is the Shepherd and King over one kingdom consisting of Jews and Gentiles. Jesus' blood enacted the New Covenant, a covenant of peace that brought all His divided people into one.[25] This prophecy of the two sticks becoming one has already been fulfilled. Now, instead of waiting for the by and by, divided believers everywhere can apply this fulfillment and participate in the "one stick."

This prophecy tightly interwove the unity of God's divided people with the New Covenant. One cannot exist or be experiential without the other. The "I will put My Spirit in you" (Ezek. 37:14) is the same phrase used in Ezekiel 36:37: "I will put My Spirit within you," which clearly alludes to the New Covenant (Ezek. 36:25-30). This understanding is vital, for while most Christians desire to walk in the New Covenant, they may still treat division among diverse believers as normative – thereby perpetuating what the New Covenant was meant to heal. However, without unity, the New Covenant, which is of peace, is inoperative. The goal of the New Covenant is to have one kingdom and one King. These divided nations with the Jews became united as One Nation.

Through the New Covenant, the once competing promises of God to the nations and the 12 tribes are fulfilled. Both promises were kept. This was because 10 of those 12 tribes became Gentiles, and the Gentiles have become those "lost tribes." God made use of Ephraim-Israel's unfaithfulness to integrate them with the Gentiles so that, through Christ, both the Jews and the Gentiles can be the restored "tent" of the United Kingdom of David. The United Kingdom of David under David and Solomon consisted only of the 12 tribes. Now the restored Tabernacle of David, Tent of David, United Kingdom of David, through the Son of David, the Messiah, includes both Jews and Gentiles, fulfilling God's promises to both peoples.

The Grafting to the Olive Tree

> I say then, has God cast away His people? Certainly not! For I also am an Israelite, of the seed of Abraham, [of] the tribe of Benjamin.... 5 Even so then, at this present time there is a remnant according to the election of grace....
> 7 What then? Israel has not obtained what it seeks; but the elect have

---

25   This same thought is supported in John 10: the door of the sheepfold was opened into the pastures where there were other sheep that "were not of this fold"—them He also gathered so that there would be "one flock and one Shepherd."

obtained it, and the rest were blinded. 8 Just as it is written: "God has given them a spirit of stupor, Eyes that they should not see and ears that they should not hear, to this very day."

— Rom. 11:1, 5, 7-8

Let's consider this grafting to the olive tree since it is the closest New Testament description that expounds on the joining of the two sticks in Ezekiel 37. Paul spoke as a person with a dual identity in this chapter. He is an Israelite belonging to one of the 12 tribes, specifically from the tribe of Benjamin, which is part of the southern two tribes, Judah and Benjamin, also known as the Jews. Throughout this chapter, the term "Israel" refers to all 12 tribes, and more specifically, the Jews of Judah who had returned from the Babylonian captivity, becoming the ancestors of Jesus Christ. Those returned Jews who believed in the Messiah Jesus are the remnant chosen by grace. The twelve apostles and the tens of thousands of Jews (including Paul) who had believed in Jesus since Pentecost would be included in this "remnant chosen by grace."

Israel did their best to obtain all that God promised by working on fulfilling God's law. Eventually, just about all failed since both Ephraim-Israel and Judah-Israel were defeated and deported. Their failure was in God's plan since God hardened them — God gave them a spirit of stupor. God's purpose was that Ephraim-Israel's failure would cause their deportation to Assyria and be swallowed up by the Gentiles.

I say then, have they stumbled that they should fall? Certainly not! But through their fall, to provoke them to jealousy, salvation [has come] to the Gentiles. 12 Now if their fall [is] riches for the world, and their failure riches for the Gentiles, how much more their fullness!

— Rom. 11:11-12

In a way, God planned and allowed their fall, knowing that they would not have the strength and nature to fulfill the Mosaic Law. Nevertheless, their stumbling was not beyond recovery. Israel transgressed so that salvation would come to the Gentiles. When Ephraim-Israel became Gentiles, to recover them, God would have to save the Gentiles as well. Certainly, Israel's loss was a gain of riches for the Gentiles since God's chosen people were dispersed among the Nations/Gentiles. God's inheritance is no longer confined to the ethnic 12 tribes of Israel. It has been dispersed to the Gentiles. In Acts 26:17, Paul was sent to the Gentiles to open their eyes to see *an inheritance among those* [Jews and Gentiles] *who are sanctified by faith in Me"* (Acts 26:18). The riches of God's inheritance are now within the Gentiles. The Gentiles would participate in the Commonwealth of Israel (Eph. 2:12).

The door was opened to the Gentiles when Ephraim-Israel was defeated and assimilated by the Assyrian Gentiles. Subsequently, through the death and resurrection of Christ and the gospel preached, the Gentiles received faith and the Holy Spirit. *"How much greater riches will their full inclusion bring!"* Most Bible teachers may delay this to a future event. However, based on the words of James in Acts 15, this can be applied to the here and now. This means the "full inclusion" refers to the mystery of Christ — the threefold joining of Jews and Gentiles. There are riches of God among individual believers, whether Jews or Gentiles, but the *"greater riches"* are when they are united with full inclusion between these previously divided people. The greater riches: joint heir, joint body, and joint partakers of God's promises (Eph. 3:6).

> And if some of the branches were broken off, and you, being a wild olive tree, were grafted in among them, and with them became a partaker of the root and fatness of the olive tree, 18 do not boast against the branches. But if you do boast, [remember that] you do not support the root, but the root [supports] you. 19 You will say then, "Branches were broken off that I might be grafted in." 20 Well [said]. Because of unbelief they were broken off, and you stand by faith. Do not be haughty, but fear.
>
> – Rom. 11:17-20

> The LORD called your name, Green Olive Tree, Lovely [and] of Good Fruit. With the noise of a great tumult He has kindled fire on it, and its branches are broken. 17 "For the LORD of hosts, who planted you, has pronounced doom against you for the evil of the house of Israel and of the house of Judah, which they have done against themselves to provoke Me to anger in offering incense to Baal."
>
> – Jer. 11:16-17

Traditionally, most Bible teachers understand that the Jewish branch was broken off so the Gentiles could be grafted in. This *"broken off"* includes all the ceremonial ordinances, such as diet, Sabbath, circumcision, etc. The Gentiles may well have used this to push back on Jewish Christians, who wanted Gentile believers to also abide by the law. While the Jewish believers wanted to convert the Gentiles to come under the Mosaic Law, the Gentile believers could use Romans 11 to not only object but also tell these Jewish believers to terminate all the Mosaic practices if they were truly living under the New Covenant. Gentile believers could readily quote, as Paul did, referring to the Jews: *"Let their table become a snare and a trap, a stumbling block and a recompense to them. Let their eyes be darkened, so that they do not see, and bow down their back always"* (Rom. 11:9-10). The Gentile believers could say: "Stop being Jewish, terminate your heritage from the Old Testament, and be liberated from the Mosaic ceremonial laws like us. We can eat everything, and every day is the same to us, while you (Jews) are so restricted and enslaved."

In the days of Acts, the battle between Jewish and Gentile believers was fierce and divisive. In Romans 9, the Jews could claim their superiority to convince the Gentile believer to become Jewish in addition to faith in Christ. They had the exalted position to boast since they had *"the glory, the covenants, the giving of the law, the service of God, and the promises; of whom are the fathers and from whom, according to the flesh, Christ came"* (Rom. 9:4-5). Furthermore, they were loved and not hated, unlike the Gentiles (Rom. 9:13). However, in Romans 11, the Gentile believers have the position and reasons to be arrogant and boastful. They have the Scriptural backing to convert Jewish believers to become more like the Gentiles.

Paul's olive tree metaphor in Romans finds its roots in Jeremiah 11:16, where God first likened His people to a "green olive tree." In that context, the image encompassed both the house of Israel and the house of Judah — together representing all twelve tribes. However, all those who forsook God and worshipped Baal were branches that were broken off. This shows that the breaking off of the branches took place during a period of defeat by Assyria and then by Babylon. Contrary to traditional teachings, these branches were not cut off at the rejection or crucifixion of Christ. Rather, Jeremiah 11 shows us that the cutting off of these olive branches happened well before the birth of Jesus Christ.

Significantly, Paul said, *"**Some** of the branches have been broken off"* and not **"all."** And the Gentile or wild branches *"were grafted in among **them** [branches]"* (i.e., the "natural branches"). This makes a huge difference in understanding this portion. Who were the branches that were broken off, and who were those who remained to be among the latter grafted in Gentiles? There were two groups: some were broken off before the time of Christ, and those who remained were called the "natural branches." Traditionally, most Christians reading this portion ("and its branches are broken" — Jer. 11:16) would understand it to mean "all" the Jewish branches were broken off; not so.

According to history and Jeremiah 11:16, the northern 10 tribes were broken off during Assyria's invasion. They were discarded among the Gentiles, swallowed up, and became Gentiles themselves. If the northern 10 tribes were the "some" of the branches broken off, then who were those branches that remained? "Some" does not mean "all."

No, those natural branches that remained are the remnants of Judah that believed. Even though Judah was exiled to Babylon, a remnant remained faithful (such as Daniel, his friends, and Ezekiel). Then a remnant came back to rebuild the temple and Jerusalem. Among this remnant who came back, some continued to be faithful until the birth of Jesus Christ. Afterward, some of these Jews believed and became Christ's disciples. From the day of Pentecost, tens of thousands of Jews became followers of Jesus. This is the history of the remnant spoken of by Paul in Romans 11:5: *"This present time there is a remnant according to the election of grace."* These are the branches that remained. The Gentiles were grafted into the same root (Messiah/Christ) as wild branches — yes, into the same olive tree.

The branches grafted into this cultivated olive tree are from a wild or uncultivated olive tree. According to botany, it is noteworthy that when uncultivated (wild) olive branches are grafted into a cultivated olive tree, something marvelous takes place. It is twofold: (1) The uncultivated olive branches produce much better olives; and (2) The natural branches produce their original cultivated olives. Both maintain their distinction, but the olive tree is one, inseparable. Both branches of this one olive tree are nourished by the same root, which bears them; however, the olives that they produce are distinct. Unlike the grafting in of an orange and a tangerine, creating a tangelo (part orange and part tangerine — a completely new fruit), that is not the case when you graft in a wild/uncultivated olive branch with natural/cultivated branches, even though they have the same root. It would be like saying when the orange and the tangerine reproduce, there are some oranges and some tangerines on the same tree; no, you have tangelos. Whereas with the illustration of the olive tree, you have cultivated olives and upgraded uncultivated olives. Therefore, no one is replacing another one here; both continue in their distinctiveness and are fulfilled in the Messiah.

No other trees can be successfully grafted into a cultivated olive tree, just uncultivated/wild branches of another olive tree. This is based on the olive trees' vascular system and genetic traits. Israel, under the Mosaic Covenant, was called an olive tree — God's cultivated planting — while the Gentile nations were depicted as thorns, briers, or a great tree set for destruction (Ezek. 28:24; 31:3). This distinction rendered them unqualified for grafting into the olive tree. However, the wild olive tree mentioned here has something unique to "olive tree genetics," yet it is also described as "wild." This can refer to the "wild" Gentiles who swallowed up Ephraim-Israel, so that these Gentiles would contain genetic codes from Israel, the original olive tree, making these Gentiles a "wild olive tree." This allowed the Gentiles to have the genetic traits to be grafted and accepted by the cultivated olive tree of Christ. In other words, without the fall of the northern 10 tribes, the Gentiles would not be compatible as thorns and briers to be grafted into the olive tree. Though these Gentiles were wild, Israel has become a part of their constitution, making them compatible with the olive tree.

This cultivated olive tree now contains some original Jewish branches that remained and Gentile branches that were grafted in place of the "cut-off" 10 tribes. Christ, being the tree's root, is upholding and supplying His riches as nourishment to all the branches of this tree. Christ is the source of this entire tree, no matter which branch. Without the root, the branches are nothing. Even though the branches are many and distinct from each other, they are one and united because of their joint connection to Christ. The Gentiles are now in the Commonwealth of Israel (Eph. 2:12). There is mutual fellowship among the branches through Jesus Christ. The two sticks have become one stick in the hand of the LORD.

This olive tree is another description of the Body of Christ, His democratic assembly. The entire tree from the roots, which is Christ, to the branches, which are all His followers, is similar to the Body of Christ. The Body of Christ consists of both Jews and Gentiles with Jesus Christ as the Head. The Body does not support the Head; rather, the Head lifts up the Body (Eph. 1:22-23). However, with the tree, it is Jesus Christ at the bottom (root), supplying and upholding all the distinct and diverse branches. Both manifest the mystery of Christ.

There was a long history of animosity and warfare between Ephraim-Israel and Judah-Israel after the split at the time of Jeroboam and Rehoboam. There were wars between them for over 200 years until Assyria defeated Ephraim-Israel. Then the Gentiles who swallowed up Ephraim-Israel continued their conflict with Judah when Judah returned to rebuild the temple in Jerusalem. That enmity and hostility continued for the next 500 years until Christ. This division can be seen between the Jews and the Samaritans. Although Jesus broke down the wall of division between the Jews and the Gentiles at His crucifixion, that long history of hatred and competition continued into the "church age," or the democratic assembly of believers. In other words, solving this long history of division between these two groups, who were both chosen as God's people, is the pattern of solution for all divisions and conflicts among God's people.

Today's Christians may consider that the conflict between Jews and Gentiles is simply history from long ago, and it is not applicable today. Far from it! Their conflict can be traced to its beginning with the Mosaic Covenant until the time of Acts in the New Testament, which was about 1,500 years. This is a much longer period of a God-created division than any current divisions among Christians. Consider how long the major divisive factions within Christianity have persisted: Catholicism and Eastern Orthodoxy — divided for 1,000 years. Catholicism and Protestantism — 500 years. Anglicanism and Catholicism — also 500 years. Anabaptist movements (such as Mennonites and Amish) diverged from Protestantism — 500 years. Calvinism (with its "once-saved-always-saved" view) versus Arminianism (which holds that salvation can be lost) — 400 years. Evangelical traditions (like Methodists and Baptists) versus mainline Protestants — 200 years. Pentecostalism versus both mainline Protestant and Evangelical churches — 100 years. Additionally, in the past century alone, the world witnessed an explosion of tens of thousands of new denominations and independent churches — each blending historical traditions with fresh variations in social justice emphasis, eschatological views, church governance models, leadership personalities, musical genres, and worship styles. Therefore, if Paul's epistles solved the division of 1,500 years between Jews and Gentile Christians, all the current divisions between believers are minor in comparison.

Since multiple branches were broken off, not just one branch, the Gentiles grafted into the cultivated olive tree (Christ) must also be various branches. These branches can be viewed as individual believers who have come to faith. This would be like the Lord's description of Himself being the vine and all His believers are branches of this vine found in John 15. On the other hand, these branches can represent a diverse group of believers. Just as the broken branches were the 10 northern tribes, these branches grafted in could be groups of believers from a similar background, like a "tribe." For example, Nigerian believers can be a "tribe" or a branch. So can Catholic believers, Baptist believers, Pentecostal believers, "once saved always saved" believers, "you can lose your salvation" believers, word of faith believers, social justice believers, Reformed believers, universalists, etc. All these groups of believers may also be considered as branches grafted into the same root, Christ, the one olive tree. It's important to note that these various church organizations are not the grafted-in branches — rather, it is the believers themselves who are grafted in. Organizations are inorganic without life or faith. Nevertheless, God's people in these organizations are the ones who are ingrafted.

The point remains: None can boast or be arrogant and divide themselves from other branches. Today, there is pridefulness among believers depending on which "branch" they belong. In their arrogance, they may avoid believers in a different branch or try to convert others to their "better" branch. This was exactly what the Jewish and Gentile believers were trying to do to each other, as described in Acts and Romans. None of the branches should boast since none support the root or supply life to other branches. The same root supplies and supports every branch of this "diverse" olive tree. Jesus Christ is the source of all believers, no matter with which branch they may associate.

> Therefore consider the goodness and severity of God: on those who fell, severity; but toward you, goodness, if you continue in [His] goodness. Otherwise, you also will be cut off. 23 And they also, if they do not continue

in unbelief, will be grafted in, for God is able to graft them in again. 24 For if you were cut out of the olive tree which is wild by nature, and were grafted contrary to nature into a cultivated olive tree, how much more will these, who [are] natural [branches], be grafted into their own olive tree? 25 For I do not desire, brethren, that you should be ignorant of this mystery, lest you should be wise in your own opinion, that blindness in part has happened to Israel until the fullness of the Gentiles has come in. 26 And so all Israel will be saved, as it is written: "The Deliverer will come out of Zion, And He will turn away ungodliness from Jacob."

– Rom. 11:22-26

The warning to the ingrafted Gentiles is not to be arrogant and prideful over the Jewish branches but to fear (Rom. 11:20). Surely, the northern 10 tribes being broken off was a severe punishment by God. Paul now warns the ingrafted from among the Nations to continue in God's goodness and not fall into unbelief; otherwise, they too would be cut off. How did the Northern 10 tribes fall? Their fall was not because they had another king other than Rehoboam of the house of David, since God orchestrated the splitting of the kingdom into two. Their fall is when Jeroboam institutionalized division by permanently separating the two kingdoms and preventing the northern tribes from going to Jerusalem to worship God at the temple. That was "the sin of Jeroboam" due to his insecurity, from which Ephraim-Israel never recovered. Therefore, the warning to the Gentiles of not falling into unbelief as the 10 tribes did, includes their terminating the one place of worship, which is keeping the oneness among God's people, including the same for the Jews. If the Gentiles are boastful and arrogant in judging the Jewish branches by dividing and separating from them, that would constitute "unbelief," and they too would be "cut off."

Since there is a phrase *"cut off"* and *"grafted back in,"* this should not be understood as eternal salvation or perdition. When a branch is *"cut off,"* it is not eternal damnation, nor when a branch is grafted back in, is it eternal salvation. In this chapter, it is reasonable to understand that this matter has to do with a believer's present connection and fellowship with all the blessings of the root of the olive tree, Christ. It is related to the daily experiences of the branch, whether it is enjoying the fatness of the unsearchable riches of Christ, or it is dried up and has lost the joy, peace, and purpose of the root, Christ.

This would be like those immature believers in Corinth when they divided from each other due to their preferences for ministerial styles. Paul said that the Corinthians were building with wood, hay, and stubble, which can all be burned in fiery trials.

When their divisive work is burnt up, they will suffer loss, but they will be saved (1 Cor. 3:1-16). So, it is not a matter of eternal perdition since they will be saved, but a matter of the Lord's judgment for dividing the Body of Christ. Believers whose work builds up the oneness of the temple will be rewarded. It is a serious matter to destroy God's temple with divisions, as Jeroboam did by systematically dividing Israel and preventing the northern 10 tribes from being united with the southern tribes for worship at the temple. Continuing to 1 Corinthians 11, those divided believers who did not discern the Body of Christ are those who could experience being cut off and become weak, sick, and even die. This is also similar to those non-abiding and unfruitful branches in John 15 being cut off and withering. They will face the judging fire of the Lord (John 15:6). Again, this is not the same as being saved by faith alone from eternal condemnation (John 3:15-16).[26]

When a branch remains abiding by receiving all the other branches in humility (and becomes one stick), it would be enjoying a present salvation from the supply of riches from Christ, the root. There are tremendous blessings of the Lord upon those in unity that would be missed by those locked into divisiveness (Psa. 133). This is the salvation needed by divided believers in Romans 10. The "gospel of peace" was preached to these divided Jewish and Gentile believers (Rom. 10:15). When anyone received this gospel, they would automatically be joined together and receive all of Christ's riches.

> For the Scripture says, "Whoever believes on Him will not be put to shame."
> 12 For there is no distinction between Jew and Greek, for the same Lord
> over all is rich to all who call upon Him.
>
> – Rom. 10:11-12

The evidence is that verse 11 is a quote from Isaiah 28:18, referencing Jesus as the Foundation Stone and the precious Cornerstone for building up God's temple. Romans 10 speaks not of eternal salvation, but of a present salvation from division — where those once estranged are united in Christ, and upon Him, these diverse people are built together as the temple of God. Though there are still Jews and Greeks (producing different olives), if anyone calls upon the Lord, He, as the root of the olive tree, will be rich to them; these riches flow in and out through both Jews and Gentiles. This is the experience of those saved in the unity of the olive tree.

Gentile believers need to be "kind" to those of the Jewish branch, including those who have not yet believed in Christ, since they are the natural branches (remember back in Jeremiah 11, some of the broken branches include Judah). God has allowed

---

26   Reference the book *God's Kind* by Henry Hon, chapter 15.

blindness to come upon many of the Jewish branches who are not yet grafted in due to unbelief. This is so that the fullness of the Gentiles can be grafted in. Only God knows when the fullness of the Gentiles (aka the "Melo-Hagoyim" or the "multitude of nations") will reach its fullness, but when this happens, then the rest of the Jewish branches will be grafted back in. Then *all Israel will be saved.*

The ingrafted Gentiles into the same olive tree with believing Jews are now "all Israel." All Israel at this point refers to both the Jews (southern kingdom) and the Gentiles (the swallowed northern kingdom). The 12 tribes of Israel are no longer the original 12 sons of Jacob. The "12 tribes of Israel" now include Gentiles. Again, this was especially foreseen when Jacob gave his right hand of blessing first to Ephraim, who was half Hebrew and half Egyptian — and it was Ephraim and Manasseh, his brother, who were first blessed and adopted by Jacob-Israel to be his 13th and 14th sons. Then, after blessing Joseph's two sons, Jacob blessed his other sons, including Joseph. All the promises and prophecies concerning the Patriarch being the father of Gentile nations and Ephraim being the father of many nations have come to pass. This is the mystery that brethren should not be ignorant of. This is the mystery of Christ!

> Concerning the gospel [they are] enemies for your sake, but concerning the election [they are] beloved for the sake of the fathers. 29 For the gifts and the calling of God [are] irrevocable. 30 For as you were once disobedient to God, yet have now obtained mercy through their disobedience, 31 even so these also have now been disobedient, that through the mercy shown you they also may obtain mercy. 32 For God has committed them all to disobedience, that He might have mercy on all.
>
> – Rom. 11:28-32

The enemies of the gospel are referring to these unbelieving Jews. Nevertheless, they are chosen and beloved. What a testimony of the faithfulness of God! His gifts and calling are irrevocable. It does not depend on man's faithfulness. The history of man is one of utter failure and unfaithfulness. Through all of man's faithlessness, God shines in His faithfulness and triumph. No one and nothing can revoke God's gifts and calling, not even God Himself. *"My covenant I will not break, nor alter the word that has gone out of My lips"* (Psa. 89:34).

The Gentiles were disobedient to God. The nations have always been against God since Nimrod, who founded Babel, a city in rebellion against God. However, through the disobedience of the 10 northern tribes, the Gentiles received mercy. Their disobedience was the sin of Jeroboam's systematic division from Judah. All his sins were with one aim — to permanently divide the northern 10 tribes from a united worship of God. Their disobedience led to them being overtaken and swallowed up by the Nations. Then the Gentiles received mercy to be grafted into the original olive tree.

This is not just a historical event. There is something we must do now. *"These also have now been disobedient"* can certainly include the pre-believing Jews who are the natural branches, but it can also include today's divisive believers who have been cut off. Remember, "disobedient" here refers to the divisiveness of the sins of Jeroboam. Christians today can still operate in the principle of the sins of Jeroboam by insisting that they cannot fellowship and be united with some other branches in this olive tree. The principle of the "Breach of Jeroboam" is when a Christian leader uplifts something (a special doctrine, gift, practice, or personality) to draw people to themselves and away from the unity of the Body of Christ. Believers who are deceived by such ministers and adopt their divisive attitudes and style will experience being "cut off" from the entire Body of Christ. This is reasonable since they have cut themselves off from fellowshipping with other believers who are not like them.

Nevertheless, those who are ingrafted and enjoying the unity and fellowship of the olive tree need to show mercy and kindness to those who are disobedient. Those attached to the olive tree know they are only there due to God's mercy and not their merit; therefore, they should not condemn or judge those disobedient in their divisiveness. Any branches attached to the olive tree will show love, mercy, and kindness to all of God's people, no matter where they are. By God's mercy shown through these ingrafted branches, all the other pre-grafted or ex-grafted branches will be grafted into this wonderful olive tree.

All of God's people have been disobedient in their divisiveness at one time or another. They were all enclosed in their obstinacy against God's will concerning the oneness of His House, His Body, or this one olive tree. Every believer has fallen into divisiveness. Now God will show mercy and liberate them from this enclosure. Whoever recognizes under God's light and revelation that they have been rejecting other branches (believers) and thus experiencing being "cut off" from the fatness of the olive tree must repent. Their repentance will cause God to show mercy and graft them in again to their own olive tree. God desires to show mercy to all. His eternal purpose depends on the oneness of all the olive tree branches.

> Oh, the depth of the riches both of the wisdom and knowledge of God! How unsearchable [are] His judgments and His ways past finding out! 34 "For who has known the mind of the LORD? Or who has become His counselor?" 35 "Or who has first given to Him and it shall be repaid to him?" 36 For of Him and through Him and to Him [are] all things, to whom [be] glory forever. Amen.
>
> Rom. 11:33-36

After describing this olive tree, given the mystery and God's conflicting promises to the nations and Israel, Paul launches into praise and worship to God for His wisdom and knowledge. God solved a conundrum of universal proportion relating to His eternal purpose that needed the coming together of two enemies. *"Who has known the mind of the Lord or been His counselor?"* What He promised and ultimately fulfilled through Christ is awesome. Considering this olive tree is too wonderful for words. Whether good or evil things due to sin as witnessed through history, He uses them all for His glory: For of Him and through Him and to Him are all things!

The River of Life Flowing Out of the Temple

> Then he brought me back to the door of the temple; and there was water, flowing from under the threshold of the temple toward the east, for the front of the temple faced east; the water was flowing from under the right side of the temple, south of the altar. . . . 8 Then he said to me: "This water flows toward the eastern region, goes down into the valley, and enters the sea. [When it] reaches the sea, [its] waters are healed. 9 "And it shall be [that] every living thing that moves, wherever the rivers go, will live. There will be a very great multitude of fish, because these waters go there; for they will be healed, and everything will live wherever the river goes.
>
> – Ezek. 47:1, 8-9

Ephesians 2:14-18 speaks of the joining together of the Jews and Gentiles since Christ has broken down the hostility between these two peoples and made them one new man. This is the same as the joining of the two sticks into one and the grafting of the Gentiles into the olive tree, where the Jewish believers already reside. At the end of Ephesians 2 is the building of the temple, God's dwelling place, where Christ, as the cornerstone, joined together the Gentiles and the Jews. So here in Ezekiel 47 is the temple of God resulting from the joining of the 2 sticks in Ezekiel 37. The reality of the temple of God established the unity between previous enemies.

What a wonderful description of the temple in Ezekiel 47. Yes, the description of the New Jerusalem has similar elements; the river of life flows from the throne of God and the Lamb. However, this temple should be the experience of the Lord's Democratic Assembly (Ekklesia) today since Paul said that the Lord's Ekklesia is the House or Temple of the living God (1 Tim. 3:15). The symbolism depicts a river flowing from the temple of God, bringing life wherever it goes. "Sea" in the Bible signifies the world of death. However, this river does not avoid the sea; it flows directly into the sea. This river is not afraid of death; rather, it will flow into the world and provide healing.

The people in this world of death need healing and life. They are hopeless. When they look at all the divisions, fighting, and corruption in Christianity, they perceive that believing in God is useless. However, what would heal, encourage, and enliven them is to see previous enemies loving each other and joining together in unity. Secular people of this world desire this peace and unity. This is the temple with the river flowing to reach them that they cannot ignore. When this river comes, there is healing and everything lives. As the saying goes, resistance is futile. When the river of life, love, and oneness of God's people reaches the sea, it is no longer a sea but a place of life.

This prophecy concerning the temple with the river of life flowing out can be a fulfillment of the Lord's prayer in John 17:21, *"That they all may be one, as You, Father, are in Me, and I in You; that they also may be one in Us, that the world may believe that You sent Me."* When the world can witness the oneness of God's people from diverse backgrounds, including sworn enemies, they will believe and be healed from this deadened world. This is the mystery of Christ!

10

THE MYSTERY
OF THE GOSPEL

Now to Him who is able to establish you according to my gospel and the preaching of Jesus Christ, according to the revelation of the mystery kept secret since the world began 26 but now made manifest, and by the prophetic Scriptures made known to all nations, according to the commandment of the everlasting God, for obedience to the faith–

– Rom. 16:25-26

And for me, that utterance may be given to me, that I may open my mouth boldly to make known the **mystery of the gospel**, 20 for which I am an ambassador in chains; that in it I may speak boldly, as I ought to speak.

– Eph 6:19-20

The thesis of this book is to unveil the mystery made manifest by the prophetic Scriptures. Without Paul's gospel and the preaching of Jesus Christ, the mystery would have remained a hidden secret. The mysteries hidden in the Hebrew Scriptures can only be unraveled with the help of Paul (with the confirmation of Peter and other apostles). Paul considered the Epistle to Romans a gospel, specifically his gospel. Twice he said "my gospel" in this epistle (Rom. 2:16; 16:25). Paul stitched together the various prophecies in the Hebrew Scriptures, and, with his revelation of Jesus Christ, he developed his gospel. He owned this good news message that he preached. It was unique to him. His gospel can be likened to a stew with the prophetic ingredients he gathered, mixed with his revelation of Jesus Christ. His gospel and the preaching of Jesus Christ are the unique light and message needed to unveil the previous six mysteries hidden in the prophetic Scriptures.

The last two mysteries of this book are focused on the gospel of Jesus Christ and the faith to receive the gospel. The gospel and faith go together. The gospel and faith are also mysterious; nevertheless, the Scriptures were written to unveil all His mysteries to God's people. Reading and studying the Scriptures with the enlightening of the Holy

Spirit, these mysteries are made known to mankind (male and female) in all nations. This is God's command that humanity would understand and accept these mysteries in obedience to the faith.

Generally, the gospel is understood to be the good news of going to heaven. Repent, believe that Jesus Christ died for your sins, and accept Him as your Savior and Lord of your life; then one day you will be in heaven with Him. Where is the mystery? It seems very straightforward. Yet, here is the phrase "the mystery of the gospel" at the end of Paul's epistle to Ephesian believers, whose letter is full of the unveiling of mysteries. The word "mystery" was used five times in this epistle to the Ephesians — just six chapters. There is "the mystery of His will" in chapter 1. In chapter 3, "He made known to me the mystery," "the mystery of Christ," and "the dispensation (*oikonomia*) of the mystery." In chapter 5, "the great mystery," and finally, the last chapter (6) is the "mystery of the gospel."

Therefore, Paul's conclusion with "the mystery of the gospel" can summarize his short epistle to the Ephesians. The gospel is not superficial or elementary. It is incumbent upon every gospel preacher to reach an understanding of the mystery of the gospel distilled in the Ephesians' epistle. The gospel of God extends to the highest height of the entire revelation of God and His eternal purpose. Gospel preachers, without preaching Ephesians as the gospel, may only be preaching a small piece of the gospel at best, and at worst, they may be preaching a perverted gospel (Gal. 1:7).

Let's consider the gospel and faith revealed in the prophetic writings. Two examples will be used to show the gospel preached by God. These are essentials for preparing the gospel of Jesus Christ, which came thousands of years later. Nevertheless, these two cases express God's heart of love and mercy for humanity.

The Gospel Preached in the Prophetic Writings

The word "gospel" (Gk. *euangelion*) means "good tidings" or "good news." This gospel was not preached in clear words until the beginning of the New Testament era, since the good news was the coming of Jesus Christ. Nevertheless, it was hidden in the prophetic writings. As mentioned, God preached the first gospel as soon as man (male and female) fell into sin.

> And I will put enmity between you and the woman, and between your seed and her Seed; He shall bruise your head, and you shall bruise His heel.
>
> – Gen. 3:15

The above verse is known in theological circles as the "Protoevangelium" — the earliest announcement of the gospel message. After man partook of the tree of the knowledge of good and evil, they were afraid of God and hid from Him. God warned and forbade them to eat of that tree, saying, *"In the day that you eat of it you shall surely die"* (Gen. 2:17). Therefore, they hid, thinking that God would kill them for their disobedience. When God found them, instead of killing them, God gave them good news. The woman will have a seed which will bruise or crush the head of the snake who deceived Eve and caused Adam's disobedience in partaking of the forbidden fruit. That means that instead of death, they will have the continuation of life through their seed. Truly, this was the gospel.

Adam believed God's promise. He did not doubt God. He trusted in God's good news; therefore, Adam named his wife "Eve," which means "life-giver" (Strong's). He believed God's promise that they would have a seed, meaning, instead of death, they would live. Their lives would endure for generations. Adam acted by faith and called His wife Eve (living) because he believed the gospel of God.

This first gospel has nothing to do with going to heaven one day. It has everything to do with extending life on earth to crush Satan. The gospel is that man would stay alive to defeat and dominate God's enemy. God's concern and the destiny of their lives were to have dominion over His enemy, which was part of His intention in creating man in the first place. God said man would dominate the whole earth and have dominion over every creeping thing that creeps upon the earth (Gen. 1:26). So, there was nothing about heaven or paradise; rather, the utter defeat of Satan (the creeping snake) upon the earth.

Romans is the Apostle Paul's preaching of the gospel of God. Most Christian teachers have focused the gospel on justification by faith and the believer's destiny unto glorification. However, their glorification in Romans 8 is not the final goal — there are still eight more chapters! By chapter 15, we see believers in one accord glorifying God. Although Paul spoke of the believers' glorification in chapter 8, it was not until the saints were in one accord that God Himself received glory (Rom. 15:6). Then, at the end of Romans 16, almost the last verse, Satan is crushed under the feet of the believers (Rom. 16:20). Going to heaven or paradise was not mentioned in Romans, but glory to God while on earth, and the crushing of Satan is the goal of the gospel of God in Romans. The crushing of Satan corresponds to the gospel first preached as a promise in Genesis 3. Jesus Christ is the "seed of the woman." However, the fulfillment is orchestrated in the increase from an individual to include all of God's diverse people as the corporate seed of Jesus Christ (Gal. 3:28-29) — it is through those made one by the Gospel of Peace that Satan's head would be crushed.

The Gospel Preached to Israel

I will take you as My people, and I will be your God. Then you shall know that I [am] the LORD your God who brings you out from under the burdens of the Egyptians. 8 "And I will bring you into the land which I swore to give to Abraham, Isaac, and Jacob; and I will give it to you [as] a heritage: I [am] the LORD."

– Exo. 6:7-8

Then Caleb quieted the people before Moses, and said, "Let us go up at once and take possession, for we are well able to overcome it." 31 But the men who had gone up with him said, "We are not able to go up against the people, for they [are] stronger than we."

– Num. 13:30-31

Then Moses and Aaron fell on their faces before all the assembly of the congregation of the children of Israel. . . . 8 "If the LORD delights in us, then He will bring us into this land and give it to us, 'a land which flows with milk and honey.' 9 [Then Joshua said] "Only do not rebel against the LORD, nor fear the people of the land, for they [are] our bread; their protection has departed from them, and the LORD [is] with us. Do not fear them." 10 And all the congregation said to stone them with stones. Now the glory of the LORD appeared in the tabernacle of meeting before all the children of Israel. 11 Then the LORD said to Moses: "How long will these people reject Me? And how long will they not believe Me, with all the signs which I have performed among them? . . . 28 "Say to them, 'As I live,' says the LORD, 'just as you have spoken in My hearing, so I will do to you: 29 'The carcasses of you who have complained against Me shall fall in this wilderness, all of you who were numbered, according to your entire number, from twenty years old and above.

– Num. 14:5, 8-11, 28-29

For indeed the gospel was preached to us as well as to them; but the word which they heard did not profit them, not being mixed with faith in those who heard [it].

– Heb. 4:2

Hebrews 4 says that the gospel was preached to Israel. Going back to Exodus, God announced good news (gospel) to them: They would possess the Promised Land as their heritage. Although they were slaves in Egypt at the time, God through Moses preached the gospel: They would be liberated from the Egyptians and enter their own land. Truly, this is good news for Israel!

Moses sent spies into the promised land. These 12 spies brought back the produce of the land, testifying to its richness. Caleb, one of the spies, declared: Let's go at once, we can do it. However, 10 of the 12 spies gave an evil report, saying they could not defeat the giants in the land. This caused Moses and Aaron to repeat God's gospel to Israel. Joshua spoke up to encourage Israel again to believe in God's promise and go and possess the land without fear. However, the people refused and wanted to stone those with faith in God's promise.

God came at this juncture and said to those unbelieving: since you said you are unable to possess the Promised Land, then, according to your words, you will not go in. Instead, you will die in the wilderness. Their speaking of unbelief caused what they spoke to come to pass. All those over 20 years of age died in the wilderness from wandering for 40 years. Only Caleb and Joshua, who spoke in faith, believing the gospel of God, became leaders to bring Israel into the Promised Land.

In Hebrews 4, it continues: even though Israel (those over 20 years old at the time of their unbelief) did not get to rest and enjoy the Promised Land, *"There remains therefore a rest for the people of God"* (Heb. 4:9). The rest for Israel was a physical piece of land that they should enter. For believers today, it is not anything physical, but *"Let us therefore come boldly to the throne of grace, that we may obtain mercy and find grace to help in time of need"* (Heb. 4:16). The place of rest and plenty is the "throne of grace" where Jesus is. He is the throne of grace! Today, the gospel is that there is grace and mercy to help during all times of need. However, to receive this help, a person must come forward or "enter in," which requires faith's boldness. Israel was fearful, so they did not enter but died in their unbelief. The gospel is preached today: come forward to the throne of grace to receive help and live. Those who believe will do so and find grace (joy, pleasure, and rejoicing). Those in unbelief will remain outside the Promised Land — dying in their wilderness of unbelief.

The writer of Hebrews used the history of Israel to show that when the good news is preached, faith is needed to realize the benefit of the gospel. Without mixing the gospel with faith, the result is death. Let's juxtapose the gospel preached to Adam and the gospel preached to Israel. Adam believed God's promise of an offspring that would crush Satan's head, so he named his wife Eve (life-giving). Israel was given the gospel of a land of rest and plenty. They didn't believe, so they died. This is still the case today: Those who believe in the gospel of Jesus Christ live, and those who reject remain in death.

The gospel of God is simple, straightforward, and to the point, singularly concerning Jesus Christ: He is the Son of God who put on flesh (became a man). He died on the cross for the sins of the world and was resurrected on the third day. He ascended physically as the Lord of all, and as the Life-giving Spirit, He indwells His believers. This is the simplicity of the gospel; yet this short gospel would fulfill the mysteries described in this text. The mysteries hidden within Christ are accomplished by such brevity and plain speak that even children can grasp and believe, thus receiving salvation. How miraculously amazing is the gospel of God!

This simple gospel, which is easier for little children to accept, accomplishes God's eternal purpose. This gospel can cause men to be forgiven of their sins, justified before God, and born of God to be His children. It brings joy and purpose, tearing down the walls of hatred that once divided enemies and uniting men of vastly different socio-economic, racial, and cultural backgrounds. Together, they are built into God's House — becoming the Bride of Christ, the Body of Christ, and the Kingdom of God.

What a mystery is the gospel of God. Simple words convey understanding and touch the hearts of men. When they respond, a chain reaction of sequential transformation of sinful men occurs, and they become the fulfillment of God's eternal purpose. This is almost too awesome and wonderful to ponder. This transformation takes place without men's effort. Rather, they abide in an environment of joy, love, peace, and kindness so that God's ultimate goal emerges triumphant and glorious. The mystery of the gospel unravels and answers the quest of man's deepest longing for meaning and purpose in life.

Let's consider the various aspects of the gospel.

The Gospel of God and Jesus Christ

> Paul, a bondservant of Jesus Christ, called [to be] an apostle, separated to the gospel of God . . . 3 concerning His Son Jesus Christ our Lord, who was born of the seed of David according to the flesh, 4 [and] declared [to be] the Son of God with [Gk. in] power according to the Spirit of holiness, by the resurrection from the dead.
>
> – Rom. 1:1, 3-4

> Moreover, brethren, I declare to you the gospel which I preached to you, which also you received and in which you stand, 2 by which also you are saved, if you hold fast that word which I preached to you — unless you believed in vain. 3 For I delivered to you first of all that which I also received: that Christ died for our sins according to the Scriptures, 4 and that He was buried, and that He rose again the third day according to the Scriptures.
>
> – 1 Cor. 15:1-4

The good news is from God — the gospel of God. God wants to announce good tidings to all mankind in the world, whom He loves. Two verses in Romans encapsulate the entire gospel of God concerning His Son. *"His Son Jesus Christ"* is God's Only Begotten Son; as such, He is the express image of the invisible Father (John 1:18). God gave His Only Begotten Son to die for the sins of the world that through Him people would have eternal life (John 3:16).

To have the physical traits that can experience death, Jesus was *"born of the seed of David according to the flesh."* God's divine eternal Son was incarnated, born from the seed of David. Jesus Christ put on flesh and tabernacled (dwelt) among men (John 1:14). He had the weaknesses of men of the flesh, yet without sin. Jesus Christ then died on the cross, and in His resurrection three days later, He was declared the Son of God in power according to the Spirit.

Since He was already the Only Begotten Son of God — for there to be an Eternal Father, there had to be an Eternal Son — why, then, does He need to be *"declared the Son of God?"* When Jesus was born of the Virgin Mary, He had a dual nature: Divine and human. He was the Son of God and the Son of Man. One was uncreated and the other was created. On one hand, in His divinity, He was the Creator ("All things were made through Him, and without Him nothing was made that was made" — John 1:3). On the other hand, as a man, He was a creature (Col. 1:15). In His resurrection, His human nature was declared to be the Son of God. His human nature entered the Godhead, and God became eternally divine and human (Son of God and Son of Man, Rev. 22:3). The two natures, divinity and humanity, joined and intertwined as one. Jesus Christ's humanity was made holy *"in power according to the Spirit of holiness, by the resurrection from the dead."* This is the gospel of God: God and man are made one in Jesus Christ. What wonderful news!

This was God's intention at the creation of man (male and female): God would be the "Husband" and man would be His "wife." These two shall be joined as one. God did not want to be "alone" in the universe. He desired a match to be His counterpart. No matter the beauty, mere creatures like angels cannot match Him. He needed a partner with His image, likeness, life, and nature. The "wife" would be humanity created in His image and likeness and with His life and nature. That first man failed to be such a "wife." However, the second man succeeded when Jesus Christ became the Firstborn Son of God. He brought the rest of His brethren into God (Rom. 8:29). He made a place for all humanity to enter into God and be one with God (John 14:3, 28). Now God and man are one.

The Gospel of Jesus Christ includes His death and resurrection. Man fell into sin and needed redemption. Jesus Christ died for the sins of the world so that man is cleansed and justified before God. In His resurrection, Jesus Christ regenerated His followers. Men were reconciled to God by Jesus' death, and were also regenerated with God's divine eternal life at Jesus' resurrection (2 Pet. 1:3). John 3 shows the work of His death and resurrection. His death was typified by the brazen serpent, representing man's sinful flesh being crucified on the cross (John 3:14). His resurrection included the second birth for those who would believe on His Name — that which is born of the Spirit is spirit (John 3:6). The gospel of Jesus Christ then includes His death for the sins of the world and His resurrection which gave eternal life, a new birth to all who would call on His Name.

The Gospel of Grace

> ". . . except that the Holy Spirit testifies in every city, saying that chains and tribulations await me. 24 "But none of these things move me; nor do I count my life dear to myself, so that I may finish my race with joy, and the ministry which I received from the Lord Jesus, to testify to **the gospel of the grace of God.**"
>
> – Acts 20:23-24

> For you are saved by grace through faith, and this is not from yourselves; it is God's gift — 9 not from works, so that no one can boast.
>
> – Eph. 2:8-9, CSB

> . . . through whom also we have access by faith into this grace in which we stand, and rejoice in hope of the glory of God.
>
> – Rom. 5:2

While Paul was suffering in His journey to preach the gospel, he said he would finish his course with joy. What a contrast! Chains and tribulation await him; yet, he is joyfully running his race and fulfilling his ministry to preach the gospel of the grace of God. The word "grace" (Gk. *Charis*) means "that which affords joy, pleasure, delight, sweetness, loveliness" (Thayer's). Most Christians may define "grace" as "unmerited favor," and certainly, man's salvation is a favor from God that is unmerited. However, the literal meaning is more wonderful, experiential, and subjective. The root word for *"charis"* in Greek is the same word for "joy" in the same verse (Acts 20:24).

Paul is saying, I may have suffering and persecution, but I have joy because the gospel of God that I preach affords joy, pleasure, and delight. I do not just preach the gospel as an objective truth; I am subjectively enjoying the very gospel that I preach.

The gospel of grace brings joy, delight, and pleasure, which all men seek and pursue. "Grace" then can be the final goal of men's pursuit when they seek after money, power, sex, alcohol, or drugs, since their final desire is delight and pleasure. They would be satisfied if they could arrive at and achieve the utmost joy and enjoyment. This is the gospel: the grace of the Lord Jesus Christ is the ultimate enjoyment for men. Receive the Lord Jesus, and He will fill you with deep and eternal joy and pleasure.

In the New Testament, "grace" is exclusively related to God and Jesus Christ. This grace was non-existent until the advent of Jesus. *"Grace and truth came through Jesus Christ"* (John 1:17). The joy, pleasure, and enjoyment that came with Jesus is different than all others experienced by humans. The grace of Jesus, being eternal, surpasses all earthly joy, pleasure, and delight. The grace of the Lord Jesus works during all adversities and abysmal environments. His pleasure and enjoyment manifest and endure through trials and challenges. Because of His grace, Paul, who suffered much, could declare *"rejoice in the Lord always. Again I will say rejoice"* (Phil. 4:4). "Rejoice" has the same root word in Greek as "grace."

The gospel, being the grace of God, means it is presently experiential. The gospel is not just about the past or something in the future, with no help in the present. Instead, the gospel is grace for today, no matter life's challenges. Ephesians 2 says men are saved by grace and not by works. In Greek, "**saved** (by grace)" is a perfect participle, meaning that though salvation has taken place, it has a continuous and present impact. Believers are not waiting to see the power of their salvation in the future; salvation needs to impact them daily. Saving grace is effective during daily challenges and problems.

Paul prayed in 2 Corinthians 12 for the Lord to remove a thorn in his flesh from Satan. He desperately pleaded to the Lord "three times." The reply from the Lord and His answer to His problem, *"My grace is sufficient for you"* (2 Cor. 12:9). While Paul was struggling, the Lord's joy and pleasure were available to him and were sufficient to sustain him and bring him through. If Paul had joy and rejoicing during his present struggle, it was no longer a challenge — he was enjoying the Lord. Grace is not grinning and bearing the sufferings, but it is freedom and release into the delight of the Lord while still within one's distressing circumstances.

When Paul and Silas were in prison in Philippi, they were severely whipped, and their feet were locked in stocks. It was extremely distressing to be beaten and left in a dark, wet, dirty, rat-infested prison. Nevertheless, they were singing and praising God. Even though God miraculously unchained them, and the prison's doors were opened, they did not leave. The joy of the Lord turned this horrifying prison into a heavenly place. They were satisfied and rejoiced in the present salvation of grace. Salvation to them was not a theological doctrine or something in the future; they were saved by grace amid their dreadful environments. They did not want to leave! As those in the grace of the Lord, they were already in "heaven." They were "saved by grace."

For today's example, a Christian lost his job or has a health issue. If he becomes discouraged and starts complaining, salvation is presently ineffectual for him. However, if he turns to the Lord, he will find grace in Jesus, he maintains his joy, and continues in the delight of the Lord. He is then saved from anxiety, anger, or discouragement. His rejoicing in Christ testifies that he is saved by grace. He is not relying on past events or waiting for heaven one day to escape these earthly dramas. Due to his delight and rejoicing in Christ, he experiences a current salvation.

> Who shall separate us from the love of Christ? Shall tribulation, or distress, or persecution, or famine, or nakedness, or peril, or sword? Yet in all these things we are more than conquerors through Him who loved us. For I am persuaded that neither death nor life, nor angels nor principalities nor powers, nor things present nor things to come, nor height nor depth, nor any other created things, shall be able to separate us from the love of God which is in Christ Jesus our Lord.
>
> – Rom. 8:35, 37-39

Paul said in Romans 5:2 that through Jesus Christ, believers "have access by faith into this grace in which we stand." The position and the environment of God's people are now in grace. Stay in the joy, enjoyment, love, and pleasure of the Lord. In His joy, believers are emboldened to express the reality of the Lord's salvation. If joy is missing in your life today, then again access through faith into the grace of the Lord and abide there. This is the gospel of the grace of God. This grace not only saves us through faith in His full salvation but continues to supply us, transform us, and ultimately leads to our transfiguration, for "whom He justified, these He also glorified" (Rom 8:30).

Preach the Unsearchable Riches of Christ

> To me, who am less than the least of all the saints, this grace was given, that I should preach among the Gentiles the unsearchable riches of Christ,
>
> – Eph. 3:8

The person and work of Christ are unsearchably rich. Even though the gospel of Jesus Christ is simple, He is inexhaustibly vast, deep, and high. All His attributes of love, kindness, joy, gentleness, courage, patience, forgiveness, long-suffering, humility, and more are beyond limit and imagination. What He has accomplished through His work of crucifixion, resurrection, and ascension will need eternity to absorb and fathom. Nevertheless, each aspect of Christ necessitates preaching since they are all good news for man's experience and enjoyment.

The entire book of Romans was Paul's gospel. He preached the gospel to the saints (Rom. 1:7, 15). At the benediction of this letter in Romans 16, Paul concluded that His gospel is for the obedience of the faith. Believers need to hear his **complete gospel**. Ephesians is another aspect of the gospel, and just about all the epistles are evangelizing and explaining the riches of Jesus Christ for sinners and saints. This good news is not just for personal salvation, but also for the unity of His people to bring to earth His Kingdom and to crush His enemy, Satan. Same coin, with two sides: Salvation AND Unity.

The gospel can be considered God's entire plan for Man to fulfill His eternal purpose.

Perverting the Gospel

> I marvel that you are turning away so soon from Him who called you in the grace of Christ, to a different gospel, 7 which is not another; but there are some who trouble you and want to pervert the gospel of Christ. 8 But even if we, or an angel from heaven, preach any other gospel to you than what we have preached to you, let him be accursed.
>
> – Gal. 1:6-8

> And certain [men] came down from Judea and taught the brethren, "Unless you are circumcised according to the custom of Moses, you cannot be saved."
>
> – Acts 15:1

> to whom we did not yield submission even for an hour, that **the truth of the gospel** might continue with you. 11 Now when Peter had come to Antioch, I withstood him to his face, because he was to be blamed; 12 for before certain men came from James, he would eat with the Gentiles; but when they came, he withdrew and separated himself, fearing those who were of the circumcision. . . . 14 But when I saw that they were not straightforward about **the truth of the gospel**, I said . . .
>
> – Gal. 2:5, 11-12, 14

The gospel of Jesus Christ is simple and clear. it is His person and work. In the simplest form, the gospel of Jesus Christ can be pronounced in just a couple of sentences. Jesus Christ is God who took on flesh; He died, resurrected, ascended, and was made Lord and Christ. He now indwells his believers as their eternal life.

When Christians hear of the perversion of the gospel, they may think of a mixture of Eastern religions like Buddhism or Hinduism. The more spiritual Christians may consider perversion to be mixing humanism or philosophies with the gospel. No one would suspect that the main culprit in perverting the gospel could be God's commandments or correct doctrines from the Scriptures.

People tend to complicate the gospel. When anything more is added to the gospel of Jesus Christ, it is a perversion. Jewish believers during the time of Acts added circumcision as a requirement for salvation: *"Unless you are circumcised . . . you cannot be saved."* Understand, these Jewish believers had experienced salvation through Yeshua — they belonged to the very "household of faith." Although circumcision was a commandment of God during the time of Abraham and Moses, it was no longer a requirement — especially so, from those being called out from the Nations. These Jewish followers of Jesus, the Messiah, desired to obey God's commandment given from the time of Abram (circumcision was instituted **after** he was justified by faith), and amplified under the Mosaic Covenant; therefore, they preached circumcision in addition to Jesus Christ and Him crucified. That was a perversion of the gospel. Any requirement for salvation, which includes justification, sanctification, and glorification, other than faith in Jesus Christ, is a corruption of the gospel.

It is antithetical to the New Covenant. Again, according to Acts 15, the requirement of circumcision was not compatible with Gentile's salvation. Perverting the gospel is a serious offense before God: *"Let him be accursed"* (Gal. 1:8).

Christians today, knowingly or unknowingly, have added to the simplicity of the gospel. It may not be circumcision, but it can be baptism, holiness practices, prayer and fasting, doctrinal knowledge, spiritual gifts, discipleship principles and practices, self-denials, etc. All of these could be scriptural and helpful at one time or another. However, it is precisely because they are from God and beneficial (like circumcision) that it is easy to add them as additional requirements for salvation, instead of Jesus Christ alone. Many Christians may insist that certain doctrinal understanding, such as election or affirmation in eternal security doctrines, is needed to advance in one's salvation experience. Insistence on baptism (with its multiplicity of forms) is affirmed by multitudes of Christians as "salvific" in that it "saves us." Others may promote spiritual gifts and speaking in tongues as a necessity for sanctification. To many Christians, these issues have become extra gospel items added to their faith in Jesus Christ for "salvation."

Christians certainly can be helped by a myriad of biblical teachings and practices without perverting the gospel. What is the test for whether a Christian has been affected by the perversion of the gospel? It causes division. A perverted gospel could be so deceptive that it could even distract and stumble one of the greatest apostles, Peter. He was in Antioch eating and fellowshipping with Gentile believers since they were participating in the mystery of Christ, the threefold unity between Jews and Gentiles. Then, believers from the circumcision party (aka Judaizers, who believed in Jesus/ Yeshua) came from James in Jerusalem. **after** the breakthrough regarding the raising up of the United Kingdom of David/The Tabernacle of David — Gal. 2:1-12 [Cf. vs. 10 and Acts 11:27-30]). Peter was immediately ashamed that he was fellowshipping with Gentile believers, so he separated himself from these "Gentile sinners" ("sinners" because the Judaizers believed these Gentiles were never saved in the first place because they were not circumcised). All the other Jewish believers followed his lead and divided themselves as well. Virtually, all of them were caught up in the "hypocrisy" which denied the "truth of the gospel."

Paul rebuked Peter openly, declaring that Peter and the Jewish believers were not straightforward concerning the "truth of the gospel." They deviated from the gospel. The evidence that they had perverted the gospel is that they were divided from those uncircumcised who had accepted the gospel of Jesus Christ. This meant that the Jewish believers had added circumcision as a requirement to the gospel of Christ (i.e., faith in Christ alone). They could not be in fellowship with these Gentiles unless they, too, were circumcised. This was their addition to the gospel of Jesus Christ. Division from other believers over these additions to Christ's salvation is evidence of the perversion of the gospel.

Applying the same principle to the thousands of divisions and separations among Christians today, there is an ever-increasing number of perversions of the gospel. Theological doctrines, spiritual gifts, holiness practices, discipleship principles, social justice issues, and even politics and personalities have been elevated to the same level as the gospel of Jesus Christ. They have become so essential for many believers that they have divided believers from fellowshipping with each other. Whenever Christians have any items on their checklist for fellowship with other believers other than the gospel of Jesus Christ, they have perverted the gospel.

> But I fear, lest somehow, as the serpent deceived Eve by his craftiness, so your minds may be corrupted from the simplicity that is in Christ. 4 For if he who comes preaches another Jesus whom we have not preached, or [if] you receive a different spirit which you have not received, or a different gospel which you have not accepted — you may well put up with it!
>
> — 2 Cor. 11:3-4

The perversion of the gospel is Satan's tactic to corrupt believers' minds from the simplicity that is in Christ. It is another Jesus or a different gospel whenever something other than Christ is added. Again, these verses above refer to Jewish believers preaching Jewish laws from the Scriptures to Gentile Christians. Today, Christians can become complicated considering with whom they can or cannot fellowship. These complications are Satan's tactic to divide the Body of Christ. All believers must return to the simplicity of the gospel of Jesus Christ: Jesus' person and work, plus nothing.

The perversion of the gospel: No matter how scriptural or beneficial, lifting up something to the level of Jesus Christ in the gospel has divided and factionalized Christians into tens of thousands of denominations and independent churches (including "house churches"). It has prevented believers of Jesus Christ from fellowshipping and accepting each other as equal or legitimate members of the Body of Christ. This has trampled asunder the reality of the death of Christ and made it meaningless. This is Satan's tactic to divide and conquer. Jesus declared a truism: *"Every kingdom divided against itself is brought to desolation, and a house divided against a house falls"* (Luke 11:17). The explosion of divisions among Christians has made the kingdom of God ineffective on earth. This may delay the manifestation of the Kingdom of God at the second advent of Jesus Christ, at which time the kingdom of darkness will be abolished.

The Gospel of Peace

> having abolished in His flesh the enmity, [that is], the law of commandments [contained] in ordinances, so as to create in Himself one new man [from] the two, [thus] making peace, 16 and that He might reconcile them both to God in one body through the cross, thereby putting to death the enmity. 17 And He came and preached peace to you who were afar off and to those who were near.
>
> – Eph. 2:15-17

As discussed in earlier chapters, there was deep enmity or hatred between the Jews and the Gentiles. Jesus died to break down this separating wall to create in Himself one new man. God's eternal purpose is to have the corporate new man consisting of all those who were previously enemies. His crucifixion put to death all enmity or hostility between His people, who, without His cross, were enemies. Contrasting with the "new man," the "old man" is the fallen man of sin, dividing and causing wars between peoples and nations. The old man is terminated on the cross (Rom. 6:6). Then God created the new man in Christ's resurrection, consisting of every tribe, tongue, people, and nation (Rev. 5:9). This composition of diversity is dramatically signified by the unity of the 12

Tribes of Israel (Rev. 7:1-8) and amplified in the great multitude before "God who sits on the throne, and to the Lamb" (Rev. 7:9-17).

However, due to Satan's tactic to divide God's people by the preaching of another, different, distorted, perverted gospel (Gal. 1:6-9), most Christians today are divided from those who are not from the same church or under the same theological persuasion. Therefore, the gospel of peace is necessary to bring believers into the **completion** of the gospel (Rom. 15:29). The gospel of peace targets believers who are divided or dividing the Body of Christ. Ephesians 2:17 shows that peace needs to be preached and announced to those not yet enjoying fellowship with others who are contrary to themselves. Since it is easy to stay segregated from enemies, peace needs to be preached. God's people may be ignorant of this good news and thus remain in their segregated state. So, there is a dire need to preach the gospel of peace!

Remember, Paul wrote his letter to the believers in Rome with this initial greeting: *"To all who are in Rome, beloved of God, called saints"* (Rom. 1:7). In other words when Paul in that same chapter says: *"So, as much as is in me, I am ready to preach the gospel to you who are in Rome also"* . . . (and then says) . . . *"the gospel of Christ is the power of God to salvation for everyone who believes, for the Jew first and also for the Greek"* (Rom. 1:15-16). He was writing to the Jews and Greeks who were already saints — they were already saved. So, what power of the gospel was he talking about? The power that not only brings salvation through the blood of Christ, but the power which binds together as one the people of God — the segregated Jews and Greeks!

Let's consider the gospel of peace preached by Paul in Romans 10.

> But the righteousness of faith speaks in this way, "Do not say in your heart, 'Who will ascend into heaven?' " (that is, to bring Christ down [from above]) 7 or, " 'Who will descend into the abyss?' " (that is, to bring Christ up from the dead). 8 But what does it say? "The word is near you, in your mouth and in your heart" (that is, the word of faith which we preach): 9 that if you confess with your mouth the Lord Jesus and believe in your heart that God has raised Him from the dead, you will be saved.
>
> – Rom. 10:6-9

Romans 10 sits between Chapter 9, where Jewish believers have reasons to consider themselves superior to Gentile believers, and Chapter 11, where the Gentile believers can boast over Jewish believers. This division was obvious when Peter and all Jewish believers divided from the Gentiles in Galatians 2. Romans 10 is the practicality of the preaching of the gospel of peace. Paul broke down the middle wall of partition with the gospel.

In Romans 10, the gospel of peace is exactly the gospel of Jesus Christ: *"to bring Christ down from above"* is the incarnation of Christ when God put on flesh and became a man. *"To bring Christ up from the dead"* refers to His death and resurrection. "In your mouth and in your heart" is the indwelling Spirit of Christ after His resurrection. Notice that the living Word is already in their hearts since Romans was written to believers with the Spirit in them already (aka "saints" already set apart as "holy"). Now, if they would come back to this simplicity by confessing and believing in the resurrection of Jesus Christ, they would be saved. But saved from what? This salvation is not from perdition in the future but from their current divisions. These divided believers needed to be saved in the here and now.[27]

Romans 10:11 shows conclusively that salvation in Romans 10 is to save believers from their divisions: *"For the Scripture says, 'Whoever believes on Him will not be put to shame.'"* This verse is quoted from Isaiah 28:16: *"Behold, I lay in Zion a stone for a foundation, a tried stone, a precious cornerstone, a sure foundation; whoever believes will not act hastily."* Paul quoted a verse that speaks of Jesus Christ being the foundation stone in Zion, the place of oneness. The Lord's Democratic Assembly (Ekklesia) is built on the foundation of Christ as the Rock (Matt. 16:18). He is also the precious Cornerstone, the One who joins two walls for the building. The Jews and Gentiles (Jews and Greeks) represented the two walls. They would remain separate if the Cornerstone did not join them together. Paul intentionally quotes Isaiah to show that salvation is in being joined together for God's temple.

Paul exchanged "hastily" with *"not be put to shame."* He applied the Isaiah verse to the experiential situation between Gentiles and Jews – they were ashamed to be in the presence of each other. Consider again the case with Peter and Jewish cohorts in Galatians 2. These Jewish believers were embarrassed to be seen with these "Gentile sinners." They did not want to be seen fellowshipping and having a meal together with them. It was a shame for them to be joined to these "unclean" Gentiles. Therefore, Paul says, *"Whoever believes on Him will not be put to shame."* Faith in Christ should erase all the shame of being joined in fellowship with those with animosities toward each other. For the building up of God's temple, the Cornerstone joins His diverse people and saves them from the shame of associating with each other.

---

27   At the time of Paul's writing, Rome was a bustling metropolis, the capital of the Roman Empire, with as many as one million inhabitants, the center of trade for the Empire's vast commercial and governmental interests. The inhabitants included Jews, Greeks, Romans, slaves from everywhere, and scores of Barbarians—one incredible hodgepodge full of Roman citizens and a multitude of non-citizens. Do you think, just maybe, folks "clung to their own" amid this maelstrom of people? Yes, even after getting saved—people still like to be "with our kith and kin." Don't we have more "in common" and feel more "comfortable" around "our own?" Imagine a Barbarian sitting down at the Lord's communion table with a cultured Greek or authoritarian Roman citizen—not easy. Worse, a Jew "in the know" with a philosophical Greek who thinks he knows, but the Jews know he doesn't! Paul decisively was calling them out by preaching the Gospel of Peace, almost as if saying: You "saints" say you're saved, let's see if you can live and meet like you are.

Today's situation among Christians can be very similar. Believers from one Christian faction may be embarrassed to be in fellowship or be seen with believers from a contrary faction. Evangelical believers may be dishonored if seen by fellow evangelicals if they are in fellowship with Catholic believers. A Baptist believer may be ashamed when fellow Baptists observe that he is having fellowship with a Pentecostal Christian. Today, politics can also play a big part: A politically conservative Christian may be defamed when seen sharing Christ with a liberal believer. These kinds of shame keep believers in their sectarian silos (although they would rarely admit they are being sectarian — just careful to keep their faith "pure"). To be saved from shame is to intentionally reach out to those "different believers" who may be contrary to themselves by having meals and fellowship with them.

Paul continued with the gospel of peace:

> For there is no distinction between Jew and Greek; for the same Lord is Lord of all, bestowing his riches on all who call on him. 13 For "everyone who calls on the name of the Lord will be saved."
>
> – Rom. 10:12–13, ESV

"No distinction" — To suggest that "some are more saved than others" is utterly contradictory, even anathema, to the Gospel of Christ. He is the same Lord of all. All who call on Him or who have called on Him are rich with His salvation. When it comes to our "standing in Christ," we're all rich! Some are not richer than others. Stop with the comparing who's richer! Just enjoy the "same Lord" with all the brethren.

The same gospel and the same Lord are for both Jews and Gentiles. No matter which sect of Christians one may identify with, the Lord is rich to all who call upon Him. Remember, when division sets in among Christians, the blessings of God are withheld. This was the story of Israel's journey in the Old Testament. When there is division, God's blessings are gone. When there is unity, God's blessings are poured out. Call on the Lord to be saved from disunity and be blessed by His riches in every brother and sister.

> How beautiful are the feet of those who preach the gospel of peace, who bring glad tidings of good things!
>
> – Rom. 10:15

In just four verses, the gospel preached in Romans 10 is so simple and to the point concerning Jesus Christ and the way to salvation. **The same gospel of grace is the gospel of peace.** While multitudes preach the gospel of grace to rescue unbelievers from perdition, a minuscule number proclaim the gospel of peace to reconcile the fractured body of Christ. Most Christians are unaware that divided believers must hear the gospel of peace. Most are numb and have accepted that divisions among Christians are normal and unavoidable. Most are repeatedly told that "' down here' we are divided, but 'up there' we will finally be united." No, this cannot be! The oneness of God's diverse people must be manifested on earth before the Second Advent of Christ. The gospel of peace must be preached!

Jesus said, *"Pray earnestly to the Lord of the harvest to send out laborers into his harvest"* (Matt. 9:38). There is a desperate need for preachers of the gospel of peace. Divided believers need to hear the simplicity of the gospel of Jesus Christ again, but how can they hear without a preacher? Believers need to arise to preach the gospel of peace to heal the breach between divided Christians. "O Lord, send forth gospel preachers of peace for the end-time harvest."

In the last chapter of Ephesians, Paul said: *"As shoes for your feet, having put on the readiness given by the gospel of peace"* (Eph. 6:15 ESV). For a warrior, shoes are critical equipment for moving forward in battle. Unprotected feet can quickly cripple a soldier from sharp objects. The gospel of peace is needed as shoes for God's move in battle. Believers cannot fight as God's warriors without knowing or preaching the gospel of peace. Satan's work is to divide God's people. Therefore, the only way to move forward and win the battle against Satan's sectarian devices is the gospel of peace.[28]

The Gospel of the Kingdom

> And they sang a new song, saying, "Worthy are you to take the scroll and to open its seals, for you were slain, and by your blood you ransomed people for God from every tribe and language and people and nation, 10 and you have made them a kingdom and priests to our God, and they shall reign on the earth."
>
> – Rev. 5:9-10, ESV

---

28   Yes, "peace with God," but what about "peace with your brothers and sisters?" Isn't that what Paul was saying throughout the book of Ephesians? The incessant theme has to do with the One New Man—so making peace. Now, all of a sudden, Paul's talking about simply going forth with the gospel of salvation to the ends of the earth. No, in full context, we are that One New Man, in full priestly armor, and carried forth on feet that are shod with the Gospel of Peace. Why? Because we know that the principalities and powers in high places are infuriated at such a movement. They know it is utterly impactful when we are shod with the preparation of the Gospel of Peace—ONWARD BRETHREN, now He's got them on the run!

The gospel of the kingdom is domiciled, centered, in the Lord Jesus Christ. When John the Baptist said that the kingdom of God is at hand, he was referring to the coming of Jesus Christ. Jesus Himself said the kingdom of God cannot be physically observed (it is without observation) since He is the kingdom of God in their midst (Luke 17:21). Then He said to His disciples that some of them would not taste death until they see the kingdom of God in power. Six days later, Jesus was transfigured before Peter, James, and John on the Mount of Transfiguration, displaying the glory and power within Him (Mark 9:2). These passages convincingly display that Jesus Christ is the reality of the Kingdom of God in our midst.

However, the Kingdom of God does not stop there since one person does not ultimately constitute a kingdom. After His death and resurrection, men were born from above (born again) into God's Kingdom. They were born of the Spirit with a new birth (John 3:5). Being born of God transferred men (male and female) from darkness into the Kingdom of Jesus Christ (Col. 1:13). The Kingdom of God is no longer one person but comprises millions upon millions of God's children. God's Kingdom expanded to include every tribe, language, people, and nation. This makes the Kingdom of God the most diverse in the history of kingdoms.

Every earthly kingdom typically comprises people from a similar ethnicity or language, making up one nation. However, God's Kingdom is tremendously diverse with a mix of people, including those who are polar opposites (Jews, Gentiles, masters, and slaves). Therefore, God's people, when immature in Christ, are susceptible to falling into Satan's scheme to divide. In man's natural fallen nature, separating from those viewed as undesirable comes easily.

> But He, knowing their thoughts, said to them: "Every kingdom divided against itself is brought to desolation, and a house [divided] against a house falls."
>
> – Luke 11:17

Satan's focus is to divide God's people. Christians seem to be divided into a multiplicity of silos with a shrinking number of people in each. If Satan can keep God's Kingdom divided and His people fighting each other, then his kingdom of darkness will be prolonged. Since God's people are divided, God's Kingdom is ineffective on earth, with little impact on the people.

According to Jesus in Matthew 16 and 18, the building of His democratic legislative assembly (Ekklesia) is the coming of the Kingdom of God. His Ekklesia is to legislate on earth, binding and loosing, and heaven follows these decisions made by His Ekklesia.

The authority of His Kingdom comes from the harmony of His diverse people (Matt. 18:17-18). Like the Greek ekklesia, the Lord's Ekklesia is diverse and inclusive, but far more inclusive. However, unlike the secular ekklesia, legislation is not majority wins, but all His diverse people resolve such decisions in harmony. Their decision-making is in symphony, in one accord, and the heavens listen and act. Prayers are much more stupendous, spectacular sounding, when it is prayed in concert, in symphony, with the orchestra, the Body of Christ!

> for the kingdom of God is not eating and drinking, but righteousness and peace and joy in the Holy Spirit.
>
> – Rom. 14:17

The result of the gospel of peace preached in Romans 10 is the kingdom of God in Romans 14. Romans 14 describes a Democratic Assembly where presumably Jewish and Gentile believers were gathered for a meal and fellowship. Instead of gathering and fellowshipping in the comfort of those with the same diet or keeping of days, they could come together at the same time and in the same place. Due to different convictions and measures of faith, they were warned not to judge and stumble one another (Rom. 14:13).

It is a momentous event anytime believers who traditionally do not associate come together for fellowship and break bread. How easy, relaxed, and non-threatening it is for those similar to gather and avoid those who are contrary. Remember, back in biblical times, even though both had the same faith in Jesus Christ, Jews and Gentiles were opposites with contradictory convictions and habits. It was incomprehensible for them to have a meal together (witness Peter in Galatians 2). The same would be true for slaves and masters to become equals in the Lord's democratic assembly (especially in a place like Rome). Their testimony in Romans 14 is a pattern to show that every other division among Christians is solvable. The unity of the Body of Christ and the Kingdom of God can be realized and manifested in this dark world.

This democratic assembly in Romans 14:17 is referred to as the "Kingdom of God." All the differences in doctrinal convictions and perspectives on the non-essentials are not the Kingdom of God, but "**righteousness** and **peace** and **joy** in the Holy Spirit." **Righteousness** can refer to the gospel of grace through faith, as preached by Paul in Romans 1 through 8. These chapters trace the arc from justification to glorification (Rom. 8:30), affirming that faith in Jesus Christ alone sustains the believer from the first step to the final consummation. That is the justification by faith acceptable to God, which would carry believers to their destination.

Peace can refer to the gospel of peace preached in Romans 10, which results in peace and fellowship between these boastful enemies. Peace is the focus of Romans 9-16 where God ultimately receives glory from those in one accord (Rom. 15:6). It is here, and now, that Satan is crushed by the God of peace (Rom. 16:20). Imagine, by our unity where all divisiveness is extinguished (Rom. 16:17-19), then, and then only, can the "God of peace crush Satan under your feet shortly" (vs. 20). Remember, these are the same feet shod by the preparation of the Gospel of Peace in Ephesians 6. The gospel of peace alone can break down the partition of hostility between all divisions among God's people so they rise up fully clad in the armor of God, able to crush Satan as His One New Man — so making peace!

The result of righteousness and peace is inexplicable **joy** and rejoicing. This joy originates from the fulfillment of God's pleasure. God is joyful, and His joy is transferred and experienced by believers who dwell together in unity. The unity of God's people is the Bride of Christ prepared for the marriage of the Lamb (Rev. 21:2). God rejoices over His wife as the bridegroom rejoices over the bride (Isa. 62:5). God's rejoicing is the cause of His people rejoicing in unity. This is reflected in Zion, where her saints shall shout aloud for joy (Psa. 132;16). Immediately following, in Psalm 133, the people of Zion sang: *"How good and how pleasant it is for brethren to dwell together in unity."*

Such joy, which brings glory to God, cannot come until there is righteousness and peace. It's akin to turning on the light bulb. First, we must have electricity (righteousness); next, a conduit to transfer the electricity (peace); and finally, it's time to turn on the lights ("joy in the Holy Spirit"). Now the world can see God's Kingdom manifested. This is the lampstand (God's Ekklesia) shining, giving light to this dark world!

> And this gospel of the kingdom will be preached in all the world as a witness to all the nations, and then the end will come.
>
> – Matt. 24:14

Therefore, at the end of this age, the gospel of the kingdom must be preached. Like the gospel of peace, the gospel of the Kingdom is the preaching of Jesus Christ with a view to the building up of God's Kingdom. Whereas the gospel of peace is focused on bringing peace among God's people so that they become one, the gospel of the kingdom is focused on the result of this oneness being the coming manifestation of God's eternal Kingdom. The kingdom of God prevails over Satan's kingdom of this world and will usher in the millennial kingdom where Jesus Christ and His saints openly reign with Him (Rev. 11:15). Yet, today, we stand as one as "ambassadors for Christ" (2 Cor. 5:20) representing the Kingdom of God in the here and now — we are united under one King Who is Lord of All, our Lord Jesus Christ.

In 1 Corinthians, believers started in divisions (1 Cor. 1:10). Due to their divisions, there were an assortment of problems: immorality, lawsuits among Christians, idolatry, abusing food, marriage issues, etc. However, if they would be willing to come together in their factions (and rid themselves of their **factious** ways) by remembering the Lord Jesus at the Lord's supper (1 Cor. 11:17-34), then they, though being many and diverse, would become one (1 Cor. 12). Love would be manifested among them even when every spiritual gift and knowledge has failed (1 Cor. 13). Their democratic assembly, with everyone participating and contributing, displaying unity among diverse believers would cause unbelievers and "unlearned" (those who do not know the ways of the unity of the Body of Christ) to believe and worship God (1 Cor. 14). This is the power of the Kingdom of God which Paul preached (1 Cor. 4:15-20). The gospel of the kingdom is manifested by the diversity of God's people in unity, and this is ushered in at the end of the age — Jesus' prayer in John 17 will be manifested.

The Kingdom of God Manifested in Glory:

> Now this I say, brethren, that flesh and blood cannot inherit the kingdom of God; nor does corruption inherit incorruption. 51 Behold, I tell you a mystery: We shall not all sleep, but we shall all be changed — . . . 53 For this corruptible must put on incorruption, and this mortal [must] put on immortality.
>
> — 1 Cor. 15:50-51, 53

After 1 Corinthians 14, where the Lord's Ekklesia (Democratic Assembly) is manifested, the next chapter is the manifestation of the kingdom of God coming in all His glory. The gospel of the kingdom is for building up the Lord's democratic assembly to bring the glory of the Kingdom of God to earth.[29] This is the preaching of Jesus Christ with a view toward the building up of His Ekklesia. When His Ekklesia is built, the gates of Hades (the power of death) is crushed, and the glory of God's eternal Kingdom is manifested.

---

29   Today, there is in many ministries an emphasis upon the Kingdom of God. In particular, well-intentioned brethren preach the Great Commission is to overtake at least seven mountains of culture and civilization to bring forth the Kingdom of God on earth—i.e., to "disciple nations." Though well intentioned, such efforts without the reality of the unity of the Body of Christ will fall far short of God's glory. Indeed, we have witnessed consternation and division from such emphasis in the Body of Christ. Let us embrace the Gospel of Peace for the Kingdom. This is not ethereal or some utopian fascination somewhere off into infinity—it is here and now. Yes, the Kingdom is Now but not what some have imagined—it is found in bringing glory to God alone by His people in unity.

The Kingdom of God started with Jesus Christ's incarnation. Through His death and resurrection, the Kingdom of God expanded to include innumerable numbers of His children. As immature babes, these children succumbed to Satan's tactics and became divided. However, through the gospel of peace, they grew unto maturity and unity, becoming a living expression of God's Kingdom on earth. This built-up Ekklesia will be the final preparation of the Bride of Christ at the end of this age. The *"corruptible must put on incorruption, and this mortal put on immortality."* Christ and His Bride together will manifest the glory of the Kingdom of God in the millennial kingdom and for eternity.

Therefore, the gospel is extensive and inclusive. It includes all the mysteries the Apostle Paul unveiled in His writings.

1. The mystery of God — Christ;
2. The great mystery — Christ and His Ekklesia (Democratic Assembly);
3. The mystery of Godliness — God manifested in the flesh;
4. The mystery of God's *oikonomia* (economy);
5. The hidden mystery — Christ in you;
6. The mystery of Christ — the threefold oneness between Jews and Gentiles.
7. The mystery of the Gospel (the consummation of all the mysteries)

All these mysteries are good news for preaching to believers and unbelievers. The gospel is truncated if preachers only announce that the sum and substance of the gospel of Jesus Christ entails going to heaven one day. These mysteries must be proclaimed since they can be even better news than going to a future heaven.

This concludes the mystery of the gospel. The simplicity of the good news of Jesus Christ and His unsearchable riches can rescue sinners and deliver them into God's oneness — no longer a divided people. It brings forth among humanity justification, regeneration, growth, maturity, unity, and ultimately the glory of the Kingdom of God. What a complete (7 is God's number of completion), wonderful, and glorious mystery is His Gospel!

11

THE MYSTERY OF THE FAITH

Holding the mystery of the faith with a pure conscience.

–1 Tim. 3:9

The phrase *"the mystery of the faith"* shows that faith is also a mystery. It is hidden and requires revelation from God's light to see and understand. What is "the faith," and where does faith come from? What must Christians believe if they claim to embrace "the faith"? After all, faith is not generic; it demands an object — viz, "faith in." What then is the object of this faith? How can a person come to have faith? Faith is one of the most fundamental aspects of being a believer. It could mean eternal life or perishing (John 3:16). It is essential, yet it is a mystery. No one can work for it or obtain it by merit. Therefore, it is crucial to explore this topic of faith's mystery and look to the Scriptures, depending upon the Spirit of God for light and understanding.

The context of this verse speaks to the qualifications of deacons, a person who serves under a master (Thayer's). This is a minister, especially one who serves food. Speaking about the deacons, it starts with "likewise," which refers back to elders (1 Tim. 3:8). In other words, elders should have the same quality: *"holding the mystery of the faith with a pure conscience."* However, elders are examples to all believers (1 Pet. 5:3). Elders are not extra spiritual or gifted individuals. They are simply more mature in Christ and have become examples to younger believers of how they all can be as they mature. Every believer having the same eternal life and divine nature can attain the pattern of elders. Therefore, *"hold to the mystery of the faith with a pure conscience"* is not required only for a few elders, deacons, "clergy members," or extraordinary Christians but is essential for all believers.

The subject of faith can be classified into two aspects: objective and subjective. Objective faith refers to the things in which one believes. What are the items that Christians believe in? These are outside a person. Subjective faith refers to a person's internal experience and belief. 1 Timothy 3:9 speaks of both aspects. "The faith" is objective, referring to the fundamental items in which Christians are to believe. These items relate to the person and work of Jesus Christ. However, holding it "with a pure conscience" shows this faith is also subjective and aligns internally with the conscience of a believer.

Objective Faith Is the Things Believed

> To Titus, a true son in [our] common faith: Grace, mercy, [and] peace from God the Father and the Lord Jesus Christ our Savior.
>
> – Titus 1:4

All Christians, regardless of denominational affiliation, should have this common faith. This faith, the foundational item relating to Jesus Christ, saves a person unto eternal life. Here are the essential items that all followers of Christ must believe in; otherwise, they are without "the faith."

- Jesus Christ is God, the Son of God, who came in the flesh as a genuine man. (Matt. 1:23; John 1:14; 20:31)
- Jesus Christ died on the cross for the sins of the world and was buried, and He was resurrected on the third day. (1 Cor. 15:1-4)
- Through His resurrection and ascension, Jesus Christ became Lord of all. Confessing Him as Lord makes one a believer. (Acts 2:32, 36; Rom. 10:9)
- Jesus Christ indwells all His believers, making His home in their hearts (2 Cor. 13:5; Col. 1:29; Eph. 3:17)

Read the referenced verses. It will become clear that these are the objective items of the truth of Jesus Christ that one must believe to be saved. The above four items ("four essential items of the faith") are the distillate of the person and work of Jesus Christ. This is the common faith which is also called the doctrine of Christ (2 John 1:9). In other words, this faith is common for all believers whether they are Catholics, Orthodox, Baptists, Pentecostals, Methodists, Presbyterians, Evangelicals of all stripes, those done with "organized" church, those who have never been to church, no matter ethnicity, males or females, children or those about to pass on, as long as they accepted this faith of Jesus Christ, they are children of God and fellow brothers and sisters in Christ.

What about the doctrine of the Trinity, the Bible being the infallible word of God, the second advent of Christ, baptism, holy living, Pentecostal gifts, and many other doctrines and Christian practices? They can be beneficial and have their rightful place, but according to the Scriptures, none of them are necessary for salvation. The common faith that brings about common salvation (Jude 1:3) is so simple that even little children can understand and accept it. All believers are saved in the same way and to the same extent. At the end of their salvation journey, they will ultimately bear the image of Jesus Christ (Rom. 8:29-30). Common means there is nothing special or unique concerning faith and salvation among God's children. Nevertheless, many ministries and churches do their best to preach or show that they have something unique to draw adherents. These extras can be helpful, but can also be the very factors that divide believers from one another.

Growing in the Knowledge of the Faith

> In him you also, when you heard the word of truth, the gospel of your salvation, and believed in him, were sealed with the promised Holy Spirit,
>
> – Eph. 1:13, ESV

> . . . that you stand fast in one spirit, with one mind striving together for the faith of the gospel.
>
> – Phil. 1:27

> But they were hearing only, "He who formerly persecuted us now preaches the faith which he once tried to destroy."
>
> – Gal. 1:23

Ephesians 1:13 says that the word of truth is the gospel. Then Paul says, "the faith of the gospel," and finally "preaches the faith." The truth, the gospel, and the faith are interrelated and, at times, interchangeable. The truth can be learned and assimilated through knowledge: therefore, God desires all men to come to the knowledge of the truth (1 Tim. 2:4). Even though the saving faith is so simple, it is like a seed within which are the "unsearchable riches of Christ." Paul did not just preach a simple gospel that was good enough to save people from damnation; he preached the unsearchable riches of Christ as the good news to consummate Christ's corporate Body and Bride (Eph. 3:8). As previously discussed, the gospel includes all the various mysteries consummating in God's eternal purpose. Therefore, the gospel is the good news spread concerning the truth of Jesus Christ, which is the faith (objective) for people to trust and obey. Although it starts with the simplicity of the "seed" of the saving faith, it includes the unfathomable knowledge concerning the truth of Christ's person and work as described throughout the Bible.

Let's break this down further. According to Vine's Expository Dictionary, truth (Gk: *alethia*), used in the New Testament, means "the reality lying at the basis of appearance and manifestation." According to this definition, truth is far more than refraining from lies or stating facts — it is the very reality of the universe. Truth is eternal. When a person realizes what is hidden behind what appears or what is manifested, that is the truth. No wonder "truth" has such prominence! It is one of two profundities that came through Jesus Christ — Grace and truth (John 1:17). It is important to elevate the understanding of the word "truth" to a high and spiritual level and not relegate it to a simple secular concept, such as "Tell me the truth! Did you take a cookie?"

Let's briefly consider the major items of the truth as defined by the Scriptures. First and foremost, God is truth. *"In the beginning was the Word and the Word was with God, and the Word was God . . . and the Word became flesh . . . full of grace and truth" (John 1:1, 14).*

Second, Jesus Christ, God in the flesh, is the truth. The truth was revealed in Jesus Christ. Jesus said, *"I am the truth"* (John 14:6), and Paul declared, *"the truth is in Jesus"* (Eph. 4:21).

Third, the Spirit is Truth. The Scriptures declare the Spirit of truth (John 14:17, 15:26, 16:13; 1 John 4:6); this Spirit is truth (1 John 5:6). The Spirit of Truth guides believers into all truth by declaring and infusing the reality of all Who the Father and the Son are within believers (John 16:13–15).

Fourth, the truth is all that the Father, the Son, and the Spirit have accomplished in the New Covenant for His eternal purpose. This encompasses the death of Jesus Christ on the cross, His resurrection, ascension, and enthronement, along with His redemptive work — bringing forgiveness of sins, justification, sanctification, the regeneration (new birth) of believers, and ultimately, their glorification. Therefore, the person of the Triune God dwelling bodily in Jesus Christ (Col. 2:9) and His work of redemption and regeneration is the Word of truth — that is, the gospel of salvation. It is through believing the truth that people are saved and sealed by the indwelling Spirit (Eph. 1:13). It is this truth whereby God and humanity are joined and unified together to be the Lord's Ekklesia, His body — the new man spoken of in Ephesians 2:15. This is God's eternal purpose: A corporate entity, ultimately the New Jerusalem, created and built up into maturity in truth (Eph. 4:24).

Finally, the Word as recorded in the Bible is truth. The Bible conveys the truth; therefore, in Daniel 10:21, the term "Scripture of Truth" is used. Truth is the possessor of the Scriptures. This means if one reads the Scriptures and only understands law, history, ceremonies, ethics, or morality, and misses the truth, then they miss the entire point of the Scriptures — "I will show you the Scripture of Truth." Therefore, when reading or studying the Scriptures, it is critical to know the embedded Word. Truth is experienced when the Word is made real to a person. The Word, the logos, speaks to people and communicates to their reasoning. It is truth when the Word is received, understood, and becomes real in a person. That is why people need to know and come to the full knowledge of the truth (2 Tim. 2:25, 3:7; 1 Tim. 2:4).

Hebrews 11:3 says: *"By faith we understand that the worlds were framed by the Word of God, so that the things which are seen were not made of things which are visible."* The word of God, being the truth, is the invisible power and reality framing the entire universe. The universe and all physical items in it can be seen through scientific observation. However, there is something invisible holding everything together — that is the Word of God, the truth. That invisible "glue" holding the physical universe together can only be understood by faith, not by science.

This is also the case concerning Christian things such as baptism, a holy lifestyle, the Lord's supper, dietary restrictions, liturgical practices, and everything else visible. All these items, which can be vital and concerning to various groups of Christians, so much so that they are eager and willing to debate and divide over such items. However, such issues given to debate are not the truth. Christians would become united if they focused on the truth. For example, many divisions have been created over how to baptize. Is it immersion or sprinkling, and if immersion, what kind of water should be used, and what are the qualifications for the person being baptized and the baptizer? All these visible practices relating to baptism have caused many factions among Christians. However, the truth of these outward practices is that through faith, believers are identified with Christ's death and resurrection (Rom. 6:4). All Christians agree with this invisible truth; yet, many have been divided over the appearance of baptism. Therefore, the gospel (good news) is not how to get baptized, but the reality of being one with Christ in His death and resurrection. Man's fallen nature is terminated. Now they can live in the newness of God's divine eternal life.

The truth, as outlined above, is the gospel which we should be preaching. Who God is and what He has accomplished for humanity in Jesus Christ is good news. The truth should not be hidden and kept secret. Rather, it needs to be heralded and preached everywhere. Every single item of the truth is good news since God desires all men to be saved. In their ignorance, men misunderstand God and are fearful of Him; therefore, they hide from Him or detest Him, thinking God's heart is ill-will toward them. Men need to hear the truth, so preaching is necessary to broadcast the truth since it is good news (gospel).

since we heard of your faith in Christ Jesus and of the love that you have for all the saints, 5 because of the hope laid up for you in heaven. Of this you have heard before in the word of the truth, the gospel,

– Col. 1:4-5, ESV

Every item of the truth, being the gospel, comprises the faith (objective) that men should believe. The four essential items of faith, itemized above, are encapsulated as the "seed" of faith needed for salvation. However, the appreciation of additional items of faith should increase and expand as believers hear and understand the knowledge of truth. Every item of the truth preached as the gospel becomes another item of faith for believers to accept and receive as their reality.

For example, the seed of faith is that Jesus Christ, the Son of God, died and resurrected as the Lord for the forgiveness of man's sins. Believing in this is enough to receive justification and eternal life. However, there is much more to this truth. When Jesus died through crucifixion, He buried the "old man," man's fallen nature (Rom. 6:6). Satan was defeated, and Jesus' death took away the fear of death (Heb. 2:14-15). Additionally, His crucifixion broke down walls of hatred between divided peoples and created one new man (Eph. 2:14-16). In His resurrection, He did not just come alive again but became the indwelling Spirit (John 14:16-18). His followers became regenerated with the life of God (1 Pet. 1:3). And as the Head, all His resurrection power is available to His Body, His democratic assembly (Eph. 1:22).

All these other items of truth (and there are many more) are good news for preaching and announcing. Simultaneously, these rich matters of the truth become expanded items for believing. They are a growing body of faith for Christians to receive and believe.

The truth, though holding the universe together, is outside and invisible to man. Man's scientific and research mind cannot observe or experience this hidden universe of truth. Nevertheless, it exists eternally, whereas the physical universe — governed by entropy — is limited by both time and space. What mystery that man, though finite, can connect and fellowship in the eternal realm of truth. Man can receive, experience, and have a relationship with the reality of God, all He is and has accomplished. Without knowing the reality of the universe, man simply remains unfulfilled and in a state of vanity. The reason man was created is to know God by being joined in fellowship with Him (2 Peter 1:4: *"Partakers [koinonia] of the divine nature"*).

The Subjective Faith to Experience the Truth

Faith in the Greek means conviction or belief (Thayer's). Faith in the subjective sense is the inward conviction or belief within a person. This is different than the things believed in as the object of faith. In the New Testament, having faith or the ability to believe is essential and foundational. Without faith, one cannot be considered a Christian or a believer since *"without faith it is impossible to please God"* (Heb. 11:6). Furthermore, the entire basis to be right or justified before God is by faith alone (Rom. 5:1). Likewise, man's salvation can only come by faith (Eph. 2:8).

Faith, as seen in the four gospels, when Jesus was physically on earth, was different from the faith described in the epistles after Jesus' death and resurrection. Faith during the gospels can be summarized by Jesus speaking to a blind man: *"Do you believe that I am able to do this? They said to Him, 'Yes, Lord.' Then He touched their eyes, saying, 'According to your faith let it be to you'"* (Matt. 9:29). This was a faith or a trust in the supernatural ability of Jesus to heal, raise the dead, and perform miracles. In the gospels, the focus on faith was that Jesus is recognized as the Son of God, and as such, He can perform miracles at will. The physical miracles convinced people that He is the omnipotent Son of God (John 20:30-31). This faith during the four gospels was focused on affecting the physical realm — faith to move mountains (Matt. 17:20). However, the Lord desires that His followers progress toward a faith that is not physical and cannot be observed: *"Blessed are those who have not seen and yet have believed"* (John 20:29).

Therefore, after Jesus' death and resurrection, faith in the epistles is defined by:

> Now faith is the substance of things hoped for, the evidence of things not seen.
>
> – Heb. 11:1

This faith is the ability to substantiate the invisible world of the truth. The unseen frame of the universe is real, and it is only by faith that a person can have an overwhelming conviction that it is so. What is commonly known as the five senses — hear, see, taste, touch, and smell — are used to substantiate the physical world. For example, color exists in the physical realm, but if a person is blind, they cannot substantiate color. Color is not "real" to the blind. This is also true for a person who loses their sense of taste — sweet or salty is not a substance that can be perceived. Beyond the physical realm is the invisible and spiritual. This realm is more real than the physical realm, but only a person with faith can substantiate things in this realm. Just like a person without sight will think that color is unreal, a person without faith will consider that God is not real and can only be conjured up in one's imagination.

They will say, "Where is God? We can't see Him." That is because God is not in the physical realm. If they had faith, they would have the ability to have the conviction of the reality of the invisible God. Here's another example: radio waves broadcasting music and television programs are invisible to the five senses. If a person who has never experienced or understood such signals were told that there is music and videos in the air, they would think it absurd and impossible. However, with a proper receiver, such as a radio or television can readily pick up these invisible waves so they can be realized. Faith, as defined in Hebrews 11, may be considered as the sixth sense, the ability to know and experience the unseen spiritual truth of the universe.

Abraham, the Father of Faith

(As it is written, "I have made you a father of many nations") in the presence of Him whom he believed — God, who gives life to the dead and calls those things which do not exist as though they did;

– Rom. 4:17

Abraham was childless, and he wanted an heir. He asked God to make his trusted servant, Eliazer, his heir, but God did not allow it. Then God announced the gospel to Abraham (Abram): *"Look now toward heaven, and count the stars if you are able to number them." And He said to him, "So shall your seed be"* (Gen. 15:5). Thus, when Abram heard this promise in Genesis 15:5, it was music to his ears. He desired an heir. Now, God tells him that he will have generations of offspring as numerous as the stars filling the sky. Like the gospel to Adam and Eve, Abraham, being childless, will have offspring.

Abraham believed this gospel and God counted that faith as righteousness — *"And he believed in the LORD, and He accounted it to him for righteousness"* (Gen. 15:6). Although God already counted Abraham (Abram) as justified by faith in Genesis 15, Abraham did not live according to that faith. He could not wait for God to fulfill His promise; therefore, he followed Sarah's suggestion to have a son with Hagar (Sarah's maidservant), and his name was Ishmael. However, this effort of the flesh was not the heir produced by faith. God rejected Ishmael as an heir. By then, Abraham was 99 years old and Sarah was 89, so there was no hope for Abraham to have a son when God preached the gospel to him again in Genesis 17.

Although Abraham had strayed by using his efforts to produce an heir, he continued his faith in God. This may be the experience of most Christians. They received faith in Jesus Christ for a new birth, but they could not wait for God's timing to transform them into the image of Christ. Therefore, they relied on self-effort in the flesh to modify their behaviors. Though their behavior may change, it does not last, even when they exert more effort. When they lost hope, the Lord came again to preach the gospel to them. In this way, they cannot boast of their eventual transformation into the image of Christ, knowing that it was all God's doing, simply through faith in Jesus Christ.

Romans 4:17 reflects Abraham's faith to be a "father of many nations" in both aspects: the faith of substantiating the unseen reality and the faith in God's supernatural power. *"Calls those things which do not exist as though they did"* refers to God's creative power. He spoke, as recorded in Genesis 1, and they were. *"Let there be light,"* and light came into being. *"Let the earth bring forth the living creatures according to its kind,"* and it was so. He called things into being that were not. This was the same power Jesus possessed to heal the sick, give sight to the blind, and raise the dead. This is the belief that Jesus is God.

"Giving life to the dead" is deeper and more precious. This is not just the miracle of raising the dead, as was the case of Lazarus in John 11. This is giving life to dead humanity. Due to sin, starting from Adam, humanity has been dead in relation to God — death reigned (Rom. 5:17). Though man can be physically and psychologically alive, man is still spiritually dead (Eph. 2:1). When Christ resurrected from death, He didn't simply become physically alive again. He gave life to dead humanity. Ephesians 2:5 continues: *"Even when we were dead in trespasses, made us alive together with Christ."*

Jesus Christ's death and resurrection are in the eternal realm outside the limitations of time and space, in the unseen eternal dimension, which occurred from the foundation of the world (Rev. 13:8).

Abraham saw Jesus, even though Jesus was born about 2000 years after Abraham. *"Your father Abraham rejoiced to see My* [Jesus'] *day, and he saw* [it] *and was glad"* (John 8:56). Abraham saw Jesus with the eyes of faith. Jesus, as the Son of God, existed from eternity in the invisible dimension. Nevertheless, Abraham saw Him and was glad. Therefore, to Abraham, believing that God gives life to the dead was not "blind faith." By faith, he saw and enjoyed the reality in the eternal realm.

This is the same faith that enabled all the Old Testament saints described in Hebrews 11 to endure and triumph in their sufferings. The many grueling journeys, persecutions, trials, and warfare these saints in the Hebrew Scriptures went through were able to do so "by faith" and "through faith." Faith caused them to be unburdened with the physical world but allowed them to focus on the spiritual. Faith was the means for them to triumph while in distress. Although they were journeying and suffering in the physical dimension, by faith and through faith, they were living in the reality of the invisible. This verse concerning Moses captures the experiences and reality of these suffering saints: *"By faith Moses, when he became of age, refused to be called the son of Pharaoh's daughter, choosing rather to suffer affliction with the people of God than to enjoy the passing pleasures of sin, esteeming the reproach of Christ greater riches than the treasures in Egypt; for he looked to the reward. By faith he forsook Egypt, not fearing the wrath of the king; for he endured as* **seeing Him who is invisible***"* (Heb. 11:24-27).

This is the meaning of faith as defined by Hebrews 11: **the ability to substantiate the reality in the invisible realm where Christ is, with all that He has accomplished in eternity**. This faith operated in the Old Testament as a precursor. However, it was not until the enactment of the New Covenant by the blood of Jesus, according to God's schedule, that His people from the least to the greatest fully entered the age of faith. Therefore, speaking of these great men and women of God in the Old Testament:

"All these, having obtained a good testimony through faith, did not receive the promise, God having provided something better for us [in the New Covenant], *that they should not be made perfect apart from us"* (Heb. 11:39-40). What a wonderful privilege to live in the New Covenant age and enjoy the fullness of the gift of faith. These pre-New Covenant saints are waiting for believers today to grow and mature in faith.

Now, His "brethren" (Heb. 2:12; Psa. 22:22) enjoy the reality of Jesus Christ and all that He has accomplished through His death and resurrection: This includes His people's forgiveness of sins, justification, glorification, Satan's defeat, the oneness of His people, and even the consummate Holy City, New Jerusalem. Though these items of truth are more real than the physical universe, only faith can bring conviction and substantiate their reality. A person with faith is bold toward God because of justification (Heb. 4:16). This person is seated in the heavenlies with Christ in the power of resurrection with all things subdued (Eph. 1:20-21). This person loves all other believers since the love of Christ is present and experiential (John 13:34). This one enjoys the new man in unity with his previous enemies (Eph. 2:14-15), and a vast universe of other spiritual realizations and experiences due to faith.

This is the mystery of faith. This faith has been hidden with the gospel (truth) in the invisible realm. Now the truth is being preached as the gospel — it is the object of faith. The inward subjective faith substantiates the objective faith so that all the items of truth are realized. The truth outside of man becomes real and experiential within man by subjective faith. Now, the objective truth outside becomes the subjective experiential truth inside of man. What a wonderful mystery!

Receiving and Growing in Faith

> looking unto Jesus, the author and finisher of [our] faith, who for the joy that was set before Him endured the cross, despising the shame, and has sat down at the right hand of the throne of God.
>
> – Heb. 12:2

> For by grace you have been saved through faith, and that not of yourselves; [it is] the gift of God,
>
> – Eph. 2:8

There is a direct connection and relationship between objective and subjective faith. Objective faith is essentially Jesus' person and work. He is the truth and the gospel. When a person focuses their inner eyes and sees Jesus ("looking unto Jesus"), He authors or transmits subjective faith within that person. As they look to Jesus and consider the wonder of His person, they become enthralled that He is both God and man; that He determined to suffer in shame and was unjustly murdered, and now He is resurrected and seated as the universal authority on the throne of God. This kind of contemplation initiates and creates faith within man. This faith originates in Jesus Christ and is imparted into the human spirit — his innermost being — through divine infusion. Man's spirit, once deadened by sin, becomes alive with faith — "spirit of faith" (2 Cor. 4:13).

This faith is a gift. It cannot be bought. All the riches in the entire universe are not enough to buy this faith. It cannot be earned through good deeds or holy behaviors. It is simply God's gift that man should receive with thanksgiving (Eph. 2:8).

Man cannot work up faith. He is not the source of faith. No matter how much he tries to invoke it within himself, it is impossible to have self-generating faith. Faith is not in his mind, emotion, or resolve. This faith is not to be confused with the American idiom "keep the faith, baby," which simply refers to staying hopeful in the face of adversity. No, the faith of Jesus can only originate from Him and be transmitted to those looking unto Him. He is the author and perfecter of the faith, which is the ability to substantiate the invisible.

> So faith comes from hearing, and hearing through the word of Christ.
>
> — Rom. 10:17, ESV

> Most assuredly, I say to you, the hour is coming, and now is, when the dead will hear the voice of the Son of God; and those who hear will live.
>
> — John 5:25

Unlike seeing, breathing, and eating, hearing is effortless. When a person is too weak or sick, he will not be able to open his eyes, he will need a breathing machine, and be fed intravenously. However, even when a person is in a coma kept alive by machines, that person can hear. There is no muscle needed for hearing. The Lord made the transfer of His life and faith so effortless that a person only needs to hear His word. As they hear the gospel, the truth, they may not understand how it can be that Jesus died and resurrected, but they start to appreciate and welcome the message. They start to have a stirring within to respond to the gospel of the truth. At a certain point, an inward conviction that Jesus is real and a desire to receive Him grow. Eventually, they may just mutter, "Lord Jesus, I need You. Thank you for dying for my sins. Come into my heart." Such a simple prayer was faith-generated in this person, and a spiritual transaction happened.

There was a friend of ours who simply could not believe, although he wanted to believe. He would often say: "Guys, I just don't have the faith like you bros. I'm sorry, I just don't." His honesty was refreshing — he just could not believe. We prayed for him; actually, for decades. Then, at 97 years of age, the Lord came to him through an amazing encounter initiated by the Holy Spirit. His faith exploded, and he declared that he was finally a "born-again Christian." Where did he get that faith? He got it from God Almighty. It was one of those: "Lord, I believe, help thou my unbelief" (Mark 9:14-29). No, he was not passive; he really wanted to believe, but needed faith to believe, and the Lord came to him.

As people hear the word of Christ, faith is transferred to them (Rom. 10:17). The "word of Christ" grammatically here can be understood as "words concerning Christ." In context, Romans 10:6-13 in the same chapter speaks of Christ's incarnation, crucifixion, resurrection, Lordship, and His indwelling in His believers. Any portion of this sequence and its expansive richness throughout the Scriptures are words concerning Christ. As a person hears these words, faith is transferred to them. This could be unbelievers hearing the "word of Christ," or, in this case, even more so, believers continually need to listen to the "word of Christ." They must hear the preaching of the truth to grow in faith.

Most Christians are satisfied with the rudimentary gospel of how Jesus died for their sins and are saved to go to heaven one day. Yes, this has generated faith in people, but it is quite superficial. They need to hear more of the truth of the gospel for their faith to grow. If their faith stagnates at a childish level, then they will struggle in their life journey and their relationship with other believers in the Body of Christ.

> Grace and peace be multiplied to you in the knowledge of God and of Jesus our Lord, 3 as His divine power has given to us all things that [pertain] to life and godliness, through the knowledge of Him who called us by glory and virtue, 4 by which have been given to us exceedingly great and precious promises, that through these you may be partakers of the divine nature, having escaped the corruption [that is] in the world through lust. 5 But also for this very reason, giving all diligence, add to your faith virtue, to virtue knowledge, 6 to knowledge self-control, to self-control perseverance, to perseverance godliness, 7 to godliness brotherly kindness, and to brotherly kindness love. 8 For if these things are yours and abound, [you] will be neither barren nor unfruitful in the knowledge of our Lord Jesus Christ.
>
> — 2 Pet. 1:2-8

Here is a wonderful portion relating to the growth in faith where Peter spoke to those who had started their journey of faith. Faith is the most basic and essential requirement to begin this journey. However, consider how many times knowledge is mentioned for faith to grow. In verse 2, the knowledge of God and the Lord Jesus Christ is needed for grace and peace to multiply. Then verse 3, the divine power of life and godliness is given through the knowledge of Him. In verse 4, a person needs to know the exceedingly great and precious promises to partake of the divine nature and escape corruption. In verse 5, though the gift of faith was given freely to believers, they needed to add whatever little virtue they may have to it. This is their cooperation to provide diligence and excellence in their character to do something, primarily to add knowledge. They use their virtue to gain more knowledge. By adding knowledge, the seed of faith in them will develop self-control, perseverance, godliness, brotherly love, and eventually God's agape love. Finally, they will not be unfruitful in the knowledge of the Lord Jesus Christ.

Knowledge of God and Jesus Christ, and knowing God's promises, was mentioned 5 times throughout this journey of growth from the seed of faith to God's unconditional love. Living and expressing God's love is the final fruit of the seed of faith. This shows that the knowledge of the truth needs to be preached and taught to Christians and unbelievers. Remember that the knowledge of the truth is objective faith. The more this rich truth is preached, objective faith becomes subjective faith within believers. As the truth becomes their experience, they grow and develop the riches within the seed of faith.

Christians can be very knowledgeable about the Bible, but may miss the truth. They may know history, law, ethics, miracles, and many "how-tos" — family, marriage, finance, holy living, even spirituality. Nevertheless, they may be woefully short of knowing God, Christ, the Spirit, their accomplished work, or God's eternal purpose of His one Body. As believers read and study the Bible, they must concentrate on knowing Jesus as the truth.

Prayers to Grow in Faith

You search the Scriptures, for in them you think you have eternal life; and these are they which testify of Me. 40 But you are not willing to come to Me that you may have life.

– John 5:39-40

But you, beloved, building yourselves up on your most holy faith, praying in the Holy Spirit.

– Jude 1:20

When believers come to seek the knowledge of the truth in the Scriptures, they must turn their hearts to Jesus. This is looking at Jesus while searching the Scriptures; otherwise, eternal life is missed. Neglecting Jesus in the Scriptures is missing eternal life since knowing Jesus is eternal life (John 17:3). The best way to turn one's heart in a desire to fellowship with the Lord is to pray in the Holy Spirit. The word pray (Gk. *proseuchomai*) has the meaning of "toward" God and "pray." Prayer is not just making requests but includes thanksgiving, adoration, and fellowship. It is a continual conversation toward and with the Lord, expressing what is on one's heart and hearing what is on His heart. So, the Scriptures command: "pray without ceasing" (1 Thess. 5:17).

As believers read and study the Scriptures, they are conversing with the Lord and hearing the Lord's heart and desire. That is fellowship — a two-way sharing or communication. Jesus, being the Word of God, is embedded in the Scriptures. God speaks to His people through His Word. There are two Greek words for "word" — *Logos* and *rema*. These two verses can highlight the two meanings:

> In the beginning was the Word [logos], and the Word was with God, and the Word was God.
>
> — John 1:1

> "It is the Spirit who gives life; the flesh profits nothing. The words [rema] that I speak to you are spirit, and [they] are life.
>
> — John 6:63

Logos means "those things which are put together in thought . . . i.e., gathered together in the mind, are expressed in words." (Thayer's). Remarkably, God is the Word. The invisible God is expressed and declared as the eternal Word (John 1:18). The word (*logos*) refers to God communicating to man with reasoning and logic. God's entire revelation concerning Himself in His relationship with man is embedded in the Scriptures. God's total revelation about His heart's desire is complete in the Scriptures (Rev. 22:18). No one can add any new revelation that is not already in the Bible. If a "revelation" takes place in an assembly of believers, as in 1 Corinthians 14:26, it is predicated upon the inspired Word of God. Therefore, there is a need to read and study the Scriptures with a seeking heart to know God and His purpose. Thus, *logos* refers to the objective knowledge of God that is universal and unchanging.

As believers pray and converse with the Lord while considering the knowledge derived from *logos*, the Spirit speaks words (*rema*) of Christ to their spirit and heart. This present word from the Spirit is "*rema*." The Greek word "*rema*" means "that which is or has been uttered by the living voice" (Thayer's). This refers to a timely message from the Spirit by a portion of *logos* coming alive in a particular situation. This *rema* word of Christ is Spirit and life to the hearer. It is an instant application of God's Word (*logos*). As believers pray and converse with the Lord, their faith is strengthened as the Spirit speaks back, as certain Scriptures come alive. Both *rema* and the *logos*, being God's word, are two sides of the same coin. *Logos*, being the constant and universal truth, and *rema*, being the applied truth by the Spirit, is present and situational.

John 16:13 says: *"When He, the Spirit of truth, has come, He will guide you into all truth."* As believers pray in the Holy Spirit, the Spirit guides them into all truth, building up their faith. Remember, faith is the ability to substantiate all the truth in the spiritual, invisible realm. A believer's subjective faith increases as they are led into the realization and experience of the truth.

For example, one can know this item of truth that took place in the past: *"made us alive together with Christ (by grace you have been saved), and raised us up together, and made us sit together in the heavenly places in Christ Jesus"* (Eph. 2:5-6). However, something happened in this person's environment. They became discouraged and dejected. People tried to encourage this believer, but could not help their situation and attitude. Then they turned their heart to the Lord and began to fellowship with Him in prayer. As they spoke to the Lord, the Lord spoke back to them. These verses are brought to remembrance and stir the discouraged heart. The Spirit of Truth is working to guide them into the reality of these verses. Although nothing changes outwardly, inwardly, they realize that they are seated with Christ on the throne and all things are under their feet. Being above all in the heavenly places with Christ is not a fantasy or imagination. It is more real than any depressive state of mind. By praying in the Holy Spirit, one is actively speaking Christ into themselves through the enlightening and application of this logos word in Ephesians. Their faith is strengthened, and they experience the reality of the invisible realm triumphing over the discouraging situation in the physical realm.

The more believers know the truth as conveyed by God's Word (logos), the more opportunity for the Spirit to speak to them as they pray. Reading and studying the Logos is essential; yet equally vital is prayerful attentiveness — actively listening for the present and living voice of Christ as He speaks through the indwelling Spirit.

The Testing of Faith More Precious than Gold

> Wherein ye exult, for a little while at present, if needed, put to grief by various trials, 7 that the proving of your faith, much more precious than of gold which perishes, though it be proved by fire, be found to praise and glory and honor in [the] revelation of Jesus Christ: 8 whom, having not seen, ye love; on whom [though] not now looking, but believing, ye exult with joy unspeakable and filled with [the] glory,
>
> — 1 Pet. 1:6-8, DBY

The various trials believers encounter in their journey through life are to prove their faith. The word "proves" in Greek means something that is tried or tested to be genuine. The trials are in the realm of the physical and physiological, with many challenges and difficulties. During such periods, does their faith work? They need to prove and test their faith. If their faith does not work, they remain struggling in the realm where the trials are. However, if their faith works, they will substantiate the invisible spiritual realm even though nothing changes outwardly.

When they prove or test their faith and it works, they are brought into the revelation of Jesus Christ, who is in the unseen realm. Seeing Jesus, they exult with unspeakable joy and full of glory. Amid their trials, they love and triumph with indescribable joy and glory. People around them will consider it impossible since these believers are still in their distressing situation; yet, they are liberated from it. Their faith gave them the ability to come into the revelation of Jesus. They no longer suffer in the trials, but are now in joy and glory, seeing the one they love. They are overflowing with love because they are enjoying the present love of the Lord. Their abounding love flows toward all those around them, even those who may be causing the trials.

For example, a Christian is being persecuted for their faith or rejected by other Christians due to church or ministry associations. They have every reason to become downcast and discouraged. Instead, this is an opportunity to prove their faith. They use their spirit of faith to pray and turn their heart to the Lord. Soon, their faith enables them to see the invisible Jesus. In the unseen realm, they realize that they have died with Christ; Satan's sting of death is powerless, and the middle wall of division is broken. They find themselves in the power of the Lord's resurrection. Instead of dejection, they are looking at Jesus and exulting with joy and glory. Additionally, they express love and kindness to those who intend to harm or reject them. They care for them and forgive them. If they become sad and discouraged, people will view them in shame and humiliation. However, they describe the wonder of Jesus and His resurrection. Those witnessing their joy and grace are amazed, appreciating them with praise, glory, and honor.

This is faith in action. It is truly miraculous how faith transfers a person into the reality of the invisible realm of the Spirit. Even though they are still in the physical world, wherein nothing outwardly seems to have changed. Now, faith has brought them to see the unseen Jesus and everything eternal that the Trinity has accomplished.

Speaking by the Spirit of Faith

> But we have this treasure in earthen vessels, that the excellence of the power may be of God and not of us. 8 [We are] hard-pressed on every side, yet not crushed; [we are] perplexed, but not in despair; 9 persecuted, but not

forsaken; struck down, but not destroyed — 10 always carrying about in the body the dying of the Lord Jesus, that the life of Jesus also may be manifested in our body. 11 For we who live are always delivered to death for Jesus' sake, that the life of Jesus also may be manifested in our mortal flesh. 12 So then death is working in us, but life in you. 13 And since we have the same spirit of faith, according to what is written, "I believed and therefore I spoke," we also believe and therefore speak,

— 2 Cor 4:7-13

Paul and his team were suffering many difficulties and persecutions that were devastating and debilitating. They should have been in despair and crushed, unable to move forward. However, that did not happen because they had the treasure of Christ in them, giving them the power of God. This power is not the miraculous power to improve and change their physical environment so they would no longer suffer. Instead, this was the power of resurrection. This resurrection life does not simply overcome their own "death" situation, but it spiritually enlivens people around them.

The difficulties surrounding them were leading to death. They were bearing the cross of Jesus for the benefit of others, and experiencing the afflictions of Christ for the building up of the Lord's Body (Col. 1:24). While they were bearing the killing of Jesus, the life of Jesus was manifested in their mortal bodies. People were being enlivened as they observed the speaking and actions of these ministers. The witnesses were receiving life and encouragement. Paul's environment did not change for the better, but people watching and hearing them were coming alive. So, while death worked in the ministers, life was being ministered to others.

Life was ministered because they were speaking via the spirit of faith. They were preaching Christ and His accomplished work in faith. Even though their physical situation was dismal, their faith substantiated an invisible and spiritual environment of glory and victory. In reality, they were in the heavenly realm. They spoke from an exalted position, and speaking by the spirit of faith gave life to those listening. Their words astonished the hearers; no one expected them to proclaim the victory and glory of Christ amid suffering. Yes, physically, they were perplexed and cast down, but that was not their reality. Their conviction and reality, by their sense of faith, was that they were on the throne with Christ and everything under their feet.

When Paul and his fellow ministers were struck down by their persecutors, what if they started murmuring and complaining, wishing that they hadn't followed Christ? If they were downcast and in despair, their witnesses would not receive any life. Instead, they would mock and ridicule the apostles, saying: "They preach Christ, but only know how to moan and whine when things don't go their way." Instead of receiving life, those watching would be completely blind to the reality of Jesus. However, by faith, they spoke in the reality of glory, joy, and resurrection; the hearers receive life. Whatever suffering these saints endured, they were dwelling in heaven with His Name and His Tabernacle, where His glory abides — they are with Him in the glory!

Therefore, believers are challenged to learn from the apostles to always speak by the spirit of faith. Their speaking of Christ's person and work while in challenging situations is exactly when life is ministered. No matter the dreadful environment, use faith to substantiate the reality of the invisible realm and speak forth by the spirit of faith. Describe the glory of the Lord, the defeat of His enemy, and the saints' victory in the unseen eternal reality. Their faith will grow, and those who witness and hear will receive life.

The Oneness of the Faith and the Knowledge of the Son of God

> . . . till we all come to the unity of the faith and of the knowledge of the Son of God, to a perfect man, to the measure of the stature of the fullness of Christ; 14 that we should no longer be children, tossed to and fro and carried about with every wind of doctrine, by the trickery of men, in the cunning craftiness of deceitful plotting, 15 but, speaking the truth in love, may grow up in all things into Him who is the head — Christ.
>
> — Eph. 4:13-15

At the beginning of Ephesians 4, Paul told all Christians, *"Endeavoring to keep the unity of the Spirit in the bond of peace"* (Eph. 4:3). The unity of the Spirit existed with them at the time of receiving their common faith. He then listed what every Christian has accepted as common: *One body and one Spirit, just as you were called in one hope of your calling; one Lord, one faith, one baptism; one God and Father of all, who [is] above all, and through all, and in you all* (Eph. 4:4-6). At the time of any believer's new birth in Christ, they are all born of the same heavenly Father. Therefore, every believer possesses the oneness of the Spirit at birth, which they should endeavor to keep. However, since they all began as babes in Christ, they were susceptible to being blown by winds of teachings into various systems of division (Eph. 4:14). Most Christians, as babes, end up in various silos of division (1 Cor. 3:4).

Satan is cunning in dividing God's children. He can use personalities, biblical doctrines relating to salvation, holiness, end-time prophecies, Christian lifestyles, and many more facets of various teachings to blow believers back and forth into sundry factions. Therefore, they need the help from those five-fold ministers as described in Eph. 4:11 to equip or perfect them so that they can function within the entire Body of Christ, not just within a particular church. True five-fold ministers are not interested in gathering a group around themselves but continually release believers into the entire Body of Christ.

The result in equipping saints in ministering in the Body (rather than only in their own church or ministry) is that they come to or "arrive into" the unity of the faith and the knowledge of the Son of God. They are to return to the simplicity of their common faith in Christ. Believers start their journey with the simplicity of common belief; then they get distracted and blown about by various winds of doctrines into divisive silos. Now they need to grow and mature and return to the unity of the faith. Believers can have differing convictions regarding so many facets of biblical teachings; nevertheless, oneness is not about agreeing to embrace the same set of doctrines — aside from the "doctrine of Christ" (2 John 1:9). There should be liberality among believers, allowing for various doctrinal understandings and convictions on personal holiness. Diversity must be expected in the Body of Christ (1 Cor. 12). The many facets of believers' differences are the beauty of His Body in unity based on one common faith.

The place of unity is also in the unrelenting pursuit of the knowledge of Christ. A mature believer will treasure the faith as unique for the unity in the Lord's Body. They will not contend or divide over any doctrine or practice beyond the simple common faith. Nevertheless, the initial faith is the seed containing the unsearchable riches of Christ. It embodies the entire knowledge of the truth concerning Christ's person and work. Much of Christians' pursuit may be related to the "how tos": how to be holy, how to be a disciple, how to be blessed, how to have a growing church, how to receive spiritual gifts, etc. Or "what does it look like," such as: Baptism, the Lord's supper, a godly family, a Spirit-filled church, a doctrinally correct church, etc. Focusing on "how tos" or "what does it look like" has blown about babes into various factions.

Mature believers have a singular mind: forget their past religious attainments and pursue Christ. Paul said:

> Yet indeed I also count all things loss for the excellence of the knowledge of Christ Jesus my Lord, for whom I have suffered the loss of all things, and count them as rubbish, that I may gain Christ.
>
> – Phil. 3:8

He continues:

> I press toward the goal for the prize of the upward call of God in Christ
> Jesus. Therefore, let us, as many as are mature, have this mind; and if in
> anything you think otherwise, God will reveal even this to you.
>
> — Phil. 3:14-15

The prize Paul was pursuing is Christ alone. Everything was a loss to him for the excellence of the knowledge of Christ. This is the mind of a mature person. God needs to enlighten everyone who has not yet arrived at such a mindset. Only those with such a focus can have the openness to receive all kinds of believers in the oneness of Christ.

Mature believers are in a place of unity — faith and the knowledge of Christ. In this sphere, they welcome all believers, no matter whether they are babes or mature in Christ, into the unique fellowship of the Spirit. These mature believers have the entire Body of Christ in view.

The seed of faith with the unsearchable riches of the knowledge of the Son of God, embodied in the faith, is the truth in Ephesians 4:15. Instead of using biblical doctrines to blow young believers into one side or the other, mature believers speak the truth in love. Speaking of truth, which is both the faith and the knowledge of the Son of God, will cause the speakers and the listeners to grow up into Christ the Head in all things. As Christians, many topics can and have divided believers. There is a critical need for those who can speak the simplicity of the faith and the riches of the knowledge of the Son of God amid divisive environments. This brings believers into unity and helps them grow into the Head, Christ.

Faith Producing Works

> What [does it] profit, my brethren, if someone says he has faith but does
> not have works? Can faith save him? 15 If a brother or sister is naked and
> destitute of daily food, 16 and one of you says to them, "Depart in peace, be
> warmed and filled," but you do not give them the things which are needed for
> the body, what [does it] profit? 17 Thus also faith by itself, if it does not have
> works, is dead.
>
> — James 2:14-17

James seems to contradict the doctrine of "justification by faith" by saying that faith without works is dead. James's point is that if one possesses true faith, actions will be taken based on such faith. Since the understanding of faith is seeing or substantiating the invisible, a person with faith can move and negotiate around obstacles and arrive at their destination. A person in a pitch-dark environment without a sliver of light would be frozen in a place full of obstructions or holes. He would not be able to accomplish a task like building a house. Similarly, without faith, a person is spiritually blind; faith enables a person to accomplish God's will in the invisible, spiritual realm. If a person says that he has faith yet is immobilized as if in a dark place in fear of tripping and falling, his faith cannot be real; it is dead faith.

James makes a valid point of balance that genuine faith results in works. He uses examples from the Hebrew Scriptures: Abraham and Rahab. Abraham offered up his only son on the altar, believing that God would raise him from the dead (Heb. 11:19). Because of Abraham's faith, he performed this work of sacrificing his only son. Since Rehab believed that God had given the land to Israel, she did the work of hiding the spies (Josh. 2:9). If she did not have faith, she would not have taken the risks to hide the Israelite spies. Due to this work of faith, she and her entire family were saved when Jericho's walls collapsed.

Noah was also a man of faith, and due to his faith, he spent about 120 years building the ark (Heb. 11:7). Abraham and Rahab performed acts of faith for only a short period. Whereas Noah kept his belief that God would judge the world and that his salvation would come through the building of the ark. It was not only his family's salvation, but through the ark he built, a new world was brought forth. God told Noah the following, *"The end of all flesh has come before Me, for the earth is filled with violence through them; and behold, I will destroy them from the earth. Make yourself an ark of gopherwood"* (Gen. 6:13). With such a short word, it sustained Noah for about 120 years to fulfill his task of building the ark.

Unless faith sees the unseen reality, Noah could not have labored for 120 years simply from a memory of what God said. God's speaking would have been a distant memory after 50 years without signs of God's judgment. Certainly, after 100 years without seeing God's judgment, he would have doubted about building the ark since those around him probably mocked him for a century for forecasting rain when it had never happened. By year 100, whatever God said 100 years ago and wasn't fulfilled should have caused him to forget the coming judgment and succumb to the pleasures of the world around him. However, since faith means seeing the hidden reality, it enabled Noah to see eternal things beyond time and space. He saw beyond the eating, drinking, and marrying that were going on in the physical world (Matt. 24:38). By faith, he saw that judgment was coming, even though it was not there for 120 years. Since God spoke of it, it had already happened. His conviction of the unseen judgment strengthened him to relentlessly build the ark, which saved his family of eight and all the creatures into a new world.

What did Noah's ark prefigure? Certainly, it is Jesus Christ. It is in Him that all believers pass through the judgment of God (1 Pet. 3:20-21). Through faith, believers entered Him and in Him there is a new creation where old things have passed away and all things have become new (2 Cor. 5:17). Jesus spoke of salvation in Him: *"For God so loved the world that He gave His only begotten Son, that whoever believes in* [Gk. into] *Him should not perish but have everlasting life."* However, it does not quite fit since Jesus Christ does not need to build from scratch. He is eternal and does not need anyone to create Him. So, what else could Noah's ark prefigure?

The only thing that matches would be the Lord's Democratic Assembly (Ekklesia), His Body. His Body is Christ's increase and expansion, which needs building. Jesus said, "I will build my Ekklesia" (Matt. 16:18). Jesus went to the cross to build His democratic assembly. Jesus did His part by His death and resurrection to build His Body, but He also told Peter to follow Him to build His Ekklesia by picking up his cross. Paul did just that when He said that He suffered the afflictions of Christ for the sake of the Lord's Body, His Ekklesia (Col. 1:24). He suffered and filled up what was lacking in the afflictions of Christ.

In 2 Corinthians 14, building up believers is mentioned twice. Building up the Lord's Ekklesia is mentioned three times. This was in the gathering where each diverse believer contributed to speaking forth the Lord in His democratic assembly. When their speaking unveiled and uplifted Christ, participants in the Ekklesia were comforted and encouraged through prayers, singing, teachings, fellowship, and testimonies. These times of edification of the Lord's Ekklesia require actions from everyone: *"Whenever you come together, each one has a psalm, has a teaching, has a revelation, has a tongue, has an interpretation. Let all things be done for building up"* (1 Cor. 14:26). In the Ekklesia where saints are being built up, there is salvation even for the unbelieving. It says that *"some unbeliever or unlearned person enters, he is convicted by all, he is examined by all; the secrets of his heart become manifest; and so falling on his face, he will worship God, declaring that indeed God is among you"* (1 Cor. 14:24). This is the saving "ark" experience. In this environment, diverse believers are united in their speaking and lifting up of Jesus as Lord — that is the ark built up for salvation.

The Lord Jesus was sent to build up His democratic assembly; therefore, He died and resurrected for this purpose. Now that He has resurrected, ascended, and poured out His Spirit upon His followers, they are to continue building up His Ekklesia until His Body is mature and His Bride is prepared.

> For we are His workmanship, created in Christ Jesus for good works, which God prepared beforehand that we should walk in them.
>
> – Eph. 2:10

Martin Luther once said, "St James' epistle is really an epistle of straw, compared to these others [such as Paul's], for it has nothing of the nature of the Gospel about it."[30] That was a brutal critique. This was due to James's emphasis on work. Luther considered that such a focus takes away justification only through faith alone. Most Bible teachers would quote the Apostle Paul when teaching that salvation is only from faith and not of works. This could be the most popular verse for this support: *"For by grace you have been saved through faith, and that not of yourselves . . . not of works, lest anyone should boast"* (Eph. 2:8-9). Nevertheless, the very next verse, Paul says: *"For we are His workmanship, created in Christ Jesus for good works, which God prepared beforehand that we should walk in them"* (Eph. 2:10). Clearly, God desires and expects those saved by faith to have works; not just do some good works as events or occasional actions, but "to walk in them." These good works become their living and lifestyle.

Most Christians have relegated these "good works" to generally doing anything good for people and society. This would include donating money or efforts to help the poor, build schools and hospitals, visit the sick, preach the gospel, build churches (buildings), and anything else deemed "good." However, in the context of this chapter, Paul speaks of preparing believers for "good works" in specific terms. It is not simply doing anything good. It is to build up the oneness of His Body with once divided enemies into the temple of God!

Some translations use the word "masterpiece" instead of "workmanship" in Ephesians 2:8. God created a work of art; His "masterpiece" is the reason for His salvation. This creation or masterpiece is not referring to the creation of Adam in Genesis 1, but was created in Christ Jesus through His death and resurrection. God's masterpiece is His New Creation. A few verses later, Paul explained what was created: *"Create in Himself one new man from the two, thus making peace"* (Eph. 2:15). This masterpiece is the new man composed of both Jews and Gentiles. Jesus Christ died to break down the wall of hatred between people to unite them into a new man.

In 2 Corinthians 5:17, it says: *"Therefore, if anyone is in Christ, he is a new creation, old things have passed away; behold, all things have become new."* Most believers may apply this verse to their individual experience, that they, individually, are a new creation. This is partially true; however, they are only part of His New Creation — that makes somewhat of a huge difference. The verses before verse 17 continuously speak of "all" as "we're all in this together" (e.g., "if One died for all, then all died" vs. 14). A believer divided from other believers is still holding on to the "old" and cannot truly enjoy the full new creation since this new creation is composed of all of God's people united. That is the reason that immediately the next verse says: *"Now all things are of God, who has*

---

30   https://zondervanacademic.com/blog/martin-luther-james-bible?form=MG0AV3

reconciled us to Himself through Jesus Christ, and has given us the ministry of reconciliation" (2 Cor. 5:18). The new creation needs reconciliation, not only to God, but also to one another. The ministry of reconciliation is necessary to unite believers who are divided.

This is the "good works" God requires that those saved by faith should walk in them. It is not just random good works Christians are to do, but specifically, their lifestyle should be one of working out the peace between God's divided people, which Christ accomplished through the cross. They are called to join the Lord in proclaiming His peace to those still estranged in fellowship with other believers (Eph. 2:17). Christ did His part of crucifixion, resurrection, ascension, and pouring out of the Spirit. Now, it is time for all those saved by faith to do their part; to do the work of peacemaking for the building of the "ark."

Eventually, by the end of Ephesians 2, all of God's people who were previously enemies are together as God's household, family, which is the Lord's democratic assembly (1 Tim. 3:15). They are no longer fighting and divided, but together as God's family joined by Jesus Christ, the Cornerstone. This is God's living temple made up of living stones, the habitation of God (Eph. 2:21-22). The good works include feeding and nourishing believers around them so that they may grow. Only by growth into maturity can God's temple be built.

Now that believers are saved by grace through faith, there is much to do. "Don't be lazy and wait for heaven in the sweet by-and-by." Today, the followers of the Lamb must have a lifestyle of doing good works. They are to join in fellowship with other believers whom they have ignored or counted as enemies. They are to preach the peace of Christ in uniting divided believers based on Christ's accomplished work. They are to nourish and help those in their surroundings to grow into God's temple. This is the work of building the "ark." Through the building of this ark, they will be saved and usher in the new creation in fullness at the second advent of Christ.

Therefore, there is no conflict between Paul and James. Faith is not passive but actively living a life of "good works." When there are eyes of faith, seeing the hidden eternal things behind the physical world, then, like Noah, believers will spend the rest of their time on earth building up the Lord's Ekklesia, the real ark of God. Yes, though justification and salvation are by faith alone, it is not idle or passive. It is not "since I believe, I will wait for heaven one day." This kind of passivity is not faith at all; it is death. True faith will cause believers to do something, and that something is to build up God's eternal purpose, which is His Ekklesia (Democratic Assembly). Yes, it's an "enduring race" but well worth it. The building up of God's temple, the Bride of Christ, and the Spirit's Body is the manifestation of a person's faith for today.

12

CONCLUSION, THE GOLDEN LAMPSTANDS

The summation or conclusion to our study of the mysteries — and comparing and contrasting the New Covenant with the Mosaic Covenant — would be wholly inadequate without an exposition of what can only be termed the "All-Inclusive Lampstand" of Zechariah 4 with the Unveiling of the Son of Man standing amidst the Seven Golden Lampstands of Revelation 1-3.

What is in view in Zechariah 4 is far more that the "glory of the latter house" (Hag. 2:9, or the rebuilding of the Second Temple after the return of Judah to Judea from Babylonian Captivity), but Zechariah's vision prophetically extends to the glory and completion of God's Ekklesia expressed as the "Seven Golden Lampstands" of Revelation 1-3. The two are intrinsically united in revelation, past and future, by the Spirit (Rev. 4:5; Zech. 4:6) regarding God's eternal plan and purpose for the ages. What John saw when he *"was in the Spirit on the Lord's Day"* concerning the seven golden lampstands utterly comports with and amplifies Zechariah's vision of the *Universal Menorah (lampstand)*.

In Revelation 1, the resurrected victorious Jesus (the Son of Man) stands in the midst of the seven golden lampstands. These lampstands are His Ekklesias on earth (Rev. 1:20). It is significant that in the age of Revelation, the Lord's Democratic Assembly is prominently unveiled as the working of the Spirit among united believers shining on earth — just as it was prophetically seen by Zechariah in chapters 4 and 6 wherein *"the counsel of peace shall be between them"* (6:13). In both visions, the centrality of Christ, the Messiah (i.e., the priesthood and kingship in Zechariah 4 and the Son of Man in Revelation 1-3), supplies the surrounding Lampstand(s) with His eternal Spirit (viz., the golden oil shall never cease to emit His eternal flame).

In the previous chapters, the mysteries unveiled in the prophetic writings have much to do with the Lord's Democratic Assembly.

- The great mystery is Christ and His Ekklesia (Eph. 5:32)
- The mystery of Godliness is the House of God, which is the Ekklesia of the living God (1 Tim. 3:15-16)

- The mystery of Christ: the threefold unity between the Jews and the Gentiles in His Ekklesia (Eph. 3:4-6).

Therefore, it is fitting that the Lord's democratic assembly would have prominence alongside Christ as the unique topic in Revelation concerning the present age on earth. Those who miss the significance of the Lord's Ekklesia, which Jesus said He would build in Matthew 16, could readily miss the reward of what is coming in the future. Caring and building His democratic assembly today is the preparation needed and the ushering in of the Kingdom Age — both now and into the future.

The Work of the Spirit is the Two Olive Trees and the Lampstand

> And he said to me, "What do you see?" So, I said, "I am looking, and there [is] a lampstand of solid gold with a bowl on top of it, and on the [stand] seven lamps with seven pipes to the seven lamps. 3 "Two olive trees [are] by it, one at the right of the bowl and the other at its left." 4 So I answered and spoke to the angel who talked with me, saying, "What [are] these, my lord?" . . . 6 So he answered and said to me: "This [is] the word of the LORD to Zerubbabel: 'Not by might nor by power, but by My Spirit,' says the LORD of hosts. 7 'Who [are] you, O great mountain? Before Zerubbabel [you shall become] a plain! And he shall bring forth the capstone with shouts of "Grace, grace to it!" ' " 8 Moreover the word of the LORD came to me, saying: 9 "The hands of Zerubbabel have laid the foundation of this temple; His hands shall also finish [it]. Then you will know that the LORD of hosts has sent Me to you. 10 For who has despised the day of small things? For these seven rejoice to see the plumb line in the hand of Zerubbabel. They are the eyes of the LORD, which scan to and fro throughout the whole earth."
>
> – Zech. 4:2-4, 6-10

What a mysterious sight seen by Zechariah! He saw a golden lampstand (menorah) with 7 lamps and each made up of 7 flames, making 49 points of light, and two olive trees pouring their golden oil directly into the golden bowl in the center.[31]

---

31   Most other versions describe a lampstand with 49 flames as per NLT: "I see a solid gold lampstand with a bowl of oil on top of it. Around the bowl are seven lamps, each having seven spouts with wicks." Think of each lamp has seven flames. 49 (7x7) signifies absolute completion and perfection. It is the cycle of Jubilee, *"And you shall count seven sabbaths of years for yourself, **seven times seven years**; and the time of the seven sabbaths of years shall be to you **forty-nine years**"* (Lev. 25:8).

Zechariah asked, *"What are these?"* referring to both the lampstand and the two olive trees. The answer is *"Not by might nor by power, but by My Spirit."* The obvious interpretation of this "might" and "power" is referring to human might and power. However, we will explore later that this "might" and "power" includes God's supernatural might and power. In any case, Zechariah was seeing and witnessing the Spirit of God in His ultimate work and purpose – supplying the golden oil to enflame the menorah with 49 lamps.[32] The Spirit is operating in both the olive trees and the lampstands, for, as well, consider this verse in Revelation: *"To Him who loved us and washed us from our sins in His own blood, and has made us **kings and priests** to His God and Father"* (Rev. 2:6) – such are the two olive trees of Zechariah 4.

At the time, Zerubbabel, the governor, and Joshua the High Priest were sent by Cyrus the Great, the second King of Persia (2 Chronicles 36:22-23), to go back to Jerusalem to rebuild God's temple. They laid the foundation, but due to significant opposition from the local Samaritans, Persia's withdrawal of support, and the returnees' internal discouragement, they halted the rebuilding (off and on) for a total of 28 years. Therefore, God sent Zechariah to encourage both Zerubbabel and Joshua with this vision so that they could be encouraged and strengthened to continue rebuilding the temple until completion.

The prophet was saying, "Zerubbabel, it is not by power or might that the temple can be rebuilt; it is only by the Spirit of God. All the difficult mountains in your way will come down, and you will have 'plain' sailing to finish this work." Zechariah continued that the "capstone," the last stone to finish the temple, is *"grace, grace to it."* It starts in grace and is finished in grace. The very stone that completes the rebuilding is the Lord Himself, the capstone of grace. The Lord Jesus is the foundation and cornerstone; now He is also the top or capstone (cf. Isa. 28:16, 1 Cor. 3:11, Eph. 2:20, John 1:16). The entire building consists of the Spirit and the Lord together with human cooperation and effort.

Although they were, at the time, rebuilding a physical temple, these striking allusions to Christ show that Zechariah and the other prophets were foreseeing the building of a *spiritual temple in the future*. A temple where Jesus Christ is essentially embedded and integrated into the building. No wonder the glory of the "latter house" would be "greater than the former" (Hag. 2:9: *"'The glory of this latter temple shall be greater than the former,' says the LORD of hosts. 'And in this place I will give peace,' says the*

---

32   It is of keen historical interest that during these 49 years the fourth King of Persia (aka, the "third king" of Daniel 11:2) known as Darius II (aka Artaxerxes the Great – reigning from 521-485 B.C.) was greatly influenced by Queen Esther (his wife) by protecting the Jews throughout the Persian Empire and with little doubt enabled the Jews to complete their Second Temple in Jerusalem in 488 B.C. Yes, the "Year of Jubilee" (short-count) was 49 years, which comports with the 49 conduits streaming from the bowl's golden oil secured from the Two Olive Trees into 49 flames of light—how glorious is this vision!

LORD of hosts."). Since the Second Temple is much inferior to Solomon's Temple, it is "prophetically mandatory" that the Ekklesia (Democratic Assembly) Jesus would build is the "greater temple."

During the period of David and Solomon leading up to the building of the Solomonic (first) Temple, there was significant power and might displayed both by God and man. David, the most powerful King, conquered all His enemies. Solomon mightily kept the peace throughout his reign. God supported them through His prophets with His supernatural might and power in numerous incidents, such as the defeat of Goliath, miraculous escapes from King Saul, winning other battles against all odds, stopping the judgment of a plague, Solomon's supernatural wisdom, and finally, God's glory and power filled the First Temple (2 Chron. 7:1-3). Power and might were visibly displayed during that period.

In contrast, the return from the 70-year Babylonian Captivity was a meager 50,000 people who were, as well, subjects of a foreign king. They were a defeated people, returning to rebuild a temple under the auspices of foreign rulers (Cyrus, Darius, and Artaxerxes). Zerubbabel, the Governor (kingship), and Joshua the High Priest (priesthood) were insignificant officials serving at the pleasure of those who conquered them. The prophets during that period (Ezra, Nehemiah, Haggai, Zechariah, and Malachi) only spoke words and visions of encouragement, but did not perform any supernatural or miraculous feats of support. Neither man nor God displayed any power or might. Yet, the Spirit of God was working hiddenly and providentially to help and finish the rebuilding work.

At the time, it would have been easy to despise *"the day of small things"* because everything about the rebuilding situation was disappointing and discouraging. No wonder they stopped their rebuilding efforts (on and off) for 28 years. Therefore, Zechariah encouraged them not to despise the small things. He was saying, "Don't look for and expect power and might, appreciate the small things." Even just the simplest act of holding a plumb line, which is about the easiest action for construction, the Lord rejoices. His seven eyes (the perfection of completion) are scanning specifically for those building the temple. Ultimately, the Lord's Spirit is only interested in the rebuilding efforts among His people. The vision of this "all-inclusive lampstand" and the olive trees was designed to encourage the building and completion of God's dwelling place.

The Spirit's work, represented by the two olive trees and the seven-fold lampstand, was not of human power and might; nor was it akin to His supernatural power as manifested in His original creation. According to Zechariah 9:11-17, it would be related to the Blood Covenant — harkening to the New Covenant inaugurated by Christ. This is the indwelling Spirit as prophesied in Ezekiel 36:26, *"I will put My Spirit within you."* This is the "drinkable" Spirit as promised by the Lord in John 7:39, *"This He spoke concerning the Spirit, whom those believing into Him would receive; for the Holy Spirit was not yet, because Jesus was not yet glorified."* The indwelling Spirit of God was released at the Lord's glorification through His death and resurrection; thus, the *"blood of your covenant."* This is the indwelling life-giving Spirit released through the Lord's death and resurrection (1 Cor. 15:45).

Juxtaposed with "power and might" is the Spirit, revealing that His primary role is not one of force, but of indwelling to provide light and understanding. As shall be demonstrated, the Spirit required for the present is ultimately the unifying Spirit. Additionally, unity is not primarily accomplished by "power and might," but by love and light supplied by the indwelling Spirit.

In Zechariah's vision, these two olive trees pour their oil through two separate conduits into the bowl, which sits atop a Menorah. It is obvious to interpret these two olive trees as Zerubbabel and Joshua — the "two sons of oil" — anointed figures representing the kingship and the priesthood (Zech. 4:14). That message brought hope to the people rebuilding after exile at the time. However, since this is a prophetic vision, it should also reveal something more about the future.

> Then speak to him, saying, 'Thus says the LORD of hosts, saying: "Behold, the Man whose name [is] the BRANCH! From His place He shall branch out, And He shall build the temple of the LORD; 13 Yes, He shall build the temple of the LORD. He shall bear the glory, and shall sit and rule on His throne; So He shall be a priest on His throne, and the counsel of peace shall be between them both.
>
> – Zech 6:12-13

The Branch is the coming Messiah. The imagery of branching out is likened to Jesus saying, "I am the vine, you are the branches" (John 15:1). The Branch is branching out through all His believers. That is how He will build God's temple. In the Mosaic Covenant, the priesthood and the kingship are separate and distinct offices, such as Zerubbabel and Joshua. However, Jesus Christ is eternally the glorious King and High Priest. He is Melchizedek, King of peace and the Priest of the Most High God (Heb. 7:1).

The obvious reading of "the counsel of peace shall be between them both" is referring to the priesthood and kingship being brought together as one in Christ. However, both offices are appointed by God to work together symbiotically for His purpose and people's well-being. It is abnormal for them to have conflict with each other. Therefore, it seems anti-climactic and raises questions as to why a counsel of peace — typically reserved for deep-rooted and enduring conflicts — would be necessary for the Messiah to reconcile the priesthood and the kingship. A second layer of interpretation beyond the obvious text must be considered.

Continuing to Zechariah 9, the Messiah came to solve a centuries-long and deep, insoluble conflict between Judah and Ephraim (who had been estranged at the "Breach of Jeroboam" after King Solomon's reign). Through the work of His blood covenant (by death and resurrection), Jesus Christ brought together two divided, warring people. Instead of fighting each other, God uses Judah as a bow and Ephraim as an arrow, working through both as one to defeat His enemies (Zech. 9:13). Again, supporting that unity is not uniformity, but each with distinctive roles working together to defeat God's enemies. The work of the "counsel of peace" brings Judah and Ephraim together, resulting in the proclamation of peace to all nations. Fascinating that although Ephraim, who was "swallowed up of the nations/Gentiles" (Hos. 8:8), reappears via the "blood of the covenant" (Zech. 9:11) to be the "arrow" in the bow of Judah!

Because the Spirit in Zechariah 4 is closely tied to the "blood of your covenant," prophetically, the two olive trees, upon further revelation found in Zechariah, can readily represent Judah and Ephraim — two parts of God's people, joined together, displaying the work of His Spirit. These former enemies united around a shared purpose, working together to supply oil to the bowl through 49 conduits, sustaining 49 flames atop a lampstand with sevenfold lamps. What a powerful image of the Messiah's "counsel of peace," magnifying the work of the Spirit in uniting distinct peoples and becoming a light to the world.

This vision further supports this: while Zerubbabel belonged to the tribe of Judah and Joshua the High Priest to the tribe of Levi, the first person named Joshua — son of Nun — was from the tribe of Ephraim and led Israel into the Promised Land. The Tabernacle at Shiloh was located in Ephraim's territory, where Joshua's inheritance was located — that is where the Ark of the Covenant was initially housed for some 396 years before its capture by the Philistines. The glory, or Ark of the Covenant, was retaken by King David and housed in the Tabernacle of David for some 32 years before it was relocated to Solomon's Temple for an additional 396 years.[33]

---

33   These calculations/chronologies cover a period 396+27+396 years or some 792 years + 27 years = 819 years or from 1405 B.C. (the crossing of the Jordan River by the Israelites) until 586 B.C. (1405 B.C. less 819 years = 586 B.C.). These calculations can be found in *Signs in the Heavens and on the Earth, Man's Days are Numbered and he is Measured*, by Douglas W. Krieger, 2024, Tribnet Publications, Sacramento, CA. The interim 27 years signify the 27 books of the New Testament (the full revelation of Jesus Christ) and the 792 years, evenly split between Ephraim and Judah, are a resemblance/fractal of the edge of the New Jerusalem or 12,000 furlongs * 660 ft. = 7,920,000 liner feet or "792" ~ "792" (Rev. 21:16; and one furlong is 660 linear feet. – Wikipedia @ https://en.wikipedia.org/wiki/Furlong)

Therefore, although Joshua (the priesthood) in the book of Zechariah was from the tribe of Levi, he could readily be seen as one representing Ephraim, the 10 Northern Tribes. Then Zerubbabel (the kingship) is representative of the tribe of Judah (the 2 Southern Tribes). Zerubbabel and the name Joshua predict the working together of Judah and Ephraim for God's testimony, through the "blood of the covenant," brought together in peace or in full reconciliation — this is the work of the Spirit, not by "power or might" could this happen.

Originally, God saw both Judah and Ephraim-Israel as one olive tree (Jer. 11:16). Together, they were His anointed ones (Ps. 105:15). But by the time of Zechariah's prophecies, that unified tree had split into two branches: Judah and Ephraim were long divided, and Ephraim was scattered among the nations, absorbed into their midst. At that point, Ephraim-Israel essentially became part of the nations (the Gentiles) — the so-called "10 lost tribes," while Judah — along with Benjamin and the Levites — came to represent the remainder of Israel or Judah.[34] It is noteworthy that Joseph's son, Ephraim, was one-half Hebrew-Israelite and one-half Egyptian.

This breach became the very way God began fulfilling His original twofold covenant with Abraham: *"I will make you into a great nation" (Judah-Israel), and "in you all the families of the earth shall be blessed* (the nations)" (Gen. 12:2-3). Through this unfolding, the one olive tree can be seen as having become two — Judah and Ephraim among the nations — yet both remained under the covering of God's covenant with Abraham.

In Zechariah's vision, two olive trees poured their oil into a single lampstand — an image of the Spirit. This symbolizes that both the Jewish people (Judah/Zerubbabel) and those called out from the nations (Gentiles/Joshua/Ephraim) are essential in supplying oil into God's unique and universal lampstand. Together, they are called to be the light of the world. This unity is echoed in the New Covenant given to both houses of Israel (Jer. 31:31), and in the prophetic joining together of the "two sticks" found in Ezekiel 37:15-28. The Spirit's light shines into a darkened world through the reconciliation of former enemies — both bearing God's covenant and anointed by faith — now united to bear one testimony. The lampstand does not manifest might or power (whether human or divine), but reveals the Spirit of God working through the restored unity of His once-divided and resurrected people (Ezekiel 37:1-14 — the Valley of Dry Bones, which have been resurrected to be His Mighty Army).

---

34   With the Northern Kingdom dissolved (722 B.C.) and Judah later exiled (586 B.C.), יְהוּדִי [Yehudi] became the prevailing self-designation in Babylon. Jeremiah speaks of "the Jews who live in the land of Egypt" (Jeremiah 44:1), showing its early expansion beyond strict territorial borders. (Source: https://biblehub.com/hebrew/3064.htm)

The Lampstands are the Seven Ekklesias ("Churches")

> Then I turned to see the voice that spoke with me. And having turned I saw seven golden lampstands, 13 and in the midst of the seven lampstands [One] like the Son of Man, clothed with a garment down to the feet and girded about the chest with a golden band. . . . 17 And when I saw Him, I fell at His feet as dead. But He laid His right hand on me, saying to me, "Do not be afraid; I am the First and the Last. 18 "I [am] He who lives, and was dead, and behold, I am alive forevermore. Amen. And I have the keys of Hades and of Death. . . . 20 "The mystery of the seven stars which you saw in My right hand, and the seven golden lampstands: The seven stars are the angels of the seven churches [ekklesia], and the seven lampstands which you saw are the seven churches [ekklesia].
>
> – Rev. 1:12-13, 17-18, 20

Zechariah saw the image of this all-inclusive lampstand as the work of the Spirit, and John saw the same in Revelation. However, the vision seen by John has evolved to express the ultimate plan and purpose of the ages, the Lord's Ekklesia (Democratic Assembly). She is the Bride of Christ in the great mystery (Eph. 5:32), God's Household in the mystery of godliness (1 Tim. 3:15-16), and the joining together between Jews and Gentiles in the mystery of Christ (Eph. 3:4). The one lampstand likened to the Spirit is now manifested as seven practical Ekklesias in seven cities. They are not in heaven but on earth in this darkened world. These Ekklesias were constituted of diverse people shining out the very Spirit of God.

Just as the Messiah in Zechariah 6 brought together in Himself both the Priesthood and Kingship, the Son of Man is both priest and King, standing amidst the seven golden lampstands. He wore a long priestly robe and the golden band or sash of a king across His chest. He is also the Shepherd with the staffs of grace and union caring for His one flock in His Ekklesias (Zech. 11:7). Being the Priest, He restored and maintained grace between God and man. As the King, He rules with peace in the hearts of believers to preserve unity among diverse believers in the Ekklesias (Col. 3:15). Grace and peace are interconnected; God's people cannot have one without the other. No wonder that "Grace to you and peace" is the common salutation used by the apostles in every epistle.

The lampstands are the seven Ekklesias, and the seven lamps of the lampstand are the seven Spirits of God (Rev. 4:5), which are also the eyes of the Lamb (Rev. 5:6). What a sight! Since the imagery of the lampstand in Zechariah represents the Spirit, it is reasonable that the seven lamps are the seven Spirits of God. Since the Lamb (Jesus) and the Sprit are one, by extension, it is not surprising that the eyes of the Lamb are the seven Spirits of God (Rev. 5:6). Just like in Zechariah 4, the Lamb with His eyes which are the seven Spirits are searching, enlightening, and strengthening believers for the building up of His dwelling place, temple.

It would have made more sense to say the seven golden lampstands represent God's Holy Temple, Christ's victorious Body, or His perfect Bride. Instead, the golden lampstands are Ekklesias! Surprise, ekklesia is appropriated from the idol-worshipping Greek polity's chaotic democratic forums. The imagery of the golden lampstand (Grk. *luchnia*) being the Lord's Ekklesias is astonishing, since His democratic assembly consists of people on the earth that are of the flesh in various conditions, from those defeated, immature, and sinful to those victoriously overcoming whatever degradation. These are the constituents of the Lord's Ekklesia; they are members of His Body. They became members solely through faith in Jesus Christ, by which they were regenerated – born anew – and transferred into God's Kingdom, His Democratic Assembly. Since faith is the sole qualifier, the "ekklesiastical" community reflects a striking diversity – across race, gender, age, politics, ethnicity, socio-economic status, religious background, and more. Additionally, many are still struggling with the things of this sinful flesh. Their actions would not be considered righteous or holy. Yet, amazingly, in God's eyes, they make up His golden, shining lampstands – His Spirit on earth. Yes, the Spirit commends and rebukes these seven in Revelation 2-3 – notwithstanding, all seven are GOLDEN LAMPSTANDS. They express God's perfect divine nature.

No matter their condition, the Lord is amidst His Ekklesias on earth, caring for each one, and esteeming them highly as golden lampstands representing the Spirit of God shining on the earth. In Revelation 1-3, John was instructed to write to each of the seven Ekklesias, sending a letter to every city where believers were located: Ephesus, Smyrna, Pergamos, Thyatira, Sardis, Philadelphia, and Laodicea. Seven Ekklesias in seven cities; one Ekklesia according to a city. In God's eyes, all His people within the jurisdiction of a city are one Ekklesia. There is only one per city! This exactly matches the original Greek practice of their democratic legislative assembly (ekklesia): Only one democratic decision-making body in each city-state, representing the entire community or city.

The nature and definition of the Greek ekklesia require the inclusion of all its diverse citizens with equal rights to speak forth. A quorum of representatives from the various factions of society was needed to legislate. Likewise, 1 Corinthians 11:19 states that when the Lord's Ekklesia assembles, there must be (of necessity) factions (diversity). Believers with preferences for Paul, Peter, and Apollos must be represented; even those "of Christ." In addition to these four factions, Jews and Greeks, rich and poor, must be included to remember the Lord (the Lord's Supper) as one Ekklesia. It is natural for the Pauline "tribe" and the Petrine "tribe," the Jewish and Gentile "tribes," as well as the rich and the poor "tribes," to gather normally in their distinctively divided groups. Now, they are being called out of the comfort of their factions to the Lord's Ekklesia (Democratic Assembly), where all the "tribes" are to gather to feast and worship. This is the New Jerusalem on earth in each city, where all of God's people, representing the various factions, come together in unity to share Christ. Yes, there must be such factions that assemble; however, none should be "factious," to cause divisions in the assembly (like Corinth).

Due to mistranslating the word *"ekklesia"* to *"church,"* much confusion among believers and unbelievers has been created. The meaning of the word *"church"* refers to the physical building used for worship.[35] Therefore, churches are the physical buildings where various ministries do their work. Since there are differing ministries, gifts, and activities given by the Trinity (1 Cor. 12:4-6), there are many churches where people can go to receive services. The different churches have distinctive focuses depending on the leadership of the ministry that owns the church building. These are the specialties in addition to the faith in Christ that they espouse. For example, the Catholic church may focus on historical orthodoxy, the Baptist churches may emphasize baptism by immersion and biblical knowledge, and the Pentecostal churches may attend to helping believers experience the gifts of the Spirit. Therefore, "churches" housing ministries can be many, but the Lord's Ekklesia consists of all His followers — they are one.

Believers of various stripes go to different churches. They may become siloed in these churches without fellowshipping with those attending other churches. These silos are artificial barriers separating God's people. God not only sees all His people as one Ekklesia, a golden lampstand, in a city, but it is manifested when believers from various factions assemble to celebrate the work and victory of His Son, Jesus Christ. This is the display of unity in diversity that causes the world to believe in Jesus Christ (John 17:21, 1 Cor. 14:25). This is the pattern of diversity in unity shown in 1 Corinthians 11:17 through chapter 14, where each distinct believer can come with something to contribute and prophesy or speak forth the riches of Christ (1 Cor. 14:26). It was a democratic assembly where no one dominated, and everyone discerned to receive that which is profitable (1 Cor. 14:30-31).[36]

What Made the Ekklesias Golden Lampstands

Among the seven Ekklesias, the collective of all believers scattered in the seven different cities, only one was praised as positive (Philadelphia), another one was satisfactory (Smyrna), but the remaining five were negatively chastised. The degraded

---

35   Etymonline.com

36   The book *One Ekklesia* by Henry Hon is an in-depth study of God's Ekklesia

ones included those who left loving the Lord and His people first (Ephesus), those who were "worldly" and compromised (Pergamos), ones who were corrupted by Satan (Thyatira), those who were spiritually dead (Sardis), and lukewarm ones, thinking they were rich, but poor and blind (Laodicea). In such awful conditions, the Lord was still in their midst, and they were maintained as golden and shining.

What was the condition that made them shine as golden lampstands expressing the Spirit on earth? It could not be their righteous deeds, their holiness, their purity, or their fervency. The only item left that would cause God to consider them as shining lampstands is their unity; they continued their love and care for one another, no matter the condition of the individuals. The believers in these cities functioned as one Body, even though among these cities, many were in degraded conditions; those who overcame would have reasons to divide from those in degradation. It would be natural for the "overcomers" to form their own group and separate and depart from those criticized by the Lord. They could even say to believers, "Come out from among these weak and corrupted churches." No, they remained in fellowship and cared for those around them. This diversity in unity is the very definition of the Lord's Ekklesia. The stronger "overcoming" believers were exemplary when compared with those in Corinth who considered themselves more spiritual and divided themselves from others as the "of Christ" group.

There was only one Ekklesia out of seven in danger of having its lampstand taken away by the Lord. It was Ephesus. What was their condition that would cause them to lose the testimony that the Spirit was working among them? Revelation 2:2-3 showed that the saints in Ephesus labored for the Lord, endured sufferings, could not bear evil men, and were knowledgeable with discernment to try apostles and found them to be false. That means they were fervent and holy people with correct doctrinal knowledge and discernment. Most would consider them mature and a model "church." However, the Lord said He is/was about to take away their lampstand. They would no longer shine with the Spirit as God's testimony on earth. What was the reason? The Lord had only one thing against them: They left their first (or "best") love.

Most Bible teachers interpret this to mean that they stopped loving God first. Therefore, "repent and love the Lord as the priority above all else, return to the first and fresh love for Jesus." They may even say: "God does not care for your works; He wants you to love Him first." This sounds correct. Who can argue against loving God first? However, the repentance is to "do the first work" (Rev. 2:5). Normally, love is not equated to work, but here, first love depends on first work. It is not loving the Lord with words, but with deeds, with works. There must be evidence of love, but they were working! It was because they loved God that they were laboring and enduring. They hated evil and exposed the false because they love the Lord.

What is the *"first work"* for them to return to? According to Jesus, the evidence of loving Him is feeding and caring for His people. He asked Peter three times: Do you love Me? If you do, feed and shepherd My sheep (John 21:15-17). The *"first work"* is caring and nourishing God's people. He desires this unique evidence and result of loving the Lord. There are many works Christians can do in service to God, but they could miss the "first work." Loving the Lord, without knowing His heart and requirements, could lead to a condition similar to the saints in Ephesus. Therefore, *"repent and do the first works."*

The believers in Ephesus could not bear evil men. They were able to test apostles and expose the false. They were very strict and severe with anyone evil or false among them. If they put apostles on trial, they could just as well put one another "on trial" — critiquing whether someone had labored sufficiently, measuring endurance, probing doctrinal correctness, and judging who may be "evil" or fallen short. Since that is the case, the atmosphere would not be conducive to feeding and loving one another. It would be one of fear, suspicion, and separation among the saints.

Among most Christians today, the typical experience is that those belonging to one church are either judging or being judged by those in another church. Their suspicion of one another is motivated by measuring holiness, rejecting evil, and exposing false teachings. Each could declare that such works are because they love the Lord. While they are doing these works, their lampstand might have already been taken away. No wonder the light in the world is dim since the testimony is gone.

The greatest commandment in the Mosaic law is *"you shall love the Lord your God with all your heart"* (Matt. 22:37). However, Jesus' new commandment did not include such a requirement; rather, it is, *"love one another as I have loved you"* (John 13:34). John continued, *"for he who does not love his brother whom he has seen, how can he love God whom he has not seen"* (1 John 4:20). Therefore, having left their "first love" means that they were judging and dividing from one another rather than loving and caring for one another. *"Repent and do the first works."*

The love for one another is taught regularly within all churches. However, loving one another within the same church or community is akin to what Jesus said: *"If you love those who love you, what reward will you get?"* Rather, *"love your enemies"* (Matt. 5:44). In God's view, He does not see His people siloed in various churches, but they are all one Ekklesia. Their love and care for one another must cross all doctrinal or denominational boundaries.

In contrast to the saints in Ephesus, only one Ekklesia received the Lord's praise — Philadelphia, whose name means *brotherly love*. As discussed previously, they were not strong or great (no power or might), but with "little strength." Nevertheless, being kept in the Lord's word and name was enough to fulfill the commandment to love one another. While Ephesus was about to lose its shining lampstand due to having left their "first love" — love for one another — Philadelphia was praised for brotherly love.

In any city with believers, there are bound to be many who are spiritually weak, those struggling with holiness, and having contention with one another. Among such diversity, the uniqueness of these lampstands is the expression of the Spirit's work of unity among assorted believers, from the weak to the strong. Therefore, Ephesians 4:3 says, *"keep the unity of the Spirit in the bond of peace."* The Spirit's work is uniting diverse and even contrary believers, no matter their condition. Therefore, His lampstands must have such a testimony that those who normally do not associate with each other due to differences are now loving and caring for one another. To be in unity, at least some of these believers are those *"with all lowliness and gentleness, with longsuffering, bearing with one another in love"* (Eph. 4:2). These are overcomers uniting believers. This is the expression of the power of the Spirit working among conflicting believers.

Again, all of the above corresponds with the vision in Zechariah 4, where Judah and Ephraim are the olive trees supplying oil to the lampstand. Here in Revelation's vision of Zechariah's all-inclusive, sevenfold lampstand, diversity has multiplied — drawing together former enemies, now united by the Spirit of God into one radiant witness.

Calling for Individuals to Overcome

Since the Lord's Ekklesia is constituted with individual believers, the believers' spiritual condition in a particular city is the condition of that Ekklesia. As mentioned, five of these cities had believers in awful conditions: having left their first love, worldly and compromised, corrupted with idolatry and the depths of Satan, spiritually dead, and lukewarm and self-deceived. Only one was praised by the Lord, and the other (Smyrna) was satisfactory. In any case, to all seven Ekklesias, all the believers in each city, no matter their condition (good or bad), the Spirit of God was speaking to all who had an ear to hear. Each believer could respond and overcome.

It is crucial to acknowledge that the Spirit was not speaking specifically to any leaders or a mediatory class, but to every individual. The only qualification to hear the speaking Spirit is having an ear. These Ekklesias in Revelation showcase the various conditions of God's people on earth today; most are spiritually frail and sick. Unlike the period of Acts and the epistles, it is striking that at the later stage of His democratic assembly, there was no mention of any of the five-fold ministers (apostles, prophets, evangelists, pastors, and teachers), and no mention of elders or deacons. The Spirit bypassed them and spoke directly to all individual believers, treating everyone the same, no matter their spiritual situation.

This is contrary to the importance of the leadership role of the clergy class (including "elders" and "disciplers"), which plays out among common believers today. Most believers hear and obey their leaders in their Christian journey as expected. Sadly, far too many would rather trust their leaders than the speaking of the Spirit. Nevertheless, if the leaders are doing their job per God's purpose, then why are most of these Ekklesias in such horrible spiritual conditions? Something is wrong. This is not intended as a critique or condemnation of all leaders, but rather a reminder that true spiritual leadership is marked by equipping the saints — empowering them to hear the Spirit directly and independently, so that each member may function fully within the one Body of Christ. Believers must recognize Paul's warning that even among the "elders" he appointed, there were wolves drawing people to themselves (Eph. 20:30). People, even Christians, can change; Not only some of these elders changed, but even some that were numbered among the apostles became antichrists to isolate believers from their anointing (1 John 2:18-20).

The call went out to every believer, without exception, directly from the Spirit: "overcome." Don't place blame on the leaders; that is not an excuse because the Spirit is speaking directly to each believer. Saying, "It is my elders' fault" or "I just followed my pastor" will not alleviate serious judgments upon believers of sickness, tribulation, death, shame, and the Lord's absence as outlined in these seven letters. Whatever negative environment there is, overcome it. And if it is positive, like Philadelphia, the call is to hold fast, since the natural inclination is toward spiritual entropy or decay. It takes strengthening — just a little strength to overcome passivity and stagnation.

In Revelation 2, Jesus said twice to two different Ekklesias that He hated the deeds and teaching of the Nicolaitans. This is a critical matter worthy of consideration. Other than these two mentions in Revelation, there are no other records of Nicolaitans in the entire Bible. So, who are they? The only understanding available is based on this word "Nicolaitans." The word itself means "to conquer the people."[37] It is a compound Greek word from *nikan*, which meant "to conquer," and *laos*, which meant "people." *Laos* is where the word "laity" or "common people" comes from. The Lord hated the deed and doctrine of having any sort of conquering of His people. This is a direct challenge to the detriment of ekklesia, which is democracy, rule by the people.

The Lord elevating "ekklesia" (democratic assembly) to such a height as His Spirit on earth is strategic but also counterintuitive. Here are some of the arguments against ekklesia. Isn't God the one ruling? How can His purpose be built around "people rule?" Without leaders, it would be chaotic and confusing. People will just run wild if no one

---

37   The Nicolaitans in Revelation: Bible Story and Meaning | Christianity.com, Nicolaitans - Encyclopedia of The Bible - Bible Gateway

is in charge. Consider how today's democracies have amplified divisions, hatred, and corruption in society. God's Kingdom can never be democratic.

However, one essential matter is missed in this conjecture: the life of Christ or the indwelling Spirit within each believer. His Ekklesia is His organic Body with His nature. The problem with secular democracy is not that people have the freedom to be who they are and pursue happiness. It is the fallen nature of sin. Due to man's sinful nature, there is an innate tendency toward disorder. Therefore, external forces and rules are necessary for order in society. Whereas God's Ekklesia (democracy) is a new creation constituted with people born anew with the life of God, and their old sinful man is crucified. What is needed in this new creation is for each individual to be nourished and given the liberty to grow and live according to the life-gifting (Christ's DNA) received in their unique environment.

According to Paul, the Lord's Ekklesia is the Body of Christ, with each member having different gifts (Eph. 1:22). Since there is a fear of chaos in the Lord's democratic assembly if every believer is liberated to speak and serve without control, the "chaos theory" would be fittingly explored and applied. It is a mathematical theory derived from the scientific study of natural phenomena, including the formation and development of physical bodies. Scientists have used this theory to understand and model various systems that are governed by deterministic rules in components (cells) that work and behave independently and unpredictably based on their unique environment and connections with surrounding components. Let's assume that every believer is a cell in the Body of Christ, and the deterministic rules are the law of the Spirit of life (spiritual DNA). Though each cell has the same DNA, depending on its placement and connections with other cells, they will develop differently with distinct functions (eyes, heart, brain, muscles, etc.).

Each believer carries the **life of Christ** within them — like spiritual DNA. That inner pattern guides how they grow, serve, and relate to others. But the way that pattern unfolds will look different for each person. The Spirit works through their unique stories, cultures, and relationships. When they are free to respond to that inner guidance, the result is a diverse, vibrant community — full of grace, peace, creativity, and beauty.

According to Chaos Theory, when outside forces try to control or standardize that process through strict rules, rigid programs, or institutional pressure, the life begins to break down. It's like forcing every cell to behave the same way: the body loses its ability to adapt, and things start to fall apart. What was once alive and dynamic becomes rigid and fragile. This is why the Lord hates those "Nicolaitans" who exert control and rule over believers. The Lord's Ekklesia is the environment for all His members (cells) to grow and develop organically in the freedom of the Spirit and form His one Body.

True spiritual growth and building come from trusting the inner rule — the Christ-pattern — and creating space for people to respond freely. Instead of managing people, nurturing environments where life can flourish is what is needed. Chaos isn't something to fear — it's the signature of a living, Spirit-led Democratic Assembly.

In Chaos Theory, there are several other critical concepts: the Butterfly Effect and Fractals. The Butterfly Effect says that one small change can radically affect the entire system. It came from this metaphor: "A butterfly flapping its wings in Brazil might set off a tornado in Texas." Tiny changes can lead to massive, unpredictable consequences. Remember what the Lord said to Zechariah: *"Who has despised the day of small things"* (Zech. 4:10). How encouraging, even if one believer does just a little gyration, they can have an astounding impact. Whatever little bit of peace-building and breaking down walls for fellowship among siloed believers could have a global impact.

Fractal means its structure or characteristics repeat themselves in different scales — whether large or small, zoom in or out, the same pattern resembles the whole. This means that the local Ekklesias, as described in Revelation 2 and 3, have the same fractal as the universal Ekklesia that the Lord Jesus said He would build in Matthew 16:18. Moreover, it is the same for Ekklesias with a limited number of people assembled in various homes, whether in Asia, Africa, Europe, or the Americas. In other words, what is in view in any given local Ekklesia is, in point of biblical fact, a picture of its entirety; that is, you're viewing the universal Ekklesia Jesus said He would build. This fractal would contain the following pattern:

1. Expression of the fruit of the Spirit is love, joy, peace, longsuffering, kindness, goodness, faithfulness, gentleness, self-control (Gal. 5:22)
2. Diversity of believers (the more the better) from differing factions can immediately fit in
3. Equal rights and freedom for each believer to speak and fellowship
4. No one person or subset of people dominating (this would define a cancer in the body)

Since it is the same fractal, any believer is immediately welcomed without any other agreements other than the person and work of Jesus Christ (the common faith). From first-time participants to those hosting Ekklesia in their homes, all share the same care for one another. Indeed, those whom the majority may consider less desirable would be given more honor (1 Cor. 12:23).

In such a democratic environment, the Chaos Theory is in effect. Juxtapose the Lord's Ekklesia with churches where ministries operate, and there are stark differences. Positively, ministries have their distinct messages, demographic targets, and methods for achieving their goals. Therefore, rightly so, leadership is indispensable. Without firm leadership, there would be confusion, and the ministry (church) would cease to exist. When there is disagreement that cannot be resolved with leadership, there will be two ministries (example: Paul and Barnabas). Therefore, leadership in a church (i.e., ministry) cannot allow people to voice their divergent opinions in its ministry since it would create confusion. This is not to disparage churches (ministries). This is the nature of ministries, and when there is a multiplication of ministers, an explosion of churches follows.

Due to the lack of focus and understanding concerning the Lord's Democratic Assembly (Ekklesia) since the dominance of the Roman Church from around the 4th century until today, gifted ministers since the Reformation have primarily focused on building their own ministries or churches (e.g., denominations). Since then, men and women of God have reacted to the degraded states of believers by introducing helpful teachings and practices. However, in doing so, they have also raised up churches to spread their ministries. For example, to help believers that justification is by faith alone and not due to indulgences, Martin Luther started the Lutheran Church. John Calvin taught his brand of Reformed theology, and many churches were built to spread his doctrines.

Over the centuries, even till now, successive men and women of God, having a heart to help God's people to improve their spirituality, have started more and more churches. Ministers recognizing the spiritually weak and deadened situation of God's people have started more ministries to teach people how to fast and pray, receive spiritual power and gifts, live a holy life, etc. While this is commendable, the mistake of these ministers is to create a group or a church of "overcomers" and separate from their "weaker and degraded" brethren. The desire to start a better, stronger, holier, more spiritual, or overcoming "church," by dividing from those that are less so, has obscured God's lampstand. God's lampstand requires love and unity among believers of all kinds.

Though motivated by sincere convictions, some believers — perceiving "compromise" among those they deem less committed — opt to "come out from among them and be separate," aspiring toward a more purified ecclesial expression. However, such separatist impulses, however well-intentioned, are not reflective of the inclusive and participatory nature of the ekklesia as envisioned in the New Testament.

This does not suggest that in Chaos Theory pandemonium persists when the Ekklesia assembles. No, *"For God is not the author of confusion* ["disorder"], *but of peace, as in all the Ekklesias of the saints"* (1 Cor. 14:33). Even by observing nature and the physical body, it is a beautiful mosaic of God's work. Therefore, the Lord's Ekklesia, though seemingly chaotic, expresses the functioning of a unified Body for God's glory.

Nor is this a suggestion that there should not be an increase in the number of ministries and churches (buildings) where people can go for help and services. That by itself should not cause divisions if all believers fellowship with each other regardless of what church they may or may not attend. God's Ekklesia, the lampstand, is one, regardless of the number of believers or churches in a city. Consider the democratic assembly in Corinth, where some were divided due to their preferences for Paul, Cephas, or Apollos. Some believers, considering themselves more spiritual, aligned themselves with the designation "of Christ" (1 Cor. 1:12), thereby distinguishing themselves from others. While all believers are indeed "of Christ," this group was regarded as divisive — not for affirming Christ, but for separating themselves as a spiritually superior faction, implying greater accuracy or purity than the rest. There is nothing wrong with desiring and seeking to "overcome," obeying the Spirit's calls. However, an "overcomers" group or church, even if they did overcome the degradation spoken of by the Lord, is no longer representative of the Lord's lampstand. They have separated themselves from the other members of the Body who are less spiritual and have not yet "overcome."

Other men of God have also trumpeted the need for unity and proposed "the ground of oneness" where all Christians should meet. However, to meet on this ground, they need to come out of all other churches or denominations. Additionally, this "ground of unity" is typically dominated by a ministry; therefore, conformity to this ministry is necessary to be accepted into this unity. This method of "unity" has caused division among believers and does not reflect the vision and practice of the Lord's Ekklesia.

Over the centuries, men and women of God have desired to build a better "church". This has spawned competition among ministers, each claiming to be more holy, spiritual, victorious, and doctrinally more accurate than others. The promotion of their "overcoming" is to draw more men to themselves. Even if successful, and they develop a group of "overcomers," inadvertently, they will inevitably become another division or sect opposing the Spirit's work in the building of His lampstand, Ekklesia.

Who Are the Overcomers

The Lord did not request those who overcome to separate themselves from those who are defeated or degraded. They live their overcoming lives amid those whom the Lord is chastising. They are still in fellowship, loving, and caring for those who need strengthening to repent. Regardless of which church or group a believer attends, each must hear the Spirit's call to overcome — even those in Philadelphia were called to overcome by the Spirit (Rev. 3:12). Those who overcome will break free from any limitations to fellowship with believers in other churches or those disenfranchised from churches. They will seek to be in unity with other believers simply because they are in the one Body of Christ. Additionally, they will influence others who may be siloed to do the same: break out and fellowship with diverse believers in the Lord's Ekklesia.

How blessed are those ministries or churches with gifted leaders who have seen and practiced the unity found in His Ekklesia in their community. They have discovered by the Spirit's prompting that their ministries commend themselves to the building up of saints who, in turn, commit themselves to the building up of His entire Body.

There are rewards to those who overcome, as described in Revelation 2 and 3. Many of these are rewarded in the coming Messianic Kingdom — Millennial Kingdom. However, believers today have received the Spirit as a guarantee, a pledge, or a foretaste of the coming full-taste (2 Cor. 1:22). In other words, whatever is in the future is already here for believers to enjoy and experience. The guarantee that you will have the reward in the future is to have them as a foretaste today. Therefore, those who overcome and anticipate a future reward must be those already participating in its foretaste today. If one is not enjoying these rewards today, there is no guarantee they will have them in the future.

Let's consider the overcoming in Ephesus. Here, to repent and return to their first love and begin again to feed and care for other believers. The reward is: *"I will give to eat from the tree of life, which is in the midst of the Paradise of God"* (Rev. 2:7). As they overcome to feed others, they are being fed themselves. They are not waiting to go to paradise one day, but are enjoying peace and rest in God's presence today. This is a peace shared among and between brethren — a true foretaste of His Covenant of Peace.

To those overcoming in Smyrna, although they are suffering persecution, tribulation, which could readily lead to their physical ("first") death, they have no fear. They are experiencing Christ in resurrection since He has already triumphed over the second death, which is the eternal death (Rev. 2:11). This was the Apostle Paul's experience amid his tribulations and sufferings in 2 Corinthians 4; he was living in resurrection and giving life to those around him. He could not be "hurt by the second death." Those receiving life from him can witness him wearing "the crown of life" (Rev. 2:10).

To those overcoming the doctrine of Balaam and Nicolaitans in Pergamos, they are to eat of the hidden manna and receive a white stone (Rev. 2:17). Balaam was the prophet who prophesied for profit and eventually caused Israel to compromise by committing fornication with women outside God's Covenant, which led to idolatry. When Christians are in a weakened condition, it is easy to hire and pay someone to speak on their behalf for God (Balaam) and simultaneously allow a stronger person to dominate and control them (Nicolaitans). Individual believers are called to overcome; their reward is to partake of the hidden manna and be shaped into a living stone for God's Ekklesia — echoing the transformation of Peter, whose name means "stone" (Matthew 16:18).

To those overcoming the doctrine of Satan, which is idolatry in Thyatira, they will rule over the nations and have the Morning Star (Rev. 2:28). Ruling over nations should be in the future, but having the Morning Star should be experienced today.

Jesus is the Bright and Morning Star bringing a new day, a new beginning (Rev. 22:16). To those who overcome, they do not just hope for a future new day, but He arises in their hearts bringing newness and freshness now, every day (2 Pet. 1:19).

Most of the saints in Sardis have a name that they are spiritually living, but they are actually dead. The reward for overcoming deadness is to have their names remain in the Book of Life (Rev. 3:5). They may participate in activities and live a "holy" life, giving the appearance that they are alive. However, they can be spiritually dead with no expression of the fruit of the Spirit and no genuine works like feeding and caring for others' salvation or growth. If they are to remain in the Book of Life in the coming kingdom, they need to live the life of Christ today.

The Lord praised the believers in Philadelphia. Nevertheless, they still needed to overcome by holding fast to loving one another and not growing weary. The reward is that they would become a pillar in God's temple — His Ekklesia — transformed into the image of Christ as an eternal foundation of peace, bearing the name New Jerusalem (Rev. 3:12). Such an overcomer carries a presence that immediately impacts those around them, even now.

Finally, the believers in Laodicea are called to overcome their passivity and pride, thinking that they are rich, but actually miserable, poor, blind, and naked (Rev. 3:17). Those who, in their own minds, consider themselves superior to others are proud and judgmental. Such believers are often the source of division in the Body. The Lord is outside, knocking on the door of their hearts for them to repent and open to Him. He will come in and dine with all those who will respond. This can refer to the Lord's supper. In 1 Corinthians 11, the Ekklesia assembled to partake of the Lord's Supper; however, their divisions nullified the intended blessing and resulted instead in judgment. They missed dining with the Lord. Overcomers ("approved") are those who usher in the blessing of dining with the Lord at His supper by making peace between diverse believers gathered as His Democratic Assembly.

The Manifestation of the Lord's Democratic Assembly (Ekklesia) Today

The Lord's Ekklesia has its beginning on the day of Pentecost.

> So continuing daily with one accord in the temple, and breaking bread from house to house, they ate their food with gladness and simplicity of heart, 47 praising God and having favor with all the people. And the Lord added to the church [ekklesia] daily those who were being saved.
>
> – Act 2:46-47

Jesus said in Matthew 16:18 that he would build His Ekklesia, and immediately he said that He had to die and be resurrected. That was His way of building His Ekklesia. The second and last time the Lord mentioned His Ekklesia is in Matthew 18. That was to show that the decision-making of His Ekklesia is in unity and harmony. His Ekklesia on earth legislates — makes decisions — like a symphony, with heaven responding to accomplish their deliberations through fellowship and prayer. This is His Kingdom on earth, governing as promised when He said He would build His Ekklesia (Democratic Assembly).

The fulfillment came in Acts 2 when the Spirit was poured forth and the apostles started to preach the good news of Jesus Christ. After 3000 men came to repent and were baptized, His Ekklesia was formed, and was constituted with all those saved by faith. At that time, the temple was where the apostles were preaching and teaching about Jesus. It was an open public area for their ministry. The Lord's Ekklesia took place in the believers' homes from house to house. Though thousands had come to believe — and more were being saved each day — the one Ekklesia gathered in homes: sharing meals, remembering the Lord, fellowshipping around the apostles' teaching, and praising God. When Saul persecuted the Ekklesia in Jerusalem, he went from house to house since those were their places of assembly (Acts 8:3).

Acts 2 was a wonderful beginning, but it was not diverse since it consisted only of Jewish believers. The next description of the Lord's Ekklesia, the Kingdom of God, was in Romans 14. Here, those who had dietary restrictions (derived from Jewish ordinances) and those who did not (presumed Gentiles) gathered to have a meal and fellowship together. In this setting, judging and rejecting one another would be instinctive. As seen previously, each group had justifiable reasons to boast in being either Jewish or Gentile — if they focused on their distinctives. Therefore, they were told that the Kingdom of God was not based on their distinctives, but on righteousness, peace, and joy in the Holy Spirit.

> For the kingdom of God is not eating and drinking, but righteousness and peace and joy in the Holy Spirit. 18 For he who serves Christ in these things [is] acceptable to God and approved by men. 19 Therefore let us pursue the things [which make] for peace and the things by which one may edify another.
>
> – Rom 14:17-19

These diverse believers, who were enemies, coming together for fellowship, define the Lord's democratic assembly, the Kingdom of God. This was the practical expression of the Lord's lampstand. For this to happen, there were some in their midst who were serving in the way of the Kingdom. They kept the focus on righteousness, peace, and joy through the person and work of Christ alone. When those around them had reasons to judge each other, then the ones who were able to maintain peace and edify, rather than succumbing to the divisiveness of distinctives, became the ones who were acceptable to God and approved by men. If there were no one doing such a service, it could well become a situation like Galatians 2, where the Jewish believers separated themselves from the Gentile believers. Similarly, since no one did this service in the Ekklesia in Corinthians 11, the rich and poor were separated and received judgment from God.

Neither group of believers had to change their conviction about whether to eat meat or not. Whatever conviction they maintained was between them and God (Rom. 14:22). They did not need to condemn themselves or others based on their differences. They kept their distinctiveness, yet they fellowship with one another. Instead of judging and rejecting each other, they desired to please and build up one another. Now, with one mind and one mouth, they glorified God. Their unity was not uniformity; neither did they have to conform to each other. The resulting charge to them was, *"Therefore receive one another, just as Christ also received us, to the glory of God"* (Rom. 15:7).

> For first of all, when you come together as a church [ekklesia], I hear that there are divisions among you, and in part I believe it. 19 For **there must also be factions** [*hairesis*] among you, that those who are approved may be recognized among you.
>
> – 1 Cor. 11:18-19

Romans 14 was an example of the Lord's Ekklesia; however, 1 Corinthians is the only detailed instruction of the Lord's Ekklesia functioning in a city with many diverse factions. This is a serious portion in light of understanding that the Lord's Ekklesias are His lampstand, God's Spirit shining on earth. It is so essential that Paul spent three-and-a-half chapters (from 1 Cor. 11:17 through to the end of chapter 14) describing in detail what the Lord's Ekklesia looks like and how it is practiced. After all, this is the manifestation of God's eternal purpose on earth. Through His ekklesia, He is glorified; and Satan, though still ruling in a darkened world, is put to shame.

Since churches historically have consistently ejected (disfellowshipped) those who have caused divisions, 1 Corinthians 11:19 is problematic and incomprehensible: *"when you come together as a church . . . there must be factions among you."* How can that be? History is replete with church splits due to differing opinions and perspectives. Yet, here Paul says there must be, or it is necessary to have, factions. Having such differences is a far cry from blatant heresy where, for example, the deity of Christ is rejected outright.

15

Due to the KJV translating the Greek word *hairesis* to "heresy" instead of "factions" or "sects" (Thayer's), traditional theology has taught that false believers are bringing in false teachings so that the genuine believers will be recognized. This line of teaching often stirs suspicion, prompting efforts to identify and root out perceived false Christians and doctrines within the church. That usually falls on those who do not have the same doctrinal understanding as the prevailing theology of that church. This leads to distrust and rejection of those who disagree within a church.

However, once the meaning of ekklesia as a democratic assembly is understood, it is obvious that there must be believers included from the various factions. They are "called out" from the comfort of their silo to assemble as the Lord's Ekklesia. By definition, the factions must be included in a democratic assembly. Consider Corinth, there are at least eight factions of believers mentioned: Those "of Paul," "of Cephas," "of Apollos," "of Christ," Jewish, Gentiles, the rich, and the poor. A permutation of these eight will produce many more factions. It would not be the Lord's Ekklesia if any identifiable groups were excluded.

There may well be a ministry (church) for the Jews, the poor, a house church for Apollos' preferred Christians, and even a gathering for those thinking they were superior since they were "of Christ." In any case, none of these distinctive groups is the Lord's Ekklesia. Since they are believers, they are members of the Ekklesia. However, if there is no assembly of a democratic forum for believers from all the various factions, the Lord's Ekklesia is not manifested in that city. If each faction is siloed in the comfort of their own "tribes" or "clan", then the Lord's Ekklesia is under a bushel, and there is no shining lampstand! Just like the Greek ekklesia has requirements of diversity (inclusion) and free speech, the Lord's Ekklesia has the same as described in 1 Corinthians 11:17 through chapter 14.

When believers from diverse factions gather, those approved are readily recognized. "Approved" in the Greek is *"dokimos,"* which means tested and found to be genuine. Amid believers from various factions coming together, it is a testing environment. Who will pass the test and be peacemakers? Those who do not take sides in disputes, but are focused on God's Kingdom. In a typical church group, any contrarians are usually over minor points. Anyone with major disagreements would have already left that church. In the Lord's Ekklesia, having believers from different factions is necessary, and some of these differences could be enormous. Then every democratic assembly becomes a test for those to manifest genuine love, kindness, patience, forgiveness, and humility.

Every ekklesia is a test since it is participatory and democratic, so anyone can show themselves "approved" by serving righteousness, peace, and joy in the Holy Spirit. Being approved is not the same as being appointed as an elder or a pastor. There is no such thing as an "approved" appointment, certificate, or stamp. It is situational whether one will pass the test amid believers of contrary perspectives. For example, there is a division between two Christians in an assembly over the doctrine of "once saved always saved" or "one can lose salvation by choice." A peacemaker must guide both parties to center their attention on the person and work of Jesus Christ, breaking down walls and cultivating fellowship in peace. Moreover, there will undoubtedly be Christians divided over politics. The one who makes peace earlier may now take a political side and join the conflict. So, another person would need to step in to heal this breach and bring those with opposite political views into fellowship. The person who can do that will be recognized as approved in that situation. Therefore, every democratic assembly with diverse believers is an opportunity to manifest those approved. This is profound, not simple, but obtainable through the Spirit of Christ that arises in approved brethren.

Like "overcomers" in Revelation, anyone can qualify to rise up and be recognized as approved. This function of a peacemaker edifying believers is open to all: young, mature, male, female, rich, poor, and all ethnicities. In Paul's major epistles — Romans, 1 & 2 Corinthians, Galatians, Ephesians, Colossians, and Philippians — He wrote to the saints in that particular location or region. His instructions were addressed to all believers and not to any leaders. While he called those who made peace and served the Kingdom as "approved," John in Revelation called them overcomers or *"he who overcomes."*

In 1 Corinthians 11, those who brought much food (the rich) got "drunk," and those who brought little (the poor) went hungry. They should have shared and eaten together, just as the feasts in Jerusalem were practiced under the Mosaic Covenant. These two factions, the rich and the poor, staying divided, meant no "approved" person was manifested between them. Therefore, according to Paul, they were not having the Lord's supper. Instead of a profit, receiving blessings, it was worse for them; some received judgment (1 Cor. 11:30). They should have shared and remembered the Lord together in a worthy manner by discerning that the Body of Christ is one. Each believer needed to "examine" or "approve" themselves that they were not excluding or dividing from any other member in the Body of Christ.

In 1 Corinthians 12, supporting his statement that there must be factions (differences) in the democratic assembly, he used the physical body as an example. Each member of the body is gifted and diverse. No matter the extreme difference between an eye and a foot, they are necessary in the body. No member or part should be dishonored or considered unnecessary. Each is needed just as they are, as the Lord made and placed them. The entire body hurts when one member hurts. Therefore, *"have the same care for one another."* Although Paul used one body as a metaphor, the individual distinctiveness should not be ignored or rejected but appreciated (1 Cor. 12:27).

In such a disparate environment as His democratic assembly, it is natural for the spiritually immature to divide and judge others who are different. So, Paul in 1 Corinthians 13, focuses on and describes in detail the Lord's new commandment: *"love one another as I have loved you."* The love described by Paul was not among people who would naturally love one another, such as when Jesus said, *"If you love those who love you, what credit is that to you? Even sinners love those who love them."* The love characteristics described in 1 Corinthians 13 are needed in a conflicting and testing environment since people with differences have assembled. Please note that 1 Corinthians 13 (although commonly read at weddings and similar events) is at the heart of a functioning Ekklesia.

> Love is patient and kind; love does not envy or boast; it is not arrogant 5 or rude. It does not insist on its own way; it is not irritable or resentful; 6 it does not rejoice at wrongdoing, but rejoices with the truth. 7 Love bears all things, believes all things, hopes all things, endures all things.
>
> – 1 Cor. 13:4-7, ESV

The characteristics of love are put to the test in a democratic assembly. An "approved" or an overcoming person will manifest such characteristics when tested. If their love is genuine, then all these characteristics will be expressed. If not, they must return to their first love, doing the first work; otherwise, their lampstand is in jeopardy of being taken away by the Lord. The more difficult the situation among immature believers, boasting of their distinctives, the more patience, kindness, not irritable, bearing is needed. No matter how gifted, powerful, or knowledgeable a person is, without this divine love, he is nothing. He could even be the most sacrificial to the point of giving all and dying for Christ, but without love, he gains nothing (1 Cor. 13:2-3). This is love toward one another and especially toward those who are difficult and contrary. This is the love that the saints in Ephesus left and were enjoined to return to it. This demonstrates that love needed for unity is treasured above all gifts and sacrifices.

Finally, in 1 Corinthians 14, free speech, being the second pillar of democracy, is described in the Lord's Ekklesia. Everyone speaks and contributes their riches of Christ. The entire chapter encourages each member to speak, pray, and sing to build up one another. Here are the key portions.

> How is it then, brethren? Whenever you come together, **each of you has** a psalm, has a teaching, has a tongue, has a revelation, has an interpretation. Let all things be done for edification.
>
> – 1 Cor. 14:26

> But if [anything] is revealed to another who sits by, let the first [speaker-prophet] keep silent. 31 For you can **all prophesy one by one**, that all may learn and all may be encouraged.
>
> –1 Cor. 14:30-31

When coming to the Lord's democratic assembly, each believer should already have something to contribute. The atmosphere is contributory, participatory, diverse — no one dominating, no one controlling, everyone gracious and encouraging, even willing to be interrupted (1 Cor. 14:30). This is exactly like the feasts under the Mosaic Covenant, where no one should appear before the Lord in Jerusalem "empty-handed" (Deut. 16:16). They were to bring their offerings to share at the feasts. This is the enjoyment of the entire Promised Land. Likewise, it is through each believer having prepared to share their revelation and experiences of Christ that the assembly will apprehend the vast dimensions of Christ and His knowledge surpassing love (Eph. 3:18-19).

Since Christians commonly view themselves as those going to "church" to receive ministry, there is scarcely a thought that they should prepare to speak and contribute a word of Christ when gathered with other believers. They do not consider themselves as workers for building up, but as those watching and listening to others more qualified — to the mature or professional ministers. Nevertheless, the Lord's democratic assembly requires the fellowship of all believers. Everyone partakes of each other's sharing of Christ and His work in their lives. A radical change of concept is needed; otherwise, the Lord's democratic assembly will be poor or an invitation for an outspoken, controlling person or sub-group to dominate. This would erase the manifestation of the Lord's Ekklesia and revert to a gathering for a person's ministry, like all the other churches.

Jesus said, "I will build My Ekklesia," My Kingdom, in Matthew 16:18, and here in 1 Corinthians 14 is the only other portion of Scripture using the same phrasing of building His Ekklesia (Democratic Assembly). This should be an immense revelation: Jesus went to build His Ekklesia through His death and resurrection, and now it is the direct activities of believers in His democratic assembly that are building His Ekklesia, His Kingdom. In other words, without such a democratic assembly as described in chapters 11 through 14, the Lord's Kingdom is practically not being built. This should wake up and shake up believers considering only going to church. The building up of the Lord's Ekklesia is His majestic mission; yet, all are needed to contribute. How awesome and applicable that even the youngest and newest believers are responsible and can participate in this eternal work, even if they only have "five words" to say (1 Cor. 14:19).

All are welcome to the Lord's democratic assembly, including unbelievers and the uninstructed (1 Cor. 14:24).[38] They are there to witness an amazing testimony of unity in diversity, and come under the shining of the Lord's lampstand. Light penetrating their hearts, they bow down to worship, declaring that God is truly present among His people (1 Cor. 14:25). This fulfills the Lord's prayer in John 17, where He said that when the world sees the unity among His diverse people, they will believe. The most powerful gospel is preached in His democratic assembly.

This is radical (but Scriptural) when compared to traditional "church" practices, where communion or the Lord's Supper is restrictive. Each church, including "house churches," typically has qualifications as to who can participate in its "Lord's Table." Unbelievers, uninstructed, or non-members are generally precluded from participation. Whereas the Lord's democratic assembly, which began from chapter 11 with an assortment of distinctive individuals, was broad and welcoming to all. This reflects God's heart of love for the world and desiring all to be saved. God's House reflects His openness for all to come and rejoice (Isa. 56:6). Jesus Christ is not fenced in; He is the Vine of life spreading out and reaching to all.

Restoration movements, those desiring to return to New Testament practices, including "house churches," have focused on 1 Corinthians 14 to teach the "priesthood of all believers," where all believers can speak without relying on one minister/pastor. They have criticized "institutional churches" for having one person preach and not allowing others to speak freely in their services. However, what has generally been missing in their teachings and practices is the need for believers from sundry factions in 1 Corinthians 11 (the 12 tribes at the place God chose). Without an intentional inclusion of differences among believers, these "restoration groups" normally and ultimately result in being another sectarian group. Their "free" speaking, without diverse perspectives, becomes one-dimensional. Eventually, their speaking, even though from many in their gatherings, only reinforces a similar perception whereby those with different views will find themselves excluded or will have to conform or convert. A "group-think" develops — and here, it is not "being of the same mind and spirit," but contrariwise, a rigid conformity that stifles the multifaceted grandeur and wisdom of the New Creation, His One Body, His Ekklesia.

Therefore, the two characteristics of a democratic assembly must be proactively maintained and encouraged by those "approved" (peacemakers) or "overcomers": diversity (inclusion) and freedom of speech (no person dominating). This is the practical manifestation of God's eternal purpose on earth and the fulfillment of the

---

38   There are four types of people excluded from the Lord's Ekklesia according to the New Testament. Please read appendix: People Excluded from the Lord's Democratic Assembly.

mysteries as unveiled in the prophetic writings. God, as the searching Spirit, is looking for and functioning on behalf of His lampstand on earth.

In these days when the knowledge and practice of the Lord's Ekklesia is deficient among Christians, the "five-fold" ministries are necessary. They are to equip believers to function and serve in the Lord's democratic assembly, Body of Christ, so that believers become one in the faith (Eph. 4:11-13). These gifted ministers should not work for themselves but for the Lord's Ekklesia. If they become a cause for believers to stand apart or divide from other Christians, they become those as described in Romans 16:

> "Now I urge you, brethren, note those who cause divisions and offenses, contrary to the doctrine which you learned, and avoid them. For those who are such do not serve our Lord Jesus Christ, but their own belly, and by smooth words and flattering speech deceive the hearts of the simple"
>
> – Rom. 16:17-18

When their labor shifts toward personal gain rather than guiding believers to prioritize the building up of the Lord's Ekklesia, they begin retaining people to expand their own church or group (*"their own belly"*). Historically, this has been the case due to the lack of knowledge and understanding concerning the Lord's democratic assembly. In these last days, the revelation of the Lord's democratic assembly is being unveiled, and believers are responding.

These are the beginnings of the prophetic days of Revelation. Now is the time for the Lord's Ekklesia to emerge and be manifested city by city around the globe where Christians reside. The Lord prayed desperately for this visible unity so that the world would believe. The Spirit is working and speaking to all God's people to overcome and have His democratic assemblies shine as lampstands. Believers' blessings and strengthening depend on this, and God's glory awaits the manifestation of it.

No wonder Satan is using all his wisdom to keep God's people divided. Do not be ignorant of his devices. Now is the time for each of Jesus' followers to hear the Spirit and overcome. It is time to build His Democratic Assembly today!

Conclusion

God's singular, eternal purpose is a profound and extraordinary thread woven throughout the entire Bible: to establish His Democratic Assembly, the **Ekklesia, as His Bride and Kingdom on earth**. This is not a tangential concept but the very essence of God's plan, unveiled progressively through the prophetic Scriptures and fully disclosed by Christ and His apostles.

God's Ekklesia embodies God's Mysteries. His divine purpose is revealed through these eight interconnected mysteries, each defining the identity, mission, and ultimate glory of His Democratic Assembly. These mysteries converge to highlight God's desire for a diverse, unified people who manifest His glory and overcome His enemy, Satan:

- **Mystery of God, Christ**, makes God intimately knowable and approachable to humanity. (Col. 2:2-3)
- **The Great Mystery** is the astonishing joining of Christ, the Husband, with His *Ekklesia*, the wife, fulfilling God's desire for a divine counterpart. (Eph. 5:25-32)
- **The Mystery of Godliness** reveals God manifested not only in Jesus Christ but also in His Household (*Ekklesia*) — a body of redeemed sinners, diverse yet unified, becoming His dwelling place on earth. (1 Tim. 3:16)
- God's *Oikonomia (economy)*, His household management, involves the continuous dispensing of the unsearchable riches of Christ (grace) to mature His Democratic Assembly, enabling her to bring Him glory and shame to His enemies. (Eph. 3:2, 9-10)
- **The Hidden Mystery** is "Christ in you (plural)," literally indwelling every believer through the Spirit, empowering them to live supernaturally human and enabling unity amidst differing views. (Col. 1:27)
- **The Mystery of Christ** proclaims the threefold oneness of historically hostile Jews and Gentiles as joint heirs, a joint body, and joint partakers in Christ, creating "one new man" through the cross. Together, they declare that all diverse and previous enemies can be united, still retaining their distinctions, to manifest God's wisdom to the universe. (Eph. 3:4-6)
- **The Mystery of the Gospel** is God's comprehensive plan for mankind, going beyond individual salvation by grace to achieve glory to God on earth and the crushing of Satan's kingdom through His unified Democratic Assembly. It includes the Gospel of Peace for uniting divided believers and the Gospel of the Kingdom, which manifests "righteousness and peace and joy in the Holy Spirit" on earth through His people's oneness. (Eph. 6:19)
- **The Mystery of Faith** is the gift of faith from God that substantiates the unseen reality of Christ's person and accomplishments. Genuine faith is active, resulting in "good works" that specifically involve working for peace and unity among God's people and building His Democratic Assembly. (1 Tim. 3:9)

God's Shining Lampstand on Earth is a metaphor that aptly describes the Lord's Democratic Assembly. It signifies the *Ekklesia's* core identity as a radiant bearer of divine light and love in a "dark and hopeless world." This radiance flows from Christ's presence in her midst. It is the visible expression of God's glory and multifaceted wisdom, demonstrating His ultimate triumph over sin and Satan through His unified people. Remarkably, this radiance shines forth even when many local assemblies are in degraded conditions, as seen in the seven Ekklesias in Revelation (e.g., Ephesus having left its "first love," Pergamos and Thyatira committing immorality and idolatry). This shining was not due to their righteousness or holiness, but because of God's continuous presence, the collective unity, and the brotherly love exemplified by those like Philadelphia. Furthermore, the Lord's hatred for the doctrine of the Nicolaitans, which means "to conquer the people," underscores the truly democratic, non-dominating, and non-hierarchical nature of His Democratic Assembly. It is the Kingdom of God manifested now, a living testimony to the world.

The spiritual journey of every believer is one of profound transformation, moving beyond individual spiritual progress to a corporate partnership with Christ in fulfilling His eternal purpose. This progression, epitomized by the Shulamite's journey in the Song of Songs, leads from personal love for Jesus to a corporate-minded self, a peacemaker, and an army for God's eternal purpose, culminating in the Holy City, New Jerusalem — the eternal dwelling place where God's people, made one in Christ, manifest His glory for eternity.

In light of these profound mysteries, a dynamic **call to action** emerges for every believer:

- **Prioritize and Pursue Unity**: Actively resist and reject all forms of division within the Body of Christ (among believers, not among "churches"). Divisions, whether doctrinal, cultural, social, or political, undermine God's Kingdom and grieve the Holy Spirit. Embrace diverse believers, seeking fellowship and reconciliation as a powerful witness to the world. Remember, as Paul stated, "there must also be factions" (*hairesis*) in His Democratic Assembly, so that "those who are approved" (peacemakers, those who show genuine love, kindness, and forgiveness amidst differing views) may be recognized. This recognition occurs in the testing environment of God's Democratic Assembly.

- **Live an Active Life of "Good Works"**: Do not remain passive or merely self-focused in your faith — no matter how busy or self-constrained your life may be. Engage in the "good works" God prepared for you, which fundamentally involve building up the Lord's Ekklesia. This means serving, nourishing, comforting, and seeking unity with fellow believers, especially those with whom you differ, transforming individual experiences into corporate manifestation. This active laboring should echo the encouragement given to Zerubbabel and Joshua to "not despise the day of small things" when rebuilding the temple, knowing that God rejoices even in seemingly small efforts to build His Ekklesia on earth. The "purpose-driven life" (centered on you) has its merits; however, "the purpose-driven Christ" is all about His Ekklesia; it's all about what He's focused upon.

- **Pursue a Deeper Knowledge of Christ:** Move beyond elementary understanding. Diligently immerse yourself in the Scriptures to uncover the "unsearchable riches of Christ," allowing the Holy Spirit to transform objective truths into subjective, living experiences. This continuous "eating and drinking" of Christ will nourish your faith, enable you to manifest the "Christ-in-you" life in all circumstances, and empower you to speak forth His victory. Hear the calling of the Spirit to "overcome" and be rewarded not merely a future hope but a present "foretaste" — such as opening the door for Jesus to come and dine at the Lord's supper. And experiencing Jesus as the Morning Star now, bringing newness and freshness every day.

- **Proclaim the Complete Gospel:** Share the comprehensive good news of God, encompassing not just individual salvation by grace but the Gospel of Peace and the Gospel of the Kingdom. This "Completion Gospel" preached will crush Satan's kingdom under their feet. Practically, believers are commanded to go greet (spend time in fellowship) those outside one's normal and familiar circle of Christians. They should proactively seek out believers in other "tribes" and bring peace where there might have been a wall of division.

- **Host or facilitate a democratic assembly.** God's Ekklesia, His Kingdom and Bride, needs to be practically manifested in every locality by those in the faith of Christ. The love and unity between desperate believers in their various spiritual conditions is God's lampstand shining His Spirit on earth. This is the most powerful testimony, causing the world to believe. Those "approved" and "overcoming" need to do this building work and be an open door for both the Lord and believers to dine together at the Lord's supper.

By embarking on this transformative journey, guided by the Holy Spirit and patterned after the Shulamite's growth, you will not only fulfill your individual calling but also actively contribute to the glorious manifestation of God's eternal purpose on earth. This leads to the ultimate divine romance: the eternal union of God and man in the New Jerusalem, a destiny awaiting all who are His.

"But you have come to Mount Zion and to the city of the living God, the heavenly Jerusalem, to an innumerable company of angels, to the general assembly and church [ekklesia] of the firstborn who are registered in heaven, to God the Judge of all, to the spirits of just men made perfect, to Jesus the Mediator of the New Covenant, and to the blood of sprinkling that speaks better things than that of Abel" (Hebrews 12:22-24).

APPENDIX
(In Alphabetical Order)

Believers Excluded from the Ekklesia

Those Who Divide Should Be Marked and Avoided

> Now I urge you, brethren, note those who cause divisions and offenses, contrary to the doctrine which you learned, and avoid them. For those who are such do not serve our Lord Jesus Christ, but their own belly, and by smooth words and flattering speech deceive the hearts of the simple.
>
> – Romans 16:17–18

> But shun foolish questionings, and genealogies, and strifes, and fightings about the law; for they are unprofitable and vain. 10 A factious man after a first and second admonition refuse;
>
> – Tit. 3:9–10, ASV

A person who causes division in the Body through differing teachings, diverting believers away from the focus on Jesus Christ's person and work, needs to be avoided, even rejected. "Division" in Romans 16:17, in Greek, is *dicostasia*, a strong word meaning *"to stand apart."* Those under the influence of this person's teaching will stand apart from simply being believers in common fellowship with other believers in the Body of Christ. They will consider themselves different, superior, and special from other believers. These divisive teachers are not motivated to build up the oneness of the Body of Christ; rather, they purposely want to cause a separation among believers. They may want to have their own group of followers, or they may simply want to be contentious in showing they are right, as well as superior, while others are wrong and inferior. Either way, through their speech and actions, they oblige believers to choose between one group and another group — to be on one side or another.

All believers should be on the same side, for we are all members of the same Democratic Assembly, because there is only one Jesus Christ, one Spirit of God, one fellowship, and one Body of Christ. Therefore, any divisive teacher (after two admonitions to point out their damaging and divisive actions) should stop their destructive ways or be rejected from the fellowship of that Ekklesia.

Yes, all believers may associate themselves with a group or a "tribe," but they should assemble as the Lord's Ekklesia, similar to gathering in Jerusalem for the feasts. The Lord's Ekklesias should include believers from various factions ("tribes"). However, it is altogether unacceptable to be **factious**, a person actively causing divisions among brethren when assembled to remember the Lord. They are not satisfied that brethren from various factions are gathered; they sabotage the unity by intentionally causing believers to take a side against another. They are to be refused from the Ekklesia after two warnings to stop such divisive behaviors.

Those Who Do Not Teach Jesus Christ Is God in the Flesh

> For many deceivers have gone out into the world who do not confess Jesus Christ [as] coming in the flesh. This is a deceiver and an antichrist. . . . 9 Whoever transgresses and does not abide in the doctrine of Christ does not have God. He who abides in the doctrine of Christ has both the Father and the Son. 10 If anyone comes to you and does not bring this doctrine, do not receive him into your house nor greet him; 11 for he who greets him shares in his evil deeds.
>
> – 2 John 1:7, 9-11

It can be assumed that these deceivers John referred to in 2 John 1 considered themselves Christians. They were not unbelievers, since unbelievers by definition do not believe Jesus is God come in the flesh. Moreover, in 1 Corinthians 14, we read that there were *unbelievers* in the assembly; therefore, these deceivers must have been people who passed themselves off as Christian teachers. They probably used the Bible to teach, for they could deceive. However, they did not teach that Jesus Christ is God becoming flesh (man). This is the very essence of our faith concerning the person of Jesus Christ — He is both one hundred percent God, and one hundred percent man. He is altogether God and, simultaneously, genuinely man. Anyone identified as a Christian teaching Jesus Christ is either not eternally God or not eternally man, is against the person of Jesus Christ — this is the spirit of antichrist. Such a teacher should not be received.

One Living Habitually in Sin

Believers who habitually and openly practice sin and immorality, which can no longer be tolerated by love, should not be received into the assembly.

> Above all, keep loving one another earnestly, since love covers a multitude of sins.
>
> – 1 Pet. 4:8, ESV

> Let no corrupting talk come out of your mouths, but only such as is good for building up, as fits the occasion, that it may give grace to those who hear.
>
> – Eph. 4:29, ESV

Due to the closeness in fellowship in God's Democratic Assembly (viz., life between believers), there will be opportunities to know each other's faults, even sins. There will be times when believers will hear of, or even witness, a failure or a sinful fall of another believer. In all such occasions, Scriptures instruct believers to cover their brother or sister with love – not to spread in gossip the weaknesses of other believers. In some situations, believers may have to share what has been learned with another believer, to pray for and support the believer with a certain weakness. In any case, we are not to spread news of another's failure – it should be contained and covered so believers in the assembly will not know of each other's faults, weaknesses, failures, and sins. They should not spread such information to others, since it could corrupt and damage the assembly. This has nothing to do with "hiding in darkness" but everything to do with "love covers a multitude of sins." Nevertheless, if someone commits a crime, there may be a legal obligation to report.

> It is universally reported *that there* is fornication among you, and such fornication as is not even among the nations, so that one should have his father's wife. And you are puffed up, and you have not rather mourned, in order that he that has done this deed might be taken away out of the midst of you.
>
> Your boasting is not good. Do you not know that a little leaven leavens the whole lump? Purge out the old leaven, that you may be a new lump, according as you are unleavened. For also our Passover, Christ, has been sacrificed.
>
> I have written to you in the epistle not to mix with fornicators; not altogether with the fornicators of this world, or with the avaricious [covetous] and rapacious [extortioner], or idolaters, since *then* you should go out of the world. But now I have written to you, if any one called brother be [a] fornicator, or avaricious [covetous], or idolater, or abusive, or a drunkard, or rapacious [extortioner], not to mix with him; with such a one not even to eat. For what have I *to do* with judging those outside also? you, do not you judge them that are within? But those without God judges. Remove the wicked person from amongst yourselves.
>
> – 1 Cor. 5:1–2, 6–7, 9–13, DBY

When a believer's failures become habitual, universally known, wherein they can no longer be considered as an occasional sin able to be covered by love, the assembly should not tolerate or accept this believer as if everything is okay. The assembly in Corinth boasted that it had such a sinful brother in their midst. The apostle Paul likened this openly sinful brother's behavior to "leaven," which would corrupt the entire assembly, because other believers who were witnesses to such "leaven" would be encouraged to cave in to sin's temptations, thinking this sinful practice to be acceptable behavior in the assembly.

Therefore, this brother could no longer be welcomed into the Ekklesia or participate in its meals. This does not mean caring believers could not visit this brother by helping him to repent of his sin; however, this does mean he should be excluded from gathering together with the Democratic Assembly. This exclusion includes all those believers who are known to be people who live in the manifestation of their sinful nature in various ways, as listed in 1 Corinthians 5:11.

This exclusion, however, should not include unbelievers or those new in the faith, since they don't know better. These unbelievers or new believers living in sin should still be welcomed; otherwise, they will not receive the Word of faith nor encouragement in the assembly for them to come to Christ and grow in the faith. Functioning in this way reveals the heart of the Lord. On one hand, He reaches out to all people for them to be saved from their sinful practices; on the other hand, He protects the assembly from corruption.

One Who Is a Busybody, Not Working

> But we command you, brethren, in the name of our Lord Jesus Christ, that you withdraw from every brother who walks disorderly and not according to the tradition which he received from us. For you yourselves know how you ought to follow us, for we were not disorderly among you; nor did we eat anyone's bread free of charge, but worked with labor and toil night and day, that we might not be a burden to any of you, not because we do not have authority, but to make ourselves an example of how you should follow us. For even when we were with you, we commanded you this: If anyone will not work, neither shall he eat.... And if anyone does not obey our word in this epistle, note that person and do not keep company with him, that he may be ashamed. Yet do not count him as an enemy, but admonish him as a brother.
>
> – 2 Thess. 3:6–10, 14–15

What an example the apostle Paul gave to believers! He labored in preaching the gospel; therefore, he had the right to receive financial support from those he was spiritually helping. Nevertheless, he purposely worked to support himself materially so he would not be a burden to any of the believers under his care. Consequently, he strongly asserted every believer should work to support themselves without being a burden on others, limiting leisure time, which could lead to becoming a "busybody" bothering others. It can be assumed that Paul was referring to people with able bodies who could work to support themselves.

Although believers who are not willing to work should be put to shame, they should still be cared for in love, encouraging them to repent of their ways and bring their lives into order.

In the Old Testament, everyone should labor on their portion of land and bring their produce to the feast for sharing. None can come empty-handed; They cannot be a "free loader." Today, for the meal in the Lord's Democratic Assembly, everyone should bring something to share, whether a little or much. None should be a "busybody" and only eat other people's food.

Beware of Wolves – Serving Their Own Belly

> "For I know this, that after my departure savage wolves will come in among you, not sparing the flock. 30 "Also from among yourselves men *will* rise up, speaking perverse things, to draw away the disciples after themselves.
>
> – Act 20:29-30

The Apostle Paul was warning that even among elders, there are wolves who draw disciples to themselves, juxtaposing elders serving the entire Body of Christ. These wolves are similar to the teachers in Romans 16:17-18, who deceive the simple to *"serve ... their own belly."* This descriptive language tells us that they are far more interested in feeding themselves than in feeding others in the whole Ekklesia. Tragically, they are prone to gathering brethren to themselves rather than simply gathering God's people together for common fellowship around the Head of His One Body. Far too often, "gifted ministers" are more than predisposed to gather for discourse and "expressions of unity" in a pastoral/ministry association, but in the name of "protecting their own sheep" (lest they be stolen by another "ministry"), discourage the sheep in their own fold from fraternizing/fellowshipping with sheep which allegedly "belong to pastor so-and-so's flock."

Isn't Christ the Shepherd of the sheep? If God's people wish to meet and greet brethren from different churches "at random" to fellowship and share in the riches of Christ in whatever venue they desire, is that somehow "suspicious" or repugnant to those who "shepherd the flock" in a given locality? Under the guise of "wolves in sheep's clothing," those who should be pastoring, teaching, evangelizing, missionizing, and prophesying on behalf of God's people, assiduously, in the name of "protecting their own," tenaciously hold on to their own sheep lest they run off to another minister/ministry. This kind of attitude is repugnant to the "*ekklesia* of the First Born" (Heb. 12:23) and most assuredly to the "Great Shepherd of the sheep" Who, through the blood of the everlasting covenant, is more than capable of watching over His "one flock" (John 10:16).

Ironically, wolves can be those holding on to the sheep so tightly in the name of protection against false doctrine and "wolves in sheep's clothing." They may have a noble justification among caring shepherds of the sheep by discouraging diverse meetings and greetings in His One Flock. True shepherds should grasp the biblical reality that there is but One Good Shepherd Who is well-able to gather the sheep in His arms and is the ultimate guardian of His Ekklesia. Have you ever viewed a large number of sheep in the open pasture – they're grazing all over the place, hardly in a protected fold. But guess what, the Good Shepherd is there, carefully watching for wolves and those wandering off from the flock. Christ is the door of the sheep – allow them to "go in and out and find green pasture" – and know this, the "other sheep which are not of this fold" are outside the fold where there is One Shepherd and One Flock!

Ekklesia Amplified – the Original Vision & Ultimate Manifestation

Revelation 7: The Ultimate Manifestation of the Original Vision
Revelation 11: 2 Olive Trees, 2 Lampstands, 2 Witnesses, 2 Martyrs, 2 Prophets

Again, our stress upon "democratic" assembly is manifold: It not only highlights the participatory/contributory nature of the Ekklesia Jesus said He would build as these New Covenant believers gathered together (and as understood in the context of the so-called Greco-Roman world relative to community governance), but likewise stressed Jehovah's original intent to make all members of the Twelve Tribes of Israel into a "kingdom of priests and a holy nation" before God (Exo. 19:5-6). As they say: "We're all in this together!" Sadly, only the tribe of Levi, who stood with Moses during a rebellion, became the priests (Numbers 7:5-22). Now, bless God, as Peter's epistle declares: *"But you are a chosen generation, a royal priesthood, a holy nation, His own special people, that you may proclaim the praises of Him who called you out of darkness into His marvelous light"* (1

Peter 2:9); and John's Revelation echoes those New Covenant realities: *"Jesus Christ . . . has made us kings and priests to His God and Father"* (Rev. 1:4-5 NKJV). The "you" and "us" here connotes both Jew and Gentile.

Revelation 7: The Ultimate Manifestation of the Original Vision

Quite possibly, this threefold recognition may be seen in Revelation 7, where we have, finally, the unity of all 12 tribes (Judah and Ephraim) and then the great multitude that no one could number.

Isn't it amazing that the Twelve Tribes of Israel are mentioned in Revelation 7:1-8 — inclusive of Manasseh and Joseph (the "stick of Joseph is the stick of Ephraim") . . . while immediately *"after these things I looked, and behold, a great multitude which no one could number, of all nations, tribes, peoples, and tongues, standing before the throne and before the Lamb, clothed with white robes, with palm branches in their hands, and crying out with a loud voice, saying 'Salvation belongs to our God who sits on the throne, and to the Lamb!'"* (Rev. 7:9-11). At this stage of the Revelation, one simply cannot separate the 12 tribes of the sealed upon the "earth" (vss. 1-4) from the "heavenly" throng of Revelation 7:9-17. Earth and heaven, as displayed in John 1:51, are united together by the Son of God, the King of Israel (vs. 49) as the very Son of Man, linking the two realms together in Jacob's vision of the angels ascending and descending upon the Son of Man — bringing God to man (Son of God) and bringing man into God (the King of Israel). So glorious is this vision of the oneness of His people that the New Jerusalem is described as the "**twelve gates** of the Holy City bear the names of the Twelve Tribes of Israel and the **twelve foundations** bear the names of the Twelve Apostles of the Lamb" – To God be the Glory (Rev. 21:12-14)!

Revelation 11 – 2 Olive Trees, 2 Lampstands, 2 Witnesses, 2 Martyrs, 2 Prophets

Although an extensive subject, we can fortify the defeat of the powers of darkness, the victory over the Dragon, the Beast, and the False Prophet when the Wrath of God and the Lamb are poured out upon the "kingdoms of this world" AFTER the prevailing testimony of the Two Witnesses is given. In Greek, the word used for "Witness" is the same for "Martyr" in the book of Revelation. Yes, this is controversial; however, the identity of the Two Witnesses, we affirm, is far more than two X-Men like Moses and Elijah with fire breathing out of their mouths. The only identification given to the Two Witnesses is the following: "**These are the two olive trees** (Israel as His witness is the "green olive tree" — Jer. 11:16) *and the two lampstands* (the Church or churches/ Ekklesia are His witness as His "lampstands" or "luchnia" in Greek for *"the seven lampstands* (luchnia) *are the seven churches* (Ekklesias) (Rev. 1:20; 11:4). It is when these Two Witnesses are raised from the dead in front of the whole earth when His "loud voice" is heard: *"Come up here,"* and *"they ascended to heaven in a cloud, and their enemies saw them"* (vs. 12). It is then we read: *"In the same hour there was a great earthquake, and a tenth of the city fell"* — this is the Wrath of God and the Lamb (Rev. 11:13). Then, and only then, we read: *"Then the seventh angel sounded* (the last trumpet): *And there were loud voices in heaven, saying, 'The kingdoms of this world have become the kingdoms of our Lord and of His Christ, and He shall reign forever and ever!"* (Rev. 11:15).

Ezekiel's Holy District - Future Enjoyment of the Riches of Christ

It is in this light there is the revelation of this difference: Although manna and the "produce of the Good Land" BOTH represent the enjoyment of Christ, one (manna) is freely given and unilateral — no work is needed aside from gathering it; however, the "produce of the Promised Land" necessitates bilateral cooperation wherein the believer must labor (work the land) in order for the Lord's Appointed Times (Modim/ Feast Days) to take place.

The Israelites entered the Land of Promise and were to incorporate the "Feast Days" or "Modim" as the Lord's appointed times. For what purpose? At least three times each year, the 12 Tribes were to come to Zion (Jerusalem) to express the unity of His people and to share in the abundance of the Good Land. It was an "agrarian society" in which the agriculture of the Land upon which the Children of Israel labored brought forth its nourishing riches. The Book of Hebrews affords us an abundant understanding that this Good Land is our Rest upon which we labor, and the surplus of the cultivated land reveals the "riches of Christ" for all believers — riches that are shared at the Lord's appointed times.

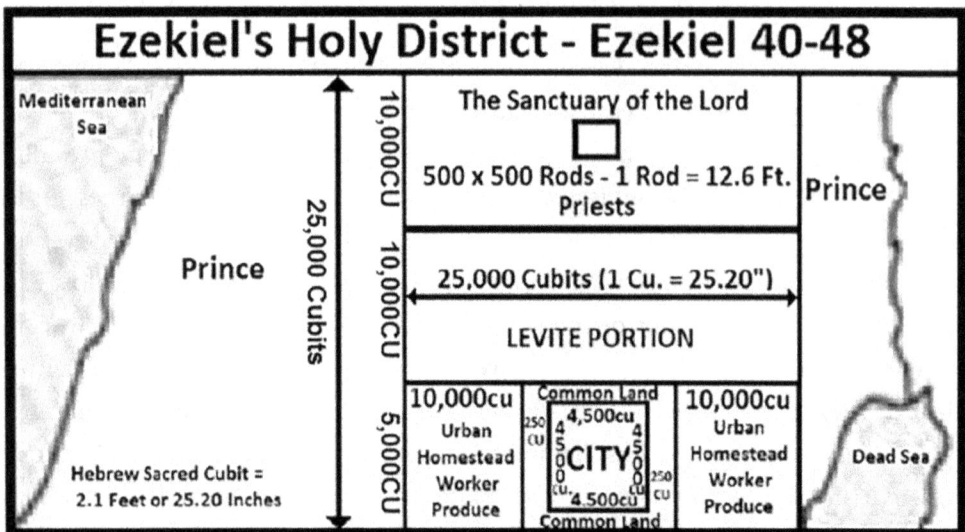

Ezekiel's Holy District - Ezekiel 40-48

The age of "Millenarian Bliss" clearly advocates the bilateral enjoyment of the Son of David, our Lord Jesus Christ. This is abundantly seen in the description of the "Holy District" found in Ezekiel Chapters 40-48, where we read:

> 15 "The remaining area, 5,000 cubits wide and 25,000 cubits long, will be for the common use of the city, for houses and for pastureland. The city will be in the center of it 16 and will have these measurements: the north side 4,500 cubits, the south side 4,500 cubits, the east side 4,500 cubits, and the west side 4,500 cubits. 17 The pastureland for the city will be 250 cubits on the north, 250 cubits on the south, 250 cubits on the east, and 250 cubits on the west. 18 What remains of the area, bordering on the sacred portion and running the length of it, will be 10,000 cubits on the east side and 10,000 cubits on the west side. **Its produce will supply food for the workers of the city. 19 The workers from the city who farm it will come from all the tribes of Israel**" . . . "And the name of the city from that time on will be: **The Lord is there (Jehovah Shamma)**"
>
> – Ezek. 48:15-19, 35

Don't we want to be where the Lord is? Absolutely! To visualize the above, we have provided a graphic to comprehend the location of the Holy District with the site of the Holy City and the surrounding grazing land (viz. "common land") and the "produce plots" on either side of the Holy City:

The "divine order" is absolute: All the workers of the City (for they are "from the City" and from "all the tribes of Israel") will eat of both the produce of the land (the "produce plots") and enjoy the animals (as food) from the immediate "grazing areas" immediately surrounding the City (viz. "common land"). The obvious is in view — the "workers" are to **work the Land** (Christ) and to **enjoy this abundance**; moreover, "workers" connote that if the workers do not work, they don't eat! You might say there are no "freebies" in the Millenarian state. What an incredible picture of the futurity of eternity — we will forever work the Promised Land to enjoy the riches of Christ, our Sacrifice (grazing land), and our eternal nourishment (produce plots).

Some vehemently reject the futurity of Ezekiel's description of the Temple, the Lord's Dwelling Place and the elaborate depictions of the Millennium Altar and offerings mandated thereon cannot possibly be efficacious because of Christ's once for all sacrifice — as in "How can these offerings in Ezekiel 43 'make atonement' (vs. 20) when His atonement has already taken place at Calvary (Heb. 10:1-18)"? Burnt offerings and the "sprinkling of blood" – sin offerings and peace offerings – wouldn't they be unnecessary, superfluous, and worse, antithetical to the New Covenant? No, what is in view is the "forever" — perpetual:

> "And He said to me, 'Son of man, this is the place of My throne and the place of the soles of My feet, where I will dwell in the midst of the children of Israel forever. No more shall the house of Israel defile My holy name, they nor their kings, by their harlotry or with the carcasses of their kings on their high places . . . Now let them put their harlotry and the carcasses of their kings far away from me, **and I will dwell in their midst forever**"
>
> *– Ezek. 43:7-9*

No, once we realize these "types and shadows" will forever amplify the once for all sacrifice to be enjoyed by His people, then there is absolutely no biblical contradiction; again, this Holy District with its sacrifices and feast days (Ezek. 34:18-25, including Passover and the Feast of Unleavened Bread), is described as follows: *"And the name of the city from that day shall be: THE LORD IS THERE (lit. YHWH [Jehovah] IS THERE."*

Feast of Tabernacles

Is there, then, any wonder that in "Millenarian Bliss" the nations are enjoined to go up to Zion/Jerusalem year after year to enjoy the Feast of Tabernacles – Feast of Nations?

> "And it shall come to pass that everyone who is left of **all the nations** which came against Jerusalem shall go up from year to year to worship the King, the LORD of hosts, and to keep the **Feast of Tabernacles**. And it shall be that **whichever of the families of the earth** do not come up to Jerusalem to worship the King, the LORD of hosts, on them there will be no rain. If the family of Egypt will not come up and enter in, they shall have no rain; they shall receive the plague with which the LORD strikes the **nations** who do not come up to keep the **Feast of Tabernacles**. This shall be the punishment of Egypt and the punishment of all the nations that do not come up to keep the **Feast of Tabernacles**"
>
> *– Zech. 14:16-19*

A picture of the Hebrew Festival Calendar will aid in our understanding of these three major Feast Days:

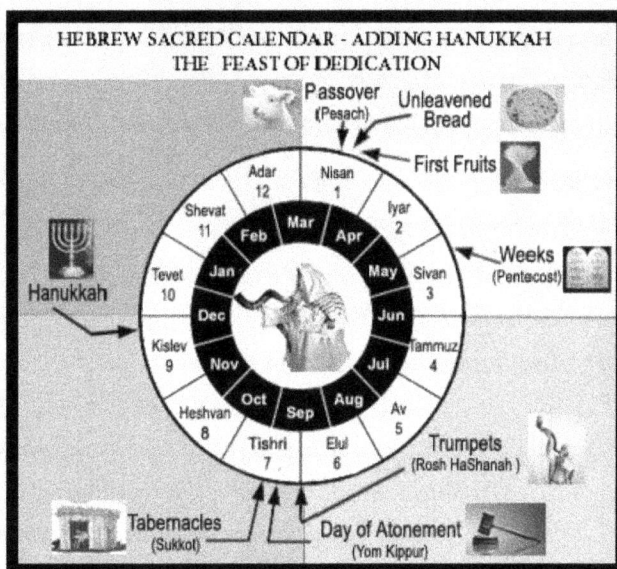

HEBREW SACRED CALENDAR - ADDING HANUKKAH
THE FEAST OF DEDICATION

God's Eternal Purpose – Making of the Two, One New Man, So Making Peace

God's Eternal Purpose on Display Before Principalities and Powers
John 6 and the New Covenant

"As it has now been revealed by the Spirit to His **holy apostles and prophets**: that the Nations (Gentiles) should be fellow heirs [both Jew and Gentile], of the **same body**, and **partakers of His promise in Christ** through the gospel. . . that I should preach among the Nations **the unsearchable riches of Christ**, and to make all see what is the **oikonomia** (fellowship/dispensation), which from the beginning of the ages has been hidden in God who created all things through Jesus Christ; to the intent that now the manifold wisdom of God might be made know by the church [ekklesia] to the principalities and powers in the heavenly places, according to **the eternal purpose which He accomplished in Christ Jesus our Lord**"

– Eph. 3:5-11, excerpts

It is a divine imperative that we capture His purpose in that *"We love Him because He first loved us"* – what shall be our response, and is it embedded in His determination? *"Having made known to us **the mystery of His will**, according to His good pleasure which **He purposed in Himself** . . . that in the dispensation of the fullness of the times He might **gather together in one all** *things in Christ*, *both which are in heaven and which are on earth* — *in Him* . . . *according to the purpose of Him* *who works all things according to the counsel of His will*, *that we who first trusted in Christ should be to the praise of His glory"*

– Eph. 1:9-12, Excerpts

His *purpose* (Grk. πρόθεσις – "a setting forth" as in the "shewbread") connotes a divine display motivated by *"the counsel of His will,"* no doubt before the *"heavens and the earth,"* wherein the result of *"gathering together in one all things in Christ"* will result *"to the praise of His glory."*

We can grasp the "dispensation (or "administration/stewardship") of the mystery" when we take hold of this: *"And to make all see what is the dispensation of the mystery . . . to the intent that now the manifold wisdom of God might be made known by the Ekklesia (aka "church") to principalities and powers in heavenly places, according to the eternal purpose, which He accomplished in Christ Jesus our Lord"* (Eph. 1:9-11). The Almighty definitely wants to exhibit His eternal purpose, *"which from the beginning of the ages has been hidden in God"* to all — especially, to these principalities and powers with whom we, His Ekklesia, wrestle (Eph. 6:12).

God's Eternal Purpose on Display Before Principalities and Powers

The obvious confronts us: His Eternal Purpose is known through the Ekklesia Jesus said He would build and that the *"gates of Hades"* (i.e., these same "principalities and powers") would not prevail (Matt. 16:18) against her. This eternal purpose is on display through the New Covenant's promise found in Ezekiel 36.

Coupled with Ezekiel's disclosures in Ezekiel 36:26-27, the same verbiage is found in Jeremiah in relationship to the coming New Covenant: *"I will make a New Covenant with the house of Israel and with the house of Judah . . . No more shall every man teach his neighbor, and every man his brother, saying, 'Know the LORD,' for they all shall know me, from the least of them to the greatest of them, says the LORD. For I will forgive their iniquity, and their sin I will remember no more"* (Jer. 31:31, 34 – NKJV).

When Christ presented Himself as the "manna from heaven" – as the Bread of Life in John 6 – He disclosed the following from the prophets as to how this reality could take place: *"It is written in the prophets, 'And they shall all be taught by God"* (John 6:45 – NKJV) . . . but how could "all be taught by God"? Only under the aforesaid New Covenant found in Ezekiel 36 and Jeremiah 31 could this happen.

How could it ever be that *"No more shall every man teach his neighbor, and every man his brother, saying 'Know the LORD,' for they all shall know Me, from the least of them to the greatest of them, says the LORD"* (Jer. 31:34 – NKJV)?

Isn't this what John, the Apostle, declared in 1 John 2:27 (NKJV): *"But the anointing [of the Holy Spirit] which you have received from Him abides in you, and you do not need that anyone teach you; but as the same anointing teaches you concerning all things, and is true, and is not a lie, and just as it has taught you, you will abide in Him"*?

John 6 and the New Covenant

Moreover, isn't it altogether the revelation of the New Covenant when four times it was introduced to His disciples that the ultimate empowerment of the New Covenant would advance from (1) *"everyone who **sees the Son** and believes in Him may have everlasting life and I will raise him up at the **last day**" (John 6:40)*; to (2) *"No one can come to Me unless the **Father who sent Me draws him**, and I will raise him up at the **last day**"* (John 6:44); to (3) *"... It is written in the prophets, '**And they shall all be taught by God**' ... (4) I am the bread of life ... your fathers ate the manna in the wilderness, and are dead ... Most assuredly, I say to you, unless you eat the flesh of the Son of Man and drink His blood, you have no life in you. .. whoever eats My flesh and drinks My blood has eternal life, and I will raise him up at the **last day** ... It is the **Spirit who gives life**; the flesh profits nothing. .. The words I speak to you are spirit and they are life"* (John 6:44-45, 48-49, 53-54, NKJV).

Brethren, do we see this? The Triune God (the Father, the Son, and the Spirit, under the impress of the New Covenant) longs to bring us into eternal fellowship that the Father and the Son enjoy by seeing the Son, being drawn by the Father, and by eating and drinking via the Spirit the body and blood of the Son of Man — that's being taught by God; that's by partaking of the Son of Man in Spirit; and that is precisely how intimate the New Covenant is vs. the Mosaic Covenant.

Tabernacle of David

Once each year the High Priest under the Mosaic Covenant ministered his priestly duties in three parts of the Tabernacle in the Wilderness, and then the Tabernacle was established in Shiloh, Ephraim/Israel in the Good Land; and, finally, the Solomonic Temple in Jerusalem. Those three places were the Outer Court, where the Altar of Sacrifice was found; the Holy Place, where the Menorah, Shewbread Table, and Altar of Incense were; and then the Holy of Holies, where the Ark of the Covenant — housing the Glory of God — was placed. Once each year, the High Priest (under the Aaronic Priesthood/Mosaic Covenant — Heb. 9:7-11; Lev. 16:14-15) would enter through the veil (which purposefully concealed the Ark of the Covenant — acting like a barrier). That veil was completely torn in the Temple (Herodian Temple) from top to bottom when the "Messiah was cut off" (Exo. 26:31-33; Dan. 9:26; Matt. 27:51; Mark 15:38; Luke 23:45 — even though the Ark of the Covenant no longer was concealed behind the veil). His crucifixion gave all access to the Most Holy Place, the Holiest of All, through the blood of Jesus (Heb. 10:19-22).

It is most significant that during the time in the Good Land, when the Ark of the Covenant was no longer in Shiloh's Tabernacle (in Ephraim/Israel), and prior to having the Ark of the Covenant (bearing the glory of God) moved by King Solomon into the Solomonic Temple in Jerusalem some 33 years later, that there was what was known as the Tabernacle of David or Tent of David. This intermediate location was in the City of David, immediately south of the Temple Mount, which, again, housed the Ark of the Covenant for up to its 33rd year (21 years under King David's rule and 11 years under King Solomon's rule, prior to it being brought into the Temple built by King Solomon). Likewise, King David ruled from Jerusalem for 33 years (1 Kings 2:11). There is sufficient evidence that when Jesus was about 30 years of age (Luke 3:23), He began His earthly ministry and ministered for three-and-a-half years or until He had reached the age of 33. Moreover, most biblical scholars place the date of His crucifixion and resurrection in the year 33 A.D. This Tabernacle of David did NOT have a curtain or veil concealing the Ark of the Covenant — all could see it. It was amazingly accessible.

During the early stages of the Ekklesia in the NT, there arose a contestation between the followers of Yeshua among the Pharisees and others who had ministered to the Gentiles (Grk. "ethnos" or "nations"), at the "Church Council" in Jerusalem in Acts 15. These Pharisees contended that those among the Nations/Gentiles who claimed forgiveness through the Blood of the Messiah were not even saved, because they were not circumcised (Acts 15:1-5). The followers of Yeshua, like Peter, Barnabas, and Paul, *"had no small dissension and dispute with them"* in that they contended that the Spirit of God fell on these uncircumcised Gentiles just as the Spirit fell upon the Jewish people (Acts 15:2-4, 6-11 - found in the summary of the Apostle James as to why the Spirit was poured out on the Nations). James stood up and summarized the contentions in this manner:

> "Men and brethren, listen to me: Simon (Peter) has declared how God at the first visited the Gentiles to take out of them a people for His name. And with this the words of the prophets agree, just as it is written: 'After this I will return and will rebuild the **TABERNACLE OF DAVID**, which has fallen down; I will rebuild its ruins, and I will set it up; so that the rest of mankind may seek the LORD, even all the Gentiles who are called by My name, says the LORD who does all these things'"
>
> – Acts 15:14-17; Amos 9:11-12

James was not forecasting an event that would take place in millennial bliss, but a present phenomenon was happening in the "here and now." The Tabernacle of David was uniquely manifested at the outset of the United Kingdom of David (all 12 tribes under King David). This unification of God's people demonstrated the diversity, distinctness, and unity of God's people (inclusive of Jew and Gentile), and was foretold by the prophets. This was staring the early Ekklesia/"Church" smack dab in the face. Also, it clearly displayed that there was no longer a veil/curtain between the Holiest of All and the Holy Place or Outer Court — all could enter into His Glory! They had all become "priests and kings unto God" (1 Peter 2:9; Rev. 1:6).

BIBLIOGRAPHY

Anderson, Sir Robert. *The Coming Prince*. Grand Rapids: Kregel Publications, 1954.

Armerding, Carl. "The Coming of the Son of Man," *Moody Monthly*, 51 (1951), pp. 787, 788, 809.

Barnhouse, Donald Grey. *Revelation . . . An Expositional Commentary*. Grand Rapids: Zondervan Publishing House, 1971.

Bullinger, E. W. *Number in Scripture . . . Its Supernatural Design and Spiritual Significance*. Grand Rapids, MI: Kregel Publications, 1967.

Bullinger, E. W. *The Apocalypse*. London, UK: Eyre & Spottiswoode, 1909.

Capt, E. Raymond. *Jacob's Pillar: The Stone of Bethel*. Muskogee, OK: Artisan Publishers, 17 Edition, 2009.

Cheney, Johnston M. and Ellisen, Stanley. *"Harmony of the Gospels" — The Greatest Story — a Unique Blending of the Four Gospels*. Portland, Oregon: Multnomah Books, 1994.

Church, J. R. *Daniel Reveals the Bloodline of the Antichrist*. Oklahoma City, OK: Prophecy Publications, 2010.

Cirlot, J. E. *A Dictionary of Symbols* (Translated from the Spanish by Jack Sage). Mineola, New York: Dover Publications, Inc., 2002.

Clawson, Clarence. *Mathematical Mysteries: The Beauty and Magic of Numbers*, New York and London: Plenum Press, 1996.

Coneybeare and Howson. *Life and Epistles of St Paul*. Grand Rapids, MI: WM. B. Eerdmans Publishing Co.

Culver, Robert D. *Daniel and the Latter Days*. New York: Fleming H. Revell Co., 1954.

Daniel, Grady and Abrams, Cooper. *What Day Was Christ Crucified?* Portland, Oregon: Multnomah Books, 1994.

Eusebius. *The Preservation of the Gospel*. Grand Rapids, MI: Baker, 1982.

Feinberg, Charles L. *Millennialism . . . The Two Major Views*. Chicago: Moody Press, 1980.

Flynn, David. *Temple At The Center of Time*. Crane, MO: Anomalos Publishing House, 2008

_____ *The David Flynn Collection*. Crane, MO: Defense Publishing, 2012.

Gaebelein, Arno C. *The Harmony of the Prophetic Word*, New York: Our Hope, 1907.

Garnier, Colonel J. *Great Pyramid: Its Builder & Its Prophecy*. Netherlands: Fredonia Books, 2001.

Ginzberg, Louis. *The Legends of the Jews*. Philadelphia: Jewish Publication Society, 1909-1938.

Gray, James M. *Synthetic Bible Studies*. New York: Fleming H. Revell Company, 1923.

Green, Jay P. Sr. *The Interlinear Bible – Hebrew-Greek-English* (With Strong's Concordance Numbers Above Each Word). Peabody, Mass. Hendrickson Publishers, 2005

Gregg, Steve. *Revelation – Four Views – A Parallel Commentary*. Nashville, TN: Thomas Nelson Publishers, 1997.

Gundry, Robert H. *The Church and the Tribulation*. Grand Rapids, MI: Zondervan, 1976.

Gundry, Stanley N. *Four Views on the Book of Revelation*. Grand Rapids: Zondervan, 1998.

Hamp, Douglas. *Corrupting the Image . . . Angels, Aliens, and the Antichrist Revealed*. Crane, MO: Defender Publishing LLC, 2011.

_____ *The Millennium Chronicles*. Costa Mesa, CA: CreateSpace Independent Publishing Platform (Self-Published), 2013.

Hancock, Graham. *Fingerprints of the Gods*. New York: Three Rivers Press, 1996

Hayer, Joseph Henry. *A Greek-English Lexicon of the New Testament*. A translation, revision and enlargement of Grimm's Wilke's Clavis Novi Testamenti. Fourth edition. Edinburgh: T. & T. Clark, 1953.

Hon, Henry. *Galatians: Uniting Divided People: The Truth of the Gospel*. One Body Life, 2022.

_____ *God's Kind: The Glory and Triumph of God's Kingdom*. One Body Life, 2023.

_____ *ONE EKKLESIA: The Vision and Practice of God's Eternal Purpose*. One Body Life, 2018.

_____ *One Life & Glory: Miraculously Normal Living and Service*. One Body Life, 2020.

_____ *One Truth: Liberating — Nourishing – Unifying*. One Body Life, 2019

_____ *The Gospel of the Kingdom in Romans*. One Body Life, 2023.

Hooper, Francis John Bodfield. *Palmoni: An Essay On the Chorographical and Numerical Systems*. London: Longman, Brown, Green, and Longman, 1851.

Ironside, H. A. *Lectures on the Revelation*. New York: Loizeaux Brothers, 1919.

Josephus, *The Works of Josephus*, both the Harvard Loeb editions and the Whiston translation. Peabody, Massachusetts: Hendrickson Publishers, 1987

Klausner, Joseph. *The Messianic Idea in Israel*. Translated from the third Hebrew edition by W. F. Stinespring. London: George Allen and Unwin Ltd., 1956.

Krieger, Douglas W. *The Two Witnesses, Volumes 1* and 2. Sacramento, California: TribNet Publications, 2014.

_____ *Signs in the Heavens and on the Earth . . . Man's Days are Numbered and he is Measured*. Sacramento, California: TribNet Publications, 2024 (10th Anniversary Edition

_____ *Commonwealth Theology*. Sacramento, CA: Tribnet Publications, 2018.

_____ *Commonwealth of Israel Theological Review*. Commonwealth of Israel Fd. @ https://commonwealthofisrael.com/coi_theological_review.html (Retrieved on October 15, 2025). Authors: Dr. Gavin Findley, Dr. Douglas Hamp, Chris W. Steinle, Gianluca Morotti, Ed Doss, Scott Horrell

_____ *So, You Want to do Ekklesia?* Sacramento, CA: Tribnet Publications, 2019.

Ladd, George Eldon. *The Blessed Hope*. Grand Rapids: Wm. B. Eerdmans Publishing Co, 1956.

_____ *A Commentary on the Revelation*. Grand Rapids, MI: Eerdmans Publishing Company, 1972.

Larkin, Clarence. *The Greatest Book on Dispensational Truth*. Larkin (Publisher), 38th Edition, 1920.

Lee, Witness. *The Economy of God*. Anaheim, CA; Anaheim, CA: Living Stream Ministry, 1968.

_____ *Life-Study Series*. Anaheim, CA: Living Stream Ministry, 1974-1995.

Liddell, Henry, George, Scott, Robert. *A Greek-English Lexicon*. Revised and augmented by Sir Henry Stuart Jones with the assistance of Roderick McKenzie. Oxford: Clarendon Press, 1948.

Mackintosh, C. H. *Genesis to Deuteronomy*. Neptune, NJ: Loizeaux Brothers, 1972.

_____ *The Mackintosh Treasury*. Neptune, NJ: Loizeaux Brothers, 1978

Maimonides, Pines, Shlomo, *The Guide of the Perplexed*, Chicago: University of Chicago, 1963.

Martin, Ernest L. *The Temples that Jerusalem forgot*. Portland, Oregon: ASK Publications, 2000.

McGee, Dr. J. Vernon. *Daniel . . . Thru The Bible Commentary Series, The Prophets*. Nashville, TN: Thomas Nelson Publishers, 1991.

_____ *Revelation Chapters 14-22 . . . Thru The Bible Commentary Series, The Prophecy*. Nashville, TN: Thomas Nelson Publishers, 1991.

Michell, John. *The Dimensions of Paradise . . . Sacred Geometry, Ancient Science, and the Heavenly Order on Earth*. Rochester, Vermont: Inner Traditions, 1971.

Murray, Andrew. The Two Covenants. New Jersey: Spire Books

_____ *The Spirit of Christ*. Minneapolis, MN: Bethany House Publishers

Nee, Watchman. *The Normal Christian Life*. PA: CLC

_____ *The Normal Christian Church Life*, Colorado Springs, CO: ISP

_____ *The Song of Songs*, Anaheim, CA: Living Stream Ministry, 1993.

Osborne, Grant R. *Revelation . . . Baker Exegetical Commentary on the New Testament*, Moises Silva, Editor. Grand Rapids, Michigan: Baker Academic, 2006.

Payne, J. Barton. *The Imminent Appearing of Christ*. Grand Rapids: Wm. B. Eerdmans publishing Co., 1962.

Pember, G. H. *Earth's Earliest Ages . . . and Their Connection with Modern Spiritualism, Theosophy, and Buddhism*. Grand Rapids, Michigan: Kregel Publications, 1975.

Pentecost, J. Dwight. *Things to Come*. Findlay, Ohio: Dunham Publishing Co., 1958.

Robinson, E., *Biblical Researches in Palestine, Mount Sinai and Arabia Petra*, New York: Reprint, 1977.

Rosenberg, Joel C. *Epicenter . . . Why the Current Rumblings in the Middle East will Change Your Future*. Carol Stream, Illinois: Tyndale House Publishers, Inc., 2008.

Schmitt, John W. and Laney, J. Carl. *Messiah's Coming Temple: Ezekiel's Prophetic Vision of the Future Temple*. Grand Rapids, MI: Kregel Publications, 1997.

Scofield, C. I. *The Scofield Reference Bible*. New York: Oxford University Press, 1945.

Scott, Walter. *Exposition of the Revelation of Jesus Christ*, Fourth Edition, New York: Fleming H. Revell Publishing, 1968.

Seiss, Joseph A. *The Apocalypse . . . An Exposition of the Book of Revelation*. Grand Rapids, MI: Kregel Publications, 1900.

_____ *The Apocalypse: Lectures on the Book of Revelation*. Grand Rapids, MI: Zondervan Publishing House, n.d.

Shearer, Douglas Ray. *The Great Unraveling — Facing the Storm . . . An Exposition of Matthew 24 & 25*. Sacramento, California: Self-Published, 2015.

Sparks, T. Austin. *The Centrality and Supremacy of the Lord Jesus Christ*. Online Library of T. Austin-Sparks.

Stedman, Ray C. *God's Final Word, Understanding Revelation*. Uhrichsville, Ohio: Discovery House/Barbour Publishing, Inc., 1991.

Thayer, Joseph H. *Thayer's Greek-English Lexicon of the New Testament* (Coded with Strong's Concordance Numbers). Peabody, Mass: Hendrickson Publishers, Fourteenth Printing — June 2019.

Tregelles, S. P. *The Hope of Christ's Second Coming*. Los Angeles: The Sovereign Grace Advent Testimony, Sixth Edition, 1959.

Ussher, Archbishop James. *The Annals of the World*. Copyright, Larry and Marion Pierce. Green Forest, AZ: Master Books, Inc. First Printing, 2003.

Vine, W. E. *Vine's Complete Expository Dictionary of Old and New Testament Word, With Topical Index*. Copyright, Ltd. of Bath, England. First Published in 1985 by Thomas Nelson, Inc. With Merrill F. Unger and William White, Jr.

Viola, Frank. *Reimagining Church*. Colorado Springs, CO: David C. Cook

Walvoord, John F. *Daniel — The Key to Prophetic Revelation*. Chicago: Moody Press, 1971.

_____ *Every Prophecy of the Bible*: Colorado Springs, CO.: Chariot Victor Publishing/ Div. of Cook Communications, 1999.

_____ *The Church in Prophecy*. Grand Rapids, MI: Zondervan Publishing House, 1976.

Warner, Tim. *Mystery of the Mazzaroth . . . Prophecy in the Zodiac*. Oakfield, Maine: The Wild Olive Press, 2010.

Wigram, George V. *The Englishman's Hebrew Concordance of the Old Testament* (Coded with Strong's Concordance Numbers). Peabody, Mass.: Hendrickson Publishers Marketing, LLC. Ninth Printing — September 2018.

Yadin, Yigal. *Jerusalem Revealed*. New Haven, CT: Yale, 1976.

OTHER BOOKS BY HENRY HON

One Ekklesia: The Vision and Practice of God's Eternal Purpose. The apostle Paul declared that God's *Ekklesia* manifests His multi-faceted wisdom according to His eternal purpose (Eph. 3:10-11). His *Ekklesia* was central to Jesus Christ's mission. Therefore, immediately after Peter proclaimed Jesus as "The Christ, the Son of the living God," Jesus said, "I will build My *Ekklesia*," which has been mistranslated to "church" (Matt. 16:18).

Ekklesia was the forum for democracy invented by the Greeks BC 600. While secular democracies are increasing with divisions, hatred, and corruption, Jesus' *ekklesia* (Democratic Assembly) cultivates acceptance, forgiveness, love for one another, and unity among His people of uniqueness and diversity.

This book distinguishes between "church" as a place for ministry for preaching and teaching, and God's *Ekklesia*, which is also identified as the Body of Christ, God's Household, the Bride, the New Man, and the New Jerusalem. While churches have benefited many of God's people, they have also unwittingly caused much division among Christians.

Jesus is calling His followers to join Him in building His "democratic" Kingdom. This is not a call to start a new church or to improve churches, but for individual believers to fellowship with one another and manifest their organic unity in Christ no matter which church they attend or not attend at all. This call is in fulfillment of the Lord's prayer: " . . . that they may be one in us, that the world may believe . . . " (John 17:21).

Jesus Christ died and resurrected for His *Ekklesia*. This practical oneness of diverse believers serves as a light to the world, igniting the holy fire of God, spreading uncontrollably – the next and final revival. (336 pages)

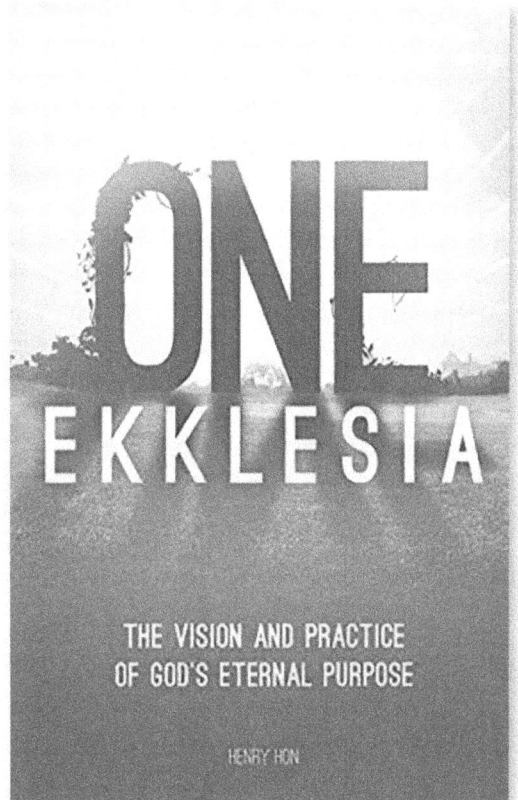

One Truth: Liberating – Nourishing – Unifying. Jesus said: The truth shall set you free, and if the Son sets you free, you shall be free for real. When Jesus declared these words in John 8, the religious people of His day were first condemning an adulterous woman to death, and then, after Jesus saved her, they wanted to kill Jesus.

Truth liberates people from religious condemnation and its zeal that's ready to kill — if not physically, then at least psychologically or spiritually.

The word "truth" in the Greek (*alethia*) means "the reality lying at the basis of appearance." People are caught up with appearances, both in the secular and religious world. There is a hunger within every person for what is real. Your inner being is drained by vanity; truth is needed to nourish, sustain, and energize your soul. The world is full of hostile separations. Jesus, in John 17, gave the gift of truth so that the most hostile and divided people may become united. Religious dogma and ceremonial practices divide, but truth unites.

A person who has received logic and life from truth can love, forgive, and express kindness to all, especially those different or contrary to himself. Jesus answered: "I am the way, the TRUTH, and the life" (John 14:6).

Bonus: Introducing the Completion Gospel, which is needed today for the ending of the age. Most of the gospel heard by people today is basically only half of it. The entire gospel needs to be preached! *ONE TRUTH.* (278 pages)

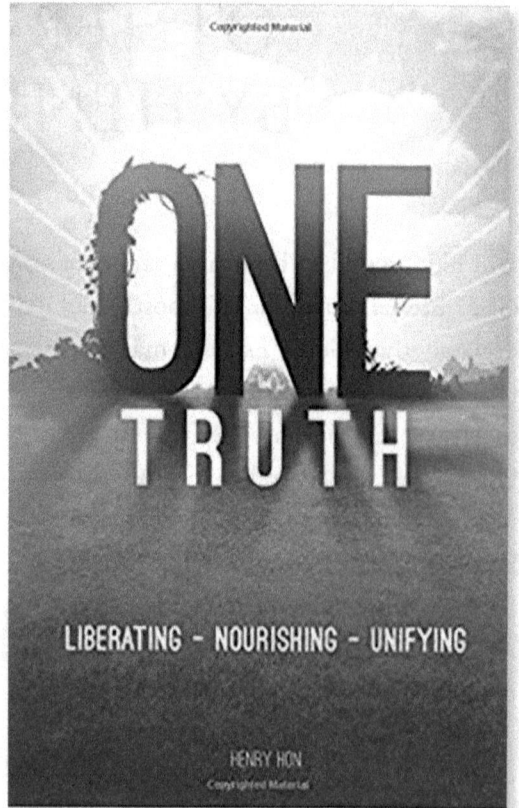

One Life & Glory: Miraculously Normal Living and Service. Both Christians and non-Christians like to witness the supernatural, miraculous actions taken by God. Certainly, God can do miracles to heal your loved ones from terminal diseases or to solve all your financial worries with a lottery win. However, God's desire with humanity is not to be their "Santa Claus"; His desire and purpose are wonderful beyond imagination: He wants to be "miraculously normal" in humanity. Not just hit and miss miraculous events here and there, but miraculous every day, such that it is normal and ordinary.

This is God Himself being the source, empowering humanity to live by His divine-eternal life through faith in Jesus Christ. Being miraculously normal means it will be indistinguishable whether it is you or God who is loving, caring, forgiving, enduring, and living in this present world. Moreover, services rendered to both God and humanity can likewise be miraculously normal.

Ordinary words can be spoken; yet, they can give eternal life to the hearer. Through normal interactions, peace can be made between people previously divided and hostile with one another; they are brought into fellowship. This book, *One in Life and Glory*, is the third in this series, forming a Trilogy together with *One Ekklesia* and *One Truth*. This Trilogy of *ONE* expounds on the Lord's prayer in John 17 for all His people to become one — as one as the Father and the Son are one. In His prayer, He gave three gifts to accomplish the oneness of His people: eternal life, truth (the "logos" or His Word), and His glory. When previously divided, even hostile people can become one in this present conflicting and confusing age; then the people of the world will believe "the Father sent the Son" — our Lord Jesus Christ. One Life & Glory (332 pages)

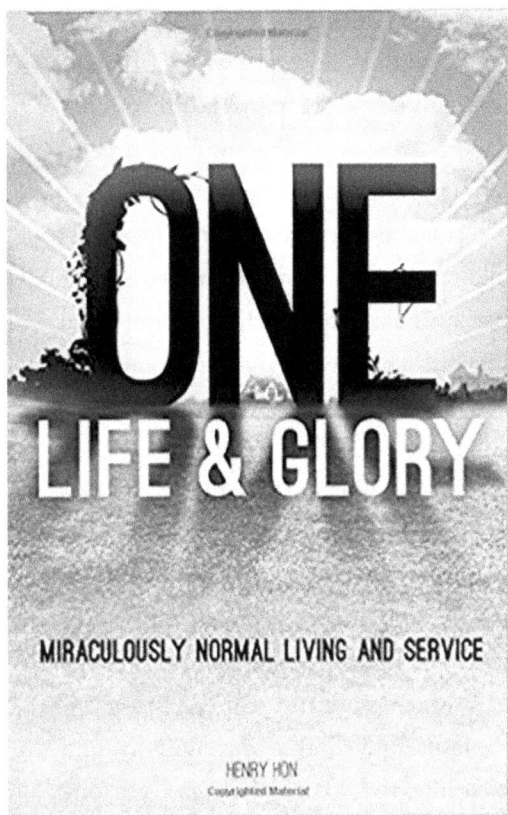

Galatians: Uniting Divided People. This book examines how and why Christians have unknowingly played into Satan's plan of division by de-emphasizing and even ignoring Jesus' heart for unity.

This is the gospel that unites us: Jesus followers by faith. However, most overlook that Jesus died not only for our individual sins but also "to gather into one the children of God who are scattered abroad" (John 11:52, ESV).

This book exposes Satan's craftiness in using the gifts of God and laws in Scripture to create divergent brands of churches and groups. Christians have unwittingly distorted the gospel, resulting in more and more divisions.

Jesus prayed that our unity would look like the Trinity: diverse yet one (John 17:22, 23, ESV). This is good news! Christians can have opposing perspectives and experiences but still love, respect, serve, and forgive one another, as one.

When followers of Jesus Christ are more divided than the secular world, Galatians provides the solution. God reveals this reality as a light: "There is neither Jew nor Greek, there is neither slave nor free, there is no male and female, for you are all one in Christ Jesus" (Gal. 3:28). Galatians: Uniting Divided People (95 pages)

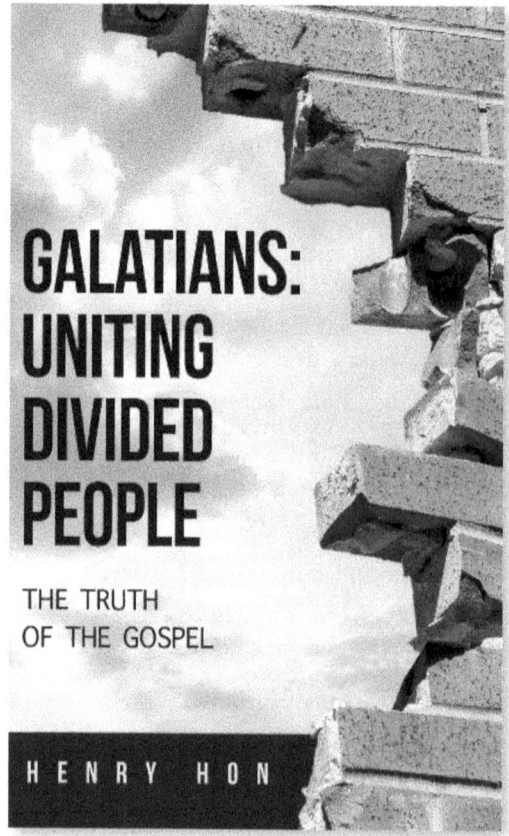

GOD'S KIND: THE GLORY AND TRIUMPH OF GOD'S KINGDOM.

"God's Kind" here does not mean "God is kind," even though He certainly is. Rather, it refers to God's species or children. Using "God's Kind" to expound on the Kingdom of God is new and bold. The hope is to jolt readers to think outside the "Kingdom of God box," which has been rigidly constructed within the various perspectives of major theological schools and has continued to divide Christians.

Satan's attack on God's *kind* is focused on this truism spoken by Jesus: "Every kingdom divided against itself is laid waste, and a divided household falls" (Luke 11:17b ESV). Satan manipulates immature believers to increase division in God's Kingdom. Consequently, divided believers are made weak, sickly, poor, and ineffectual.

This comprehensive study of God's Kingdom from Genesis to Revelation exposes Satan's tactics of dividing God's children and should motivate them to grow to maturity. God's Kingdom is not a "theocracy," as most would assume. Rather, His desire is for a diverse democratic Kingdom where each of His *kind* can be liberated as distinct individuals. Yet, they love one another in fellowship, expressing the oneness of the Trinity.

Love and oneness express the divine life (DNA) within God's *kind* — God's Kingdom. Seek first His Kingdom, and He will richly provide all things needed for the present life and a rich entrance into the coming Kingdom of God in glory. Immature believers may find themselves unfavorably judged at the Judgment Seat of Christ. Instead of reigning with Christ in the Millennial Kingdom, those who stay babes may need another period to grow before the Eternal Kingdom.

Being a child of God is an awesome privilege; nevertheless, each person is responsible for building God's Kingdom. Bringing God's Kingdom to earth in the present age is an abundant blessing of life, grace, and purpose. God's *kind* will triumph over Satan's kingdom and ultimately give glory to God. GOD'S KIND (250 pages)

These books and their e-book companions, as well as AUDIO on these books, can be found @www.onebody.life and on Amazon.com.